PLAYING
THE CHANGES

PLAYING THE CHANGES

▲ ▲ ▲ ▲ ▲ ▲ ▲ ▲

FROM AFRO-MODERNISM TO THE JAZZ IMPULSE

CRAIG HANSEN WERNER

UNIVERSITY OF ILLINOIS PRESS
Urbana and Chicago

Library of Congress Cataloging-in-Publication Data

Werner, Craig Hansen, 1952-
   Playing the changes : from Afro-modernism to the jazz impulse /
Craig Hansen Werner.
      p. cm.
   Includes bibliographical references (p.) and index.
   ISBN 0–252–02112–6
   1. American literature—Afro-American authors—History and criticism.
2. American literature—20th century—History and criticism. 3. Afro-
Americans—Music—History and criticism. 4. Music and literature—History—
20th century. 5. Modernism (Literature)—United States. 6. Afro-Americans in
literature. 7. Afro-American aesthetics. 8. Jazz in literature.
I. Title.
PS153.N5W38 1994
810.9′896073—dc20   94–711
                                                                                    CIP

To Leslee Nelson
(from Chance Music to
The House of Dreams)

I think that all theories are suspect, that the finest principles may have to be modified, or may even be pulverized by the demands of life, and that one must find, therefore, one's own moral center and move through the world hoping that this center will guide one aright.

James Baldwin, *Notes of a Native Son*

Proverbs for Paranoids, 3: If they can get you asking the wrong questions, they don't have to worry about answers.

Thomas Pynchon, *Gravity's Rainbow*

Contents

▲ ▲ ▲ ▲

Acknowledgments
▲ ▲ ▲ ▲

The writing of *Playing the Changes* was supported with research funds and release time provided by the Graduate School and the Center for the Study of Southern Culture at the University of Mississippi; the Graduate School Summer Research Support program, the Institute for Research in the Humanities, and the Vilas Fellows program at the University of Wisconsin; the Ford Foundation; and a National Endowment for the Humanities Summer Research Fellowship. In particular, I would like to thank Sheila Biddle of the Ford Foundation; John Pilkington and Ann Abadie of the University of Mississippi; and, from Wisconsin, David Cronon, Charles Read, David Ward, Phil Certain, and Donna Shalala, whose appointment to the Clinton cabinet holds out some hope of a public life sensitive to the importance of diverse voices and complex understanding.

"Revolution Is One Form of Social Change," "Prologue," "New York City," "Now" from *Undersong: Chosen Poems Old and New,* by Audre Lorde, by permission of W. W. Norton & Company, Inc. Copyright © 1992, 1982, 1976, 1974, 1973, 1970, 1968 by Audre Lorde.

Portions of several chapters are revised versions of previously published essays:

Chapter 1: "The Framing of Charles W. Chesnutt: Practical Deconstruction in the Afro-American Tradition," *University of Mississippi Studies in English,* n.s., 9 (1991): 1–25.

Chapter 2: "Minstrel Nightmares: Black Dreams of Faulkner's Dreams of Blacks," in *Faulkner and Race,* ed. Doreen Fowler and Ann J. Abadie (Jackson: University Press of Mississippi, 1987), 35–57; "Tell Old Pharaoh: The Afro-American Response to Faulkner," *Southern Review* 19 (Autumn 1983): 711–35.

Chapter 3: "The Briar Patch as Modernist Myth: Morrison, Barthes, and Tar Baby As Is," originally published in *Critical Essays on Toni Morrison,* edited by Nellie Y. McKay. Used by permission of G. K. Hall & Co., an imprint of Macmillan Publishing Company.

Chapter 4: "On the Ends of Afro-Modernist Autobiography," *Black American Literature Forum* 24, no. 2 (Summer 1990): 203–20.

Chapter 5: "Dumas, Nationalism, and Multicultural Mythology," *Black American Literature Forum* 22, no. 2 (Summer 1988): 394–99.

Chapter 7: "Blues for T. S. Eliot and Langston Hughes: The Afro-Modernist Prosody of Melvin B. Tolson," *Black American Literature Forum* 24, no. 3 (Fall 1990): 453–72.

Chapter 8: "Bigger's Blues: *Native Son* and the Articulation of Afro-American Modernism," in *New Essays on Native Son,* ed. Keneth Kinnamon (New York: Cambridge University Press, 1990), pp. 117–52.

Chapter 9: "James Baldwin: Politics and the Gospel Impulse," *New Politics* 2, no. 2 (Winter 1989): 106–24.

Chapter 11: "The Burden and the Binding Song: August Wilson's Neoclassical Jazz," in *May All Your Fences Have Gates in Them: Essays on the Drama of August Wilson,* ed. Alan Nadel (Iowa City: Iowa University Press, 1993), 21–50.

Many thanks to those who helped me come out roughly even in my ongoing war with the word processors: Jo Failing, Marj Haanstad, Pat Newell, and, above all, Maggie Brandenburg, without whom I would probably still be trying to print out a copy of the title page.

I extend my gratitude to Ann Lowry, Alan Nadel, Michel Fabre, and Becky Standard for sheparding the manuscript through the publication process.

There are so many people whose voices sound throughout these pages that it seems nearly futile to even try to name them all. Yet and still . . . gratitude, respect, and love to:

The folks back home in Colorado, who never let me forget that it's not just about tenure: Mike DeLong; Brian Berry; my brothers Brian and Blake, along with the newer Werners, Wendy, Ellie, Kiel, Shannon, Shelby, Chelsea, Taryn; and my father, Ray, a Republican economist ("I learned the value of money, not that money is the only value") who brought James Baldwin's books into my life. And, always, to my late mother, Donna, whose spirit watches over the little ones.

The teachers who inspired my passion for intellectual dialogue: Bob Smith, Frank Krutzke, and Dan Tynan of Colorado College; Emily Watts, Chuck Sanders, Richard Barksdale, Nina Baym, Edward Davidson, Berni Benstock, and Ken Kinnamon at the University of Illinois.

The colleagues who have challenged me to extend my boundaries: Barbara Ewell, Bill Ferris, Evans Harrington, and "Daddy" Ben Fisher of the University of Mississippi; and Nellie McKay, Sandy Adell, Bill Van Deburg, Herb Hill, Ron Radano, Frank Gilliam, Eugene Redmond, Clovis White, Laurie Beth Clark, Prospero Saiz, Mary Layoun, Susan Friedman, Thomas Schaub, Rafael Perez-Torres, and Amy Ling at the University of Wisconsin.

The students who remain the source of energy, inspiration, correction, and hope: Sue Christel, Cathy Kasper, and Brian Shaeffer from the "Doom, Gloom, and Despair" class at the University of Illinois; Kevin Stewart, Karah Stokes, Jonny Duvall, and Mike Reese (gone too soon) from the Southern Studies marathons at the University of Mississippi; Judylyn Ryan, Eli Goldblatt, Jane Splawn, and John Gruesser from the "Afro-American Modernism" seminar in which I first realized I was writing this book, and Melvina Johnson Young, Amy Bowles, and Yasmin Cader, from the seminar in which I realized it had stopped being about "Afro-Modernism"; Glenn Berry and Gant Johnson (who taught me to hear the gospel in house), Eric Rasmussen and Brian Bischel (who make the Mudcats the most interesting softball team in the upper Midwest), Mikki Harris and Kern Jackson (who persevered), Aja J'ielle Brown and Wendy Schneider (who made it real), Donia Allen and Lorrae Watters (the next generation of African-American women's voices), Julie Skemp and Mel Nickerson (whose collaborative video should turn some heads around), Damon Harrell—probably the only Big Ten center to interpret the game in terms of *Gravity's Rainbow*—Duer Sharp, and Howard Moore (who reveal the stereotypes of student-athletes for the nonsense they are), Rebecca Johnson, Howard Shack, Ari Kelman,

Victor Jew, Adam Chern, Anne Borden, Anthony Stockdale, Larry Rodgers, Dan Schultz, Juan Avila, Sam Chaltain, Todd Hansen, Beate Gersch, Bob Trondson, Kevin Evanco, Pat Shea, Lori Leibovich, David Wright, Robin Reddeman, Tom Cavanaugh, Malin Walther . . . the list could go on forever, but I'll conclude it with Ed Pavlick, whose insights into the Yoruba concept of *iwa* exerted a decisive impact on the way this book came together.

The people whose voices keep me (relatively) sane: Barbara Talmadge, Robert Philipson, Scott Sherman, Steve Schultz, Geoff King, and Missy Dehn Kubitschek.

And, finally, to my wife, Leslee Nelson, whose sculptures shimmer with the energies of the orisha, and our daughters Riah and Kaylee, whose sparkling spirits are always in my heart.

Introduction:
(Re)Phrasings and the Study of African-American Literature

▲ ▲ ▲ ▲

A radical aesthetic acknowledges that we are constantly changing positions, locations, that our needs and concerns vary, that these diverse directions must correspond with shifts in critical thinking. Narrow limiting aesthetics within black communities tend to place innovative black artistry on the margins.

—bell hooks, "An Aesthetic of Blackness"

[Prophetic pragmatism seeks] a reconception of philosophy as a form of cultural criticism that attempts to transform linguistic, social, cultural, and political traditions for the purposes of increasing the scope of individual development and democratic operations. Prophetic pragmatism conceives of philosophy as a historically circumscribed quest for wisdom that puts forward new interpretations of the world based on past traditions in order to promote existential sustenance and political relevance.

—Cornel West, "Tragedy, Tradition, and Political Praxis"

Two fundamental goals inform this book: the search for a "moral center," for values supporting "individual development and democratic operations," and the attempt to phrase questions in ways that support the emerging values while maintaining a complex awareness of our "constantly changing positions, locations . . . needs and concerns." *Playing the Changes: From Afro-Modernism to the Jazz Impulse* consists of a sequence of phrasings centered on the relationship between two superficially disparate traditions: European-American (post)modernism and African-American culture in both vernacular and "high art" forms. Although most of the essays in this book subvert this racialized dichotomy, each tradition occupies a specific place in my intellectual development. If (post)modernism encouraged me to develop a complex apprehension of the uncertainties of experience and to value innovative aesthetic forms, African-American culture continually reminded me of the moral foundations of my intellectual interests and their relationship to my overlapping communities. To borrow a phrasing from the black women critics and writers who play such a central role in my intellectual community in the Department of Afro-American Studies at the University of Wisconsin, African-American culture reminds, requires, us to honor the sources of our being and to accept responsibility for passing our traditions on to the children, our next generations.

From Afro-Modernism to the Jazz Impulse

In the decade since I began work on the issues that would eventually take the form of *Playing the Changes,* my phrasings of the basic questions concerning (post)modernism, African-American culture, and their historical and potential relationships have undergone several changes, including that reflected in the subtitle, *From Afro-Modernism to the Jazz Impulse.* (If I had waited another year to put the final manuscript together the subtitle might well have been *From Afro-Modernism to West Afrocentrism,* reflecting my growing sense of African-American music as part of a larger West African and diasporic *gnosis.*) The parts of this study that were written first—the prosodic/thematic analyses of Gwendolyn Brooks, Etheridge Knight, and Audre Lorde—were intended as part of a book tentatively titled "New Democratic Vistas: The Whitman Tradition in American Poetry." Like my first book, *Paradoxical Resolutions: American Fiction since James Joyce,* "New Democratic Vistas" was conceived not as a study of "influence"—especially not in Harold Bloom's patriarchal sense of the term—but as an exploration of the continuities and discontinuities of the American literary tradition carried out in the populist spirit of Whitman's "Democratic Vistas." As my interests began to shift to broader questions of Afro-American culture (not just literature), largely as a result of my participation in Robert Stepto's NEH summer seminar "Written and Folk Voices in Afro-American Letters," my phrasing of the question concerning the intersection of (post)-modernism and African-American culture underwent a fundamental change. No longer centrally concerned with the role of the European-American "masters," though still interested in what I now conceived as cross-cultural "dialogues" such as those between Faulkner and various Afro-American novelists, I rephrased the central problem of what I still thought of as "New Democratic Vistas" in terms of comparative American literature.

After a transitional stage focused on extending and revising

Stepto's paradigm of "ascent and immersion," the comparative emphasis coalesced around the idea of "Afro-Modernism." At its inception this "Afro-Modernist" project was equally concerned with demonstrating the importance of African-American culture to canonical modernist works and with casting light on the complexities of innovative Afro-American texts. As the project progressed, however, I became increasingly frustrated with the tendency of academic discussions of (post)modernism to marginalize issues of community access and politics (in anything other than abstract ideological terms). By the time I had completed the studies of "Afro-Modernist" autobiography (chapter 4) and Melvin B. Tolson (chapter 7), my phrasings had begun to foreground the underlying process of negotiating difference, of translating between different vocabularies (not just between, but within, Afro- and European-American communities) in a way that frees the energies of repressed experiences and traditions.

This interest in the critical process as a form of cultural negotiation, or—to use a phrasing highlighting the problematic nature of all European-American contact with multicultural traditions—"mediation," refocused my attention on African-American musical aesthetics. Phrasing questions in terms of the gospel, blues, and jazz impulses, this stage of my process developed as a response to several synergetic calls: the cultural criticism of Ralph Ellison and Zora Neale Hurston; the emergence of rap music as a central element in urban African-American culture; the public flowering of African-American women's thought; and the explosion of "Afrocentric" criticism, both the relatively polemical style championed by Molefi Kete Asante and the more traditional academic research of Anthony Appiah, Patricia Hill Collins, and Robert Farris Thompson. Pioneered by writers and musicians with synthetic multicultural sensibilities (Ellington, Hurston, Hughes, Brooks, Armstrong) the jazz impulse (grounded in blues and gospel) engages basic (post)modernist concerns including the difficulty of defining, or even experiencing, the self; the fragmentation of public discourse; and the problematic meaning of tradition. The jazz impulse engages the question of how to communicate visions of new possibilities—psychological, aesthetic, or political—to audiences and communities that frequently seek release from the dislocations of (post)modern life by retreating to superficially reassuring, if fundamentally outmoded and often counterproductive, cultural attitudes and forms. A decade after I started work on "New Democratic Vistas," I see the complex process embodied in the three impulses as a useful way of engaging the complexity of experience, a way that, unlike some versions of European-American (post)modernism, maintains a grounding in moral values and living communities. Seeking to increase access to the intellectual and cultural energies that will certainly be necessary if we are to come to terms with what Manning Marable calls the "crisis of color and democracy," *Playing the Changes* in its current form is my way of paying tribute to the ancestors—both my intellectual predecessors and the members of my family who have passed on—and of honoring the multiple energies that texture my experience—whether phrased as the West African orisha or aspects of a fragmented (post)-modern psyche.

Calls and Responses

This book makes no attempt to develop a theory of African-American literature. Rather, it responds to what I hear as the fundamental calls of the African-American (and I use that phrasing to emphasize the African elements of a profoundly American synthesis) cultural tradition: to clarify realities (understood as broadly as possible) and to envision possibilities. Grounded in West African conceptions of the interrelationship of individual and community, the concept of "call and response" resonates throughout these essays. As Harold Scheub demonstrates in his germinal work on African oral traditions, call and response begins with the call of a leader who expresses his/her own voice through the vehicle of a traditional song, story, or image. This call, which provides a communal context for exploration of the "individual" emotion, itself responds to a shared history that suffuses later stages of the process. If the community, as it exists in the ever-changing present, recognizes and shares the experience evoked by the call, it responds with another phrase, again usually traditional, which may either affirm or present a different perspective on the initial call. Whether it affirms or critiques the initial call, however, the response enables the leader to go on exploring the implications of the material. Rich in political implications, this cultural form enables both individual and community to define themselves, to validate their experiences in opposition to dominant social forces. When working most effectively, this process requires individuals not to seek a synthesis, to deny the extreme aspects of their own experiences, but to assert their subjectivity in response to other, equally personal and equally extreme, assertions of experience. Call and response, then, is African-American analysis: a process that, by admitting diverse voices and diverse experiences, supports a more inclusive critique than any individual analysis.

Alan Nadel, whose sensitive critique helped me clarify the theoretical dimensions of *Playing the Changes,* provides a provocative and insightful commentary on the relationship between call and response and contemporary critical theory:

> By understanding African-American music as an historically situated text that manifests and reasserts aspects of African-American culture, we can develop understandings that identify the aspects and strategies of cultural critique in much 20th-century African-American literature. If we recognize deconstruction as an act of rampant recontextualizing so as to reveal the logical flaws in the foundation for any form of authority—social, theological, economic, political, rhetorical, grammatical—then we can recognize the deconstructive energies of African-American art and culture, in the context of the dominant discourse of American culture. To see this, we need to see the ways in which music can provide an alternative authority, one composed of subversive strategies drawing from African-American traditions of "call & response," "signifyin'," and "loud talking." These strategies have in common with deconstruction the constant undermining and reconfiguring of the audience-text-performer relationship, so as to reveal the instability of the assumptions that give each of those positions its positionality, its center. (The "response" of "call & response," for example, turns the audience into the performer, and the authority of the performer derives from his/her ability to shift his/her role to the audience, i.e., to decenter that authority.)

Framed in these terms, *Playing the Changes* can be seen as a series of responses to (as opposed to theoretical interrogations of) a variety of calls, many of them responsive to W. E. B. Du Bois's formulation of "double consciousness," which asserts the importance of both African and European traditions to Du Bois's vision of a "better and truer" American self. Applying Du Bois's formulation to Afro-American culture, Robert Stepto explores literary history in terms of narrative patterns of "ascent" and "immersion," increasingly (self)-conscious literary responses to the "quest for freedom and literacy," a quest articulated not only in formal literature but also in animal tales, sermons, and the spirituals and work songs that gave form to gospel, blues, and jazz. An extremely useful way of framing Afro-American literary studies for students from widely divergent cultural backgrounds, Stepto's definition of ascent and immersion bears quotation in full:

> The classic ascent narrative launches an "enslaved and semi-literate figure on a ritualized journey to a symbolic North; that journey is charted through spatial expressions of social structure, invariably systems of signs that the questing figure must read in order to be both increasingly literate and increasingly free. The ascent narrative conventionally ends with the questing figure situated in the least oppressive social structure afforded by the world of the narrative, and free in the sense that he or she has gained sufficient literacy to assume the mantle of an articulate survi-

vor. As the phrase "articulate survivor" suggests, the hero or heroine of an ascent narrative must be willing to forsake familial or communal postures in the narrative's most oppressive social structure for a new posture in the least oppressive environment—at best one of solitude; at worst, one of alienation. This last feature of the ascent narrative unquestionably helps bring about the rise and development of an immersion narrative in the tradition, for the immersion narrative is fundamentally an expression of a ritualized journey into a symbolic South, in which the protagonist seeks those aspects of tribal literacy that ameliorate, if not obliterate, the conditions imposed by solitude. The conventional immersion narrative ends almost paradoxically, with the questing figure located in or near the narrative's most oppressive social structure but free in the sense that he has gained or regained sufficient tribal literacy to assume the mantle of an articulate kinsman. As the phrase "articulate kinsman" suggests, the hero or heroine of an immersion narrative must be willing to forsake highly individualized mobility in the narrative's least oppressive social structure for a posture of relative stasis in the most oppressive environment, a loss that is only occasionally assuaged by the newfound balms of group identity. (167)

These narrative patterns can be seen as responses to the pressure of Du Boisean double consciousness: ascent as an engagement with a hostile white world that forces African-Americans to look at themselves "through the eyes of others"; immersion with the "veiled" black self that experiences "two warring ideals in one dark body, whose dogged strength alone keeps it from being torn asunder" (364–65).

Stepto's formulation suggests the underlying connection between the chapters of *Playing the Changes* that focus on Afro-Modernism (which requires the type of literacy Stepto associates with ascent) and those that focus on blues and gospel (the forms that most clearly encode the "tribal literacy" fundamental to immersion). It is not my intention to provide a critique of either Stepto's paradigm or "double consciousness," which has been subjected to rigorous (but sympathetic) philosophical critiques in Arnold Rampersad's *The Art and Imagination of W. E. B. Du Bois* and Sandra Adell's *Double-Consciousness/Double Bind,* as well as in the more personal meditations of Asante, Henry Louis Gates, Darlene Clark Hine, Toni Cade Bambara, Glenn Loury, Wanda Coleman, and others in Gerald Early's anthology *Lure and Loathing: Essays on Race, Identity, and the Ambivalence of Assimilation.* Rather, my focus on the multicultural, (post)modernist, and yet very black "jazz impulse" seeks to contribute to the development of what Antonio Benitez-Rojo describes as a polyrhythmic approach to literature as "a stream of texts in flight, in intense differentiation among themselves and within whose complex coexistence there are vague regularities, usually paradoxical" (27). As Benitez-Rojo observes, the point of a jazz-inflected polyrhythmic discourse is not to destroy or replace binary discourses but to understand them as part of a larger structure in which other voices sound freely. This formulation suggests the appropriateness of employing diverse critical methodologies (as opposed to generating a single alternative methodology) based on the polyrhythmic structures of oral traditions.

In relation to (post)modern concerns, these issues coalesce around the changing significance of the "jazz impulse" in African-American culture. Ralph Ellison, the most insightful and influential theorist of the relationship between African-American music and literature, defines the jazz impulse as a way of defining/creating the self in relation to community and tradition. Applicable to any form of cultural expression, jazz as Ellison defines it provides a way for new ideas to enter the tradition. Ellison writes: "true jazz is an act of individual assertion within and against the group. Each true jazz moment (as distinct from the uninspired commercial performance) springs from a contest in which each artist challenges all the rest; each solo flight, or improvisation, represents (like the successive canvases of a painter) a definition of his identity: as individual, as member of the collectivity and as a link in the chain of tradition" (234).

Almost all successful jazz is grounded in what Ellison calls the "blues impulse." Before an artist can hope to create a meaningful new vision for individual and communal use, she must acknowledge the full complexity of her experience. In his classic essay on Richard Wright, Ellison defines the blues impulse as "an impulse to keep the painful details and episodes of a brutal experience alive in one's aching consciousness, to finger its jagged grain, and to transcend it, not by the consolation of philosophy but by squeezing from it a near-tragic, near-comic lyricism" (78–79). Although the blues impulse is based on intensely individual feelings, these feelings, for most black American blues artists, can be traced in part to the brutal racist context experienced in some form by almost all blacks. Substituting the less "philosophical" term "affirmation" for Ellison's idea of "transcendence," Albert Murray emphasizes that, especially when her call elicits a response from a community that confirms a shared experience, the blues artist becomes "an agent of affirmation and continuity in the face of adversity" (*Hero* 38). Both the individual expression and the affirmative, and self-affirming, response of the community, then, are crucial to the blues. Seen in relation to the blues impulse, the jazz impulse provides a way of exploring implications, of realizing the relational possibilities of the (blues) self, and of expanding the consciousness of self and community through a process of continual improvisation.

Although it has received less attention as a literary resource, the "gospel impulse" grounds both the blues and jazz impulses in West African values and cultural forms. Centered in the black church—the institutional space furthest removed from the attention and mediation of whites—religious music and speech allowed African-American communities to develop appropriate expressions of their experience with relative autonomy. Expressing West African values in a Christian vocabulary acceptable to surrounding white communities, the gospel impulse resists, though it has always felt the effects of, the oppositional structures of the European-American analytical tradition. Aware that most whites, because they accept the authority of binary structures, behave as if they are "devils," the gospel impulse nonetheless holds out the possibility of universal salvation while providing an institutional setting for the communal affirmation of individual experience.

Asserting the African dimension of Du Boisean double consciousness, the gospel impulse keeps alive the concept of difference from and within the white world. As Amiri Baraka notes in *Blues People,* both the call-and-response structure of the secular work songs and the AAB form of the classic blues can be traced to sacred forms that encode West African understandings of self, community, and spiritual energy. If the blues impulse can be described as a three-stage process—brutal experience, lyrical expression, affirmation—then the gospel impulse can be described in parallel terms derived from the sacred vocabularies of the African-American church: the burden, bearing witness, the vision of (universal) salvation. Bearing witness to his/her experience of the "burden," the gospel artist—possessed by a "Spirit" transcending human categorization—communicates a vision affirming the possibility of salvation for any person willing, as Leon Forrest phrases it, to "change their name." Whether phrased as "burden" or "brutal experience," as "near-tragic, near-comic lyricism" or "bearing witness," as existential "affirmation" or spiritual "vision," the blues/gospel process provides a foundation for African-American artists' explorations of new possibilities for self and community.

Playing the Changes

The choice of the specific topics considered in *Playing the Changes*—focusing on August Wilson and *Tar Baby,* say, rather than

Ntozake Shange and *Philadelphia Fire*—represents both my personal response to a variety of professional calls (for essays, lectures, seminars, etc.) and my call for further attention to writers whose work responds most usefully to the subversive calls of West African and African-American cultural traditions. Because I am more interested in exploring processes than in establishing foundations or advancing a theory, I have left the labels used to identify racial/cultural groups in the particular essays as originally written, reflecting the (re)phrasings of nearly fifteen years: Black, black, white (never, I believe, White), mainstream, Afro-American, Euro-American, European-American, African-American, etc. Similarly, rather than providing a global definition (thereby delimiting the range of potential response), this book allows the meaning(s) of (post)modern—the two "poles" of which, from most African-American perspectives seem more continuous than not—to emerge from the specific senses invoked in the individual chapters.

The four essays included in part 1, "Afro-Modernist Dialogues," address the question of why it makes sense to juxtapose African-American and (post)modern perspectives. Concluding that black folklore and the formal literature derived therefrom anticipate many of the potentially subversive insights of contemporary critical theory, "The Framing of Charles W. Chesnutt" emphasizes the need to negotiate literary texts with a broad awareness of the cultural frames circumscribing the meanings available to their changing audiences. "Endurance and Excavation: Afro-American Responses to Faulkner" approaches the Afro-Modernist dialogue through Stepto's paradigm of ascent and immersion, highlighting the "minstrel show" dynamic of cross-cultural communication. Like Faulkner's "narrative of endurance," the minstrel show begins with white artists distorting black cultural practices in ways that reveal specifically European-American psychological (and, indirectly, political) needs. Psychologically demeaning and historically destructive in its impact on black communities, the minstrel show dynamic, paradoxically, provides a useful image of how imitation, a way of testing the limits of understanding and personal identity, plays an inescapable role in all cross-cultural communication, including this book. "The Brier Patch as (Post)modernist Myth: Morrison, Barthes, and *Tar Baby* As-Is" brings the theoretical insights of Roland Barthes into dialogue with the work of our greatest living American writer. Confronting an implicitly (post)modern dilemma in a way that both casts light on and is clarified by the process of historical repression described in Barthes's "Myth Today," Morrison focuses on the attempts of Jadine (an ascent figure in Stepto's terms) and Son (an immersion figure) to come to terms with a world characterized by the intricate interaction of seemingly incompatible mythic understandings. Along with the chapter on Melvin B. Tolson's *Harlem Gallery,* "On the Ends of Afro-Modernist Autobiography" represents the culmination of my interest in "Afro-Modernism" as a primary phrasing. Reflecting the central role teaching has always played in my critical writing, several University of Wisconsin seminars on Afro-American modernism highlighted the limitations of (post)modern vocabularies even for audiences of intellectually talented and disciplined nonspecialists. Seriously addressing the fundamental issues even as they resisted what many students saw as unnecessarily arcane terminology, those seminars played a crucial role in redirecting my attention to African-American music as a way of phrasing Afro-Modernist issues in a more accessible, though equally rigorous and complex, manner.

Even prior to this reorientation, black music had played a major role in shaping the work on prosody included in part 2, "Studies in African-American Poetics." Both "Black Blues in the City: The Voices of Gwendolyn Brooks" and "Blues for T. S. Eliot and Langston Hughes: Melvin B. Tolson's Afro-Modernist Aesthetic" respond to Joyce scholar Bernard Benstock's admonition that "all literature is comparative literature" by examining the tension between European-American written and African-American oral forms. Paying close attention to details of diction, syntax, and rhythm, prosodic analysis focuses attention on the intricacies of the linguistic fields in which cross-cultural literary engagements take place. Complementing the formal methodology of these studies, "Black Dialectics: Kennedy, Bullins, Knight, Dumas, Lorde" links the detailed issues of technique raised in the prosody studies to a more general consideration of the premises and potential uses of Afro-American writing. Asserting the continuing importance of the Black Arts Movement (despite its sexist and homophobic articulation and flawed realization), this chapter examines five writers' engagements with the intersection of culture and politics: Adrienne Kennedy's critique of mainstream (post)modernism; Ed Bullins's attempt to forge a theory of "Black Dialectics" capable of turning a complex (post)modern consciousness to revolutionary uses; Etheridge Knight's populist vision of the poet as singer/warrior; Henry Dumas's celebration of a multicultural black nationalism; and Audre Lorde's insistence, informed by her experience as a black lesbian feminist mother, on a continuing awareness of ourselves as ancestors for future generations. "Black Dialectics," then, suggests that the roots of a dialectical, feminist, multiculturalism—the approach I believe offers the best chance of addressing contemporary activist concerns—lie in the Black Arts Movement, that while we should learn from the singer/warriors' mistakes, we should continue to honor them as ancestors.

Part 3, "Playing the Changes: Gospel, Blues, Jazz," consists of four essays exploring the relationship between African-American musical aesthetics and the issues introduced in the "Afro-Modernist Dialogues" and "Studies in African-American Poetics." "Bigger's Blues: *Native Son* and the Articulation of Afro-American Modernism" marks the transition from Afro-Modernist to musical phrasings. Where "Bigger's Blues" concentrates on the challenges facing Wright's protagonist in the blues-riddled secular world, "James Baldwin: Politics and the Gospel Impulse" concentrates on the sacred dimensions of black music, pointing toward the West Afrocentric visions discussed at greater length in "Leon Forrest and the AACM: The Jazz Impulse and the Chicago Renaissance" and "The Burden and the Binding Song: August Wilson's Neoclassical Jazz." Providing the context for my discussion of Forrest, one of the most powerful and undervalued Afro-Modernist writers, Robert Bone's documentation of the cultural flowering that took place in Chicago between the mid-1930s and mid-1960s marks the most significant revision of African-American literary history since the recovery of black women's writing sparked by June Jordan's "Notes toward a Black Balancing of Love and Hatred" (1974).

In addition to exploring the values underlying my West Afrocentric phrasing—functionality and a form of call and response that encourages individuals to pursue the outer ranges of their subjectivity (understood communally)—"The Burden and the Binding Song" anticipates a "new"—in the jazz sense—form of academic writing. This form responds to the lessons I have learned in the classroom, where I typically present contextual information, suggest alternative phrasings for questions concerning the relationship between texts and contexts, and then call for student responses, which almost inevitably highlight the different perspectives of blacks, whites, Asian-Americans; of men and women; of students from reservations, small towns, and big cities. The juxtaposition of contexts with exploratory improvisations (rather than focused theses) in this chapter suggests one way of adapting the call-and-response dynamic to the written critical text. Ideally, this structure will encourage freer responses from individual readers, who I hope will be encouraged to participate in the text by creating their own juxtapositions and recombinations of the framing devices and textual analysis. Combined with the discussions of Brooks and Tolson, part 3 is intended to clarify the underlying premises and possible functions of a process grounded in African-American musical aesthetics. The implicit foundation of what Amiri Baraka refers to as the "changing same" of black music, this process combines a West African spiritual vision (the gospel impulse), an unremitting honesty about the complexity and brutality of individual experience in an oppressive context (the blues impulse), and a constant struggle for self-definition and communal transformation (the jazz impulse).

In conclusion I would like to quote the call that has remained most insistently in my mind from the time I first encountered African-American literature in my father's library and in classes taught by Dan Tynan and Frank Krutzke at Colorado College through my graduate education under the guidance of Richard Barksdale, Bernard Benstock, and Keneth Kinnamon, whose scholarly rigor and integrity provide an inspirational model for white scholars of African-American culture, to my ongoing dialogues with Nellie McKay, Ron Radano, Herb Hill, Sandra Adell, and the many students who make the Department of Afro-American Studies at the University of Wisconsin an ideal environment for committed scholar-teachers. Near the end of *The Fire Next Time,* James Baldwin sounds a call for individual and social renewal: "If we—and now I mean the relatively conscious whites and the relatively conscious blacks, who must, like lovers, insist on, or create, the consciousness of the others—do not falter in our duty now, we may be able, handful that we are, to end the racial nightmare and achieve our country, and change the history of the world." Baldwin's concluding warning—"If we do not now dare everything the fulfillment of that prophecy, recreated from the Bible in song by a slave, is upon us: 'God gave Noah the rainbow sign, No more water, the fire next time'"—has never seemed more pressing or relevant than in the wake of the Los Angeles uprising, a conflagration predicated on the horrifying and destructive hypocrisies characterizing much European-American intellectual life (and I would not limit that characterization to the political Right) during the Reagan/Bush era. Concerned only secondarily with redefining the literary histories of either (post)modernism or African-American culture, *Playing the Changes* is my attempt to find a phrasing that helps make Baldwin's visionary, interracial "we" our reality.

PART 1

AFRO-MODERNIST DIALOGUES

▲ ▲ ▲ ▲

1

The Framing of
Charles W. Chesnutt

▲ ▲ ▲ ▲

First, three quotations.

"Under exegetical pressure, self-reference demonstrates the impossibility of self-possession. When poems denounce poetry as lies, self-referentiality is the source of undecidability, which is not ambiguity but a structure of logical irresolvability: if a poem speaks true in describing poetry as lies, then it lies; but if its claim that poems lie is a lie, then it must speak true."—Jonathan Culler, *On Deconstruction: Theory and Criticism after Structuralism* (202).

"They ain't no different from nobody else. . . . They mouth cut cross ways, ain't it? Well, long as you don't see no man wid they mouth cut up and down, you know they'll all lie jus' like de rest of us."—Zora Neale Hurston, *Mules and Men* (22).

"The text is a beautiful, slender stream, meandering gracefully through a wide meadow of margin."—Charles Waddell Chesnutt, "Baxter's *Procrustes*" (419).

As the Signifying Monkey and Brer Rabbit have always known, as Charles Chesnutt knew in 1890, as academic literary theorists working in the wake of Jacques Derrida have discovered, truth lies in a lie. By focusing on the writing of Chesnutt, one of the most enigmatic figures of the post-Reconstruction era, I hope to prefigure a politically significant discourse between Euro-American literary theory and the Afro-American expressive tradition it has excluded from its premises.

But before I begin, two remarks on the premises. First, an anecdote explaining a certain hostility toward the theoretical enterprise that may emerge throughout this study. As a graduate student at the University of Illinois, I participated briefly in a critical theory reading group. At one meeting, a prominent theoretician responded to Missy Dehn Kubitschek's question concerning the relevance of theory to a nonspecialist audience with the contemptuous statement, "I don't much care what the guys at the corner garage think about my work." Juxtaposed with the frequently recondite and exclusive vocabulary of theoretical writing, this dismissal highlighted what I perceived, and to some extent continue to perceive, as an elitist stance that bolsters the institutions deconstruction ostensibly calls into question. As an aesthetic populist who takes James Joyce, Aretha Franklin, and George Clinton with equal comico-seriousness, I consigned the whole enterprise to the nether regions and went about my business. Only gradually, under the gentle chiding of autodidacts Geoff King and Charles Weir and academics Kathy Cummings of the University of Washington and Robert Stepto of the Afro-American Studies Department of Yale—a ritual ground given over to unspeakable forces in my neo-populist demonology—did I begin to realize that, professional argot and elitist individuals aside, the guys at the corner garage may have been telling lies about their true theoretical knowledge all along.

Second, and perhaps the paranoia inheres in the populism, during the early 1980s I felt that I was standing alone in my reading of Chesnutt as an exceptionally complex (post)modernist ironist situated on the margins of a literary marketplace conditioned first by the plantation tradition stereotypes of Thomas Nelson Page and later by the virulent racist diatribes of Thomas Dixon. Standard literary histories evinced almost no awareness of Chesnutt's complexity; *The Cambridge History of American Literature* (edited by Carl Van Doren, et al., 1917) omits all mention of Chesnutt while the fourth edition of *The Literary History of the United States* (edited by Robert Spiller, et al., 1974) dismisses him as a minor plantation tradition figure overshadowed by Joel Chandler Harris. Even William Andrews's sensitive study *The Literary Career of Charles W. Chesnutt* credits Chesnutt with relatively little awareness of structural irony or metafictional subtlety. Aesthetic isolation mocks my populist soul; on the other hand, originality intrigues my academic mind. Fortunately, beginning with John Wideman's "Surfiction" (1985) and culminating in the trickster deconstructions of Darius James's *Negrophobia* (1992), it became apparent that the growing dialogue between Afro-American literary culture and various types of (post)modern/structuralist theory was creating a space within which my reading makes a different kind of sense. Maybe there's a point to conversing with demons after all. With these positions in mind, we can begin.

"Baxter's Procrustes"

"Baxter's *Procrustes*," the last story Chesnutt published prior to the literary silence of his last twenty-seven years, reflects his growing despair over the absence of an audience sensitive to his concerns. Not coincidentally, the story provides clear evidence that, even as he wrote the "conventional" novels (*The House behind the Cedars, The Marrow of Tradition, The Colonel's Dream*) that have veiled the complexity of the works which frame them, Chesnutt continued to develop his awareness of theoretical concerns that have entered the mainstream of Euro-American literary discourse only recently. To a large extent, the issues raised in "Baxter's *Procrustes*" are those described in Jonathan Culler's discussion of the "Critical Consequences" of deconstruction. Culler catalogs four levels on which deconstruction has affected literary criticism, the "first and most important [of which] is deconstruction's impact upon a series of critical concepts, including the concept of literature itself" (180). Among the specific results of deconstruction, he lists the following propositions. Deconstruction focuses attention on the importance and problematic nature of figures, encouraging readings of "literary works as implicit rhetorical treatises, which conduct in figurative terms an argument about the literal and the figural" (185); "intertextuality," the "relations between one representation and another rather than between a textual imitation and a nontextual original" (187); the gap between signifier and signified, leading to the conclusion that there "are no final meanings that arrest the movement of signification" (188); the *parergon*, the "problem of the frame—of the distinction between inside and outside and of the structure of the border" (193); and the problematic nature of self-reflexivity, which implies "the inability of any discourse to account for itself and the failure of performative and constative or doing and being to coincide" (201).

"Baxter's *Procrustes*," a parody of a literary club tricked into publishing and giving glowing reviews to a book that contains no words whatsoever, reads from a contemporary perspective as a treatise on the deconstructive issues Culler identifies. The "figural" descriptions of the reviewers, including the narrator, entirely supersede the book's "literal" contents, underlining the problematic relationship between signifiers and signified. The text's emphasis on the value of "uncut copies" of the book, ostensibly a printing of a poem parts of which Baxter has presented orally, draws attention to the problem of intertextuality. In Chesnutt's configuration, written copy and verbal "original" assume significance only intertextually, as they relate to one another; the probability that no "original" of Baxter's *Procrustes* exists renders the concept of "final meanings that arrest the movement of signification" absurd. Even the critical attempts to construct a final meaning are presented in terms of intertextuality. Responding to the comments of a fellow critic, the narrator observes: "I had a vague recollection of having read something like this somewhere, but so much has been written that one can scarcely discuss any subject of importance without unconsciously borrowing, now and then, the thoughts or the language of others" (419). Especially in regard to a "text" consisting entirely of absence, the most promising field of play for original critical thought, no definitive interpretation is possible. At his most insightful, the narrator half-recognizes the distance between his figuration and the text, writing that he "could see the cover through the wrapper of my sealed copy" (420). Chesnutt seems aware that this parody of critical/philosophical certainties implies a parallel deconstruction of the idea of the unified transcendent subject. The interrelationship between psychological and linguistic realities assumes a foreground position when the narrator claims that Baxter "has written himself into the poem. By knowing Baxter we are able to appreciate the book, and after having read the book we feel that we are so much the more intimately acquainted with Baxter—the real Baxter" (418). Baxter's significance can be perceived only through recognition of his absence.

The most interesting aspects of "Baxter's *Procrustes*," however, involve framing and self-reflexivity. Tracing the concept of the *parergon*—the "supplement" or "frame" of the aesthetic work—to its ill/logical extreme, Chesnutt again anticipates the deconstructive perception summarized by Culler as follows: "The supplement is essential. Anything that is properly framed . . . becomes an art object; but if framing is what creates the aesthetic object, this does not make the frame a determinable entity whose qualities could be isolated" (197). "Baxter's *Procrustes*" foregrounds this issue; frame and object simultaneously give one another significance—a significance derived purely from the traces each leaves in the other's field of absence—and deconstruct the hierarchical relationship between "ground" and "figure." The binding, which is the sole concern of the narrator's "review," is decorated with the fool's cap and bells, in effect becoming the "work" that derives its meaning from the *parergonal* absence of the empty pages. The narrator's description of the form of the words on the page in Baxter's *Procrustes* is based entirely on intertextual hearsay: "The text is a beautiful, slender stream, meandering gracefully through a wide meadow of margin" (419). This recognition in turn suggests an awareness of context as frame. Extending the concern with the audience introduced in Chesnutt's early work *The Conjure Woman,* which I will discuss in detail below, "Baxter's *Procrustes*" presents a model of a literary discourse in which cultural frame and literary text cannot be clearly distinguished from one another.

Published in the *Atlantic Monthly,* this openly self-reflexive text anticipates deconstruction's concern with the way "texts thematize, with varying degrees of explicitness, interpretive operations and their consequences and thus represent in advance the dramas that will give life to the tradition of their interpretation" (Culler 214–15). Sharing a title with an empty book reviewed by fools who drive the author out of their community while they continue to profit from his production—a "sealed copy" of Baxter's *Procrustes* is sold for a record price at a club auction after Baxter's expulsion—Chesnutt's "Baxter's *Procrustes*" anticipates its own "misreadings." Interestingly, it also anticipates future "positive" readings in the club president's suggestion that Baxter "was wiser than we knew, or than he perhaps appreciated" (421). The retrospective appreciation of Baxter's "masterpiece" (420), however, relates solely to its economic value. Suspended in a context in which Uncle Julius's original auditors, Chesnutt's contemporary readers, and, perhaps, even his future critics share an inability to perceive the true value of an Afro-American text, (")Baxter's *Procrustes*(") seems acutely aware that its self-reflexivity does not transcend the gap between signifier and signified, attain closure, or imply self-possession. In this recognition, as in so much else, Chesnutt seems much more proto-deconstructionist than the marginal plantation tradition figure he has traditionally been seen to be.

Signifying and Minstrelsy

Henry Louis Gates suggests the implicit connection between the Afro-American folk tradition from which Chesnutt drew many of the figures prominent in his early work and a certain type of deconstructionist sensibility. Gates presents "the Signifying Monkey, he who dwells at the margins of discourse" as a figure embodying the "Afro-American rhetorical strategy of signifying [as] a rhetorical act which is not engaged in the game of information-giving. Signifying turns on the play and chain of signifiers, and not on some supposedly transcendent signified" (129–31). Locating his own position in the space between Euro-American theory and Afro-American signifying, Gates applies his insights concerning what might be called "folk deconstruction" to Afro-American literary history in a diagram centering on Hurston and including Jean Toomer, Sterling Brown, Ralph Ellison, Richard Wright, and Ishmael Reed. In response to this diagram—clearly intended by Gates as provisional rather than definitive—I would suggest that, especially in "Baxter's *Procrustes*" and *The Conjure Woman* (1899), Chesnutt prefigures both the Afro- and Euro-American understandings of literary signification in a way that we have only recently begun to comprehend. In advancing this argument, I am suggesting not simply that theoretical insights can be profitably applied to Chesnutt's work or that a general parallel exists between the Afro-American tradition and Euro-American theory. Rather, I am suggesting that Chesnutt anticipates constructive approaches to several issues that remain extremely problematic in contemporary theoretical discourse. From a deconstructionist perspective, for example, it should come as no surprise that focusing on the excluded margin, the Afro-American literary tradition, which has never enjoyed the social privilege allowing it to dismiss the masters from its awareness, should help cast light on the blind spots of Euro-American theory.

By focusing on a general (and to the extent possible, shared) understanding of deconstruction in contemporary academic discourse —and I am aware that such a generalized understanding inevitably simplifies any particular critical practice—I hope to lay some groundwork for future cross-cultural discussions. Terry Eagleton's chapter "Post-Structuralism" in *Literary Theory: An Introduction* and Culler's chapter "Critical Consequences" in *On Deconstruction*, two works that diverge sharply in their political and institutional commitments, share a number of premises I shall treat as consensual positions. Both understand deconstruction as a philosophically grounded approach that: emphasizes the problematic relationship between the linguistic signifier and the "transcendent signified" (Eagleton 131; Culler 188); challenges, and ultimately decenters, hierarchies of thought or expression based on binary oppositions that privilege one term over its ostensible opposite (Culler 213; Eagleton 132); focuses on the "marginal" terms excluded from the discourse in order to recognize the way in which the text subverts its own meaning (Culler 215; Eagleton 132–33); recognizes that all signifiers derive their meaning from "traces" of other signifiers; and concentrates on the "play of signifiers," creating a theoretically endless chain that frustrates attempts at closure (Eagleton 134; Culler 188). Eagleton summarizes the deconstructive project as follows: "Deconstruction tries to show how such oppositions, in order to hold themselves in place, are sometimes betrayed into inverting or collapsing themselves, or need to banish to the text's margins certain niggling details which can be made to return and plague them. . . . The tactic of deconstructive criticism, that is to say, is to show how texts come to embarrass their own ruling systems of logic" (133). Culler echoes this understanding when he writes of the deconstructionist interest in "previous readings which, in separating a text into the essential and marginal elements, have created for the text an identity that the text itself, through the power of its marginal elements, can subvert" (188). Generalizing this approach in a manner consistent with Eagleton's insistence on the contextual determinants of textual meaning, Culler asserts, "one could, therefore, identify deconstruction with the twin principles of the contextual determination of meaning and the infinite extendability of context" (218).

Although his active publishing career had ended by the time Ferdinand de Saussure delivered the lectures that would become the *Course in General Linguistics* between 1907 and 1911, Chesnutt might well have understood these principles, albeit in a different specific vocabulary. Chesnutt derived his awareness of the problematical nature of binary oppositions, hierarchies in discourse, and the signifier-signified relationship from two basic sources: the folk tradition on which he drew and the literary context in which he wrote. As Hurston, Ellison, Lawrence Levine, and Gates have noted in quite different contexts, the Afro-American folk tradition encodes a profound suspicion of and resistance to Euro-American expression. Placed in a marginal position enforced by institutional structures and physical violence, Afro-Americans, especially those *without* access to the mainstream educational system, have always been acutely aware of the radical inadequacy of white figures for black experience. Experiencing what W. E. B. Du Bois called *double consciousness*—"this sense of always looking at one's self through the eyes of others, of measuring one's soul by the tape of a world that looks on in amused contempt and pity" (17)—Afro-Americans, individually and communally, learned quickly to exploit the gap between signifier and signified. Constructing elaborate verbal "masks" in everyday discourse as well as in the spirituals and animal tales, "slaves" (to use the Euro-American signifier) continually (and because of their political oppression, implicitly) subverted the oppositional racist association of *white* with such privileged terms as "good," "God," "mature," and "civilized," and *black* with such excluded terms as "evil," "devil," "child-like," and "savage." Focusing on the "marginal" elements of the dominant discourse (i.e., themselves), they learned to decenter social and political hierarchies in order to survive, psychologically and physically. Ultimately, as Ellison notes in his wonderfully titled essay "Change the Joke and Slip the Yoke," this shaped an expressive tradition based precisely on the closure-resisting play of signifiers articulating "a land of masking jokers" in which "the motives hidden behind the mask are as numerous as the ambiguities the mask conceals" (70). Chesnutt, one of the first Afro-American writers to assume the truth lying behind Ellison's signifying, incorporates this folk sensibility into his literary productions in a highly self-conscious manner.

The specific manifestations of this self-consciousness, however, derive directly from the tradition of racial signification in Euro-American writing of the 1880s and 1890s. When Chesnutt began to publish in mainstream magazines such as *Family Fiction* and the *Atlantic Monthly* in 1886 and 1887, he encountered editors and readers deeply influenced by Joel Chandler Harris's tales of Uncle Remus and Brer Rabbit. Harris remains one of the least understood, and perhaps least understandable, figures in one of the least understood/standable currents of the southern literary tradition: that of minstrelsy. On the surface, Harris appears to articulate a straightforward version of the plantation tradition in his tales of an essentially childlike black man gently harassed into telling charming animal stories by a young white boy who brings sweets and affection from the big house. Occupying the center of the American consciousness of Harris—the Disney minstrel show *Song of the South* is only the most obvious of many examples—this image would seem to dictate dismissal of the Uncle Remus tales as the type of "blackface minstrelsy" Berndt Ostendorf describes as "a symbolic slave code, a set of self-humiliating rules designed by white racists for the disenfranchisement of the black self" (66).

Beneath both the benevolent and maleficent surfaces of the minstrel tradition, however, lie unsuspected depths where Harris joins William Faulkner and Derrida to comprise a significant genealogy in which Chesnutt is the crucial, and crucially unrecognized, missing relation. The most powerful recent Faulkner criticism, that written by John Irwin and Eric Sundquist, recognizes a troubling link between the irresolvability of the Faulknerian text—Irwin calls Quentin's narration of *Absalom, Absalom!* "an answer that doesn't answer— an answer that puts the answerer in question" (8)—and unresolved psychological tensions originating in miscegenation, the denied actuality that unrelentingly subjects racial oppositions to subversive interrogation. Orienting his discussion specifically toward Faulkner's rejection of the binary oppositions inherent in "Manichaeanism," Sundquist writes: "The gothicism of *Absalom, Absalom!* is not by any means the sentimentality of a minstrel show—not the benign dream in which 'all coons look alike'—but the nightmare in which black *and* white begin all too hauntingly to look alike" (99). Harris and Chesnutt in fact prefigure this Faulknerian dilemma, a dilemma inherent in the minstrel show from the beginning. As Ostendorf writes,

"Minstrelsy anticipated on stage what many Americans deeply feared: the blackening of America. Minstrelsy did in fact create a symbolic language and a comic iconography for 'intermingling' culturally with the African Caliban while at the same time 'isolating' him socially. In blackening his face the white minstrel acculturated voluntarily to his 'comic' vision of blackness, thus anticipating in jest what he feared in earnest. . . . Minstrelsy is proof that negrophilia and negrophobia are not at all contradictory. Minstrelsy is negrophobia staged as negrophilia, or vice versa, depending on the respective weight of the fear or attraction" (67, 81). To state this in specifically deconstructive terms, the minstrel show—whether manifested in the Uncle Remus tales, Faulkner's novels, or, as Charles Sanders brilliantly suggests, T. S. Eliot's *The Waste Land*—subverts its own meaning by deconstructing the binary oppositions on which its hierarchical structures depend, creating a form of expression that demands confrontation with an infinitely extensive/regressive chain of signifiers. Which is to say: white minstrelsy deconstructs itself.

Uncle Remus, His Songs, and Subversions

Nowhere is this clearer than in *Uncle Remus: His Songs and Sayings*, the text through which Harris engendered a long line of Euro-American negrophiles. As Harris seems to have sensed—he attributed the writing of the Brer Rabbit tales to an internal "other fellow" who "is simply a spectator of my folly until I seize a pen, and then he comes forward and takes charge" (Martin 92)—and as Bernard Wolfe first articulated in "Uncle Remus and the Malevolent Rabbit" (1949), the volume presents a sequence of "answers that don't answer, that put the answerer in question." Just beneath the negrophiliac surface of the "charming" tales (most of them faithfully reproduced from the Afro-American oral tradition) Harris attributes to the benevolently asexual Uncle Remus lies a world of violence, sexual energy, and barely subdued racial drama in which the physically weak Brer Rabbit attains at least momentary mastery over the stronger but less aware Brers Bear, Wolf, and Fox through his manipulation of the gap between verbal signifier and concrete action. Encoded within the ordered hierarchy of the plantation tradition, the trickster figure delights in the disruption of hierarchies, textual or contextual, almost without reference to their apparent significance. At times, as in "The Wonderful Tar-Baby Story," this radically subversive delight works to Brer Rabbit's detriment. When Brer Rabbit takes on the role of the "master" demanding respect from the tar baby—a profoundly charged figure for the "black" pole of oppositional racist thought (stupid, lazy, very black, a thing)—his discourse subverts his own claims of privilege as surely as his ability to turn Brer Fox into a riding horse elsewhere decenters the plantation tradition hierarchy. This aspect of the Brer Rabbit tales is particularly important in relation to the development of Afro-American discourse because it protects against substituting one set of privileged terms for another. Although Wolfe's reading of the animal fables as allegories of racial hatred and sexual competition seems accurate, the random and frequently self-destructive manifestations of Brer Rabbit's deconstructive energies makes it clear that the tales privilege *neither* the black nor white position.

An understanding of Chesnutt, however, requires some attention to Harris's adaptation of this material in *Uncle Remus: His Songs and Sayings,* which subverts its own intended meanings by encoding several thoroughly contradictory versions of its Afro-American subjects. The tension emerges clearly in a comparison of the three major sections of the book. The irascible minstrel show darky signified by the name "Uncle Remus" in "His Sayings" and the loyal slave presented in the plantation tradition short story "A Story of the War" evince nothing of the creative energy of the storyteller of "Legends of the Old Plantation." Within the "legends," on which Harris's reputation depends almost entirely, a similar tension exists between the frame tales, written in standard English, and the animal tales, written in a linguistically accurate dialect that Harris's introduction contrasts with "the intolerable misrepresentations of the minstrel stage" (39). As Harris's comment concerning the "other fellow" intimates, an anxious but not quite articulated awareness that the linguistic and thematic tensions of the book cast his own identity as a unified subject into doubt permeates *Uncle Remus.* The opening "legend," "Uncle Remus Initiates the Little Boy," establishes not one but two narrative frames, suggesting the unbridgeable distance between Euro-American signification and Afro-American experience. The most obvious frame tale concerning Uncle Remus and the seven-year-old boy establishes a symbolic equality between the ostensibly child-like black man and the actual white child. Like Mark Twain's *Tom Sawyer,* Harris's pastoral version of an earlier self reveals a deep longing for the Old South (Martin 92–96). Alongside this frame, however, another frame, almost entirely unrecognized, presents a "mature" perspective that "explains" how the collaboration between the two "childlike" figures happens to have been written down on paper. Presented only at the beginning of the first legend, this frame is in some ways as subversive of oppositional hierarchies as the Brer Rabbit tales themselves. The little boy is introduced as a figure of absence; his mother, "Miss Sally," a curiously asexual figure who will be refigured in the "Miz Meadows" of the Brer Rabbit tales, "misses" her child. Arriving at Uncle Remus's cabin, she sees her "boys" together and steps back. Harris concludes the initial frame with the sentence: "This is what 'Miss Sally' heard" (55). Although there is no evidence that he was doing so as part of a conscious rhetorical strategy, Harris has in effect decentered his presence into at least four components: Uncle Remus who as storyteller plays the role of "the other fellow" in charge of Harris's pen; the little boy who bears the most obvious biographical relationship to Harris; the passive "feminine" figure who resembles the Harris who collected the tales attributed to Uncle Remus from a number of Afro-American "informants"; and the silent scribe, Harris the *Atlanta Constitution* columnist who attributes his tales not directly to the black tellers but to a white female intermediary. In this complex configuration, neither whiteness nor masculinity possesses the significance—as signifiers invoking a range of transcendent creative attributes—attributed them by the explicitly patriarchal and paternalistic plantation tradition writers.

Given the multitude of "presences" mediating between "Harris" and his "subjects," it should come as no surprise to discover mutually deconstructing forms of awareness throughout the "legends." "The End of Mr. Bear," for example, betrays its own ruling system of logic in several ways. Most obviously, the text subverts the plantation tradition opposition between benevolent white master and happy black slave through the contrast between the superficially stereotypical frame and the vicious tale. Culminating in the death of Brer Bear (on the level of racial allegory, the symbolic white man), who Brer Rabbit tricks into sticking his head into a tree where it is stung by a swarm of bees, the text closes with an expression of barely veiled joy (attributed to Uncle Remus but consistent with the folk materials) derived from contemplation of this inverted lynching: "dar ole Brer B'ar hung, en ef his head ain't swunk, I speck I hangin' dar yit" (136). It seems almost unbelievable that no critic prior to Wolfe seems to have understood this even in part as a warning against the racial pride—ironically projected as a savage black desire for a "shrunken head"—which enforced the social privilege encoded in the black-white opposition.

Even in the frame, "The End of Mr. Bear" provides clear evidence of the tendency of Harris's text to "embarrass its own ruling systems of logic." When the little boy comes to the cabin, he finds Uncle Remus "unusually cheerful and goodhumored" (133). Signifying this good humor in the way most dear to slaveholders and plantation tradition writers who cited the slaves' oral performances as proof of their contentment, Uncle Remus sings a song, "a senseless affair so far as the words were concerned" (133). Immediately after quoting a verse of this "non-signifying" song, however, Harris contradicts himself in a peculiar manner. Unconsciously underlining Harris's ever-shifting Brer Rabbit–like relation to his text, the following passage reads:

> The quick ear of Uncle Remus, however, had detected the presence of the little boy, and he allowed his song to run into a recitation of nonsense, of which the following, if it be rapidly spoken, will give a faint idea: "Ole M'er Jackson, fines' confraction, fell down sta'rs fer to git satisfaction; big Bill Fray, he rule de day, eve'ything he call fer come one, two by three. Gwine 'long one day, met Johnny Huby, ax him grine nine yards er steel fer me, tole me w'ich he couldn't; den I hist 'im over Hickerson Dickerson's barn-doors; knock 'im ninety-nine miles under water, w'en he rise, he rise in Pike straddle un a hanspike, en I lef' 'im dar smokin' er de hornpipe, Juba reda seda breda. Aunt Kate at de gate; I want to eat, she fry de meat en gimme skin, w'ich I fling it back agin. Juba!" (133)

This curious passage begins with an intimation of a level of awareness in Uncle Remus, associated with his leporine "quick ear," that allows him to shift from the "senseless affair" into "a recitation of nonsense." The reasons for the shift, or the differences between the two levels of nonsignifying discourse, are never stated. Emphasizing the insufficiency of his written text, which can provide only a "faint idea" of the oral expression of "Uncle Remus," who exists only within the written text, Harris plunges into what, if recognized, would certainly have seemed a nightmarish minstrel show skit on the relationship between signifier and signified. Trapped within the hierarchical system that denies transcendence to the Afro-American subject, Harris can only dismiss Uncle Remus's words, albeit with a great uneasiness grounded on his sense that the black voice signifies something unavailable to any white "presence" in the text.

Clearly a version of the signifying rhetoric described by Gates, Uncle Remus's speech is best understood as a quintessentially Afro-American manipulation of the "play of signifiers," which includes numerous politically resonant images of conflict and Africanisms that subvert plantation tradition images without concern for specific referential meaning. Accepting the divergence between signifier and signified, the black voice encoded in the text subverts the previous interpretation of the words as nonsense. Immediately after the performance, which creates "bewilderment" in the young boy and, presumably, in the white readership guided by Harris's remarks, Uncle Remus proceeds "with the air of one who had just given an important piece of information" (134). The black voice, aware that the destruc-

tion of an oppositional hierarchy resting on a simplistic sense of linguistic significance does not entail the destruction of all meaning,
very nearly effects a successful revolution when Uncle Remus says:
"Hit's all des dat away, honey. . . . En w'en you bin cas'n shadders
long ez de ole nigger, den you'll fine out who's w'ich, en w'ich's who"
(134). Acutely uncomfortable with the confusion of identity established through the verbal play of the "black" voice in the "white" text,
Harris seems unable to distinguish between his own voice and the
voice of an "other"—a Jungian "shadder" figure—subverting the
hierarchical system that privileges the written expression as a mark
of civilization and humanity. Returning to the standard English of
the frame tale, Harris attempts to reassert the plantation tradition
stereotype that ascribes superior "capacity" to whites and only childlike significance to black expression: "The little boy made no response. He was in thorough sympathy with all the whims and humors
of the old man, and his capacity for enjoying them was large enough
to include even those he could not understand" (134). Even the reas-
sertion reveals subversive traces, however; the boy is silenced, uncomprehending. Shortly the angry black voice of the Brer Rabbit tales
will assume the central position in the world of the text. The deconstructive black voice renders the white personae silent, thereby creating a space for articulation of the subversive animal tale ending with
the lynching of Brer Bear, condemned by his inability to see through
Brer Rabbit's masks.

As ironic prelude, however, and apparently without any awareness
on the part of Harris, Uncle Remus effects a role reversal that places
the white child in the symbolic position of the subordinate attending
to the marginal details of the master's work: "Uncle Remus was fin-
ishing an axe-handle, and upon these occasions it was his custom *to
allow* the child to hold one end while he applied sand-paper to the
other" (134; emphasis added). The final sentence of the frame story
echoes, almost word for word, the standard plantation tradition description of slavery as a system benefiting both black and white:
"These relations were pretty soon established, to the mutual satisfaction of the parties most interested." Operating in the newly created
textual space, the final clause of the final framing sentence specifically contrasts the nonsense of the previous sections with the significance of the animal tale to come: "the old man continued his remarks, but this time not at random" (134). Even the frame tale, the
section of *Uncle Remus* in which Harris attempts to impose the oppositional order of the plantation tradition on the Afro-American folk
materials, is subject to the deconstructive energies of the black voice.
As the frame story metamorphoses into Brer Rabbit tale, the white

writer's voice surrenders itself to the black speaker's as written by the white writer. In effect, the text acknowledges a significance in the nonsignifying nonsense. This infiltration of a signifying black voice into not only the tale but the frame itself recalls Ostendorf's comments on the minstrel show and prefigures the racial and aesthetic tensions of Faulkner's greatest work.

The Conjure Woman

Appropriating the voice of the Euro-American figure who established the ground on which he worked, Chesnutt recognized and consciously manipulated the unconsciously subversive form of *Uncle Remus*. Particularly in *The Conjure Woman*, Chesnutt employs a complex rhetorical strategy, based on a deep understanding of the deconstructionist principles of the contextual determination of meaning and the infinite extendibility of context, anticipated in the southern literary tradition only by the best work of Poe and Twain. Superficially, Chesnutt's conjure stories mimic Harris's structure; a white narrator, writing in standard English, reports the charming but absurd tales of an old black man, presented in black dialect. Like Uncle Remus, Chesnutt's Uncle Julius seems motivated by childlike selfish concerns. Uncle Remus cajoles the little boy into bringing him sweets; Uncle Julius manipulates his white listeners, the relocated northern businessman John and his wife, Annie, into a variety of personal indulgences. Most critics who have discussed the relationship between frame tale and conjure story in *The Conjure Woman* concentrate on the economic dimension of the relationship between Julius and John or on Julius's attempt to educate Annie concerning the realities of slavery (Ferguson; Andrews). While these observations shed light on the mimetic dimension of the text, they typically exclude those aspects that relate primarily to the communication process itself, the aspects that intimate Chesnutt's awareness of numerous theoretical concerns.

The rhetorical relationship between John and Julius in *The Conjure Woman* comments directly on Chesnutt's own position as an Afro-American writer working in a context dominated by Euro-American oppositional hierarchies, particularly the plantation tradition stereotypes shaped by Harris, Thomas Nelson Page, and countless others publishing in the same magazines where "The Goophered Grapevine" and "The Conjurer's Revenge" first appeared. Recognition of this parallel hinges on an understanding of the significance of the "mask" in the signifying tradition. In *Mules and Men,* Hurston described masking as follows:

the Negro, in spite of his open-faced laughter, his seeming acquiescence, is particularly evasive. You see we are a polite people and we do not say to our questioner, "Get out of here!" We smile and tell him or her something that satisfies the white person because, knowing so little about us, he doesn't know what he is missing. . . . The theory behind our tactics: "The white man is always trying to know somebody else's business. All right, I'll set something outside the door of my mind for him to play with and handle. He can read my writing but he sho' can't read my mind. I'll put this play toy in his hand, and he will seize it and go away. Then I'll say my say and sing my song." (4–5)

Most immediately, this rhetorical strategy creates a space, simultaneously physical, verbal, and psychological, within which the Afro-American individual and community can survive in a hostile racist culture. At times, it can serve as a more active political tool allowing Afro-Americans access to information or situations from which they would be excluded if their true motives were recognized. Set against this background, the figure Chesnutt creates in *The Conjure Woman* comes into focus as an elaborate mask, or set of masks, designed to infiltrate Euro-American discourse and, in the long run, subvert the binary oppositions on which racial privilege depends.

It should be noted in approaching this strategy that, as soon as an audience recognizes the mask as a mask, the mask loses all possible effectiveness. The nature of the masking strategy, therefore, depends on the trickster's ability to convince the audience that it sees his/her actual face. One of the conceptually simple but practically inexhaustible methods for attaining this goal is to construct "false" masks, masks over masks, which the audience is allowed to see through in order to convince it that it has seen the trickster's face when in fact it is encountering only another mask. In effect, Chesnutt uses such a strategy to construct a complex model of subversive strategies in which the masking Julius, prefiguring the doubly conscious Afro-American modernist writer, manipulates his audience through his awareness of the structure and limitations of Euro-American oppositional thought and his understanding of the potential uses of a marginal position.

Reflecting his situation as a light-skinned "black" writer born in North Carolina but living in Ohio, Chesnutt creates two personae, textual masks: John, with whom he shares geographical residence and a Euro-American literacy based on writing and knowledge of white institutional structures (Stepto 167), and Julius, with whom he shares racial and geographical origins and "tribal literacy," based on oral expression and specifically black cultural patterns (Stepto 167). Dividing "himself" into two figures who, in the binary oppositions of the plantation tradition, are mutually exclusive and irresolvable, Chesnutt anticipates Saussure in critiquing the linguistic convention, crucial to mimetic fiction, that asserts the identity of signifier and signified. Nonetheless, Chesnutt's audience, excluding from its discourse any cultural traditions positing alternatives to oppositional thinking and assuming the identity of signifier and signified, was almost totally unprepared to understand his critique. Chesnutt's "solution" to the problem brought the implicitly deconstructive elements of the masking/signifying tradition of Afro-American culture very near the surface of *The Conjure Woman*.

In *The Conjure Woman*, Julius, like Chesnutt in the literary culture of his era, constructs a sequence of increasingly opaque masks, predicated on his knowledge of the structure of his audience's belief systems and implying a recognition of the underlying perceptions asserted in Culler's identification of deconstruction with "the twin principles of the contextual determination of meaning and the infinite extendability of context." On the surface the Julius of "The Goophered Grapevine" appears to be motivated by economic self-interest, telling the story of the haunted vineyard in an attempt to scare John off and keep the grapes for himself. But this mask is absurdly transparent. Julius, of course, has no hope of frightening John, the "hard-headed" businessman, with romantic fancy. If John grants Julius any economic concessions it is because he is an essentially well-meaning "master." In fact, Julius seems aware of the actual economic dynamic when he stresses the past bounty of the vineyard and the crucial role played by blacks in maintaining its productivity.

In addition to suggesting a less direct economic motive, this double voicing intimates Julius's awareness that his white audience is in fact less unified than it appears. Employing many of the standard images associated with the nineteenth-century sentimental fiction addressed primarily to a female audience—particularly those focusing on the division of families (Fiedler)—Julius addresses not only John but also Annie, whom he gradually educates concerning the inhumanity of the slave system of the Old South. Given the composition of Chesnutt's magazine audience, it seems likely that he perceived the parallel between Julius's rhetorical strategy and his own. Allowing male readers seeking escapist fantasy to perceive him, like Julius, as a simple storyteller who "seemed to lose sight of his auditors, and to be living over again in monologue his life on the old plantation" (12–13), Chesnutt simultaneously educated his "female" audience, which itself occupied a marginal position in patriarchal/paternalistic culture, concerning the actual brutalities of racial relations.

Adopting an essentially deconstructive narrative technique, Julius places his criticism of the romantic image of the Old South in the margins of his tale. Frequently, his most pointed criticism occurs in the background descriptions of what life was like "befo' de wah," a common formula in the nostalgic stories of Page and others. In "The Goophered Grapevine," for example, Julius says: 'I reckon it ain' so much so nowadays, but befo' de wah, in slab'ry times, a nigger did n' mine goin fi' er ten mile in a night, w'en dey wuz sump'n good ter eat at de yuther een'" (14). Contrasted with the illicit treats the boy gives Uncle Remus or with the slave banquet in Paul Laurence Dunbar's poem "The Party," the political point of Julius's marginal "literary criticism" seems unmistakable. Especially in the early tales, Julius makes political points obliquely since more direct approaches might alienate John and result in his exclusion from the situation in which he can address Annie. As Julius establishes himself within the structure of John's and Annie's lives, however, he alters his strategy. "Mars Jeems's Nightmare," the third story in the collection, focuses on a harsh master whose attitudes change substantially after he is transformed into a slave for a period of time; clearly, Julius feels free to include much more explicit social commentary than he had previously. Although John retains his condescending belief in the childlike simplicity of blacks in his ironic comment—"I am glad, too, that you told us the moral of the story; it might have escaped us otherwise"—there is no danger that he will use his social privilege to exclude Julius from the discourse into which they have entered (101). The strategy of "Mars Jeems' Nightmare" depends, therefore, on that of "The Goophered Grapevine," which disarmed John by playing on his belief that he "understands" Julius when he has actually only seen through a transparent economic mask. The long-term success of the strategy, however, requires periodic reinforcement of John's assumption, which Julius provides in "The Conjurer's Revenge" when he tricks John into buying a blind horse. The significance of Julius's interaction with John, then, lies not in the success or failure of a particular trick but in the control he attains over the context in which he can direct his "marginal" address to Annie, who frequently supports Julius's search for communal rather than purely individual benefits.

When he allows this mask to become transparent in the didactic "Mars Jeems' Nightmare," Julius creates another level of contextual complexity. By convincing relatively liberal whites such as Annie, who are willing to face the somewhat distanced reality of the brutality of the Old South (itself part of a binary opposition of North-civilized/ South-primitive), that they have seen the true face of the black "petitioner," Chesnutt creates a context in which his more radical subversion can infiltrate the literary forum. Having entered this discourse, Chesnutt may in fact discredit both conservative Old South *and* liberal New South through the structural analogy between the whites in the fables Julius tells and those in the frame story Chesnutt writes. From this perspective, John and Annie can be seen as new incarnations of the old masters subjecting Afro-Americans to a system of discourse and institutional organization that denies their humanity. Allowing his readers to penetrate a sequence of transparent masks, Chesnutt articulated an extremely intricate parody that deconstructs the ostensible opposition of "liberal North" and "reactionary South," both of which manifest a similar set of racist attitudes. Active oppression and condescending pity—recalling Du Bois's doubled consciousness of contempt and pity—are equally compatible with the binary oppositions of the plantation tradition. Perhaps Chesnutt's final target, in his immediate context, is northern readers who, like John and Annie, are willing to indulge the transparent "entertainments" of a charming black storyteller, perhaps even accepting a limited political critique, as long as the social framework remains undisturbed.

Each level of this process moves toward the actual context in which Chesnutt wrote, raising questions regarding the interaction of text and world, and implicitly repudiating the traditional view of fiction as a privileged form of discourse. Extending this approach temporally, it would be possible to see Chesnutt as attempting to educate a future audience, or perhaps future Afro-American writers, in the methods of deconstructionist/masking reading and writing. Of course such readers and writers, whites or "literate" blacks, themselves would be subject to interpretation as new incarnations of John and Annie determined to master Afro-American experience through ever more subtle techniques. At some point in this infinitely extendible context, Chesnutt's deconstructions flip over into a kind of structuralist (though not ahistorical) awareness of the persistence of the deeply ingrained oppositional structures characterizing Euro-American discourse and supporting oppressive institutions. In speculating on the long-term implications of the rhetorical structure of *The Conjure Woman,* I realize I have ventured forth onto shifting ground. The final stages of the process outlined above are unsupported and, by nature, unsupportable. The last mask must always remain opaque, at least to its immediate audience. Any evidence of its construction renders it partially transparent and subjects it to possible exclusion from the public forum, destroying any hope of political effectiveness. The play of signifiers must resist closure in order to resist the power of the dominant discourse. Nevertheless, Chesnutt provides enough textual evidence to suggest this approach is not simply a postmodernist imposition, an academic revoicing of the plantation tradition distortion of the Afro-American voice. Both the contrast between John's and Julius's linguistic practices and the specific choices of material for Julius's tales suggest Chesnutt's conscious awareness of complex theoretical approaches to discourse.

Possessing only a minimal sense of irony, John takes the identity of signifier and signified as a given. Because his attitude toward southern life has been shaped by literature, John perceives Julius in terms of plantation tradition signifiers. Rather than leading to a relaxation of his belief in the adequacy of the signifiers, perceived discrepancies between signifier and signified are resolved by adjusting his conception of the signified. John's belief in the plantation tradition stereotype attributing mental capacity solely to the white term of the white/black binary opposition leads him to create a mixed ancestry for Julius: "There was a shrewdness in his eyes, too, which was not altogether African, and which, as we afterwards learned from experience, was indicative of a corresponding shrewdness in his character" (9–10). Similarly, the frame story of "Mars Jeems's Nightmare" emphasizes the underlying structure of the binary opposition that defines blacks as subhuman. Extending the black-physical/white-mental dichotomy, John describes Julius's relationship with the "natural" world:

> Toward my tract of land and the things that were on it—the creeks, the swamps, the hills, the meadows, the stones, the trees—he maintained a peculiar personal attitude, that might be called predial rather than proprietary. He had been accustomed, until long after middle life, to look upon himself as the property of another. When this relation was no longer possible, owing to the war, and to his master's death and the dispersion of the family, he had been unable to break off entirely the mental habits of a lifetime, but had attached himself to the old plantation, of which he seemed to consider himself an appurtenance. (64–65)

In addition to supporting politically destructive institutions, such reduction of the black subject reveals John's simplistic linguistic and philosophical premises. Foregrounding the deconstructionist tendencies implicit in *Uncle Remus, The Conjure Woman* suggests ways of subverting the power of the discourse based on such simplistic premises.

Recognizing John's tendency to confuse white metaphorical signification with the actuality of the "black thing" signified, Julius bases his strategy on the manipulation of the unrecognized distance between signifier and signified. Where John assumes presence, Julius implies absence. Frequently, Julius's speech implies the inadequacy of the signifier = signified paradigm, drawing attention to the ways in which the linguistic figuration serves institutional structures whose actual operations the language veils. For example, Julius describes Mars Jeems's relations with his slaves as follows: "His niggers wuz bleedzd ter slabe fum daylight ter da'k, w'iles yuther folks's did n' hafter wuk 'cep'n' fum sun ter sun" (71). Rhetorically accepting the distinction between "daylight ter da'k" and "sun ter sun," this sentence parodies the way in which white folks, especially when they want to evade their own position in an unjust system, employ different signifiers to obscure what from the Afro-American perspective appear to be identical signifieds. Although the sun rises after light and sets before dark, the distinction, which might be emphasized by a good master as evidence of his kindness, does nothing to alter the fact that, in either case, the enforced labor is of murderous duration. Frequently Julius bases his rhetoric on the apparent acceptance of a white signifier, as in "The Goophered Grapevine," which identifies the slave Henry with the vineyard in much the same way John identifies Julius with the "things" of the plantation. By adapting John's preconceptions, Julius finds it much easier to construct an effective mask. As Gates notes in his discussion of the "Signifying Monkey," who along with Brer Rabbit provides the closest analogue for Uncle Julius in the folk tradition, "the Signifying Monkey [Julius, Chesnutt] is able to signify upon the Lion [John, the white readership] only because the Lion does not understand the nature of the Monkey's discourse. . . . The Monkey speaks *figuratively,* in a symbolic code, whereas the Lion interprets or 'reads' *literally*" (133–34).

A similar dynamic is at work in relation to the "folk" tales that charmed and fascinated both Julius's auditors in the text and Chesnutt's readership. Because the tales are presented in dialect within a frame readily familiar to readers of Harris, most contemporary reviewers assumed that Chesnutt was presenting "authentic" Afro-American folk tales; several hostile reviews criticized *The Conjure Woman* for simply repeating folk materials without adequate imaginative transformation. As Melvin Dixon demonstrates, however, only one of the tales ("The Goophered Grapevine") is an authentic folk tale. While the remainder incorporate folk elements, Chesnutt transforms them in a way that deconstructs the hierarchy on which the negative judgments rest. The recurring images of transformation in the tales—Sandy turns into a tree, Mars Jeems into a slave, Henry into a kind of human grapevine, etc.—implicitly repudiate the identification of signifier with transcendent signified. Identity is multiple, shifting, a play of forces rather than a transcendent essence. Chesnutt charmingly anticipates the Faulknerian minstrel show/nightmare in which the answers place the answerers in question; names surrender their significance, becoming a source of ironic play in which the devil turns from black to white: "Mars Jeems's oberseah wuz a po' w'ite man name' Nick Johnson,—de niggers called 'im Mars Johnson ter his face, but behin' his back dey useter call 'im Ole Nick, en de name suited 'im ter a T" (75).

Deprived of their linguistic base, dichotomies—including that of white-classical-written-civilized/black-vernacular-oral-savage—collapse. For, although Chesnutt used Afro-American folk materials, the clearest source of the stories in *The Conjure Woman* is Ovid's *Metamorphoses*. The illiterate former slave and the classical poet play one another's roles in the minstrel show in which black and white begin to look very much alike. In a rhetorical gambit worthy of "The Purloined Letter" or the Signifying Monkey, Chesnutt draws attention to the similarity between Julius's concerns and those of the Euro-American philosophical tradition. At the beginning of "The Gray Wolf's Ha'nt," John sits down with Annie and reads:

> The difficulty of dealing with transformations so many-sided as those which all existences have undergone, or are undergoing, is such as to make a complete and deductive interpretation almost hopeless. So to grasp the total process of redistribution of matter and motion as to see simultaneously its several necessary results in their actual interdependence is scarcely possible. There is, however, a mode of rendering the process as a whole tolerably comprehensible. Though the genesis of the rearrangement of every evolving aggregate is in itself one, it presents to our intelligence. (163–64)

When Annie repudiates the passage as "nonsense," John claims that this is philosophy "in the simplest and most lucid form." His failure to understand either the deconstructive implications of the emphasis on transformation and interdependence or the similarity between the philosophical passage and Julius's tales would seem clumsily ironic were it not for the fact that Chesnutt's ostensibly "literate" Euro-American readership shared the blindness. In addition, Annie's impatience with the philosophical discourse, contrasted with her eager but simplistic acceptance of Julius's oral versions, suggests intriguing approaches to the problem of audience that concerns both Afro-American writers and Euro-American theorists.

Chesnutt's Silence

To remark Chesnutt's engagement with deconstructive concerns does not imply his ability to resolve their more disturbing implications. Confronting his marginalization and the failure of his audience to respond to anything other than the surface of his texts, Chesnutt fell into a literary silence like that of another premodernist American deconstructionist, Herman Melville, or those of the women writers Tillie Olsen discusses in her profoundly moving essay "Silences." Olsen catalogs a number of professional circumstances that drive marginal writers into giving up their public voices. Among the most powerful forces are "devaluation" ("books of great worth suffer the death of being unknown, or at best a peculiar eclipsing," 40); "critical attitudes" ("the injurious reacting to a book, not for its quality or content, but on the basis of its having been written by a woman [or black]," 40); and, perhaps most important, the "climate in literary circles for those who move in them" ("Writers know the importance of being taken seriously, with respect for one's vision and integrity; of comradeship with other writers; of being dealt with as a writer on the basis of one's work and not for other reasons," 41). Chesnutt clearly confronted each of these problems without finding an adequate solution.

This breakdown (or absence) of contact between artist and audience parallels a similar situation that some observer/participants, myself among them, see as a major problem of contemporary theoretical discourse. Critics whose insights would seem to possess profound social significance find themselves in the situation of John reading to Annie; the form of their discourse and lack of contextual awareness alienate their audience and, all too frequently, the critics respond by retreating into a contemptuous solipsism that guarantees that the subversive implications of their work will have little effect on the context. One particularly unfortunate manifestation of this pattern has been the almost unchallenged alienation of Euro- and Afro-American discourse, an alienation being addressed with increasing effect by a small group of writers and intellectuals including Stepto, Gates, Adrienne Rich, bell hooks, and Cornel West. Still, further work toward a context that allows, to use Culler's phrase, "these discourses to communicate with one another," offers intriguing possibilities for avoiding the nihilistic impasse and tapping the political potential of deconstructive thought. To begin, deconstruction possesses the potential to expose the conditions that forced Chesnutt— and a long line of successors including Hurston, Wright, Baldwin, and William Melvin Kelley—into exile. By focusing attention on the margin and articulating the recurring concerns of the folk-based Afro-American tradition in a vocabulary that can be recognized by the educated Euro-American readership that continues to comprise the majority of the literary audience, deconstruction, at least theoretically, could help create an audience sensitive to the actual complexities of Afro-American expression. At present, this potential remains unrealized, in large part because the literary community in which deconstruction has developed continues to exercise its social privilege in a manner that suggests a continued belief, clearly inconsistent with its articulated perceptions, that its own cultural tradition serves as the center of serious literary discourse. In contrast Afro-American writers, experiencing the "double consciousness" that makes it impossible for them to exclude the Euro-American tradition from their expression even if they so desire, have been exploring the practical implications of the intersection of modes of thought for over a century. Opening theoretical discourse to consideration of complex Afro-modernist texts such as Melvin Tolson's *Harlem Gallery,* Langston Hughes's "Montage of a Dream Deferred," and Hurston's *Moses, Man of the Mountain* might substantially alter the "feel" if not the conceptual underpinnings of contemporary theoretical discourse.

Perhaps the most important result of such consideration, derived from Afro-American concern with both the relational conception of signification (characteristic of the African continuum) and the political circumstances of slavery and continuing oppression (based on the continuing dominance of the binary oppositions of American racial thought), would be to caution against a relapse into the solipsistic withdrawal available primarily to those capable of exercising social privilege and the separation of theoretical discourse from engagement with the institutional contexts in which it exists. Despite the prevalence of such separation in American academic discourse, it is not inherent in deconstruction, a point made by both Eagleton and Culler. Attributing such separation to Anglo-American academicians (a.k.a. the demons of Yale), Eagleton stresses that "Derrida is clearly out to do more than develop new techniques of reading: deconstruction is for him an ultimately *political* practice, an attempt to dismantle the logic by which a particular system of thought, and behind that a whole system of political structures and social institutions, maintains its force" (148). Similarly, Culler emphasizes that "inversions of hierarchical oppositions expose to debate the institutional arrangements that rely on the hierarchies and thus open possibilities of change" (179). Acutely aware of the ways in which even his sympathetic readers—and I suspect that would include many of the critics (I would not except myself) working toward an opening of discourses—continued to reenact the hierarchical minstrel show of the plantation tradition, Charles Chesnutt sensed this significance over a century ago. Like the guys at the garage—brothers of Paule Marshall's "Poets in the Kitchen"—he knew that the man's mouth is cut cross ways and that the cross cuts a figure flattering to the man. Now we can begin to figure out where the meanings lie.

2

Endurance and Excavation:
Afro-American Responses to Faulkner

▲ ▲ ▲ ▲

Go down, Moses,
Way down in Egypt land
Tell old Pharaoh
To let my people go.

—Traditional

Go up, Moses
You been down too long
You been down too long.
My people, let Pharaoh go,
You don't need him.

—Roberta Flack, Joel Dorn, Jesse Jackson

No record exists of William Faulkner's reaction to the scene in *Gone with the Wind* in which a gang of slaves marches through the streets of Atlanta to rebuild the white folks' fortifications, singing "Go Down, Moses." It would be interesting to know how much of the joke Faulkner heard. The only television film of Faulkner presents him as an incarnation of Pharaoh, kindly but stern in supervising the black workers at his Mississippi home. But his own version of "Go Down, Moses" adds a beautiful and profound white voice to the traditionally black chorus. Faulkner's voice sometimes harmonizes with, sometimes sounds dissonant notes in, on occasion runs counterpoint to the Afro-American melody. It's difficult to tell whether he could actually hear the song, or see the singers, in *Gone with the Wind*.

Not surprisingly, it seems equally difficult to determine how well Afro-American writers see or hear Faulkner. As Ralph Ellison's invisible man remarks: "I too have become acquainted with ambivalence" (10). The early response of black writers to Faulkner was surprisingly—given some later developments—positive, in large part because he was quite correctly understood in relation to the virulent racism of Mississippi demagogues Bilbo and Vardaman. Sterling

Brown's pioneering study *The Negro in American Fiction* (1937) contrasts Faulkner's accurate observations of "the bitter life [black Mississippians] are condemned to live" with the "happy-go-lucky comics" common in fiction of the era and concludes that while Faulkner "does not write social protest . . . he is fiercely intent upon the truth" (179). Commenting on Faulkner's *Go Down, Moses,* Ellison expresses the underlying premise of most affirmative Afro-American responses: "Its main concern is with the problem of American freedom as faced by a specific white Southerner in relation to his individual heritage. Here . . . Faulkner comes most passionately to grips with the moral implications of slavery, the American land, progress and materialism, tradition and moral identity. . . . Whether we accept Isaac McCaslin's solution or not, the problem is nevertheless basic to democratic man" (*Territory* 270). Fully sensitive to Faulkner's ambivalence, Ellison nonetheless credits him with a heroic engagement: "Faulkner is an example of a writer who has confronted Negroes with such mixed motives that he has presented them in terms of both the 'good nigger' and the 'bad nigger' stereotypes, and who yet has explored perhaps more successfully than anyone else, either white or black, certain forms of Negro humanity" (*Shadow* 29–30).

Ellison praises Faulkner for his *individual* heroism. When Afro-American writers view, or are forced to view, Faulkner as a representative of Euro-American—or, worse, American culture, the negative aspects of the ambivalence emerge. James Baldwin's *Just above My Head* satirizes a white named Faulkner Grey—the slang joke reduces Faulkner to racial type—who bedevils the black narrator. Baldwin first parodies the confusion of relationships in a Faulkner novel: "Faulkner was blood-relative to my boss, precisely to what legal degree I never knew: blood relative of a pirate, a cunning, hard-nosed blond. I loathed him, but I must confess that he frightened me, too—he was only about twenty, and had the moral sense of a crocodile" (288). He then condemns the literary politicians who transform Faulkner from struggling individual into cultural symbol rendering Afro-American writers invisible: "Having Faulkner call me was just one more of the little ways they had of letting me know that I might be an intelligent black cat and all, and my people might be making great strides in the kingdom, but I was still a nigger" (289). The narrator's business conversation with Faulkner Grey reflects Baldwin's own ambivalence toward William Faulkner: "I don't think about you one way or the other, Faulkner. I just don't know how to move on your word" (288).

This can be seen of course, as an indication of Baldwin's anxiety over the influence of an artistic father. No doubt, some anxiety exists; no craft-conscious postwar fiction writer can ignore Faulkner's technical achievements. That Faulkner, as Sterling Brown recognized, helped break down traditional stereotypes and introduce Afro-American folk materials into American modernism complicates the influence considerably. Nonetheless, if one wishes to apply Harold Bloom's model of influence to Afro-American fiction, Richard Wright rather than Faulkner would loom as the source of anxiety for both Ellison and Baldwin. Although gender differences complicate Bloom's paradigm, Zora Neale Hurston and Toni Morrison join Wright and Ellison as the major influences on younger writers. At any rate, for reasons to be discussed below, influence is much less problematic for writers with roots in Afro-American traditions than for those grounded in Euro-American traditions.

This ambivalence toward Faulkner rests on the limitations of Faulkner's sympathy with and understanding of distinctive Afro-American traditions. Robert B. Stepto has demonstrated that, with sources in Afro-American oral culture and the slave narratives, pre-Ellisonian Afro-American narrative generates two central patterns: the narrative of ascent, in which the protagonist progresses toward literacy and freedom (usually in the North), and the narrative of immersion, in which the protagonist returns to his/her cultural roots and reintegration with the community (usually in the South). The ascent, which can threaten the protagonist with loss of cultural identity (the passing narrative is an extreme form), necessitates a subsequent immersion. Both patterns demand movement, physical and spiritual. Faulkner's fundamental limitation regarding Afro-American characters and culture is that he rarely perceives, and never emphasizes, these kinetic narrative patterns. Rather, he substitutes a third narrative type—what I call the narrative of endurance—for those of ascent and immersion. This substitution has far-reaching effects and severely limits Faulkner's direct influence on Afro-American writers. Sharing the Afro-American commitment to a "narrative of descent" that will provide the basis for a common vocabulary of racial perception, Faulkner remains locked in a moral dilemma. Forced to distance himself from the sins of his ancestors, he is also unable to embrace the static black "other." He therefore finds himself in the symbolic underground of the "narrative of repudiation," isolated from both white and black communities, while the Afro-American writers plot a return to the surface first through "narratives of hibernation" typified by Ellison's *Invisible Man* and David Bradley's *The Chaneysville Incident* and subsequently through the creation of texts that insist on the need for a much broader actual dialogue between Faulkner, his Euro-American male descendants, and the "others."

The Narrative of Endurance

The narrative of endurance differs from both the narratives of ascent and immersion in several basic ways. First, it is static, not kinetic. Second, its temporal focus is on the past or present rather than the future. Third, it defines black characters in relation to the Euro-American rather than the Afro-American community. This generates a peculiarly Euro-American "black" protagonist. Stepto labels the protagonist of the ascent narrative the "articulate survivor" and that of the immersion narrative the "articulate kinsman." The narrative of endurance, in contrast, focuses on the "enduring saint," who is physically enslaved but spiritually free. This figure's primary commitment is to the salvation of both blacks and whites in the next world. The narrative of endurance, which conventionally ends with the protagonist in a symbolic space no less oppressive than that in which she or he began (frequently the exact same space), places little value on articulateness since the "enduring saint" possesses an inherent sense of morality that literacy may in fact diminish. Stowe's Uncle Tom and Twain's Jim precede Faulkner's Dilsey and Molly Beauchamp as "enduring saints."

Faulkner's revoicing of "Go Down, Moses" reflects this tension between narrative patterns. The original lyrics combine elements of immersion and ascent, presenting the journey into bondage as a stage in the ascent to freedom; the title section of Faulkner's novel implicitly denies the validity of both movements. Where the lyrics and the contemporary Afro-American variants focus on the articulate protagonist (the kinsman or kinswoman who *tells* old Pharaoh) and movement beyond "Egypt," Faulkner focuses on largely inarticulate blacks remaining in the South. Samuel Worsham Beauchamp's experience in the North, the resolution of the "ascent" of James Beauchamp, culminates not in literacy but in urban bondage, a life of crime and death. He returns South not in the symbolically resonant space of a Jim Crow Car, but in a closed coffin. Imaginatively denied the cycle of ascent and immersion, he perishes in a vortex. Similar fates await most Faulkner blacks who attempt to break out of static endurance. Like Samuel, Rider in "Pantaloon in Black" and Joe Christmas in *Light in August* die not while attempting the ascent but while wandering without direction.

In addition to substituting this narrative pattern, Faulkner provides his black characters with "ritual grounds" only tenuously related to those of the Afro-American tradition. Stepto identifies ritual grounds—from the slave quarters to the hill on which Atlanta University is built—as places assuming significance in relation to the narrative structure in which they exist. Faulkner's ritual grounds, taking their meaning from the endurance narrative, emphasize stasis. The church, clearly not the church militant of James Cone's black liberation theology, and the jail, clearly not the space for the nationalistic awakenings of Malcolm X and Etheridge Knight, are the chief ritual grounds of the endurance narrative. Significantly, both enforce stasis and alienate black characters from the ritual grounds associated with the movements of ascent and immersion. Molly Beauchamp and Dilsey in *The Sound and the Fury* provide the types of the enduring saint working to keep both black and white "families" within the religious space available in the endurance narrative. In *Intruder in the Dust*, Lucas Beauchamp expresses the archetypal relationship to the ritual ground of the jail. Rather than risking the death Rider finds outside his cell, Lucas remains within the jail while Faulkner's moral imagination saves him from lynching. Faulkner's description of Lucas in "The Fire and the Hearth" emphasizes the stasis enveloping the enduring saint: "a vessel, durable, ancestryless, nonconductive, in which the toxin and its anti stalemated one another, seetheless, unrumored in the outside air" (104).

On occasion, Faulkner's settings correspond to the ritual grounds that Stepto identifies as central to the Afro-American tradition. Faulkner's cabins bear some resemblance to those in the Afro-American tradition, though they rarely generate movement. The wilderness presents an interesting study in the relation of Faulknerian ritual grounds to racial groups. Clearly, Faulkner's woods are not simply a Euro-American domain. Sam Fathers is their presiding genius. But Sam's Indian heritage may be the determining factor; it is not clear whether full blacks can share the ritual insights of Ike and Sam. The runaway black in "Red Leaves" is unable to negotiate the wilderness as ritual ground; it ultimately causes his death. Frequently blacks exist in the woods only as servants; Lucas cannot shoot as well as Zack in "The Bear." At any rate, the fields and hills of the Black Belt, rather than stretches of virgin wilderness, are much more common ritual grounds within the Afro-American tradition.

The complex of images associated with the endurance narrative recurs frequently in Euro-American literature, from Stowe's enduring saint Uncle Tom (whose heroism involves his refusal to leave the prisonlike ritual ground of Legree's plantation) to William Styron's Daddy Faith (a revoicing of Dilsey in *Lie Down in Darkness*) and Nat

Turner, who accepts the ritual ground of his cell. Several treatments of blacks by Euro-American writers revoice the endurance narrative in relation to northern settings. The exotics of Carl Van Vechten and the existential hero-victims of Norman Mailer move somewhat more freely than their southern compatriots in the Euro-American imagination. In sharp contrast with their Afro-American analogues, however, their movement is aimless. Both writers appear to embrace shapelessness and to apotheosize characters who endure modern life without the anxieties—frequently similar to those of Faulkner's protagonists in what I shall discuss below as the "narrative of repudiation"—that beset the white protagonists. Therefore even though both claim to portray characters who draw their strength from the Afro-American tradition, neither shows an awareness of the movements portrayed in the experience. Within their divergent value structures, they remain "enduring saints." The negative Afro-American response to Faulkner centers much more on Faulkner Grey—the heir and perhaps unwilling perpetuator of this cultural tradition—than on William Faulkner, the individual struggling to escape its limitations.

The Broken Dialogue

In *Just above My Head,* Baldwin provides a structure for understanding both the origins and complexity of this response: "To overhaul a history, or to attempt to redeem it—which effort may or may not justify it—is not at all the same thing as the descent one must make in order to excavate a history. To be forced to excavate a history is, also, to repudiate the concept of history, and the vocabulary in which history is written" (428). In these terms, Faulkner as southerner faces the same imperative as Baldwin himself. The historian C. Vann Woodward observes that "Southern history, unlike American, includes large components of frustration, failure, and defeat" (19). Like Afro-American history, it indicates that the American historical myths of abundance, success, and innocence need to be overhauled. In essence, southerners, and Woodward recognizes Faulkner as an archetypal case, are forced to defend their own experience against imposed distortions, to rewrite the standard history. As Baldwin observes, this redemption of the history from outside definitions may or may not justify it; it may in fact merely provide a clearer vision of moral failure. The Afro-American writer and Faulkner share a similar imperative to overhaul history.

But Baldwin demands an even more profound confrontation with history: excavation, which rejects the concept of history as a social text. This is necessary, Baldwin writes, because "the written history is, and must be, merely the vocabulary of power, and power is history's most seductively attired false witness" (428). This pinpoints the origin of the Afro-American ambivalence toward Faulkner. For Faulkner not only shatters Yankee myths; he creates southern myths. As cultural avatar he bears false witness in texts that interpret ascent and immersion as endurance. The double irony of Afro-American history is that blacks have been oppressed by the oppressed. Black writers coming to Faulkner find both a fellow in bondage and a new incarnation of Pharaoh. In effect, Faulkner contributes to the "history" that forces Afro-American writers not simply to overhaul, but to excavate, their own.

The excavator descends into the burrow of Ellison's invisible man, the ritual ground where individuals can examine their relationships with history in all its textual manifestations and strive for control of the text of their experiences. The excavation, Baldwin writes, "is motivated by the need to have the power to force others to recognize your presence, your right to be here. The disputed passages will remain disputed so long as you do not have the authority of the right-of-way—so long, that is, as your passage can be disputed: the document promising safe passage . . . can always be revoked" (428). In this dispute over a passage that is at once physical and textual (Afro-American narrative since Frederick Douglass has recognized this unity), Faulkner—as Faulkner Grey—has the power to dispute the passage of ascent and immersion. Ironically, Faulkner's textual power derives from the intensity of his personal excavation. Once his text—shaped in the underground burrow, in the excavating consciousnesses of Quentin Compson and Gavin Stevens and Ike McCaslin—returns to the surface, however, it is subsumed by the institutions, social and critical, that force Afro-American writers into their own excavations. Baldwin states the paradox: "Power clears the passage, swiftly: but the paradox, here, is that power, rooted in history, is also, the mockery and the repudiation of history. The power to define the other seals one's definition of oneself—who, then, in such a fearful mathematic . . . is trapped?" (428). In these terms, Faulkner/Faulkner Grey is trapped along with Dilsey and Rider and Lucas within the enduring jail of white power. The origins of experience in social history mock the individual excavation.

Baldwin attempts to forge a solution based on active extension toward and acceptance of those most likely to be oppressed by one's own excavated text when it returns to the surface. He writes: "Perhaps, then, after all, we have no idea of what history is: or are in flight from the demon we have summoned. Perhaps history is not to be found in our mirrors, but in our repudiations: perhaps, the other is ourselves" (428). Baldwin implicitly demands that we seek the answers to questions of personal and cultural identity by examining the ways we draw lines of demarcation between self and other. This parallels Michel Foucault's inquiries into the nature of the demarcations between madness and sanity. Foucault's comment that what was once a "common language" has devolved into a "broken dialogue" applies equally well to American racial discourse. Baldwin's solution implies the necessity of excavating the paralyzing structure of definition that confines both black and white, of understanding what Foucault refers to as "the point where history is immobilized in the tragic category which both establishes and impugns it" (*Madness* xii).

In a paradox typifying this intricate rite of passage, Faulkner provides many of the insights and techniques that Afro-American writers have mobilized in opposition to the "tragic" Faulknerian repudiation of ascent and immersion. To a limited degree, Faulkner provides a base for reestablishing dialogue and reconstructing a common language concerning race. Characters such as the deputy's wife in "Pantaloon in Black" and Hawk in "Dry September" delineate the limits of white perception of and sympathy for blacks. Faulkner realizes that whites frequently fail to recognize the depth of black humanity and that a black who fulfills the endurance narrative pattern by depending on external aid may wind up at the bottom of an abandoned well. Numerous Afro-American satires on white stupidity (William Melvin Kelley's *dem,* Darius James's *Negrophobia,* and several stories by James Alan McPherson) and a host of cautionary stories on white liberalism and lynching (the archetype of which is Wright's *Native Son*) revoice these motifs.

Perhaps a more specifically Faulknerian contribution to the common language is his perception of the need for multiple voicing, especially in regard to racial concerns. Faulkner clearly realizes that no individual voice can express anything other than a partial racial truth. The confrontations between Zack and Lucas in "The Fire and the Hearth" and Roth and his mistress in "Delta Autumn" demonstrate the need for both white and black voices in any approach to such truth. Similarly, the chorus of voices in *Absalom, Absalom!* attests to the complex apprehension of race *within* the white community. This polyphonic approach, frequently tied to a strong sense of the oral traditions—Afro- and Euro-American—that pass down the various histories, recurs frequently in Afro-American fiction. Sometimes several narrative voices exist, as in *The Sound and the Fury* (Baldwin's *Go Tell It on the Mountain,* Toni Cade Bambara's *The Salt Eaters,* Kelley's *A Different Drummer*); sometimes a single voice incorporates other voices, as in *Absalom, Absalom!* (Ernest Gaines's *The Autobiography of Miss Jane Pittman,* Toni Morrison's *Jazz,* David Bradley's *The Chaneysville Incident*). In his most profound moments, Faulkner—and in this he is nearly unique in the Euro-American tradition—revoices standard Afro-American scenes in terms of Euro-American experience. Perhaps the best example involves Chick Mallison's and Roth Edmonds's recognitions of their physical and metaphorical whiteness in *Intruder in the Dust* and "The Fire and the Hearth." The dawn of racial awareness is an archetypal black scene from W. E. B. Du Bois's *The Souls of Black Folks* through Countee Cullen's "Incident," Hurston's *Their Eyes Were Watching God,* and Wright's "The Ethics of Living Jim Crow" down to Gaines's "The Sky Is Gray" and Loren Cary's *Black Ice.* While Afro-Americans do not have the option of avoiding this initiation, most Euro-American writers seem totally unaware of the significance of the parallel rite *for whites.* Faulkner is one of the few white writers who adapts aspects of Afro-American voices, rather than expecting the common language to be essentially Euro-American in structure and content.

Despite these contributions, however, Faulkner only intimates a common language. His imaginative commitment to the narrative of endurance inevitably draws the wide range of negative responses by Afro-American writers discussed below. Some of these writers focus primarily on Faulkner's limitations. For example, Baldwin images endurance as a political weapon contributing to black oppression. Kelley parodies endurance as a fantasy generated by Faulkner's ignorance of Afro-American myth. Several other writers emphasize the inherent strength of the Afro-American patterns masked from Faulkner's vision. For example, Gaines demonstrates the masked presence of an ascent in what appears to be an endurance narrative. Similarly, Gayl Jones unmasks the potential for regenerative immersion in patterns that Faulkner presents as at best endurable and at worst psychically and socially destructive. Viewed as a cohesive group, these responses make the limitations of the endurance narrative clear. As I will demonstrate in the later parts of this chapter, however, these limitations have not eliminated Afro-American interest in Faulkner. Rather, writers such as Gloria Naylor, Sherley Anne Williams, and Leon Forrest respond to those limitations by shaping post-Faulknerian narratives that seek to realize the frequently implicit constructive potential of his example.

Faulkner himself would certainly not have accepted endurance as the base for a common language intended for whites as well as blacks. His white protagonists, unlike his black saints, make the descent and attempt to excavate their histories. Frequently their excavation leads

to a complex revaluation of history, shaping the narrative of repudiation. This narrative pattern presents a physically free but spiritually
tormented figure who descends to an imaginative underground
where he can excavate his history. The repudiation narrative ends
with the protagonist spiritually purified but unable to return to the
social space from which he (and Faulkner's excavators are always
male) embarked. Many Afro-American writers rework this narrative
pattern, which in complex ways derives its form from the definitions
of the endurance narrative, into what Stepto calls the narrative of
hibernation.

Endurance, Politics, and Myth

Baldwin's 1956 essay "Faulkner and Desegregation," his 1972 essay
"Take Me to the Water," and his 1979 novel *Just above My Head* all
portray Faulkner as a representative of white political oppression.
Not that Baldwin shares Addison Gayle, Jr.'s, simplistic view of Faulkner as "a champion of white supremacy" (258). Commenting on
Faulkner and Camus, Baldwin writes: "Neither of them could accurately, or usefully, be described as racists, in spite of Faulkner's declared intention of shooting Negroes in the streets if he found this
necessary for the salvation of the state of Mississippi. This statement
had to be read as an excess of patriotism, unlikely, in Faulkner's case,
to lead to any further action." Yet, Baldwin continues: "The mischief
of the remark lay in the fact that it certainly encouraged others to
such action" (*Ticket* 473). Baldwin's scathing portrait of Faulkner
Grey originates in the fact that Faulkner gives others the leeway to
commit, in his name, acts that he would not condone. To this extent
Faulkner deserves to be treated as a representative rather than an
individual.

Baldwin also convicts the individual Faulkner of a kind of unwit-
ting hypocrisy in his resistance to forced desegregation: "He is, on
the one hand, the proud citizen of a free society and, on the other,
is committed to a society which has not yet dared to free itself of
the necessity of naked and brutal oppression" (*Ticket* 150). Baldwin
underscores the hypocrisy of this position: "The racial condition
which Faulkner will not have changed by 'mere force of law or economic threat' was imposed by precisely these means. The southern
tradition, which is, after all, all that Faulkner is talking about, is not
a tradition at all: when Faulkner evokes it, he is simply evoking a
legend that contains an accusation. And that accusation, stated far
more simply than it should be, is that the North, in winning the war,
left the South only one means of asserting its identity and that means

was the Negro" (150–51). Again, inasmuch as Faulkner justifies the denial of black passage, he invites reduction to Faulkner Grey. But, as Baldwin recognizes, Faulkner's plea for black endurance originates in the moral condition of whites: "Faulkner is not trying to save Negroes, who are, in his view, already saved; who, having refused to be destroyed by terror, are far stronger than the terrified white populace; and who have, moreover, fatally, from his point of view, the weight of the federal government behind them. He is trying to save 'whatever good remains in those white people.' The time he pleads for is the time in which the Southerner will come to terms with himself, will cease fleeing from his conscience" (151–52). Addressing the desegregation issue, Baldwin correctly prophesied that "the time Faulkner asks for does not exist" (152).

In later statements, Baldwin rejects endurance as political stance more forcefully. Even though desegregation is no longer an issue, the Faulknerian attitude still poses a political and economic threat. Faulkner "is seeking to exorcise a history which is also a curse. He wants the old order, which came into existence through unchecked greed and wanton murder, to redeem itself without further bloodshed—without, that is, any further menacing itself—and without coercion" (*Ticket* 473). Baldwin rejects this as an unrealistic fantasy: "This, old orders never do, less because they would not than because they cannot. They cannot because they have always existed in relation to a force which they have had to subdue. This subjugation is the key to their identity and the triumph and justification of their history, and it is also on this continued subjugation that their material well-being depends" (473). While Faulkner as an individual may repudiate the racist heritage, the culture for which he ostensibly speaks will not do so. Further, this blinds the individual Faulkner to the needs of the subjugated other: "One may see that the history, which is not indivisible from oneself, has been full of errors and excesses; but this is not the same thing as seeing that, for millions of people, this history—oneself—has been nothing but an intolerable yoke, a stinking prison, a shrieking grave. It is not so easy to see that, for millions of people, life itself depends on the speediest possible demolition of this history" (473).

Ultimately Baldwin criticizes Faulkner for confusing the imperatives related to the redemption of southern history with those concerning the political survival of blacks. Baldwin's fiction contains numerous portraits of blacks, articulate and morally aware, destroyed by the white culture that Faulkner would have save them and itself. Richard in *Go Tell It on the Mountain*, Rufus Scott in *Another Country*, and Arthur Montana in *Just above My Head* are repaid for their endurance with destruction. Political realities clearly demand the rejection of the Euro-American historical vocabulary, which demands black passivity. Therefore, according to Baldwin, "one finally throws Balzac and Shakespeare—and Faulkner and Camus—out" (474). Only when blacks have completed the ascent to literacy, identity, and political and economic freedom will they "welcome them back, but on one's own terms, and absolutely, on one's own land" (474). For Baldwin the clear alternative to political endurance is a rapid and insistent ascent.

A similar current informs Alice Walker's comment that "unlike Tolstoy, Faulkner was not prepared to struggle to change the structure of the society he was born in. One might concede that in his fiction he did seek to examine the reasons for its decay, but unfortunately, as I have learned while trying to teach Faulkner to black students, it is not possible, from so short a range, to separate the man from his works" (*In Search* 20). In another essay, Walker writes, "that in Mississippi no one even remembers where Richard Wright lived, while Faulkner's house is maintained by a black caretaker," and that as a result of the contextual injustice "for a long time I will feel Faulkner's house, O'Connor's house, crushing me. To fight back will require a certain amount of energy, energy better used doing something else" (58).

While echoing Baldwin's statement on endurance as a Euro-American fantasy, William Melvin Kelley takes a somewhat more ironic stance regarding Faulkner. Whereas Baldwin wishes to dismiss Faulkner, at least temporarily, from black consciousness, Kelley perceives him as locked out of that consciousness by his ignorance of Afro-American myth. This in turn renders his cultural stance somewhat comic, a fitting target for intricate black parody.

Kelley's *A Different Drummer* confronts Faulkner's fantasy of black endurance with the counterfantasy of black removal. Kelley constructs this counterfantasy, its foundation fixed in Afro-American folk motifs concerning white dependence on blacks, on the archetype of "the African." The plot of *A Different Drummer,* presented like that of *As I Lay Dying* through a variety of white consciousnesses, supports Baldwin's contention that white identity depends on blacks. When blacks reject endurance and begin a mass exodus from a small southern town, the white sense of reality collapses. Kelley's whites perceive blacks in typically Faulknerian terms: "the Calibans weren't very popular among their own people . . . their devotion to us and our love for them had separated them from other Negroes" (121). Although they define blacks only in relation to whites, Kelley's whites are dimly aware of the legendary African, who prefers death to enduring bondage. But they remain unable to understand his significance to Kelley's protagonist: "that African and his blood coming down to Tucker Caliban. That's bull if I ever heard it" (187). Ultimately they prefer to retreat into fantasies—the novel ends with Mister Leland's dream (a counter-counterfantasy) of Tucker's return—rather than confront the reality of the Afro-American drive for ascent. Kelley clearly implies that, lacking an accurate sense of Afro-American myth, no Euro-American writer—even one of Faulkner's brilliance—can understand Afro-American behavior and its relation to the white man's sense of his own identity.

Numerous writers, among them Toni Morrison and Ishmael Reed, endorse Kelley's critique of the Euro-American treatment of Afro-American myth. Echoing Kelley's insistence on the African heritage, Morrison (who wrote her M.A. thesis on the theme of alienation in Faulkner and Virginia Woolf) presents the myth of the "flying African" as the key to the immersion and ascent of Milkman Dead in *Song of Solomon*. Reed insists on the kinetic power of the Afro-American mythology in many of his parodic novels. In *Mumbo Jumbo* he creates a "black plague" called "Jes Grew" (an obvious parody of Stowe's pioneering narrative of endurance) to attack the static Euro-American cultural premises fundamental to the endurance narrative. Similarly, Reed's *Flight to Canada* parodies the white belief in the "enduring saint" by presenting a variety of black characters who manipulate the belief while expediting their own ascent. Like Baldwin and Kelley, these novelists consistently argue that the narrative of endurance is made possible only by a profound misunderstanding of the politically charged substructure of Afro-American culture.

Endurance, History, Ancestry

Like Reed, Ernest Gaines re-presents the endurance narrative as a masked narrative of ascent. To an even greater degree than Kelley, Gaines evinces an abiding respect for Faulkner's voice. Both in overall structure and in numerous details, Gaines's Bayonne resembles Faulkner's Yoknapatawpha. In addition to endorsing Faulkner's disgust with the moneygrubbers (Gaines's Cajuns are in many ways similar to Faulkner's Snopeses) who have replaced the old aristocracy in the South, Gaines shares his belief in the reality of interracial love and respect. The conversation between Jules Raynard and Jane Pittman concerning Tee Bob and Mary Agnes, destroyed by Bayonne's racial codes, is perhaps the most profound statement of the need for a common black-white vocabulary in American literature. Neither alone can do more than speculate on the emotional truth. As Jules

says, "It would be specalatin if two white people was sitting here talking." To which Jane replies, "But it's us," and Jules answers, "And that
makes it gospel truth." No one need be, or can be, ignored in this
version of history (194).

Gaines does not, however, allow his voice to be dominated by
Faulkner's. His measured rejection of the endurance narrative may
be even more compelling than Baldwin's attack or Kelley's parody.
Frequently Gaines takes a ritual ground from the endurance narrative and reclaims it for the Afro-American tradition. "Three Men," in
which a black man considers remaining in jail rather than accepting
help from the white Roger Medlow, superficially resembles *Intruder in
the Dust.* The pressure to remain, however, comes from an articulate
kinsman who insists that the choice be made for internal rather than
external reasons: "You don't go to the pen for killing the nigger, you
go for yourself. You go to sweat out all the crud you got in your system. You go saying, 'Go fuck yourself, Roger Medlow, I want to be a
man, and by God I will be a man. For once in my life I will be a man'"
(*Bloodline* 141). This jail resembles the prison of Malcolm X's self-
discovery, not that of Lucas Beauchamp's endurance. Similarly,
Gaines reclaims the church as ritual ground when he presents the
clash between Jimmy's church-based civil rights movement and the
white world that, under pressure, refuses to grant any sanctuary for
enduring saints.

Gaines's revoicing of endurance narrative images culminates in
The Autobiography of Miss Jane Pittman. Viewed from a certain angle,
Miss Jane seems a sophisticated version of the enduring saint, a reworking of the Faulknerian mammy. In fact, Jane does love her white
folks. But—and this point frequently eludes Faulkner—she loves her
black folks more. Ultimately, she refuses to grant her white folks their
fantasy of black endurance, their extra time. At the end of *The Autobiography of Miss Jane Pittman* she confronts Robert, the white man who,
in good Faulknerian manner, takes care of her physical needs in her
old age. Robert confronts her with the news that Jimmy has been
killed and warns her not to participate in the imminent demonstration. When Robert says Jimmy is dead, Miss Jane responds: "Just a
little piece of him is dead. The rest of him is waiting for us in
Bayonne. And I will go with Alex" (245). Miss Jane inspires her kinsmen to join her in confronting Pharaoh. Her final gesture leaves behind the world of endurance, of Robert's imposed pattern, and unmasks the ascent: "Me and Robert look at each other there a long
time, then I went by him" (246). Faulkner, of course, would not have
thought Jimmy was dead. For him "the past isn't dead, it isn't even
past." But for Gaines, the past not only is not past, it is not even

merely present. It takes its meaning from the future. This attitude has wide-ranging implications for the development of a common language concerning race. Without the sense of a history moving toward the future, the black community must resign itself to Egyptian bondage. Sensitive to this threat, Gaines takes an enduring saint and transforms her into an articulate kinswoman demanding that Pharaoh let her people go.

This difference in temporal movement—Faulkner moving toward the past, Gaines toward the future—reflects a deep difference of sensibility, involving perception of the past, between Faulkner and most Afro-American writers. Morrison, Alice Walker, and Gayl Jones share Faulkner's abiding concern with the relation of the individual to his/her ancestors. Further, all share Faulkner's perception that, in some sense, the individual is fated to *become* that ancestor, to relive crucial scenes from the earlier life. The best recent Faulkner criticism, especially that of John T. Irwin and Richard King, emphasizes this point. Irwin demonstrates the primary importance of patterns of repetition and revenge in Faulkner's fiction. These patterns, rooted in a narcissistic fear of sex and death, lead to a symbolic castration of the recollecting individual—Quentin Compson is the archetype. As Irwin comments, "the instruments of this castration are time and tradition." He continues: "The crux, then, of Quentin's problem is repetition, the temporal form of doubling, for it is those inevitable repetitions inherent in the cyclic nature of time that seem to rob the individual will of all potency" (37). Quentin wishes to reject the tradition that imposes this impotence, but Faulkner presents such rebellion as doomed because, as Irwin notes, "resisting an influence is just an influence in reverse . . . to resist an inheritance is to inherit the role of resistance" (38). Faulkner's relationship with the past, then, is characterized by an abiding anxiety and feeling of loss. Irwin's metaphor of "repetition and revenge" admirably expresses the nature of the relationship between the Faulknerian individual and the ancestors.

The appropriate metaphor for the analogous situation in the Afro-American tradition, however, is not "repetition and revenge" but "call and response." Jones, Walker, and Morrison focus on characters who identify too little, rather than too much, with their significant ancestors. An increasing perception of the extent and inevitability of that identification liberates the Afro-American protagonists, paralyzes Faulkner's. The sisters in Walker's epistolary novel *The Color Purple* engage in a complex call and response that leads them to a deeper apprehension of the relationship between the articulate kinsman and the articulate survivor. Morrison's Milkman Dead and Jones's

Ursa Corregidora struggle, sometimes unconsciously, to merge with, rather than separate from, their ancestors. Irwin comments on Quentin's narration of *Absalom, Absalom!*: "His narration of the story of the Sutpens is an answer that doesn't answer—an answer that puts the answerer in question" (47). In *Song of Solomon* and *Corregidora*, responding to the call of the ancestors provides the only means of resolving questions concerning the identity of the answerer. While this is not an explicitly racial issue, it reflects the degree to which Faulkner's creation of an essentially static pattern for black experience—the endurance narrative—reflects a deeply rooted difference in sensibility and cultural tradition.

It is tempting to see this difference as a reflection of the diachronous European sense of time, which contrasts with the synchronous African apprehension. As Sunday Anozie demonstrates in *Structural Models and African Poetics*, a synchronous sense of time encourages the individual to see him/herself coexisting with ancestors and descendants. This reduces the anxiety of feeling limited or trapped by a role (such as that of father or daughter) at any given instant. One coexists with spirits embodying all stages of life at all times. The diachronous sense of time serves to emphasize the *separation* of roles; the individual cannot establish meaningful contact with any aspect of heritage or self that is not immediately present. No response is possible to a call sounding from an inaccessible temporal frame.

Jones's *Corregidora* explicitly rejects the Faulknerian pattern of repetition and revenge. As long as Ursa Corregidora allows herself to brood on her personal past, obsessively replaying the moment when her husband, Mutt, pushed her down the stairs, she remains unable to respond to either the call of the familial "generations" or the call of sexual love. Breaking out of her personal obsession by perceiving her ties with the generations—identifying herself with Great Gram— gives Ursa the strength to accept Mutt. In Faulkner, similar identifications—such as that of Quentin with Henry and Charles in *Absalom, Absalom!*—lead inevitably to a sense of isolation and despair.

As in *Absalom, Absalom!* storytelling in *Corregidora* reveals the relationship between the individual and his/her past. The precise relationship involves incest in both novels. The Portuguese Corregidora who fathered both Ursa's grandmother and her mother resembles Faulkner's Carothers McCaslin. But where Quentin—like Ike in "The Bear"—sets out to uncover truths distorted or repressed by his narrative heritage, Ursa's problem centers on her unwillingness to accept the direct revelations of her ancestors. One of Ursa's earliest memories is of Great Gram providing information of a sort not easily available to Quentin, the story of the heritage of incest and slavery:

"She told the same story over and over again" (11). This directness reflects the fact that the Afro-American tradition has been shaped by the demand for realistic survival techniques while Quentin's southern heritage has frequently encouraged romantic mythmaking that pays little attention to the facts. The storytelling tradition in Ursa's family rejects the Euro-American myths, claiming passage for the "generations": "My great-grandmama told my grandmama the part she lived through that my grandmama didn't live through and my grandmama told my mama what they both lived through and my mama told me what they all lived through and we were supposed to pass it down like that from generation to generation so we'd never forget. Even though they'd burned everything to play like it didn't never happen" (9). Ursa concludes, however, with a bitter reference to the fall that rendered her sterile: "Yeah and where's the next generation?" (9). Through most of *Corregidora*, Ursa obsessively replays this incident in her *individual* history, seeing it as an insurmountable obstacle cutting her off from the family past.

This feeling of isolation and impotence leads Ursa to retreat into an emotional frigidity analogous to Quentin's virginity; neither can respond to the sexual call of self or other. In *Corregidora*, this inability expresses itself through unresolved blues stanzas in Ursa's conversations with Mutt. The end of a long ritual of call and refused response emphasizes Ursa's sexual distance from Mutt, who repeatedly undercuts the rhythm of call and response as a form of retribution:

> He made me think he was going to.
> "My pussy, ain't it, Ursa?"
> "Yes Mutt, it's your pussy."
> "My pussy, ain't it, baby?"
> "Yes."
> "Well, it's yours now."
> He turned away. (156)

Caught in this pattern of revenge within repeated scenes, Ursa resembles a Faulkner character facing a future of paralysis and death.

But the Afro-American tradition, the tradition invoked by Morrison's genealogy of witnesses in *Song of Solomon*, keeps the blues singer alive through the years of her despondence. Both from the audience at the club (one of the main ritual grounds in the narrative of immersion) and from her own mother, Ursa receives responses to her unconsciously issued calls. Her mother's response when Ursa returns home to tell her story embodies the emotional identification of the blues tradition: "When I did feel I had to tell Mama my song, she listened, but it was the quiet kind of listening one has when they already know, or maybe just when it's a song they've sung themselves, but with different lyrics" (182). This sparks Ursa's perception that her own relationship with Mutt resembles her mother's with Martin—that both women have "left a certain world behind" (182). At that point, Ursa realizes that the key to reconstructing her life lies in accepting the past, not only as the source of generations but of the call for realistic love. Coming to this perception, Ursa recovers a sense of her own identity. As Mutt says, "You've still got your voice . . . you're still Ursa" (183). When they reach Mutt's room, the present merges with the past; Mutt, who has just spoken of his great-grandfather, becomes Corregidora, Martin; Ursa becomes her three female ancestors: "It was like I didn't know how much was me and Mutt and how much was Great Gram and Corregidora—like Mama when she had started talking like Great Gram. But was what Corregidora had done to *her*, to *them*, any worse than what Mutt had done to me, than what we had done to each other, than what Mama had done to Daddy, or what he had done to her in return" (184). The anger climaxes with Mutt's orgasm at the moment Ursa tells him "I could kill you" (184), a statement that is both literally and metaphorically true.

Both statement and sexual act respond to the call of the tradition. They also recall the repetition and revenge of a Faulkner drama. The vital difference between Jones's and Faulkner's vision can be seen in the result of Ursa's act. She does not feel compelled to carry out the revenge, on Mutt or on herself. Rather, the confrontation with the past frees her for a personal response to Mutt's call. The blues patterns that Mutt previously undercut can finally be resolved:

> "I don't want a kind of woman that hurt you," he said.
> "Then you don't want me."
> "I don't want a kind of woman that hurt you."
> "Then you don't want me."
> "I don't want a kind of woman that hurt you."
> "Then you don't want me."
> He shook me till I fell against him crying. "I don't want a kind of man that'll hurt me neither," I said.
> He held me tight. (185)

Their identification with the past frees them for an embrace of life, even with the certain knowledge of pain. Both of the undercut blues conclude with ironic, vicious uses of "you"; the final response both transforms the pronoun into an affirmative "me" and unites Ursa's and Mutt's fears. Their identification with the past frees them to move together in an understanding that the fear and pain, which isolate and paralyze Quentin, actually provide the only base for a mature response to the call of love.

Interestingly, Faulkner's black characters rarely show an awareness of their black ancestors, despite the fact that, like Jones's, they quite clearly act out analogous roles from generation to generation. Benjy's black keepers in *The Sound and the Fury* and Carothers's slave mistresses in *Go Down, Moses* are examples. When a Faulknerian black *is* aware of ancestors, they are more likely to be white ancestors, as exemplified by Lucas Beauchamp's identification with Carothers. Characters with an intense awareness of black ancestors, most notably Joe Christmas and Charles Bon, almost always see the ancestry as profoundly destructive, something condemning them to endurance or death. In no case does Faulkner perceive the identification as liberating.

Endurance and Hibernation

Each of the Afro-American writers discussed above rejects the stasis—at best a form of sainthood, at worst of paralysis—associated with Faulkner and the narrative of endurance. As *Corregidora* indicates, this rejection reflects a deep difference between Euro- and Afro-American assumptions concerning the excavation of history. This difference in turn generates radically different visions of how the individual can respond to the discoveries resulting from the excavation. Ellison's *Invisible Man* and Faulkner's *Go Down, Moses* share a common language concerning the necessity for descent, but differ profoundly in their response to the descent. *Invisible Man* provides the prototype of what Stepto calls the "narrative of hibernation," while *Go Down, Moses* creates a "narrative of repudiation." Although both can be seen as variations of a "narrative of descent," the Afro-American tradition again rejects stasis—even when it is tied to the heroic morality of the Faulknerian vision—and generates a kinetic pattern calling for an ultimate return to society. Bradley's *The Chaneysville Incident*, echoing both Ellison and Faulkner, intimates the imaginative synthesis necessary to effect a meaningful return from the underground.

Ellison's departure from Faulkner's example takes on greater significance when juxtaposed with his praise for "The Bear," the prototypical narrative of repudiation. Ellison views part 4 of "The Bear" as "an argument in progress in which one voice (that of a Southern abolitionist) seeks to define Negro humanity against the other's enumeration of those stereotypes which many Southerners believe to be the Negro's basic traits" (*Shadow* 43). Ellison continues: "Thus we must turn to [Faulkner] for that continuity of moral purpose which made for the greatness of our classics. As for the Negro minority, he has been more willing perhaps than any other artist to start with the stereotype, accept it as true, and then seek out the human truth which it hides. Perhaps his is the example for our writers to follow, for in his work technique has been put once more to the task of creating value" (43). To some degree, then, *Invisible Man* itself responds to the call for value sounded by *Go Down, Moses*. Both Faulkner and Ellison perceive the necessity for the excavation of history, both view this need as an occupation of narrative space. Ike McCaslin descends into the texts of history, the ledgers that dispute his moral passage. Irwin provides a suggestive formulation of the significance of narrative space for Faulkner:

> It is tempting to see in Quentin a surrogate of Faulkner, a double who is fated to retell and reenact the same story throughout his life just as Faulkner seemed fated to retell in different ways the same story again and again, and insofar as narration is action, to reenact the story as well. And just as Quentin's retellings and reenactments are experienced as failures that compel him to further repetitions that will correct those failures but that are themselves experienced as failures in turn, so Faulkner's comments on his own writing express his sense of the failures of his narratives, failures that compel him to retell the story again and again. (42)

This repeated failure necessitates an endless series of descents, of separations from history that are simultaneously attempts to understand and recreate history.

Faulkner's desire to repudiate the sins of slavery forces Ike into a stance intriguingly resembling that of the enduring saint in the narrative of endurance. Unlike Faulkner's blacks, Ike takes possession of his own narrative space after making the descent. But his descent and repudiation divest him of his social voice. Recognizing the futility of Ike's repudiation (which costs him his future by alienating his wife, cutting him off from any hope of "generations"), Richard King argues that this action reflects Faulkner's rejection of artistic acts as sources of socially significant tradition: "That Ike fails to become the founder himself and to pass on this moral (or aesthetic) vision to anyone else implies, finally, the impossibility of founding any tradition upon art. As with Ike, the artist's epiphanic experience and accompanying vision remain private or at least not compelling for the collectivity" (116). Ironically, Ike's effective paralysis is enforced by Faulkner's limited understanding of Afro-American culture. Clearly, Ike envisions himself as a victim of his racist heritage. To that extent, his position parallels those of Faulkner's blacks. But Faulkner fails to perceive the potential for black movement and therefore fails to see that Ike's identification with blacks offers him an escape from paralysis. As Baldwin states: "The power to define the other seals one's definition of oneself" (428). Despite his repudiation Ike remains cut off from his own past and from Afro-American traditions; he must remain a saint enduring the burden of his isolation. Ike, as much as any black, is Faulkner's Moses. He goes down, but he cannot go back up.

Ellison, conversely, embraces history, sees himself in the other, and provides a basis for the return from the descent. Stepto defines the Ellisonian narrative of hibernation as that set in "a context in which the imagination is its own self-generating energy. The new resulting posture and space beyond those of the ascent and immersion narratives are ones in which the narrator eventually gains complete authorial control of the text of the narrative" (193). This hero defines his own passage. Significantly, he does so without repudiating either his past or the Euro-American culture that disputes his passage.

For Ellison, hibernation involves recognition of both the Afro-American patterns of ascent and immersion and the Euro-American patterns of endurance and repudiation. The excavation of his own history sparks the invisible man's realization that his identity is intermingled with those of the people with whom he interacts, including those who forced the excavation originally. The richness of Ellison's vision, which has made *Invisible Man* a central point of reference for both white and black contemporary novelists, results from his recognition that all truly excavated histories demand respect and that denying the other constrains knowledge of the self. This understanding allows the articulate hero to transform the narrative of descent into the narrative of hibernation. Even while admitting the necessity of descent, the invisible man insists on an ultimate return: "The hibernation is over. I must shake off the old skin and come up for breath. There's a stench in the air, which, from this distance underground, might be the smell either of death or of spring—I hope of spring" (580).

This return is in part the culmination of a narrative of endurance. The invisible man can be seen as an enduring saint, though in no simplistic sense. He grants whites time in which to realize the need for excavation. In the prologue, he holds back from killing the "tall blond" passerby, saying, "Something in this man's thick head had sprung out and beaten him within an inch of his life" (5). The perception, and the restraint, are Faulknerian.

Invisible Man also plays off the Faulknerian pattern of repudiation. When the invisible man burns the contents of his briefcase, the symbols of his invisibility, he repudiates the imposed definitions that have dominated his past. He does not, however, simply leave them behind; he turns them into the light he requires to define his narrative space. Unlike Ike, he perceives that the key to his own identity lies in his repudiations. Where Ike cuts himself off from both his Euro-American heritage and the black others whom that heritage repudiates, Ellison embraces even while he repudiates. Rather than jettison the whole of the white tradition, he identifies himself with it: "I am in the great American tradition of tinkers. That makes me kin to Ford, Edison and Franklin" (7). Significantly, each of these "thinker-tinkers," described as "kinsmen" whose tradition the invisible man articulates, provides an image of either light or motion. The invisible man carefully avoids aligning himself with the static elements of Euro-American culture.

In addition to subsuming the Faulknerian patterns, Ellison embraces the kinetic patterns of the Afro-American tradition. Far from repudiating his black ancestors, the invisible man gradually reaches an understanding that they are crucial to his identity, reflecting the immersion-narrative pattern. His simplistic attempts to repudiate even the apparently repressive elements, to shatter the darky bank for instance, end in failure. The old couple, evicted yet clinging to their freedom papers, and Brother Tarp, with his link of chain, remind the invisible man of the nurturing potential emanating even from slavery.

Significantly, Ike McCaslin's repudiation focuses on his grandfather, Old Carothers, while the invisible man's excavation leads him to a progressively more mature acceptance of the grandfather he had earlier repudiated. The invisible man's final meditation on his grandfather's command to "overcome 'em with yeses, undermine 'em with grins, agree 'em to death and destruction" (16) reflects his ability to accept even the tradition he ostensibly repudiates: "Did he mean to affirm the principle, which they themselves had dreamed into being out of the chaos and darkness of the feudal past, and which they had violated and compromised to the point of absurdity even in their own corrupt minds? Or did he mean that we had to take the responsibility for all of it, for the men as well as the principle, because we were the heirs who must use the principle because no other fitted our needs?" (574). His explanation invokes the Faulknerian concept of endurance: "because we were older than they, in the sense of what it took to live in the world with others and because they had exhausted in us, some—not much, but some—of the human greed and smallness, yes, and the fear and superstition that had kept them running (Oh, yes, they're running too, running all over themselves)" (574). Even while echoing Faulkner, Ellison makes it clear that whites are inevitably trapped in their own definitions; they are doomed to run all over themselves, as well as over the invisible man. These perceptions derive from the narrative of immersion, from the invisible man's very un-Faulknerian vision of himself as articulate kinsman revoicing his grandfather's wisdom.

Most importantly, the perception reinforces the invisible man's determination not to abandon himself to the paralysis of descent. The circle revolves, the descent becomes ascent. Obviously, *Invisible Man* embodies many of the crucial elements of the ascent narrative: the flight to the North, to literacy, to articulate survival. It also recognizes the primary danger of ascent—the loss of contact with one's tradition, which carries with it the threat of paralysis. The planned ascent to the surface, which transforms the narrative of repudiation into the narrative of hibernation, in fact revoices the most deeply rooted impulse of Afro-American culture. Ellison's imaginative space becomes a profoundly meaningful social space. The passage he successfully disputes is at once literary and political. Moreover, his dispute—dated 1952—played a crucial part in clearing passage for younger contemporaries including Morrison, Leon Forrest, and David Bradley.

Bradley's *The Chaneysville Incident* recognizes both the danger of repudiation and the liberating potential of hibernation. Bradley focuses on John Washington, a young black historian who descends into a symbolic underground to excavate the history connecting him with his ancestors. John's father, Moses Washington, a revoicing of Faulkner's Ike McCaslin, insists on the bond between man and the land and excavates the history of his own father, C. K. Washington. Unlike Ike, Bradley's Moses—neither enduring nor a saint—lives fully in the world of practical politics. Rather than repudiating ownership, he gradually gains economic control over the land on which the black community lives. Having completed an economic ascent, Moses strikes directly at the Pharaoh's source of power. The purpose of John's hibernation is to enable him to respond fully to the ancestral call. At the beginning of his excavation, John interprets Moses' death—which takes place at the site of C. K.'s death—as a Faulknerian suicide brought on by the repudiation of history. Finally, however, he understands the death as Moses' articulation of an *African*-American vision of the reality of the ancestors and the responsibility of each individual as ancestor. Seen as a response to both the Faulknerian narrative of repudiation and the Ellisonian narrative of hibernation, Moses' life and death can be understood as a call for John to return to the "surface" community.

The first step of John's excavation, which superficially resembles those in *Go Down, Moses* and *Absalom, Absalom!* is an immersion that forces him to transform historical data (John is always "literate" concerning the raw facts of Afro-American history) into felt experience. Called to the deathbed of his father's friend Jack Crawley, John hears the story of the racial oppression that shaped both Moses and the local community as a whole. The evidence that John does respond is his willing exploration of the ledgers that Moses left with the white Judge Scott, ledgers that provide him with additional facts.

The most vital step of the process, however, is John's recognition that the facts are not enough. As a historian, he is theoretically aware of this from the start. He lacks, however, any sense of the imaginative process needed to animate the facts. As long as he expects salvation from the written history of his note cards, he remains locked in stasis. The sullen silence that characterizes him through much of the novel implicitly rejects both his white lover, Judith, and the Afro-American oral tradition. This repudiation resembles that which consistently dooms Faulkner's heroes to alienation. Only when he *tells* the story to Judith can he transcend Euro-American literacy and truly comprehend the history of Moses and C. K. After Judith—herself carrying out a kind of excavation—forces him to tell her as much of the story as he knows, John allows her to accompany him to the site of Moses' death. There, after he resigns himself to uncertainty, she finds the gravestones of the runaway slaves, a discovery that sparks John's return from hibernation. Repudiating simple endurance, he recognizes the kinetic potential of their excavation: "It wasn't a death somebody had marked, it was only a grave" (381).

John's subsequent articulation of his excavation frees him to return from hibernation along with Judith. In the process, Bradley extends the imaginative structure that Ellison stated in individual terms to embrace a pluralistic community explicitly including women and whites. The articulation begins with John's recognition of the limitations of Euro-American literacy, the forms of Ike McCaslin's and Quentin Compson's excavations. His measured repudiation is directed more at his own academic career than at a cultural "other." When Judith interprets Moses' excavation as a movement toward death ("he'd found C. K.'s grave"), John responds: "That's what I thought too; that's the way historians think. I assumed that if Moses Washington went looking for his grandfather he'd really be looking for signs of his grandfather: records, old campsites, markers, graves, maybe even a skeleton. And he was. So I assumed that he was acting just like a historian, and when he found whatever it was, he'd set up a marker or something and that would be it" (387). Rejecting the "marker" as a static symbol of the descent, he emphasizes the kinetic

Moses of the Afro-American tradition. Simultaneously, he embraces the Faulknerian image of the hero as woodsman. One of the clearest signs of John's successful immersion is his ability to track a deer through the snowy hills. Implicitly, Bradley repudiates the Ike of "The Bear" and embraces the Ike of "The Old People": "But I forgot that Moses Washington wasn't a historian, any more than he was a moonshiner or a real estate speculator. If he was anything, he was a hunter. And he did what any good hunter does when he's going off to trail dangerous game: He left trail markers, so that if somebody wanted to they could follow him and he more or less made sure somebody would want to" (389). This realization in turn frees John to realize that Moses' suicide, unlike Quentin's, expresses not repudiation but acceptance. "Becoming" the Moses who "became" C. K., John tells Judith the story of the runaway slaves. The tale culminates in C. K.'s suicide, which denies a symbolic victory to the white pursuers seeking to discourage ascent. Returning to his own voice, John interprets *Moses'* suicide as an immersion in the synchronous world of the ancestors and a repudiation of the stasis brought on by fear of death. Following the trail of Moses, John emerges from the underground of repudiation. His final articulation of the story to Judith becomes an encompassing act of acceptance. Shaping the story of C. K., Moses, and John, he imagines the black woman Harriette Brewer, whom he constructs as conscious kinswoman to Harriet Tubman, as the motivating force behind the communal ascent. He credits the white man Iiames with burying the bodies of the fugitives as an act of atonement and love. Finally, he accepts the white woman Judith as he returns from hibernation. His response, to the calls of the African ancestors and black women abolitionists as well as those of Faulkner and Ellison, intimates the possibilities of a truly shared language.

Like *Invisible Man, The Chaneysville Incident* echoes Baldwin's insistence that "our history is each other. That is our only guide. One thing is absolutely certain: one can repudiate, or despise, no one's history without repudiating and despising one's own" (*Ticket* 428). As Ellison's invisible man stresses, the call is urgent: "'Agree 'em to death and destruction,' grandfather had advised. Hell, weren't they their own death and their own destruction except as the principle lived in them and in us? And here's the cream of the joke: Weren't we *part of them* as well as apart from them and subject to die when they died?" (575). Only recognizing the profound link with the other can bring release from the descent that threatens physical and spiritual death. Seen in this context, Ellison's famous final line takes on a new urgency: "Who knows but that, on the lower frequencies, I speak for you?" (581). Bradley's final chapter sounds with a similarly inclusive voice, encompassing the narratives of endurance and repudiation, immersion and ascent. Bradley and Ellison sing in the streets with the slaves and listen in the big house with the masters. Individually responding to an ambiguous call, they invite Faulkner and his Euro-American descendants to join in the communal song.

Absalom, Absalom! and the Minstrel Dialogue

Each generation, of course, recreates great writers in its own image. As I have suggested, there are significant continuities between the responses to Faulkner of Afro-American writers who began their careers during the 1940s and 1950s and those who have emerged more recently. Inevitably, however, there are significant new emphases in the ways novelists such as Leon Forrest, Sherley Anne Williams, and Gloria Naylor examine the implications of Faulkner's novels, particularly *Absalom, Absalom!* The developing Afro-American response to Faulkner, like Faulkner's greatest work, pushes us to excavate the premises of our history, to focus not on the "eternal verities" that can be carved on the walls of libraries but on those aspects of our experience that we least understand. The irony here is that if Faulkner understood something adequately, the next generation can simply incorporate that understanding into its conceptual vocabulary and move on to wherever the game is actually being played. One mark of Faulkner's greatness is the extent to which contemporary Afro-American writers continue to find him worth learning from and arguing with. Aware of the complex crises confronting Afro-American communities—crises growing out of the complex relationship between race, class, and gender oppression—and of the widely perceived irrelevance of most "canonical" literature to those problems, Forrest, Williams, and others excavate a "new" Faulkner who offers important insights into the breakdown of our contextual calls and responses. For Euro-Americans, his insistence that the "past isn't dead, it isn't even past" articulates the simple, but all too often ignored, knowledge that the excavation of history is an absolute necessity if we are to make any sense of the present. For Afro-American culture, Sutpen—or more precisely Quentin's imagination of Sutpen—has something to say about the costs of leaving one's roots behind.

The most crucial recurring element of second-generation readings of *Absalom, Absalom!* however, concerns the cost of excluding "others"—either racial or sexual—from *active* participation in the excavation of history. Tapping the call-and-response dynamic of Afro-

American expression as a way of mediating between individual and communal values, these writers present images of more comprehensive dialogue/excavations. These are presented not as simplistic acceptances of the other but as attempts to conceive a process capable of supporting our own extraliterary process. The emerging consensus on the dynamic of this revised process stresses the need for an awareness of Quentin's—and I suspect they are to some extent Faulkner's—shortcomings, particularly his inability to accept the complexity and participation of the other; a determination to avoid simplistic condemnations and to seek out our own analogous blindnesses; and a commitment to putting the resulting insights to use in the world. From this perspective, resisting either Faulkner's insight or his blindness dooms us to a simplified excavation with suicidal implications.

Given the contextual focus of these issues, traditional critical concerns with "influence" hold relatively little interest. In the discussion that follows, therefore, I will not be concerned with attempting to prove that a novel is, in any narrow sense, "Faulknerian." (A term I understand to mean any story with long sentences, two narrators, italics, and incest, which is superficially more difficult to comprehend than the feature section of *USA Today*. If it is a second novel set in the same fictional county as the author's first, or involves the killing of a large nonaquatic animal, any two of the preceding provisions may be waived. All novels concerning Mississippi, of course, are automatically Faulknerian.) Although most of the writers under consideration are in fact very aware of Faulkner, my present concern is with what I see as an ongoing literary "minstrel show," a term used most effectively in Faulkner criticism by Eric J. Sundquist who writes: "The gothicism of *Absalom, Absalom!* is not by any means the sentimentality of a minstrel show—not the benign dream in which 'all coons look alike'—but the nightmare in which black *and* white look all too hauntingly alike" (99). While I agree with Sundquist's observations concerning *Absalom, Absalom!* I differ with him to the extent that I think the similarity of black and white is exactly what makes *Absalom, Absalom!* a minstrel show. Derived from the work of Ralph Ellison, Robert Toll, Charles Sanders, and particularly Berndt Ostendorf, this view of the minstrel show emphasizes the crucial roles of parody, travesty, and misunderstanding in cross-cultural communication. Ostendorf stresses that minstrelsy entailed the "blackening of America." Even though the white minstrels presented their burlesques as simple fun, they tacitly acknowledged something in Afro-American culture worthy of imitation. Ellison articulates the importance of the minstrel dynamic when he describes his response to a stage production of Erskine Caldwell's *Tobacco Road:* "It was as though I had plunged through the wacky mirrors of a fun house, to discover on the other side a weird distortion of perspective which made for a painful but redeeming rectification of vision" (*Territory* 194). Blacks and whites can move closer to mutual understanding by approximating versions of one another. Faulkner imitates blacks in his fiction; black writers imitate Faulkner's forms. Each broadens his/her knowledge and communicates, if obliquely, to his/her audience, creating a more synthetic base for the next act of the minstrel show.

Absalom, Absalom! provides Faulkner's most intricate and suggestive examination of this dynamic. As Sundquist and Thadious Davis note, the relationship between Clytie, Judith, and Rosa revolves around the difficulty of acknowledging likeness. The moment when Clytie grabs Rosa's arm to restrain her from climbing the stairs is perhaps the most intense confrontation with racial likeness in Euro-American literature. Elsewhere in *Absalom, Absalom!* Faulkner presents similarly compressed images that intimate a great deal concerning the connection between racial and sexual otherness, an issue that has been crucial to the ways Afro-American novelists have pursued their excavations. Two passages stand out. One is Quentin's speculation on Sutpen and the "monkey nigger" who puts the poor white boy in his place. The passage concludes: "He never even remembered what the nigger said, how it was the nigger told him, even before he had had time to say what he came for, never to come to the front door again but to go around to the back" (194). Forced to assume the role of the "nigger," Sutpen—curiously resembling the protagonists of Afro-American "passing narratives," a version of the ascent narrative in which the protagonist severs all connection with his/her roots—responds by creating and enforcing a vision of himself as a kind of minstrel show aristocrat. What is particularly striking about Quentin's speculation, however, is the emphasis on Sutpen's inability to speak—"even before he had had time to say what he came for"—and his subsequent silencing of the black voice—"he never even remembered what the nigger said." Although Faulkner never pursues the implications, this intimates an awareness that the silencing of the "other's" voice—his own and that of the "monkey nigger"—is crucial to Sutpen's consciousness. Much of what we know of Sutpen's "poor white" past is based on the fact that his performance as an aristocrat is not entirely convincing. From the perspective of white Jefferson, he is more minstrel parodist than accomplished actor; his failure to play an appropriate role attracts a great deal of resistance. It is certainly consistent with the minstrel dynamic of parody and burlesque that Quentin imagines that Sutpen's silence is enforced by yet another despised "other." The minstrel dynamic—a socially significant manifestation of "intertextuality," the dependence of one representation upon previous representations—recurs when Henry attempts to imitate Charles Bon. Mr. Compson says, "Henry aped his clothing and speech, caricatured rather, perhaps" (102). The "black" son, in the eyes of the "white" son, appears to be a better aristocrat than the father who derived his idea of aristocracy from the black imitation of a white who, according to W. J. Cash, was probably a criminal in the first place. The deconstructive regression does not end, it merely fades into the mind of the South.

The second crucial passage occurs when Mr. Compson tells Quentin: "The other sex is separated into three sharp divisions, separated (two of them) by a chasm which could be crossed but one time and in but one direction—ladies, women, females—the virgins whom gentlemen someday married, the courtesans to whom they went while on sabbaticals to the cities, the slave girls and women upon whom the first caste rested" (109). Sutpen's treatment of Rosa Coldfield and Milly Jones violates these distinctions. Faulkner reveals the gender codes to be as arbitrary and destructive as the racial codes which, in Mr. Compson's words, "declare that one eighth of a special kind of blood shall outweigh seven eighths of another kind" (115). Sutpen's attempt to manipulate the codes, which leads to his destruction by the poor white class he should have understood most clearly, reveals not so much his personal corruption as the absurdity of the codes. Yet the silences, the gaps in Quentin's excavation—and in this he shares much with his creator—reflect an unwillingness or inability to apply the implications of the connection between race and sex to his own process and admit the other into active dialogue. Like the blackface minstrels, Faulkner suggests a profound connection between racial and sexual insecurities; female impersonators and blackface banjo players share the same dressing room in the white male mind. Unlike the minstrel shows, however, Faulkner does not try to dismiss the tensions he articulates with facile humor. As Walter Taylor demonstrates in a perceptive discussion of the minstrel elements of *The Reivers*, his "Hee Hee Hee" is deadly serious.

The reason Faulkner's vision in *Absalom, Absalom!* continues to attract the attention of Afro-American writers rests in large part on his tentative recognition of the social nature of Sutpen's tragedy. Sutpen recreates rather than resists the sources of his own past dehumanization; his inability to conceive an alternative leads inexorably to his downfall. Further, Faulkner seems aware that coming to terms with these partially understood patterns requires a collective process, a dialogue incorporating numerous perspectives and sensibilities. Unfortunately, in *Absalom, Absalom!*, as in *Go Down, Moses* where Faulkner grants no voice to either Eunice or Tomasina, the presence of the "other" is extremely limited. Quentin, Mr. Compson, Shreve—the primary voices are those of white males. Eulalia Bon, Judith, Clytie—all are silent. The only significant female voice—there are no black voices of importance—belongs to Rosa, who remains a comparatively static figure, bearing a resemblance to the enduring saint, which is at once surprising and, given the limitations of Faulkner's vision, not at all surprising. As she tells Quentin, "I waited not for light but for that doom which we call female victory which is: endure and then endure, without rhyme or reason or hope of reward—and then endure" (144).

Toward an Open Dialogue

Concerned less with refuting Faulkner's vision of endurance than with pursuing the possibilities his work suggests, Bradley, Forrest, Naylor, and Williams—all of whom combine Faulkner's insights with those derived from Morrison, Ellison, and others—explore the applicability of Faulkner's insights, particularly concerning the nexus of race and sex, to Afro-American communities. Of this group, Forrest—whose essays and public speeches explicitly acknowledge Faulkner, Ellison, James Joyce, and Dostoyevski as crucial ancestors—revoices Faulknerian motifs in the most direct and intricate manner. One of the crucial incidents in *There Is a Tree More Ancient than Eden* concerns Jamestown Fishbond, a friend of the narrator Nathaniel Turner Witherspoon. As a young boy, Jamestown experiences a rejection similar to the one Quentin imagines for Sutpen. When Jamestown comes to the back door of what Forrest calls a "mulatto purity party" (53), Nathaniel's Uncle DuPont slams the door in his face, precipitating an argument with his wife that highlights the connection between color prejudice and sexual insecurity in the black bourgeois community: "and aunt dupont . . . saying you dirty motherless crap-eater you could let the little black bastard in his black wasn't going to rub off on your yellow white passing ass take this—and she smashes the white frosted chocolate cake into his high-creamy-yellow face even though when she was sober she hated dark people more than anyone . . . why you shit-color bitch i believe you love black men after all" (54). When, years later, Jamestown throws a cantaloupe at him, Uncle DuPont has no memory of the original incident. He renders Jamestown invisible in the same way whites render him invisible: "Why I never saw that black sonofabitch before, what the hell would he with his evil black ass have against me anyway?" (59). The black bourgeois community repeats with disturbing exactness the patterns that doomed Thomas Sutpen. By perpetuating what James A. Snead calls the "rhetoric of division," by resisting the merging that they embody less ambiguously than does Joe Christmas, they implicate themselves profoundly in their own oppression.

After a second novel, *The Bloodworth Orphans*, which recovers much of the interracially incestuous ground Faulkner explored in *Go Down, Moses*, Forrest returned to *Absalom, Absalom!* in *Two Wings to Veil My Face*, one of the finest, albeit largely unknown, works of recent American fiction. Again narrated by Nathaniel Turner Witherspoon, Forrest's equivalent of Quentin Compson, *Two Wings to Veil My Face* focuses on the relationship between the near legendary black patriarch and juror Jericho Witherspoon and his long-estranged wife, Great-Momma Sweetie Reed. Superficially Jericho occupies a position much like that of Sutpen or Old Carothers McCaslin; Sweetie, one reminiscent of both Rosa Coldfield and Dilsey. While the unraveling of the relationship is worthy of extended discussion, the process through which Nathaniel—and Forrest—comes to understand it is of paramount interest in relation to the dialogue with Faulkner. Like Rosa, Sweetie Reed—at age ninety-one—summons the young Nathaniel to explain an aspect of his past history. Unlike Faulkner, however, Forrest acknowledges Sweetie's full human complexity, as reflected in her very active and eloquent voice. Not only does she initiate Nathaniel's excavation, her own excavation of her relationship with her father and mother provides the model for his process. The women's experiences and voices are as vital as those of Nathaniel's father or any other male. This is particularly important since part of what Nathaniel must come to understand is that black women's apparent acceptance of endurance reflects their complex—and complexly understood—experience of forces of which most black men remain unaware. Nathaniel comes to understand and experience the complexity of the "other" much more fully and directly than does Quentin Compson. The process of excavation confronts Nathaniel with the uncomfortable knowledge that he is not in fact a physical descendant of Jericho or Sweetie, that his family's legend is based on a deception. More importantly, the excavation leads Sweetie Reed—and by extension Nathaniel—to comprehend the complexity of the behavior of others: her father, I. V. Reed, apparently a loyal darky in the standard plantation tradition mode, whose behavior is explained in part by the fact that he is doing penance—imposed by a conjure women—for an attempt to kill his master; and Jericho— the secular "other" to her own sacred self.

The increased understanding of the "other" and the necessity of including women's voices in any successful excavation recur as central motifs in Naylor's *Linden Hills*. Framing her story with the relationship between two young black men—the dark-skinned, streetwise Willie "Shit" Mason and the light-skinned, bourgeois Lester Tilson—Naylor excavates the history of five generations of the Nedeed family. The patriarchs of the Nedeed clan create a financial empire based in large part on their exploitation of the light-skinned women whom they, like Sutpen, perceive as means of furthering their grand design. An explicitly feminist revoicing of Faulknerian concerns, Naylor's book revolves around Willa Prescott Nedeed, the wife whom the youngest Luther Nedeed entombs along with their dead child in the basement of his funeral home as punishment for her failure to bear him an heir. The key to Willa's self-understanding, and to Naylor's excavation, lies in a diary sewn by a previous Nedeed wife into the pages of a family Bible. Like Forrest, Naylor insists that women's experiences can be understood only through recognition of the repeated historical pattern, usually invisible to males, in which black women are entombed in "otherness." Given the tendency to respond to oppression by becoming an oppressor, the frame of *Linden Hills* is particularly significant. Not only does Naylor—who has been unjustly accused of reverse sexism for the portrayal of men in *The Women of Brewster Place*—recognize the complexity of black males, she also makes it clear that light- and dark-skinned blacks, lower and middle classes, men and women, are capable of reducing one another to symbolic "others." Failure to recognize and counter this tendency leads inextricably (as in *Absalom, Absalom!*) to the final destruction of the Nedeeds' grand design. The family house burns to the ground while the black community looks on with apathy or pleasure.

Responding directly to William Styron's *The Confessions of Nat Turner,* a novel that has learned very little from Faulkner's heroic excavations, Sherley Anne Williams's *Dessa Rose* juxtaposes three distinct approaches to its historical materials. The first section is written primarily from the perspective of Nehemiah, a white man interviewing Dessa, a black woman who has been condemned to death for her part in a slave rebellion. As he gathers information for a book on the causes of slave uprisings, Nehemiah has access to most of the material necessary for a successful excavation. But he is unable to accept the simple premise that Dessa is as complex a human being as he is; as a result, he can make no sense of her words. After her escape, he feels an obsessive desire to recapture her, to reduce her again to the role of enduring "other." In a wonderful passage near the end of the book, Williams describes the cost of Nehemiah's obsession. His notes on his conversations with Dessa, which he presents as evidence to a sheriff he is trying to convince to imprison her, are totally devoid of meaning: "'Nemi, ain't nothing but a scribbling on here,' sheriff say. 'Can't no one read this.' Miz Lady was turning over the papers in her hand. 'And these is blank, sheriff,' she say. 'What?' Nemi say, still on his knees. 'Naw, it's all here'" (232). Devoid of context and cut off from dialogue with the "other," the white male excavation, like *Uncle Remus: His Songs and Sayings*, disintegrates into nonsense. Equally important in Williams's alternative excavation is her treatment of the relationship between Dessa and the white woman Ruth ("Miz Lady") who for complex reasons harbors a community of fugitive slaves on her plantation. Although Dessa at first repudiates the humanity of the white "other"—a repudiation that becomes violent when Ruth sleeps with one of the black men—she eventually comes to understand that, despite Ruth's racist responses—and it is vital that Williams does nothing to romanticize her characters' racial attitudes—Ruth is as human, as complex, as the "people."

For Williams the significance of recognizing the "other" is not abstract. Rather, it exerts a powerful influence over our way of acting in the world, helping to expand our sense of possibility. When Dessa describes Ruth's role in the westward escape of the fugitives to a group of young blacks—the actual image of dialogue/excavation in the novel—Williams provides an image of black-white cooperation much more convincing than those in Howard Fast's *Freedom Road* or Richard Wright's "Fire and Cloud."

Treating a similar set of thematic concerns, Bradley's *The Chaneysville Incident*, as noted above, emphasizes the Faulknerian theme that the understanding of history depends on constructive use of the imagination rather than on pure facts, a point reiterated by most Faulkner critics. What is unique in Bradley's treatment of the theme in regard to the open dialogue, however, is John's reluctant willingness to admit his mother's and Judith's perspectives into his excavation. Unlike Sutpen, John Washington comes to understand that he has imposed categories on women equivalent to those imposed on blacks. Finally he is able to imagine a version of history in which a black woman—his great-grandmother—assumes the traditionally masculine heroic role. What makes Bradley's novel so powerful— and I think it is the single most effective confrontation with gender ever written by an American male, a claim I make with full awareness of Bradley's problematic (I'm tempted to say Faulknerian) public comments on sexual/literary politics—is Bradley's refusal to simplify any aspect of the reality he perceives, even when it entails surrendering his privileged position in relation to the other. The point seems simple, but it is not. Simply admitting the perspective of the "other" into a text is rare enough in American literature. Treating it in relation to structures of thought other than one's own is even rarer; this is where Styron's Nat Turner fails most profoundly. Recognizing other voices as possessing a complexity equivalent to one's own—admitting the underlying likeness without denying the actual difference—is extremely rare. Figuring out what to do with the likeness is nearly unheard of. But this struggle is precisely the point of the continuing Afro-American dialogue with Faulkner.

Faulkner and the Others

In conclusion, I'd like to comment briefly on some of the implications of what I've suggested in this chapter. First, an expanded sense of dialogue contributes to the recreation of Faulkner by and for a new generation. Rereading Faulkner through the Afro-American responses to his work highlights the fact that his work is grounded in social, specifically racial, realities. This makes it difficult to accept a rhetoric of division separating narrative and social discourses. While I have no desire to deny the power or significance of *The Sound and the Fury* or *As I Lay Dying*—the books that were presented to me along with "universalist" versions of *Absalom, Absalom!* and *Light in August* as the "great" Faulkner during my graduate education—recognizing the importance of race has implications concerning which Faulkner texts belong on college reading lists. In addition to recognizing the social nature of Sutpen's tragedy, racially aware Faulkner criticism deepens our appreciation of *Light in August* and *Go Down, Moses*. Underlying this adjustment of the canon is a shift in emphasis from the primarily psychological books to the books that present models of the dialogue necessary for excavation. In addition, recognizing the connection between race, class, and gender, particularly in the dialogue works that actively explore the relationship of the spoken and the written word, will also help articulate the importance of the Snopes trilogy in Faulkner's overall development.

Second, the dialogue has implications in regard to our understanding of Afro-American literature. Many Afro-American novelists seem to believe that a point has been reached, aesthetically if not yet socially, where it is possible, to revise Baldwin's formulation, to "welcome Faulkner back on one's own terms." No longer forced to expend a great deal of energy correcting Faulkner's obvious limitations, black writers can now explore more fully the uses of his work in relation to their own concerns. On one level, this may involve "applications" of Faulknerian concepts to class or gender relationships such as those carried out by Forrest and Naylor. This in turn suggests revisions of Stepto's ascent and immersion paradigms to account more fully for the diversity of the black community. On another level, it may suggest ways of coming to terms with the white "other" as in Bradley and Williams. In addition, reengaging Faulkner on different premises can help clarify the nature of the relationship between the spoken and written word—a crucial element of a literary tradition grounded in the blues, in folk expression, in sermons. The spoken word, particularly the call-and-response dynamic, has been recognized by critics from W. E. B. Du Bois and Zora Neale Hurston to Robert Stepto and Sherley Anne Williams as central to Afro-American literary traditions. One of the ongoing problems, however, has been finding a way of translating between relatively static written forms (created primarily by individuals) and oral forms predicated on the dynamic interaction of self (the leader) and other (the congregation, the respondents). What I would suggest—and I think that Forrest's work provides a first strong intimation of the possibility—is that the Faulknerian sentence, what Irving Howe called his "stream of eloquence" style, suggests one way of solving the problem. Incorporating multiple perspectives, dictions, traditions, Faulkner's sentences—particularly in *Absalom, Absalom!* and part 4 of "The Bear"—carry on a dialogue with themselves. Similarly, passages such as part 4 of "The Bear" intimate ways of expressing the silence of writing through dialogue rendered back into writing with an awareness of its silences. Combined with the expanded sense of the "other" and conceived as an extension of the call-and-response dynamic, the Faulknerian style—far from being an archaic or idiosyncratic expression of Euro-American solipsism—can be reconstituted as an aesthetic-social instrument of profound significance.

Finally, the dialogue between Faulkner and Afro-American culture implies a sense of literature as a collective process, as an engagement with social realities. Recall the moment in Gaines's *The Autobiography of Miss Jane Pittman* when Jane and Jules Raynard discuss the relationship between dialogue and the tragedy created by the intersection of racial and sexual difference. Alone, neither Jane nor Jules can do more than speculate on the truth. As Jules says, "It would be specalatin if two white people was sitting here talking." Jane says, "But it's us," to which Jules responds, "And that makes it gospel truth." In this version of history no one need be, or can be, ignored as "other." Extending this principle, the black dialogue with Faulkner heightens, or should heighten, our Faulknerian awareness of the need to be conscious of who's speaking and, equally importantly, of who isn't. The dialogue, the excavation of America's psychic landscape, progresses—in Euro-American works such as Lee Smith's *Oral History*, Richard Powers's *The Gold-Bug Variations*, Ellen Douglass's *Can't Quit*

You Baby, Dorothy Allison's *Bastard out of Carolina,* and Russell Banks's *Continental Drift;* and those by "others" such as Leslie Marmon Silko's *Almanac of the Dead,* Bharati Mukherjee's *Jasmine,* Cristina Garcia's *Dreaming in Cuban,* Louise Erdrich's *Tracks,* Luis Valdez's *The Shrunken Head of Pancho Villa,* John Wideman's *Philadelphia Fire,* Maxine Hong Kingston's *Tripmaster Monkey,* or Xam Cartier's *Muse-Echo Blues.* All of these texts share an awareness of literature as a dialogue; all attempt to admit the voices of excluded "others." As for Faulkner's role in the dialogue with Afro-American writers, he may not have prevailed, but he has certainly endured. As for the rest of us, I suspect that we're stuck in the minstrel show. But, with the help of Forrest and Williams, of Naylor and Silko and Faulkner, we can at least come to a deeper understanding of the roles we play.

3

The Brier Patch as (Post)modernist Myth: Morrison, Barthes, and *Tar Baby* As-Is

▲ ▲ ▲ ▲

Toni Morrison remakes (post)modern myths. Shifting gradually from the conventional modernist use of myth as structure in *The Bluest Eye* to the postmodern metamythology of *Tar Baby*, Morrison recapitulates the literary/historical movement from T. S. Eliot's classic essay "Ulysses, Order, and Myth" (1923) to Roland Barthes's "Myth Today" (1957). Exploring the complex genealogy of the tar baby myth in both Afro- and Euro-American culture, Morrison's fourth novel highlights the link between Barthes's theory of myth and the Afro-American folk tradition that precedes, echoes, and revises it. Specifically, Morrison shares Barthes's concern with the "double function" of myth as something that both "makes us understand something and imposes it on us" (117). While Morrison seems aware of French literary theory—one of the characters in *Tar Baby* is named Foucault—her understanding of the way myths impose de-historicized meanings derives more directly from Afro-American culture. Attuned to both folk and literary traditions of double-voicing (masking, signifying, lying), Morrison apprehends myth both as a tool of Euro-American power and as a reservoir of historical knowledge capable of resisting that power. Significantly revising Barthes's argument that the myths of the oppressed are "rare, thread-bare myths: either transient, or clumsily indiscreet; by their very being, they label themselves as myths and point to their masks" (148), Morrison creates in *Tar Baby* a richly duplicitous text that links modernist traditions with the specific circumstances of Afro-American historical experience.

Barthes and the Revision of Modernist Myth

In "Myth Today" Barthes revises the high modernist concept of myth as a manifestation of universal values, presenting an influential theory of myth as a "second-order semiological system" (114). Analysis of first-order systems, Barthes stresses, reveals the inadequacy of signifiers (forms, words) as expressions of the signified (content, the object of discourse): "What we grasp is not at all one term after the other, but the correlation which unites them: there are, therefore the signifier, the signified and the sign, which is the associative total of the first two terms" (113). For Barthes, a particular sign has no absolute meaning. Rather, it assumes meaning from the individual and cultural processes that both clarify and impose an understanding of the relationship between signifier and signified. Building on this fundamental insight, Barthes emphasizes the peculiar nature of "myth" as both sign and signifier. As "sign," a myth derives its significance from a continuing and unfixable set of historical processes. Always subject to revision as events progress and new understandings emerge, such "myth-signs" are subject to simplification when uprooted from their context. In effect, they become signifiers encoding and serving as a shorthand representation of a particular understanding of the historical process. Barthes describes the "myth-signifier" as a "metalanguage, because it is a second language, in which one speaks about the first" (115). To avoid confusion (and because it accords more closely with common usage), I shall refer to the myth-sign (Barthes's concept) as the "sign" and the myth-signifier (Barthes's form) as "myth" for the remainder of this chapter.

As Barthes realized, the transformation of sign into myth simplifies history by repressing process and excluding alternative meanings. Myth posits "meaning [as] *already* complete, it postulates a kind of knowledge, a past, a memory, a comparative order of facts, ideas, decisions" (117). Recognizing the political implications of this process, Barthes observes that the most influential myths encode the understanding of whatever group possesses the economic, political, or military power to silence dissent. Although he recognizes that all signs are subject to such "deformation"—he writes that "the fundamental character of the mythical concept is to be *appropriated*" (119)—Barthes views myth as a potentially subversive force. Despite the repression of history by myth, the historical ambiguity of the sign cannot be fully eradicated. The myth "does not suppress the meaning, it only impoverishes it, it puts it at a distance" (118). This creates "a double system" (123). A particular myth simultaneously imposes a particular interpretation/understanding of experience and points to the more complex history behind that understanding. A comprehensive understanding therefore demands awareness of both the system that imposes the myth and the history it veils from sight.

From a viewpoint informed by Afro-American cultural traditions, Barthes's theory of myth presents few surprises. In *The Souls of Black Folk*, W. E. B. Du Bois discusses Afro-American "double consciousness" in terms applicable to Barthes's understanding of the gap between myth and sign. Forced to coexist with the Euro-American power structure in order to survive, Afro-Americans live with a constant awareness of the cultural myths of blackness that determine their meaning for whites. Designed to support the privilege of the predominantly white dominant class, racial myths discourage consideration of both racial history and the workings of the power structure. But, as both Barthes and Du Bois understood, the history is not entirely suppressed. The gaps between Euro-American myth and Afro-American experience of self suggest the inadequacy of the Euro-American understanding of history. Recalling Du Bois's description of the "two warring ideals" within the Afro-American individual, Barthes endorses a version of Du Bois's double consciousness as the crux of mythic awareness: "In order to gauge the political load of an object and the mythical hollow which espouses it, one must never look at things from the point of view of the signification [the Euro-American system which fixes the meaning of the myth], but from that of the signifier [the black individual], of the thing which has been robbed; and within the signifier, from the point of view of the language-object, that is, of the meaning [the sign which articulates the history repressed by the myth]" (145).

Barthes both extends and departs from the modernist understanding of myth as a literary device, which has itself gone through precisely the kind of mythologizing process Barthes describes. Although myth has been used in literature since antiquity, *Ulysses, The Waste Land,* and Pound's *Cantos* appear in the mythology of Anglo-American modernism as radically innovative in their use of the "mythic method." In retrospect, these texts would appear to offer a wide variety of approaches to the use of myth. If texts such as William Carlos Williams's *Paterson*, H. D.'s *Trilogy*, and Melvin B. Tolson's *Harlem Gallery* are admitted into the modernist canon, the range of "mythic methods" broadens even further. In spite of this diversity, however, histories of modernism (quite legitimately insofar as they are histories of the movement's self-consciousness) usually present a much more circumscribed approach to myth. This simplification (repression) of history stems primarily from the extensive influence of Eliot's essay "Ulysses, Order, and Myth," which in effect advanced a myth of modernist myth. Presenting *Ulysses* as a fictional analogue to *The Waste Land,* Eliot accorded Joyce's use of myth the "importance of a scientific discovery." Few would argue the point, although Joyce's employment of what Eliot called a "continuous parallel between contemporaneity and antiquity" had been anticipated both within and outside the European cultural continuum. In commenting on the significance of Joyce's discovery, Eliot issued a pronouncement that proved at least as influential as the discovery itself. Eliot described Joyce's use of myth as "simply a way of controlling, of ordering, of giving a shape and significance to the immense panorama of futility and anarchy which is contemporary history" (177). This statement claims what Eliot called the "mythical method" for the elitist strain of modernism that viewed the contemporary world, and especially popular movements, with disdain. Although Joyce did not share Eliot's conservative cultural perspective, there is no doubt that Eliot's position, especially as developed, propagated, and frequently distorted by the New Criticism, largely determined the significance of the mythical method for Anglo-American modernism.

This myth of the mythical method reinforces the modernist reticence to acknowledge the reality of history. As Frederick Karl observes in *Modern and Modernism:* "Modernists in nearly all their innovative phases view themselves not as part of a tradition but as ahistorical; as dissociated from the historical ties one expects in marketplace ideas. At any given stage, Modernism is to break not only with traditional art but with traditional humanistic culture, what is connected to historical process. The avant-garde, especially, is based on this assumption: to move so far outside the mainstream that historical development no longer applies" (xii). Grounded partially in contempt for the simplifications of popular myth, modernist myth ironically increases the Euro-American alienation from repressed historical experience. Deepening the irony is the fact that this myth of "ahistorical modernism"—as critics and historians of modernism (including Karl himself) recognize—represses aspects of literary history. Malcolm Bradbury and James McFarlane image the modernist project as an attempt to hold "transition and chaos, creation and de-creation, in suspension" (49); Hugh Kenner recognizes clearly that Joyce shared Samuel Butler's belief that "no artist can reach an ideal higher than his own best actual environment" (48).

Nonetheless, no alternative understanding seriously challenged the power of Eliot's myth in Anglo-American literary discourse prior to the postmodernist critique that Karl accurately defines as yet another manifestation of the modernist impulse. The postmodernist approach focuses primarily on the process by which signs are transformed into myths. Significantly revising Eliot, novelists such as Thomas Pynchon, Richard Powers, and Gilbert Sorrentino consider myths as manifestations of particular states of consciousness rather than pre-existing universals. Exploring these responses to the limitations of modernist myth, Robert Scholes's *The Fabulators,* Jerome Klinkowitz's *Literary Disruptions,* Raymond Olderman's *Beyond the Wasteland,* and my own *Paradoxical Resolutions* contribute to the creation of a countermyth that itself represses aspects of postmodernist/modernist history. Most frequently, (post)modernist countermyth assumes (and imposes) a radically subjective sensibility, which seriously distorts the underlying populism of Pynchon or Sorrentino. The repression of history has many implications, one of which concerns the general failure to recognize some aspects of Morrison's literary significance.

While it is obviously necessary and appropriate to acknowledge Morrison's importance in Afro-American and women's literature, her use of myth in *Tar Baby* has more in common with *Gravity's Rainbow* or Sorrentino's *Mulligan Stew* than with Richard Wright's rewriting of *Ulysses* in relation to the myth of Lincoln's birthday in *Lawd Today* or Gloria Naylor's Eliotic use of the Divine Comedy in *Linden Hills.* Aware of the way in which myth imposes meanings on experience, Morrison focuses *Tar Baby* on the processes through which individuals confront the resulting tensions. Morrison does not simply present an Afro-American version of Barthes's theory of myth; to do so would be to indirectly endorse the limitations identified by Wole Soyinka and Sunday Anozie in their discussions of Barthes in relation to the African continuum. His myth of the impoverished language of the oppressed, for example, collapses when confronted with historical evidence. Still, Barthes's limitations are neither extreme nor, given his personal history, incomprehensible. More importantly, his insights complement, and, for some audiences, clarify the folk wisdom embedded in Morrison's works.

Is-ness, Masking, and Tar Baby as Mascon

Morrison's Afro-American ancestors and relatives, in both the folk and literary communities, have explored two basic responses to the power of Euro-American myth: masking and an insistent focus on what George Kent calls "is-ness." As Jean Fagan Yellin's *The Intricate Knot* and Winthrop Jordan's *White over Black* demonstrate, Afro-Americans have for centuries encountered racial myths that deny the reality of their experience. Presented as unarguable expressions of the meaning of a historical experience ascribed to a distant past,

Euro-American racial myths are not subject to interrogation. In naive form, these myths present Afro-American characters in terms of simple stereotypes: the mammy, the black beast, etc. In more sophisticated form, they reinterpret the kinetic Afro-American cultural patterns of ascent and immersion (Stepto) as myths of endurance (see chapter 2). For blacks faced with unquestioning white endorsement of such myths, survival depended on two factors, both implicit in the mythic awareness Barthes desires: an awareness of the power system enforcing the myths, a system largely unconscious of its own myth-making processes; and the ability to use this awareness to resist (and when possible subvert) that system. Gauging their actions to accord with white expectations, blacks frequently assumed stereotypical masks to distract attention from events that Euro-American observers—unaware of even the most obvious human motives denied by the myths of animalistic blacks—had in effect trained themselves not to see.

Afro-American traditions encourage awareness of both sign and myth. To accept a myth without excavating its reservoir of repressed history, from an Afro-American perspective, would be to accept the obliteration of one's identity. Kent describes the resulting insistence on immediate experience, understood to include ideas about and apprehensions of that experience, in *Blackness and the Adventure of Western Culture:*

> From the animal tales to the hipsterish urban myth-making, folk tradition has *is-ness*. Things are. Things are funny, sad, tragic, tragicomic, bitter, sweet, tender, harsh, awe-inspiring, cynical, other-worldly, worldly—sometimes, alternately expressing the conflicting and contradictory qualities; sometimes, expressing conflicting qualities simultaneously. Thus a Brer Rabbit story is full of the contradictions of experience—an expression of the existing order of the world and Brer Rabbit's unspecific sense of something "other." And there are times in Brer Rabbit stories during which the existing order and Brer Rabbit's "other" have almost equal validity. (53)

The is-ness of the folk tradition generally and the Brer Rabbit stories in particular resists Euro-American myth. As Bernard Wolfe demonstrates in his classic essay "Uncle Remus and the Malevolent Rabbit," the animal tales encode a worldview profoundly incompatible with Joel Chandler Harris's plantation mythology. The racial animosity and sexual tensions of the tales subvert the pastoral surface, pointing to the complex racial history repressed by the frame. The is-ness of Afro-American experience survives, although it cannot be articulated directly for fear of white retribution. Asserting a high level of Barthean mythic awareness for the folk tradition, Houston Baker emphasizes that forms like the blues and animal tales mediate between competing myths through a highly developed meta-language: "Blues and its sundry performers offer interpretations of the *experiencing of experience*" (7; emphasis added).

Afro-American artists attempting to tap this metalanguage enter into a complex process involving a structural awareness of Euro-American myths; a focus on the is-ness of Afro-American experience that acknowledges the mediating power of these myths; and an awareness of the potential, and limitations, of countermyths, which may either reclaim elements of the repressed history or impose new repressions. Afro-American writers seeking to create effective countermyths typically employ some version of the masking strategy. In Barthean terms, the artist presents his/herself in a way that appears to accord with the myths of the predominantly white audience. Drawing on a wider sense of both the historical and the contemporary is-ness, however, the artist seeks to manipulate the audience's responses, inserting "masked" messages that subvert the myth or communicate with the (predominantly black) segment of the audience aware of the repressed history encoded in the mask that the white audience accepts as reality. For black audiences, this generates a countermyth that asserts an alternative to the historical understanding of the dominant myth. At their most effective, such countermyths encourage black audiences to refine their own myth-making capacities in order to discredit the racist power structure. From Charles W. Chesnutt and Hurston through Ralph Ellison and Morrison, Afro-American writers have insinuated their countermyths into the dominant discourse by appearing to endorse myths they in fact seek to subvert. The plantation tradition trappings of *The Conjure Woman,* the exoticism of *Mules and Men,* the universalist rhetoric of *Invisible Man:* all manipulate Euro-American myths of Afro-American character while calling the premises of those myths into question. Frequently, as in Hurston's *Moses, Man of the Mountain* and Chesnutt's "Baxter's Procrustes," Afro-American writers carry out what can be seen as pre-Barthean inquiries into the mythic process.

Such encounters with and revisions of Euro-American myth involve several risks. On the one hand, the writer must maintain an awareness of the historical basis of the countermyths that, however useful, are no more adequate than the Euro-American myths they challenge. During both the Harlem Renaissance and the Black Arts Movement, some countermyths assumed the power to impose a myth (or ideology) of Afro-American experience that, while preferable to Euro-American racist myths, repressed the historical experience of many segments of the community. A second potential problem stems from the difficulty of maintaining clarity while interacting with the Euro-American power structure. The creation of effective counter-myths requires mastery of what Stepto calls the "literacy" of the Euro-American world, including the myths that repress Afro-American experience. Because such literacy increases access to the material rewards of the dominant culture, Afro-American individuals may come to accept some of its myths, in effect losing the "tribal literacy" that Stepto sees as necessary to intraracial communication. The great difficulty lies in protecting the sense of is-ness while obtaining the knowledge and tools necessary for the construction of countermyths capable of altering (even minimally) the oppressive power structure.

The Afro-American countermyth of Brer Rabbit and the tar baby focuses on just such problems. Both mythic signifier and irreducible sign, the tar baby invokes the energy Stephen Henderson associates with the Afro-American "mascon": "Certain words and constructions seem to carry an inordinate charge of emotional and psychological weight, so that whenever they are used they set all kinds of bells ringing on all kinds of levels. . . . These words, of course, are used in complex associations, and thus form meaningful wholes in ways which defy understanding by outsiders. I call such words 'mascon' words. . . . I use it to mean *a massive concentration of Black experiential energy* which powerfully affects the meaning of Black speech, Black song, and Black poetry" (44).

The tar baby story has gathered a large amount of such energy as it has been recreated in a wide variety of contexts. Whatever the setting, the constituent elements and plot structure alter only minimally. Brer Rabbit (or a similar trickster figure) encounters a tar baby that has been placed in the road by a white farmer or other animals. When the tar baby fails to respond to his greeting, Brer Rabbit slaps or kicks it, becoming more and more entangled until he is finally immobilized. When his captors begin to torment him, Brer Rabbit regains his freedom by convincing them that he dreads being thrown into the brier patch. Manipulating their cruelty and shallow apprehension of his character, he thus effects his escape and runs off taunting them that the brier patch is his home. In addition to this plot, each version of the story involves one other element basic to its meaning as sign: the frame. This frame may be either textual—the scholarly apparatus of a folklore anthology or Harris's plantation setting—or contextual—the specific circumstances in which the oral tale is related.

The mascon energy of the tar baby accrues largely from its complex genealogy in African, Afro-American, and, significantly, Euro-American discourse. Assuming new meanings as its context shifts, tar baby metamorphoses repeatedly from sign to myth. Encoding several layers of repressed historical experience, each new version of the myth influences the consciousness of the individuals who, even though they accept the myths that they inherit, gradually assign them new meanings as signs that can be transformed into further myths. The tar baby myth has passed through at least four such transformations. Originating (although the concept of an origin is simply another myth in Barthean terms) in Africa, the tale assumes meaning in trickster cycles that developed prior to extensive contact with Europeans. As an Afro-American folktale, it revoices the African myth as a response to slavery. Retold in Harris's *Uncle Remus,* it enters the mythology of the plantation tradition. A fourth transformation occurs in the Walt Disney movie *Song of the South.* Morrison's novel represents only the most recent stage in an ongoing genealogical process. Each level builds on previous levels without totally comprehending them, although Morrison approximates a comprehensive metamythic perspective. Most versions of the tale adapt previous versions as if their meaning were transparent: the tar baby myth becomes a signifier rather than a sign pointing to history. The most obvious example occurs in Harris's *Uncle Remus.* Presenting Uncle Remus as the wise but childlike darky of plantation mythology, Harris seems unaware of the explosive racial anger encoded in the tales Uncle Remus tells. Similarly, Afro-American tales, framed by slavery, project a more positive view of the trickster than their African sources; the violence and dishonesty that are problematic in a context where authority comes from within the community are necessary tools for survival in the United States. Aware of the shifting meanings of the myth, Morrison reexamines its genealogy and considers its significance in the context of contemporary Afro-American culture.

The tar baby myth provides Morrison with a field of mascon energy within which numerous potential meanings coexist. As racial allegory, the myth can be understood in the following terms: White folks (the farmer, Brer Bear) set traps (the tar baby) for black folks (Brer Rabbit). The best response is to ignore them entirely. Once involved, it's best to pull out slowly since struggling only worsens the situation. Once captured, use what you know about whites—their cruelty and their ignorance of black experience (the brier patch)— to create an effective mask which will allow you to escape. While traces of this meaning persist in most Afro-American versions of the tale, each element remains open to a multitude of interpretations. The tar baby could evoke materialism or the white stereotypes of blacks (it is black, stupid, lazy, and smells bad). Similarly, the brier patch can be read as a figure for Africa, the African aspect of Du

Bois's double consciousness, the black community, the woods of the black belt, the 'hood, etc.

The presence of a Euro-American mythic frame substantially alters the meanings. Repressing the history of racial conflict that would call into question the racial harmony he associated with the (mythic) New South, Harris renders both Brer Rabbit and the tar baby as extensions of the childlike Uncle Remus. Placed in a nonracial frame, the tale can support readings as a fable of the maturing child confronting the power of the adult world; as a discussion of the problems of surviving in an amoral context; or, in Jungian terms, as a confrontation with repressed psychological impulses.

What seems to attract Morrison to the tale is precisely this multiplicity, the undifferentiated quality of the tar baby, which can support numerous meanings. Generally consistent with Barthes's theory, the consideration of individual mythic processes in *Tar Baby* seems a logical outgrowth of Morrison's previous novels. Many critics have noted Morrison's use of myth, citing the Philomela/Persephone myth in *The Bluest Eye* (Miner), the scapegoat myth in *Sula* (Lee, *Quest for Self*), the Gullah (Blake, Werner) and biblical (Rosenberg) myths in *Song of Solomon* and her continuing interest in Joseph Campbell's "monomyth" (De Arman, A. L. Harris, Lee, *"Song of Solomon"*). Focusing on individual novels, however, obscures the increasing complexity of Morrison's approach to myth. Although *The Bluest Eye* asserts the destructiveness of unquestioning acceptance of the Euro-American myth of beauty, Morrison's use of the Persephone myth to structure and clarify the meaning of Pecola's experience is generally consistent with Eliot's idea of the "mythic method." By *Song of Solomon*, however, she has begun to develop the metamythic sensibility that will emerge fully in *Tar Baby*. Juxtaposing the myths of the Flying African and the Native American "Bird" clan with the Euro-American myths of Icarus and the Cavaliers (the Byrd clan), Morrison suggests the multiplicity of repressed historical experience. Morrison's point in *Song of Solomon*, as Susan Willis observes, is that while Afro-American history may be repressed by the reifying myths, it is not destroyed. Where *Song of Solomon* emphasizes Milkman's developing understanding of this repressed history, *Tar Baby* expands the focus to involve a multitude of individuals engaged in similar processes. Morrison's panoramic presentation of the complex is-ness of Afro-American experience focuses on the way individuals—both blacks and the whites who frame their world—express and reflect on the tar baby myth, in the process reasserting its historical genealogy and renewing its mascon energy.

Tar Baby

In *Tar Baby* Morrison adapts the folk sensibility to the is-ness of contemporary Afro-American experience. Rather than employing a traditional myth or creating a countermyth to give order, Morrison explores the is-ness as a texture of competing myths and understandings of myths. The style and texture of *Tar Baby* emphasize multiplicity. When Valerian and Son think of the Isle des Chevaliers, Morrison's description highlights the split between Euro-American myth and Afro-American history/countermyth. Valerian interprets the island as a bastion of European culture, a stay against chaos: "Somewhere in the back of Valerian's mind one hundred French chevaliers were roaming the hills on horses. Their swords were in their scabbards and their epaulets glittered in the sun. Backs straight, shoulders high—alert but restful in the security of the Napoleonic code." Son thinks of the island in terms of the oppressive racial history (the jettisoning of blacks and horses from a slave ship) repressed in Valerian's myth: "Somewhere in the back of Son's mind one hundred black men and one hundred unshod horses rode blind and naked through the hills and had done so for hundreds of years" (206). Given the reality of Valerian's economic power, a comprehensive understanding of the island requires an awareness of both perspectives.

Focusing on the novel's four male-female pairs, which present a continuum spanning the Afro- and Euro-American worlds, Morrison investigates a variety of ways of understanding myth. At one extreme, Therese and Gideon are content inhabiting the mythic blackness of the islands; at the other Valerian and Margaret occupy positions in a latter-day version of the plantation myth. Poised uneasily between these extremes, Sydney and Ondine attempt to maintain their economic security in Valerian's household while preserving the core Afro-American values of family loyalty and personal dignity. Morrison's primary focus, however, is on Son and Jadine, the only characters she presents explicitly in terms of the tar baby story. Whatever their specific history, whatever racial myths they accept, Morrison's characters consistently seek to evade the painful aspects of their experience and retreat to some version of an encompassing myth of "safety." For Morrison, the myth of safety itself becomes the tar baby, the trap capable of ensnaring even the most wily trickster. In *Tar Baby,* any element of experience can become such a snare when uprooted from history. A fixed conception of masking, a total rejection of contact with whites, a romantic myth of the brier patch home: all can become traps.

Of all the characters in *Tar Baby,* Therese and her nephew Gideon view myth from the perspective most closely aligned with the early versions of the tar baby tale. Therese, especially, perceives the white world, in which she includes assimilated blacks such as Sydney and Ondine, as a tar baby to be avoided at all costs. She refuses to work inside the house, assuming an evasive mask whenever she comes into contact with its inhabitants: "[Her] hatreds were complex and passionate as exemplified by her refusal to speak to the American Negroes, and never even to acknowledge the presence of the white Americans in her world" (110). While her refusal to look at Americans reinforces white myths of black stupidity, Morrison observes that "what they took for inattentiveness was a miracle of concentration" (111). This disengagement from the white world contributes to Therese's economic survival. Gideon describes the masking strategy: "When they say to let Therese go, I say okay. But I bring her right back and tell them it's a brand-new woman" (153). Accepting the myth that all blacks look alike, the white world (including Sydney and Ondine) accepts the mask as reality, creating an absurd myth of an island populated by a multitude of Marys to avoid questioning the more basic myth of black simplicity. Although the details repress historical complexities, Therese constructs countermyths consistent with her cultural situation. Her disturbingly accurate myth of America supports her resolve to avoid contact with the tar baby: "Therese said America was where doctors took the stomachs, eyes, umbilical cords, the backs of the neck where the hair grew, blood, sperm, hearts and fingers of the poor and froze them in plastic packages to be sold later to the rich" (151).

The problem with such an extreme position, from Morrison's perspective, is that it limits the effectiveness of the Brer Rabbit strategy, which demands knowledge of *both* black and white histories. Without Gideon's knowledge of whites, for example, Therese would have lost her job much earlier. Still, Gideon shares Therese's basic attitude. Tricked into returning to the island brier patch, he has no desire to return to the American tar baby: "He could not understand why Son wanted to return to the country too terrible for dying" (218). Like Mary/Therese, Gideon remains invisible to the Americans, who call him "Yardman." Unlike his aunt, Gideon takes pleasure in using his invisibility to manipulate whites. Reveling over Son's presence in the house, he joins Therese in creating a countermyth of Son as "part-Brer Rabbit, part African spirit" (106). At times Gideon himself assumes the role of Brer Rabbit. Perceiving her black "servant" in terms of Euro-American racial myth, Ondine assumes Gideon is illiterate. However, as he tells Son, his "stupidity" is simply a mask: "I don't let on over there that I can read. Too much work they give you. Instructions about how to install this and that. I make out that I can't read at all" (154). Generally sympathetic to Gideon and Therese, Morrison also portrays their limitations. Distanced from the Euro-American world, they cannot effectively resist its power. When Therese begins to create a countermyth around Son's relationship with the black Americans, Morrison points to her limitations: "She had forgotten the white Americans. How would they fit into the story? She could not imagine them" (111).

Including the white Americans in her own version of the myth, Morrison's treatment of Margaret and Valerian concentrates on the experiences that lead Euro-Americans to create the myths of blackness that render individual blacks invisible. These racial myths, Morrison indicates, are complexly interwoven with the more encompassing myth of "safety." Shared by both Margaret and Valerian, this myth necessitates the repression of unpleasant experiences that are projected onto black scapegoats. Retiring to his pastoral greenhouse, Valerian creates a modern version of the plantation myth. Like the writers who envisioned the antebellum South as an unjustly maligned world of benevolent patriarchs, gracious ladies, and contented slaves, Valerian presents his myth as a natural signifier: "Every effort had been made to keep it from looking 'designed'" (11). Valerian plays the kindly master with Sydney and Ondine, humoring what he sees as their idiosyncracies and assuring Margaret that "I have always taken care of them" (31). Beneath this benevolent surface, however, Morrison identifies a rigid adherence to convention, a use of myth that controls behavior and represses historical realities. When Margaret and Ondine begin to develop a friendship, Valerian imposes the values of the plantation myth: "Valerian put a stop to it saying she should guide the servants, not consort with them" (59). Morrison extends this motif in a specifically postmodern fashion when she describes the relationship between Valerian's social and literary attitudes: "He read only mail these days, having given up books because the language in them had changed so much—stained with rivulets of disorder and meaninglessness" (14). For Valerian, anything that challenges his comfortable myths must be "meaningless." He does not hesitate to enforce this illusion through the economic power always present, but rarely acknowledged, in the plantation myth. When Therese and Gideon violate his rules, he fires them. When he responds to Sydney's question "Everything all right, Mr. Street?" by saying "I am going to kill you, Sydney" (33), he unintentionally reveals the historical reality behind the plantation myth.

If Valerian constructs myths to ward off meaninglessness, Margaret is unable to repress her knowledge of the ambiguous relationship between signified and signifier: "Like a blank frame in a roll of film, she lost the picture that should have accompanied the word" (32). Despite this underlying uneasiness with the meanings she has been taught, Margaret derives much of her vocabulary from conventional Euro-American myth. When she stumbles upon Son hiding in her closet, she falls back on racist cliches, referring to him as a "gorilla" (129), "literally, literally a nigger in the woodpile" (83). Still, Margaret senses the insufficiency of Valerian's plantation myth. Comparing the myth that asserts white control with her actual experience, she challenges Valerian's interpretation of Sydney's and Ondine's roles: "They tell *us* what to eat. Who's working for who?" (23). Similarly, she identifies the core of Valerian's insecurity when she says: "You're scared. Scared Kingfish and Beulah won't take care of you." After Valerian responds that he has always taken care of his loyal servants, Margaret comes close to the slave-system premises of the plantation myth: "And they will do the same for you. . . . They are yours for life." Unable to accept the implications of her insights, however, Margaret retreats to the safety of the myth, admitting, "They're loyal people and they should be" (31).

Both Margaret and Valerian endorse myths of blackness not because they are racists but primarily because such myths support the myth of safety, in which they are heavily invested. Morrison traces the racial implications of Valerian's desire for safety to his childhood relationship with a black washerwoman. In standard plantation myth style, the isolated white child seeks out the black adult for human companionship. After his father dies, Valerian's first impulse is to deny the painful reality. Only when he speaks to the black woman, whom he remembers "like a pet" (140), does he begin to realize the significance of death: "The woman looked up at him and paused for an awkward silence in which he suddenly understood the awfulness of what had happened" (141). Unfortunately, neither Valerian nor the people around him accept the is-ness of the situation. Rather, they project the reality of death onto the black woman and, as Valerian will do later with Therese and Gideon, dismiss her from their presence: "they let the woman go and Valerian never again had to say 'He's dead today'" (142). Playing a minor role in Valerian's psychic drama, blacks provide an outlet for psychological impulses excluded from the pastoral myth.

Margaret's willingness to accept racial myths can also be traced to her desire for safety. Although she comes from a "poor white" family, she accepts Valerian's values to escape from the (not purely economic) uncertainties of her family history: "The safety she heard in his voice was in his nice square fingernails too. And it was that, not his money, that comforted her" (83). The primary difference between Margaret and Valerian lies in Margaret's inability to repress her personal history indefinitely. She experiences a kind of release when Ondine reveals that Margaret had abused her son when he was a baby. No longer forced to project her own evil impulses onto blacks, she can begin to accept herself and to pursue a more normal relationship with her son (278). Valerian, on the other hand, cannot extricate himself from the tar baby of safety. When Ondine, like the washerwoman, challenges the harmonious surface of his family myth, he has no recourse. During the Christmas dinner, Sydney, Ondine, and Margaret remove masks that—held in place because the maskers feared his power—Valerian had come to accept as their true faces. Given the fact that, despite his intelligence, Valerian remains content with a superficial apprehension of his experience, it seems particularly ironic that he is attuned to some forms of double-voicing. When he tells Jadine to read *The Little Prince* as the key to understanding Michael, he cautions her to "pay attention not to what it says, but what it means" (73). Still, he is unable to apply this knowledge to his life. When his family myth collapses—in part because he listened only to what Michael was capable of saying—Valerian cannot cope with the meaninglessness that is part of Margaret's everyday reality: "He achieved a kind of blank, whited-out, no-feeling-at-all" (235). Inhabiting a mythic landscape, accustomed to repressing unpleasant realities, Valerian denies the is-ness of the world entirely: "No world in the world would allow it. So this is not the world at all. It must be something else" (234). Totally unaware of the Afro-American myths that might cast light on his situation, Valerian is hopelessly enmeshed in the tar baby he has created. Although it provides little solace, Valerian comprehends that his ahistorical myth-making process is responsible for his alienation: "[Valerian] preoccupied himself with the construction of the world and its inhabitants according to this imagined message. But he had chosen not to know the real message that his son had mailed to him from underneath the sink. And all he could say was that he did not know. He was guilty, therefore, of innocence. Was there anything so loathsome as a willfully innocent man?" (243).

Combining elements of Afro- and Euro-American mythic sensibilities, Sydney and Ondine occupy a particularly complex position in *Tar Baby*. Superficially, both play their expected roles in the plantation myth; Sydney cajoles and trades in-jokes with Valerian while Ondine plays the nurturing "mammy" when she defends her treatment of Michael saying: "You can't spoil a child. Love and good food never spoiled nobody" (35). In addition, both echo white racial myths when they condemn "low-class" blacks. Like Margaret, Sydney at first views Son as a black beast, a "stinking ignorant swamp nigger" (101), a "wife-raper" who should be shot or imprisoned (99). Similarly, Ondine perceives Son as a sexual threat to Jadine, an animalistic presence filled with "wildness. Plain straight-out wildness" (192). Re-casting racial myth in class terms, Sydney casts himself in the role of plantation master when he tells Son, "My people owned drugstores and taught school while yours were still cutting their faces open so as to be able to tell one of you from the other" (163).

Despite such attitudes, however, Sydney and Ondine do not simply or unthinkingly accept white myth. Both employ Afro-American masking techniques; both are aware of the reality of Euro-American power. Sydney recognizes the shallowness of the good master's con-cern for his loyal servants: "You ever see him worry over [Margaret]?" he asks Ondine. "No. You don't. And he don't worry over us neither. What he wants is for people to do what he says do" (163). Somewhat closer to the early versions of the tar baby myth in her basic attitude, Ondine practices the psychological disengagement implicit in Syd-ney's observation. When Sydney continues to express his outrage over Valerian's treatment of Son, Ondine insists that he "drop that bone. Drop it before it chokes you" (102). Even though he finds it difficult to dissociate himself psychologically from the white world, Sydney endorses the tar baby principle as it applies to interracial so-cial contact: "[white folks and black folks] should work together sometimes, but they should not eat together or live together or sleep together. Do any of those personal things in life" (210).

By no means unsympathetic, Sydney and Ondine nonetheless demonstrate the dangers of *any* involvement with the tar baby of ra-cial myth. Having attained a substantial degree of literacy and per-sonal freedom within the Euro-American world, they cast light on the difficulties involved in the ascent pattern that Stepto identifies as central to Afro-American culture. Their racial attitudes resemble those of the blacks who refuse to buy Valerian candy after moving from the South to the North: "They're *leaving* the South. When they move out they want to leave that stuff behind. They don't want to be reminded" (51). Even though they acknowledge some links with other blacks, Sydney and Ondine distance themselves from the ma-jority of the Afro-American community, the illiterate unnameable "niggers" such as Son, Yardman, and Mary. Their escape from the tar baby of race exists only in their minds; from Morrison's perspective, they are totally entangled in the tar baby of racist myth. There is a tragic poignancy to Ondine's realization that, from Jadine's perspective, she and Sydney share Son's position in the mythic structure they taught her to accept: "Her niece, her baby, her crown had put her in the same category as that thing she ran off with" (282). Failing to balance Afro-American history and Euro-American myth, Sydney and Ondine find themselves cast into a blackness that makes a mockery of their desire for safety and support.

Morrison's concern with the is-ness of Afro-American life—an is-ness that involves Gideon and Therese, Margaret and Valerian, Sydney and Ondine—focuses on Son and Jadine, the only characters Morrison images specifically in terms of the tar baby story. Three direct allusions to tar baby cast light on the tension in their relationship. When Jadine enters the forest while waiting for Son, she begins to sink into a substance that "looks like pitch" (185). Frightened and feeling revulsion, Jadine taps the wisdom of the animal tales—which she ironically attributes to "girl scouts"—and realizes that to escape she must quit struggling. This scene prefigures her encounter with Son and the is-ness of the Afro-American world that Jadine knows only from a distance. Jadine's feelings about blackness are amorphous; she can both "black up" and "universal out" (64). She remains unsure whether to view blackness as tar baby to be avoided or brier patch to be embraced. The realities behind the Euro-American myths that influence her own perceptions remain obscure to Jadine. They have not even crystallized into the semihuman form of the tar baby.

Presenting a sharp contrast to Jadine's racial attitudes, Son—a modern Brer Rabbit—feels at home in the black world and has little interest in the comfort and safety Jadine associates with the white world. Like Gideon and Therese, Son prefers to avoid contact with whites whenever possible. This apprehension of the folk wisdom does not, however, protect Son from the danger of entanglement in the tar baby. For him, the tar baby is associated not with racial myth, but with women. When Son thinks of the story, he associates the trap directly with Jadine who he thinks of as a "tar baby side-of-the-road whore trap, who called a black man old enough to be her father 'Yardman' and who couldn't give a shit who he himself was and only wanted his name to file away in her restrung brain so she could remember it when the cops came to fill out the report" (220). Later, Son reiterates this version of the myth directly to Jadine. Casting himself as Brer Rabbit and Valerian as the white farmer, Son condemns Jadine as an unthinking tool of the white world: "There was a farmer—a white farmer. . . . And he had this bullshit bullshit bullshit farm. And a rabbit. A rabbit came along and ate a couple of his . . .

ow . . . cabbages. . . . So he got this great idea about how to get him.
How to, to trap . . . this rabbit. And you know what he did? He made
him a tar baby. He made it, you hear me? He made it!" (270).

Spoken in a moment of passionate anger, this version of the myth
represses a great deal of Jadine's personal history. The repression
reflects Son's own desire for safety; he creates a countermyth that
would justify evading the risk and pain associated with a mature love.
In addition, Son's version of tar baby fails to address a problem more
basic than Jadine's relationship with Valerian. When Jadine tells Son
that she is unable to see lights, stars, or moon in the darkness behind
her own eyes (214), she effectively endorses the underlying structure
of Euro-American myth that associates blackness with absence. At
times, Jadine senses that such perceptions identify her as, to some
degree, a creation of the Euro-American education that veils important aspects of reality: "Too many art history courses, she thought,
had made her not perceptive but simpleminded. She saw planes and
angles and missed character" (158). When she visits Eloe with Son,
she discovers that she has lost her ability to communicate with black
people who do not share her background. In Stepto's terms, she has
lost her tribal literacy: "She needed air, and taxicabs and conversation in a language she understood. She didn't want to have any more
discussions in which the silences meant more than the words did"
(259).

Like Valerian, Jadine resists forms of communication that draw
attention to the gap between signifier and signified: the forms basic
to the Afro-American tradition. From the beginning, Jadine recognizes Son as a tar baby, a threat to her safety. When she first encounters Son, her first impulse is to dismiss him from consciousness, to
retreat to the safety and simplicity of the Euro-American world:

> With him she was in strange waters. She had not seen a Black like him in
> ten years. . . . The black people she knew wanted what she wanted—ei-
> ther steadily and carefully like Sydney and Ondine or uproariously and
> flashily like theater or media types. But whatever their scam, "making it"
> was on their minds and they played the game with house cards, each deck
> issued and dealt by the house. With white people the rules were even
> simpler. She needed only to be stunning, and to convince them she was
> not as smart as they were. Say the obvious, ask stupid questions, laugh
> with abandon, look interested, and light up at any display of their human-
> ity if they showed it. (126–27)

This alienation from Afro-American tribal literacy renders Jadine vulnerable to individuals associated with the history repressed by the
dominant myths: most notably, the African woman in yellow who
spits at her, and Son himself. Significantly, she finds it easy to dismiss

ostensibly similar criticism from Michael, whose concern with her roots derives not from an awareness of repressed history but from a myth of black primitivism. Conversely, Son continually challenges Jadine to acknowledge the realities repressed by her myths of blackness and of safety. Confronting her with her own sexual impulses, he subverts the myth that associates "funkiness" with blacks and animals. Son attempts to draw Jadine out of the safety of the white world, releasing the "night women" whom she encounters during the visit to Eloe. Although she retreats from some implications of the vision, Jadine begins to reach beneath the surface of the racial and sexual myths to the ambiguous history that has shaped her is-ness as a contemporary Afro-American woman.

At home in the Afro-American world, Son is in many respects the classic trickster; gauging all actions for survival value, he readily accepts the uncertainties that Jadine and Valerian resist. His understandings of world and self are formed in terms of relation: "He did not always know who he was, but he always knew what he was like" (165). Son recognizes that the effectiveness of his masks depends on an accurate understanding of his audience's understanding (myths) of "likeness": "The sex, weight, the demeanor of whomever he encountered would inform and determine his tale" (5). As he tells Valerian, his context determines his attitude toward any particular myth: "In a swamp, I believe" (93). For Son, masking is reflex response. Approaching all myths with caution, he attempts to keep his mind free to perceive the actual situation, which he understands to be shaped by a variety of mythic understandings.

Despite this awareness, Son contributes to the collapse of his relationship with Jadine by constructing a romantic countermyth of blackness that represses aspects of black women's experience. Son's myth centers on his hometown of Eloe, Florida. Although he describes Eloe as "all black," Jadine quickly observes its dependence on white technology (172). Holding to the folk myth of the white world as a tar baby, Son creates a complementary myth of Eloe as brier patch. In his memory, Eloe provides an image of safety, offering release from the pressure of remaining constantly on guard against the traps of the white world. Like all myths of safety in *Tar Baby*, however, Son's myth collapses. Eloe cannot comprehend or support his relationship with Jadine. Morrison makes it clear that, despite Jadine's accusations, this is not simply a matter of sexism. Thinking of the women he knew when growing up, Son thinks that "anybody who thought women were inferior didn't come out of north Florida" (268). Rather, the problem derives from Son's desire to resist changes in the is-ness. Although his Brer Rabbit knowledge should discourage such simplification, Son removes Eloe from history, freezing his idea of the brier patch rather than adapting it to changes in sexual roles. After Jadine returns to New York, Son seeks to recapture the feeling of safety in her pictures of Eloe: "he opened the envelope and looked at the pictures of all the places and people he had loved. Then he could be still. Gazing at the photos one by one trying to find in them what it was that used to comfort him so, used to reside with him, in him like royalty in his veins. Used to people his dreams, and anchor his floating days" (294). With Jadine, however, Son is no longer floating; he has entered the deep waters. His myth of safety in the brier patch evades the risk of his relationship with Jadine. By embracing a myth that dehistoricizes Jadine's complex history as a black woman, he increases the possibility of suffering the loss he most fears. Once again, Morrison implies that myths which attempt to evade reality by dehistoricizing experience are doomed to failure.

This is not to say that Morrison repudiates myth. As *Tar Baby* demonstrates, she perceives reality as a texture of competing myths that strongly influence individual and cultural behavior. In the context of Afro-American experience, almost all myths must be apprehended with a fully operating double consciousness to be comprehensible. Very few characters, however, have anything approaching an adequate understanding of both Euro- and Afro-American mythic processes. Several times, Morrison presents images that imply a full knowledge split between two characters. After Valerian fires Therese and Gideon, Morrison describes his encounter with Son as a meeting of different worlds: "The man who respected industry looked over a gulf at the man who prized fraternity" (205). Later, she writes of the tension between Son and Jadine in similar terms: "One had a past, the other a future and each one bore the culture to save the race in his hands. Mama-spoiled black man, will you mature with me? Culture-bearing black woman, whose culture are you bearing?" (269).

Morrison provides no pat answers. Like *Song of Solomon, Tar Baby* concludes with a new beginning or, to be more precise, new beginnings. Recognizing the inadequacy of the myths she has accepted, most particularly the encompassing myth of safety, Jadine takes control of her mythic environment. She determines to confront the repressed elements of her is-ness: her funky "animal" passion (associated with the "silver dogs") and the "night women" who reassert the repressed history of black women. Significantly, Jadine hopes to begin again in Paris; she realizes the impossibility of attaining safety through withdrawal: "She would go back to Paris and begin at Go. Let loose the dogs, tangle with the woman in yellow—with her and with all the night women who had *looked* at her. . . . No more dreams of safety. No more. Perhaps that was the thing—the thing Ondine was saying. A grown woman did not need safety or its dreams. She *was* the safety she longed for" (290). Morrison follows this resolve with the new myth of the female soldier ants and their queen, a myth that acknowledges sexuality, death, work, and dreams. Echoing Jadine's memory of Son, the concluding image of "the man who fucked like a star" (292) suggests that the new myth is grounded in history and confrontation. The concluding lines suggest that she will not simply create a new second-order myth repressing the reality of her past experience. While the new myth, like all myths, remains subject to eventual deformation, for the moment it marks a nearly adequate attempt to incorporate the changing is-ness of Jadine's confrontation with the myriad tar babies.

Meanwhile, Son resumes his mythic identity as Brer Rabbit, a Brer Rabbit capable of benefiting from his increased experience of both tar baby and brier patch. His encounter with Jadine has taught him that danger—the tar baby as the white world, as love, as myth—is simply a part of the is-ness. Therese's myths of disengagement, however necessary to the historical development of the Afro-American community, are no longer adequate. Like Jadine, Son resolves to confront his deepest fear, the fear of loving a woman he is afraid to lose: "Already done and he was in it; stuck in it and revolted by the possibility of being freed" (301). When Therese delivers him to the Isle des Chevaliers at the beginning of his renewed search for Jadine, she challenges him to return to the black world, the brier patch represented by the blind horsemen in the hills. Son neither accepts nor rejects the challenge. No longer limited by a dehistoricized understanding of the Afro-American countermyth, Son/Brer Rabbit provides an image of process, of a flexible encounter with the is-ness of the island that includes repressed Afro-American history and the Euro-American plantation myth. Advancing into the unsafe unknown, Son/Brer Rabbit's footsteps echo the voices of the storytellers of the Afro-American tradition as he walks toward the ever-present ever-changing tar baby that tempts him to remove his eyes from the woman who can help him forge a unified mythic consciousness: "The mist lifted and the trees stepped back a bit as if to make the way easier for a certain kind of man. Then he ran. Lickety-split. Lickety-split. Looking neither to the left nor to the right. Lickety-split. Lickety-split. Lickety-lickety-lickety-split" (306).

For Jadine, for Son, for Toni Morrison, the tar baby is everywhere. The brier patch remains to be seen.

4

On the Ends of Afro-Modernist
Autobiography

▲ ▲ ▲ ▲

A sense of endings is strong in the writing of the lives of white
folks. In the introduction to his anthology *Autobiography: Essays Theoretical and Critical,* James Olney convincingly charts a gradual shift in
the critical understanding of autobiography from *bios* (life) to *autos*
(self) to *graphe* (writing). According to Olney, the shift of attention
from the events of the writer's life to the nature of the self was
"largely responsible for opening things up and turning them in a
philosophical, psychological, and literary direction" (19). The subsequent shift of attention to the ways in which the self is mediated or
created by the act of writing initiated a view of autobiography in
which "the text takes on a life of its own, and the self that was not
really in existence in the beginning is in the end merely a matter of
text and has nothing whatever to do with an authorizing author"
(22). The resulting emphasis on writing as, to use Germaine Bree's
terms, "maze" or "game" calls the existence of a distinct autobiographical genre into question. If life and self are primarily textual
constructs, then Marcel Proust's *Remembrance of Things Past,* Samuel
Beckett's *Malone* trilogy, and John Ashbery's *Self-Portrait in a Convex
Mirror* cannot be easily distinguished, on generic grounds, from Michael Leiris's *The Rule of the Game* or *The Autobiography of Malcolm X.*
Clearly articulated in Michael Sprinker's "Fictions of the Self: The
End of Autobiography," this quintessentially (post)modernist sense
of the arbitrariness of generic distinctions frequently involves a profound challenge to the concept of "self." Perceiving traditional
genres as hopelessly entangled in social and intellectual structures
that circumscribe consciousness, modernists as diverse as John Dos
Passos, Michael Leiris, and Mark Strand—their generic differences

of minimal importance—explore the paradoxes of life, self, and writing in a textual space that, if not quite value free, is at least situated beyond the direct control of discourses that—after Nietzsche, even more after Heidegger—have lost their constituting authority. Even as he questions the more extreme manifestations of the emphasis on *graphe,* Olney recognizes that (post)modernist/poststructuralist perspectives inexorably destabilize the sense of self: "the special appeal of autobiography to students of literature in recent times . . . is a fascination with the self and its profound, its endless mysteries and, accompanying that fascination, an anxiety about the self, an anxiety about the dimness and vulnerability of that entity that no one has ever seen" (23). Taken to its extreme in the work of some poststructuralist theorists, the (post)modernist vision of *graphe* opens onto a shifting white wordscape of politically ambiguous representations.

Literacy and the Public Self

In Afro-American writing, all this is different. As Henry Louis Gates, Robert Stepto, Christopher Miller, and William Andrews demonstrate, the primary significance of *graphe* for most black writers has been that it provides proof of a self capable of participating in the discourses—literary and political—that shape the lives of that self and the community from which it cannot be separated. From its beginnings in the seventeenth century, Afro-American literary expression—and in this it differs sharply from indigenous African expression—existed in the context of "Africanist" discourse: a pervasive—if multiform—view of Africa as "void and unformed prior to its investment with shape and being" by the European (or, in a different context, Islamic) masters (Miller 13). As Gates observes, one of the primary aspects of Africanist discourse was its emphasis on the act of writing as "the visible sign of reason" (*Black Literature* xxiii). Lacking a literary tradition, as understood in European terms, Africans were assumed to be unreasonable and cast out of the human community. From an Africanist perspective, the absence of writing provides proof of the absence of reason that in turn provides the primary philosophical justification for slavery. As a result, particularly in a political context where the ability to write one's own pass or to read a road sign might mean the difference between freedom and slavery or death, a strong correlation between literacy and freedom developed as the constituting element of Afro-American letters (Stepto). Certainly an "attempt of blacks to *write themselves into being*" (Gates, *Black Literature* xxiii), Afro-American autobiography was simultaneously an attempt to write the black community into freedom.

The success of this dual project, as William Andrews demonstrates in *To Tell a Free Story,* depends largely on the ability of the autobiographer to develop a writing voice that negotiates a potentially hostile discursive environment in a manner that, in effect, *creates* a sympathetic audience. At the outset, the Afro-American writer must be aware that whatever its ostensible politics—abolitionist or apologist, conservative or liberal—the white audience is likely to have internalized, often on an un- or semiconscious level, aspects of the discursive formation that deny or question black humanity. Focusing his discussion on the antebellum period, Andrews describes a set of rhetorical strategies grounded in the folk traditions of masking and signifying and shared by black autobiographers from Olaudah Equiano to Amiri Baraka. Recognizing the absolute necessity of attracting an audience with greater access to the sources of institutional power (which must be altered if there is to be any substantial improvement in the actual living conditions of the black community), the autobiographers employ the vocabulary of "sympathetic" whites, who can use the text to support their own political agenda. The cost of this strategy is that this vocabulary only rarely challenges the deep structures of Africanist discourse. Unable to take solace from occupying the moral high ground while the larger community remained in bondage, black autobiographers (to a much greater extent than their white abolitionist colleagues) were forced to recognize that the ultimate success of the political project demanded an increase in the size of the sympathetic white audience. As Andrews observes, the appeal of the early slave narratives for the unconverted white audience derived not from their commitment to "the oratory and polemics of the antislavery press" but from their "promise of intimate glimpses into the mind and heart of a runaway slave" (5). Having attracted this internally divided audience, black autobiographers attempted to reshape its priorities, to increase awareness of and sympathy for aspects of Afro-American experience (individual and communal) alien to, and probably incompatible with, the unrecognized premises of Euro-American thought. In this extremely delicate rhetorical situation, the individual autobiographer was forced to maintain constant awareness of how each segment of the white audience was likely to interpret each statement. Any rhetorical gesture that alerted the audience to the underlying project of redefining the discursive structure risked alienating either "sympathetic" or "neutral" audiences, each of which was likely to resist direct assaults on its sense of moral (or intellectual or cultural) superiority. At the same time, failure to assault the premises of that superiority in effect doomed both black individuals and their community to continued subservience. Andrews incisively defines the underlying task of the slave narrator as "the redefining of one's place in the scheme of things by redefining the language used to locate one in that scheme" (7). In this extraordinarily complex cultural environment, awareness and mastery of writing—the *graphe* that obsessed Frederick Douglass as much as Samuel Beckett—assumes a position of primary importance in the tradition of Afro-American autobiography. Conceived as a negotiation with a plural audience for concrete purposes, Afro-American autobiographical writing consistently resists the tendency toward metaphysical abstraction that Olney identifies as the dominant current of recent white autobiography.

This is not to imply that Afro-American writers have been unwilling to explore the complex manner in which writing mediates the presentation of self and life. Andrews emphasizes that the very complexity of the situation described above dictated that black autobiographers remain "sensitive to the weaknesses of each link in the communication chain, from the writer through the linguistic medium to the audience" (9). It is not surprising, therefore, to find that early black autobiographers sought to reduce the radical uncertainty inherent in this three-variable equation by shifting attention away from the abstract philosophical problems inherent in the writing process, problems that were very much in the consciousness of contemporaries such as Hawthorne, Melville, Dickinson, Whitman, and Emerson. Developing a relatively conventional voice derived from the general—as opposed to the avant-garde—apprehension of "good writing," the slave narrators attempted to provide themselves with a fixed point of reference by deproblematizing the relationship between style and self. A complex irony adheres to this situation. At the same time that the autobiographers challenged the premises that rendered blacks invisible—in Andrews's words, they attempted "to redefine freedom as the power to integrate the unknown and the known within the self, not just the black into the white in the broader social context" (9)—they were developing a conventional voice that implied a black self acceptable to the white audience. Masking the narrator's awareness of the philosophical ambiguities of the writing process, this conventional voice in effect renders aspects of the black self invisible. The benefit of this gesture—which established the tradition of deemphasizing the importance of *graphe* in Afro-American autobiography—was to free black autobiographers to focus their energy on the political goal of establishing an institutional context in which black writers could more effectively reengage, in explicitly (post)modernist terms, the ambiguous relationship between the self in the world and the self in the text.

The Stages of Afro-American Autobiography

Recognition of this dynamic helps clarify the historical development of Afro-American autobiography. Placing the concern with *graphe* in the foreground and drawing heavily on the work of Stepto and Andrews, I would divide the genealogy of the genre into three stages: an exploratory stage during which slave narrators develop the conventions that enable them to shift attention from *graphe* to *bios* and *autos;* a long period during which black writers—however profound an understanding of the abstract problems associated with the writing process their work in other genres might reveal—rely almost exclusively on the conventional voice in their autobiographical works; and a recent stage, which I would label "Afro-Modernist," during which a variety of political and cultural forces have resulted in the reemergence of *graphe* as a central concern of Afro-American autobiographers whether or not they would associate themselves explicitly with (post)modernism.

The first stage, discussed by Stepto (whose construction of the genealogy reflects the concerns of his own study) under the rubrics of "eclectic" and "integrated" narrative (5–16), represents the search of the earliest slave narrators for a voice that would enable them to redirect the audience's attention away from the issue of writing per se and toward the practical issues of personal and individual freedom. Lacking conventions for the presentation of the black self, writers such as Henry Bibb and Solomon Northrup explore a wide variety of possible voices, shifting from journalistic to confessional to anecdotal in a manner that draws attention to the writing process. However interesting from a conceptual perspective, the strangeness of voice in the early narratives—a strangeness that implicitly questions the necessity of the conventional styles of both the popular and intellectual modes of nineteenth-century autobiography—presented a serious problem inasmuch as it suggested that blacks were essentially different (and less competent), a suggestion incompatible with either the personal or the political dimensions of the project described by Andrews.

The second stage, described by Stepto in terms of "generic" and "authenticating" narratives (16–31), culminates in autobiographical texts such as those of Frederick Douglass and William Wells Brown. Demonstrating their mastery of Victorian stylistic conventions (elevated vocabulary, formal diction, periodic syntax, etc.), slave narrators were able to shift attention away from their writing per se, in effect claiming their status as "reasonable beings" capable of fulfilling the duties of American citizens. Although it rendered aspects of black experience invisible, the conventional voice succeeded (to the degree possible in the political environment of the time) in establishing a position from which black individuals could participate in public discourse, particularly concerning topics of direct political relevance to the black community. Because such a position remained valuable to black writers who continued to confront the submerged racism of white discourse, the conventional voice persisted as a dominant stylistic gesture well into the twentieth century, even in the autobiographies of writers acutely aware of the social and philosophical problems inherent in the writing process. Even writers whose work in other genres evinces a deep awareness of and interest in modernist aesthetics chose the most "conservative" of their voices for their autobiographies. From W. E. B. Du Bois's *The Souls of Black Folk* through Richard Wright's *Black Boy,* the significance of language, as Stepto emphasizes, is a central theme in black autobiography. The relatively transparent style of both works—in comparison with, say, the autobiographical experiments of Gertrude Stein or W. B. Yeats—testifies in part to the authors' desire to demonstrate the mastery of Euro-American literacy that provided a precondition of participation in debate on other issues, *including* those identified with modernism. Similarly, although autobiographies from Du Bois's *Dusk of Dawn* through James Baldwin's *Notes of a Native Son* reiterate the ways in which selves are constructed by social and linguistic conventions, neither is written in a voice that explicitly challenges the premises of those conventions.

Perhaps the most radical examples of writers whose explicit modernist awareness contrasts sharply with their conventional autobiographical voice, however, are Jean Toomer, Zora Neale Hurston, and Langston Hughes. Toomer's autobiographical texts are written in a style that suggests little awareness of the philosophical ambiguity of the relationship between self and voice that make *Cane* a modernist classic. Although she had already conducted complex stylistic experiments in *Their Eyes Were Watching God, Moses, Man of the Mountain,* and *Mules and Men* (which she did not conceive of primarily as an autobiographical text), the voice of *Dust Tracks on a Road* gives little sense of Hurston's awareness of the deconstructive potential inherent in the intersection of Afro- and Euro-American discourse. Similarly, neither *I Wonder as I Wander* or *The Big Sea* would alert a reader to the modernist complexities beneath the tactful surfaces of Hughes's Simple stories, the effectiveness of which hinges on recognition of voice as a social construction, or his more obviously modernist epic "Montage of a Dream Deferred." Even Melvin B. Tolson, whose *Libretto for the Republic of Liberia* and *Harlem Gallery* are perhaps the most aggressively modernist Afro-American texts, assumed a conventional voice for his public presentation of self in the autobiographical fragments published in his newspaper column "Caviar and Cabbage."

As this brief invocation of the genealogy of Afro-American modernism indicates, the relative lack of emphasis on *graphe* in black autobiographies of the first half of the twentieth century should not be taken as an indication that the autobiographers were unaware of the issues foregrounded by Olney. Rather, it indicates that Afro-American writers who explore modernist aesthetics in poetry, fiction, and drama approach autobiography from different premises. Hurston, Hughes, Du Bois, and others share the slave narrators' knowledge of the need to establish and assert the reality of the self, a reality most white modernists emotionally *assume*. This is not a matter of Afro-American autobiographers raising themselves to a level where they can begin to consider the serious philosophical issues raised by Nietzsche, Joyce, and Stein: issues such as the contingency of being, the self as a construct, etc. Rather, the Afro-American tradition begins with—and for the foreseeable future will continue to be informed by—an enforced awareness that the self cannot be taken for granted. This strikes near the central irony raised by the comparative study of Afro- and Euro-American modernism. Long "free"—in an ironically contingent sense—to explore the technical subtleties of the relationship between *autos* and *graphe*, white writers have used this freedom to discover what no slave could help but know: that the self is contingent, an ever-shifting social construct. The Euro-American autobiographers discussed at length in Olney's anthology, in some senses, are just now arriving at the point where Afro-American writing begins.

The third stage of the genealogy I am constructing is characterized by the reemergence of the problem of *graphe* as a foreground concern in Afro-American autobiography of the last thirty years. This reengagement was motivated in large part by two political/cultural developments associated respectively with the civil rights movement and the black power movement. The first development concerns the shifting perception of "literacy" within Euro-American culture, particularly those elements associated with the literary/intellectual movements most likely to endorse a progressive racial agenda: radical neo-abolitionists such as the writers associated with the Beat and Black Mountain movements or conservative neo-abolitionists affiliated with academic institutions. In each case, a larger portion of the black writer's potential white audience—aware of the fundamental insights, if not the implications, of modernist thought—had begun to incorporate these insights into its implicit definition of "literacy."

As a result, in order to claim the status of politically viable subject, black autobiographers now found it in their interest to demonstrate an awareness of the centrality of writing to the presentation of self. On a deep level, of course, the dynamic remained unchanged; black deconstructionists or feminists seeking a mainstream audience, like Frederick Douglass or Harriet Jacobs, still found it beneficial to demonstrate their literacy in terms recognizable to the white audience. The only change was that what had been radical, marginal perceptions within the white community during the earlier stages of the modernist (or, in the nineteenth century, transcendental) movement, now found acceptance in enough centers of institutional power to make a change in emphasis desirable for black autobiographers. Paralleling this essentially integrationist development was a second movement toward refocusing attention on the cultural/political significance of writing, this one emanating from the cultural wing of the black power movement. Recognizing both the historical tradition of masking and the potential for co-optation in the situation described above, some nationalist writers building on the work of Franz Fanon began to assert that acceptance of white conventions—linguistic or political—inevitably circumscribes black potential and enforces a "white" identity.

The remainder of this chapter will focus on the ways in which these related, but distinct, pressures are reflected in the autobiographical writings of Gwendolyn Brooks, Samuel Delany, and Amiri Baraka. Despite their diverse political and cultural experiences, each of these writers resists the growing solipsism associated with the treatment of *graphe* in Euro-American (post)modernist autobiography. Acknowledging the central importance of the relationship between self and a community (conceived of in a variety of specific forms), all retain an awareness of the concrete political implications of the way they use writing to construct an image of their lives. Sharing a general awareness of the relationship of self and community, Brooks's and Delany's specific processes reflect their idiosyncratic relationship to the changing definitions of mainstream literacy. Where Brooks's process begins with the highly conventional literacy reminiscent of the second stage of the autobiographical genealogy outlined above, Delany is from the beginning of his career explicitly aware of (post)modernist conceptions of literacy. As a result, each addresses issues of concern to particular segments of the contemporary audience. Brooks identifies the problems of literacy for a black audience now conceived as centrally important to any political change while Delany challenges the solipsistic tendencies of the predominantly white avant-garde. Combining elements of Brooks's explicitly political perspective on *graphe* as social construct with Delany's concern with the processes informing such constructions, *The Autobiography of LeRoi Jones/Amiri Baraka* intimates the sound of an Afro-Modernist autobiographical voice that can be seen as an extension of the philosophically resonant political agenda of the earliest Afro-American autobiographers.

Report from Part One

Brooks's *Report from Part One* (1972) presents an intricate image of a poet with a well-established mainstream reputation writing her way into "the kindergarten of new consciousness" (86). Defining this new consciousness in explicitly political—black nationalist—terms, Brooks confronts the implications of what she sees as her previous, uncritical acceptance of Euro-American literacy. While she expresses a profound admiration for the younger black poets (Don Lee/Haki Madhubuti; LeRoi Jones/Amiri Baraka) who had assumed new names as they developed "blacker" writing styles, Brooks emphasizes that her "newish voice will not be an imitation of the contemporary young black voice, which I so admire, but an extending adaptation of today's G.B. voice" (183). This insistence on the continuity of the self—which can be understood and expressed in various styles of writing, each implying a different sociopolitical position—becomes a leitmotif in Afro-Modernist autobiographies. Even as she repudiates its centrality, Brooks acknowledges the importance of Euro-American literacy in her own development *and* that of younger black writers. Describing her approach to teaching writing, she insists that students in her poetry classes understand and master the complexities of the modernist tradition. Among the topics she has her students write on are "T. S. Eliot: The Rigid Rebel," "James Joyce and Symbolism: The Technical Dilemma," and "William Butler Yeats as Legacy and Launch" (80). Like Frederick Douglass and Richard Wright, she knows that failure to attain mainstream literacy severely limits the ability of blacks to survive and to instigate political change.

In *Report from Part One,* however, Brooks no longer accepts, even provisionally, the *authority* of the white masters. Requiring her students to read the poetry of Langston Hughes and the criticism of Larry Neal alongside Eliot and Joyce, she approaches *graphe* in a manner consistent with her new consciousness. Rather than repudiating the polished writing style she had developed in the aggressively "mainstream" writing workshops of Inez Cunningham Stark, Brooks reconsiders its significance by fragmenting the larger structure within which it exists. Prior to *Report from Part One,* Brooks's most direct literary treatment of autobiographical experience had been the novel *Maud Martha* (1953). Strictly linear in its plot structure, *Maud Martha*—and in this it typifies Brooks's early poetry as well as her prose—evinces little interest in the modernist problematization of *graphe*. In contrast, *Report from Part One* takes similar materials (on both the thematic and sentence levels) and places them in a form that questions their larger implications.

Structurally, *Report from Part One* revoices the questioning of the relationship between self and literary conventions implicit in the slave narratives. The six headings in the table of contents reflect Brooks's testing of a range of articulations of her doubly-conscious self: "Prefaces," "Report from Part One," "African Fragment," "Photographs," "Interviews," and an "Appendix" subdivided into "Marginalia" and "Collage." The "Prefaces" revoice the slave narrative convention of what Stepto calls "authenticating documents"—statements by whites vouching for the literacy, and by implication selfhood, of the black writer—in Afro-American terms. In place of the preface by William Lloyd Garrison and the letter from Wendell Phillips that introduce Douglass's *Narrative,* Brooks includes statements from politically committed Afro-American intellectuals Haki Madhubuti and George Kent, vouching for the reality of her "black consciousness." Reporting on her childhood and education, the "Report from Part One" section grounds Brooks's autobiography in a relatively traditional narrative structure. She describes her early life in sentences that demonstrate her mastery of mainstream literacy. The section culminates, however, in a direct challenge to the sufficiency of such literacy. Subverting the traditional narrative of a traditional self in a way familiar to the Euro-American modernist tradition, Brooks ends the section with a powerful sequence of images emphasizing the need for a new understanding of the relationship between that self and the political circumstances of black people throughout the world.

The remaining sections of *Report from Part One,* like the interpolations, documents, and digressions of the slave narratives, test nontraditional modes of presenting the self. Each of these presentations implicitly challenges the authority of the traditional style of "Report from Part One." "African Fragment" reconsiders Brooks's relationship to a black community now conceived in pan-African political terms. Like the conclusion of "Report from Part One," the fragmented montage style of "African Fragment" is a familiar modernist technique for subverting the authority of the text. More radical in their implications are the "Photographs" and "Interview" sections, both of which present alternatives to the authority of the *written* word. Invoking the African roots of Afro-American oral expression, the sequence of three interviews—originally conducted between 1967 and 1971 when Brooks was becoming aware of the limitations of her earlier literary and political stance—is particularly effective in asserting the provisional nature of each presentation of self. Struggling to find the mode of expression capable of establishing meaningful links between Africa and Afro-America, Brooks recognizes that her process has only begun, that her style and self are not yet *black* in the way her pan-African political awareness desires. Near the end of "African Fragment," she describes her feelings in a style still very much grounded in mainstream literacy: "THE AFRICANS! They insist on calling themselves Africans and their little traveling brothers and sisters 'Afro-Americans' no matter *how* much we want them to recognize our kinship" (130). Reiterating the implications of the volume's title, the "Marginalia" and "Collage" sequences of the final section reiterate the unresolved reality of a self and style in progress. Brooks, then, suggests one way in which Afro-American writers can draw on (post)modernist approaches to *graphe*—unresolved "endings," conscious fragmentation, the emphasis on the margin—to support a specifically black sense of the relationship between the individual and political needs of a community struggling for self-definition.

The Motion of Light in Water

The approach to *graphe* in Samuel Delany's *The Motion of Light in Water* (1988) is grounded in a specifically *post*-modernist sense of the irresolvable nature of self, life, and writing. In contrast to Brooks's clear vision of a definitive (if not yet clearly defined) relationship between individual self and Afro-American community, Delany, as a gay black man, apprehends a much more radically problematic situation. Like Audre Lorde's *Zami: A New Spelling of My Name*, Delany's autobiography explores the implications of living on the margins of an already marginalized group. The contrast between Brooks's title, which implies movement toward a higher level of consciousness, and Delany's, which emphasizes the difficulty of fixing meaning even provisionally, highlights the underlying difference in the strategies each employs in articulating the position of the self in (and through) a hostile discourse.

For Delany, this reflects the difference between modernism—which retains the concept of a "totalized whole" (115)—however badly fragmented—and "the hugely arbitrary post-modern" (116), which embraces the "messy and marginal" to resist the "fascist" potential of mainstream (including traditional modernist) aesthetics (156). Far from endorsing a programmatic postmodernism (to employ a phrase that is philosophically, if not functionally, a contradiction in terms), Delany emphasizes that postmodernist aesthetics could easily devolve into "rules just as codified as those by which we judge 'realism'" (147). As a result of this awareness, which he shares with some of the more solipsistic Euro-American postmodernists, Delany challenges fixed meaning both structurally and in individual sentences. Because *any* written structure simplifies the elusive reality of the living self, Delany foregrounds his own process of constructing the text. Numbering each section of his text in outline form—a representative sequence is 42, 42.1, 42.11, 42.2, 42.21, 42.3, 42.31 (135–48)—Delany forces his readers to confront the mediating presence of writing. In addition, he draws attention to the marginalizing implications of his own formal choices, repeatedly insisting on the central importance of that which *cannot* be articulated. In his early experiments with fragmented forms, Delany apprehended the unavoidable ambiguity of presenting the self in writing: "writing itself would seem to be—whether devoted to reality or fantasy, material life or lust, whether at the beginning or the end of the notebook—marginal to a vast, empty, unarticulated center called reality that was displaced more and more by it, reducing the center to a margin in its turn, a more and more tenuous split between two interminable columns of writing, one finished, one still to be begun" (37).

Delany's awareness of the problematic relationship of writing, self, and life does not result in a solipsistic stance, in large part because he cannot escape the political and psychological tensions inherent in the experience of marginality in a racist, homophobic culture. Reflecting on his first public discussion of his homosexuality, Delany concludes that "for better or worse, you use the public language you've been given. It's only later, alone in the night, that maybe, if you're a writer, you ask yourself how closely that language reflects your experience. And that night I realized that language had done nothing but betray me" (247). Yet Delany is fully aware that some forms of language encourage unconscious acceptance of the betrayal, while others—no less conventional in their philosophical implications—can be used to challenge specific types of betrayal. From some books, "we absorb the unquestioned laws of genre, the readerly familiarity with rhetorical figures, narrational tropes, conventional attitudes and expectations. From the others, however, we manufacture the dream of possibility, of variation, of what might be done outside and beyond the genre that the others have already made a part of our readerly language" (103). This awareness motivates Delany's search for a language that does not require him to repress aspects of his experience. Throughout the final sections of *The Motion of Light in Water*, Delany reiterates, in appropriately shifting phrasing, the crucial questions raised by his complex sense of his specifically textual self-presentation:

> A black man . . . ?
> A gay man . . . ?
> A writer . . . ? (212)

From a postmodernist perspective, the ellipses, which are present in the original, are as important as the words. Understanding each identity as irresolute, problematic rather than definitive, Delany frees himself to accept each as real. Recovering from a mental breakdown grounded largely in the deforming pressure of conventional attitudes on the behavior of "marginal" individuals, he can rephrase the dilemma as an assertion:

> A black man.
> A gay man.
> A writer. (242)

The formulation continues to metamorphose, but Delany has begun to approximate a style that enables him to assert the reality of fundamental aspects—which is not to say defining elements—of his life and self. Like Olaudah Equiano, an African-born black man whose autobiography *The Interesting Narrative of the Life of Olaudah Equiano, Written by Himself* provides the epigraph for *The Motion of Light in Water*, Delany reclaims his story in a context that would deny his existence. His struggle to articulate the experiences of the margins he shares with other blacks, other gays, and—crucially from a postmodernist perspective—other writers, provides insights vital to realizing the project introduced in more directly political terms in *Report from Part One*. Interacting with a Euro-American discourse in which "literacy" requires questioning the concept of a textual self distinct from the words of the text, Delany has become, to savor the ironic ambiguity of applying Stepto's term to a multicultural postmodernist context, self-authenticating.

The Autobiography of LeRoi Jones/Amiri Baraka

Combining Delany's highly developed awareness of the indeterminacy inherent in writing with Brooks's commitment to the transformation of Afro-American consciousness, *The Autobiography of LeRoi Jones/Amiri Baraka* (1984) marks a major step toward an Afro-Modernist autobiographical form. Baraka's process combines Delany's grounding in Euro-American (post)modernist discourse with Brooks's midlife conversion to a nationalist political perspective. As even a cursory examination of Baraka's poetry reveals, his writing voice underwent a major transformation after he left downtown New York City where he associated closely with avant-garde white writers such as Allen Ginsberg and Robert Creely for the aggressively black, political worlds of Harlem and Newark. What is most striking about Baraka's text as Afro-Modernist autobiography, however, is the author's re-presentation of his life and writing—including that associated with his nationalist "conversion"—as a process of accepting an elusive and frequently contradictory self. As Baraka returns to the postmodernist insights concerning the writing process—insights he had previously, at least for rhetorical purposes, rejected as impositions of a hostile white discourse—he directly and powerfully repudiates Euro-American solipsism, insisting that his process must be understood as a movement toward real understanding of, and involvement in, the political destiny of the Afro-American community.

Baraka's explicit interpretive position in the *Autobiography* reflects the Marxist thought informing his retrospective critique of the narrowness of his cultural nationalist stance. Where his endorsement of nationalism was phrased in dogmatic ideological terms, Baraka has come (back) to Delany's understanding of all positions as provisional: "All stages in illumination and from their momentary brightness now a glow of whatever relevance, as long as it remains relevant" (312). Looking back at the nationalist period, the Baraka of *The Autobiography of LeRoi Jones/Amiri Baraka*—and the recognition of both "identities" in the title is very much to the point—emphasizes the underlying connection between the earlier stages of his process: "There was a deep anti-white feeling I carried with me that had grown deeper and deeper since I left the Village. I felt it was a maturing, but in some aspects it was that I was going off the deep end. To the extent that what I felt opposed white supremacy and imperialism, it was certainly correct. But to the extent that I merely turned white supremacy upside down and created an exclusive black supremacist doctrine, that was bullshit. Bullshit that could only isolate me from reality" (245). Interpreting "reality" in materialist Marxist terms, Baraka clarifies the implications of this analysis when he writes that "much of the cultural nationalism young people fervently believe is critically important to the struggle is just a form of black bohemianism" (301). Destabilizing the authority of his past political pronouncements and acknowledging the ongoing relevance of that destabilization, Baraka attempts to bring his postmodernist insights concerning the provisionality of discourse into alignment with his increasingly flexible commitment to changing the political circumstances of blacks and poor people of all colors.

One major motif of *The Autobiography of LeRoi Jones/Amiri Baraka* concerns the changes in Baraka's perception of various forms of expression, written and oral. Growing up in Newark, and later when he began to concern himself directly with the needs of the community, Baraka realized the destructive impact of the failure to attain literacy: "Many of the kids I ran with did not have the same bulk of bodies and history and words and *articulation* to deal with that kept coming up every morning" (13). At the same time, Baraka soon learned that conventional mainstream literacy did not provide adequate forms for articulating his experience as an intellectual black man coming to consciousness during the 1950s. His early encounter with Euro-American modernism suggested alternative modes of perception and expression; as William Harris emphasizes in *The Poetry and Poetics of Amiri Baraka: The Jazz Aesthetic,* Baraka's involvement with the Village literary world was itself a rebellion against politically and aesthetically corrupt structures. Describing his initial encounters with Dylan Thomas's poetry and James Joyce's fiction, Baraka writes: "Serious, uncommon, weird stuff! At that moment my life was changed" (104). Significantly, this change was predicated in large part on Baraka's experience of the solipsism that was a central modernist concern. While still at Howard, he turned to Gertrude Stein for insight into "the isolation, the aloneness" that "was almost sweet" (88).

Following his initial exhilaration, however, Baraka gradually began to experience the white modernist voice—the constituting voice of *Preface to a Twenty-Volume Suicide Note*—as part of his isolation:

> My reading was, in the main, white people. Europeans, Anglo-Americans. So that my ascent toward some ideal intellectual pose was at the same time a trip toward a white-out I couldn't even understand. I was learning and, at the same time, unlearning. The fasteners to black life unloosed. I was taking words, cramming my face with them. White people's words. Profound, beautiful, some even correct and important. But there is a tangle of non-self in that for all that. A non-self creation where you become other than you as you. Where the harnesses of black life are loosened and you free-float, you think, in the great sunkissed intellectual waygonesphere. Imbibing, gobbling, stuffing yourself with reflections of the *other.* (120)

Words—specifically those words articulating the solipsistic confusion of *graphe* with reality—alienate "LeRoi Jones" from his grounding in communal experience, in the realities of black life. The situation, in which "words could disappear" (195), recalls his earlier dissatisfaction with the politically charged substitution of rhetoric for action that he perceived as a shaping influence on his childhood consciousness. Baraka describes "the yellow logic of my mother's prose like white twinkling distance we'd cover as easily as an amendment is written in the Constitution. 'Guaranteeing' you something you could only be guaranteed with power" (44).

The subsequent stages of Baraka's process focus on using what is useful in the postmodernist tradition without marginalizing political concerns. Recognizing Afro-American music, most specifically the blues, as "the real language of the place" (173), Baraka envisions a writing voice attuned to the "poetry we copped from the people and gave them right back, open and direct and moving" (237). Anticipated by the kinetic "voice that finally begins to emerge at the end of [*The System of Dante's Hell*]" (227), this voice should ideally articulate the experience of the community in terms recognizable to the community without the condescension implicit in the willful simplification of consciousness Baraka associated with cultural nationalism. Explicitly recognizing the solipsism of his first attempts to act on his perceptions, Baraka describes the "education I had given myself, reading and feeling myself through great parts of the Western world. I had dashed out at full speed hurling denunciations at the place of my intellectual birth, ashamed of its European cast. Arriving full up in the place of blackness, to save myself and to save the black world. Ah, the world-filling egos of youth" (227).

The Autobiography of LeRoi Jones/Amiri Baraka, then, represents a later stage of Baraka's Afro-Modernist project. Identifying itself as one stage of a process leading to further changes, the book infuses the jazz- and blues-based vocabulary of the Newark streets with a wider, for the moment Marxist, analytical perspective. At times, the new conception of *graphe* yields impressive results. Baraka's analysis of the internal structure of the Afro-American community as a continuum of "black, brown, and yellow" perspectives provides a suggestive approach to the intersection of racial and class oppression. Similarly, he returns to the (post)modernist mode of allusion—which he employed with great effectiveness in his early poetry—to invoke the shared understanding of the Afro-American community. A brief, but luminous, commentary on Smokey Robinson's "The Tracks of My Tears," for example, concludes with the line "Fuckin Smokey, the poet of the age" (234). Asserting the black community's refusal to differentiate high and popular art forms, the allusion invokes the black aesthetic tradition in which "personal" and "political" expression are so densely intertwined as to be indistinguishable. Baraka offers the allusion without explanation or elaboration. Recasting a fa-

miliar Euro-American modernist technique in black terms, Baraka
intimates the sound of a written voice grounded in the oral call-and-
response dynamic. While this intersection of written and oral forms
has long been a central issue for black poets and novelists, it is only
beginning to play a central role in the autobiographical tradition.

Baraka's "new" voice—which he knows will be "gone gone gone
again" by the time "this is a book" (319)—can be understood, like
Brooks's voice in *Report from Part One*, as an attempt to recombine his
older voices. In *The Autobiography of LeRoi Jones/Amiri Baraka*, however,
Baraka has attained a wider perspective on the origins and implications of the earlier voices, both their strengths and their unconscious
entanglement. If we accept this as analogous to the metaconscious-
ness that forms such a central part of the (post)modernist tradition,
then we can use Baraka's autobiography as a point of departure for
rereading the entire Afro-American autobiographical tradition in
Afro-Modernist terms. Baraka, like Delany, most certainly draws on
radical Euro-American techniques to help free the self in the text
from the simplifications of racist discourse. Like Brooks, and despite
the momentary (and from a postmodernist perspective, inevitable)
contradictions of a particular political stance, he acknowledges the
need for a firm (which is to say pre-ideological, nonromantic)
grounding in the actual conditions of life in the Afro-American community. What is least clear in *The Autobiography of LeRoi Jones/Amiri
Baraka* is the centrality of Baraka's Marxist perspective to the Afro-
Modernist autobiographical voice. Ideally, this voice should be as
firmly grounded in, *and* as much in advance of, the political and expressive realities of its time as were those of Anna Julia Cooper and
W. E. B. Du Bois. At points, however, Baraka loses his grounding and
relies on theoretical ideological terms that recall the solipsistic abstraction of his Village period. Yet the book also includes numerous
passages—the black, brown, yellow analysis stands out—that combine the concrete and the abstract, the philosophical and the political, the self and the community. As much as any text, *The Autobiography of LeRoi Jones/Amiri Baraka* calls for conscious development of the
Afro-Modernist potential of an autobiographical tradition that has
long been aware, to pause with Baraka's description of his own self
and life and words in process, that "life is not over. The world is still
here. There are still things that can be done. And I swear that I do
understand the world better. We will find out just how well. In words
and deeds yet to be written and realitied out" (326).

PART **2**

STUDIES IN
AFRICAN-AMERICAN POETICS

▲ ▲ ▲ ▲

5

Black Dialectics:
Kennedy, Bullins, Knight, Dumas, Lorde

▲ ▲ ▲ ▲

During the late 1970s and early 1980s, the Black Arts Movement gradually receded from a central position in academic constructions of African-American literary history. In part the result of the Reagan/Bush era hostility to any conception of "revolution" or even "liberation," the shift also reflected serious critiques from within African-American intellectual and activist communities. Reacting against what they saw as the Black Arts Movement's tendency to substitute political rhetoric for serious artistic engagement, a group of black academics with a sophisticated knowledge of critical theory asserted an alternative vision of cultural freedom in anthologies such as Robert Stepto and Michael Harper's *Chant of Saints,* Stepto and Dexter Fisher's *Afro-American Literature: The Reconstruction of Instruction,* and Henry Louis Gates's *Black Literature and Literary Theory,* which along with Barbara Smith's *Toward a Black Feminist Criticism* signaled a new era in Afro-American letters. Hailed by John Hope Franklin as the best "yardstick by which to measure the evolution of Afro-American literature and culture" since Alain Locke's *The New Negro, Chant of Saints* certainly served as a valuable caution against uncritical acceptance of cultural nationalism and opened significant new understandings of African-American culture. More recently, black feminist scholars including June Jordan, bell hooks, Patricia Hill Collins, and Patricia Williams have emphasized the ways in which the Black Arts Movement marginalized women, gays and lesbians, and older African-Americans (especially those who continued to refer to themselves as "Negroes" or attend Christian churches).

Reflecting on the "nationalism" of black women (such as those involved in the club movement), a nonideological vision articulated in the predominantly black settings of churches and homes, hooks observes: "The nationalism of the sixties and seventies was very different from the racial solidarity born of shared circumstances and not from theories of black power. Not that an articulation of black power was not important: it was. Only it did not deliver the goods; it was too informed by corrosive power relations, too mythic, to take the place of that concrete relational love that bonded black folks together in communities of hope and struggle" (36). In addition to celebrating the *real* bonds that continue to hold black communities together despite the extreme pressures generated by what Deborah King calls the "multiple jeopardy" of race, class, and gender oppression, hooks criticizes the political evasions of much contemporary academic writing about African-American (and other "marginal") cultures: "Critical pedagogy (expressed in writing, teaching, and habits of being) is fundamentally linked to a concern with creating strategies that will enable colonized folks to decolonize their minds and actions, thereby promoting the insurrection of subjugated knowledge. Trendy cultural critique that is in no way linked to a concern with critical pedagogy or liberation struggles hinders this process" (8).

Unfortunately, relatively few contemporary critics, even those committed to an activist agenda, draw actively, or even show an awareness of, the Black Arts Movement as a source of useful insights. Yet, as recent essays by David Lionel Smith and Greg Tate suggest, the time may finally be at hand when we can embrace the writers of the movement without denying their limitations. Even as he critiques "the jiver parts of their program (like the sexist, anti-Semitic, black supremacist, pseudo-African mumbo-jumbo paramilitary adventurist parts)," Tate observes that "to their credit they took black liberation seriously enough to be theoretically ambitious about it" (199). Crediting Amiri Baraka with focusing attention on jazz as cultural theory (a call I respond to more fully in the final two chapters of this book), Tate honors the Black Arts Movement for producing a "postliberated black aesthetic, responsible for the degree to which contemporary black artists and intellectuals feel themselves heirs to a culture every bit as def as classical Western civilization" (200). Part of the intellectual grounding of many contemporary intellectuals (including hooks, West, and Stepto), Michel Foucault's conception of the "insurrection of subjugated knowledge" suggests one way of reestablishing communication with the most powerful Black Arts Movement theoreticians, particularly Ed Bullins, George Kent, and Larry Neal. Describing what he calls "genealogical researches," Foucault advocates an approach to knowledge that frees repressed experiences—which in this context can be understood to refer either to the groups marginalized by the Black Arts Movement or to the movement as it has been marginalized in theoretical discourse—for use by groups or individuals resisting oppressive institutions. Foucault calls for the "painstaking rediscovery of struggles together with the rude memories of their conflicts. . . . Genealogies that are the combined product of an erudite knowledge and a popular knowledge." Such genealogies, Foucault insists, "could not even have been attempted except on one condition, namely that the tyranny of globalizing discourses with their hierarchy and all their privileges of a theoretical *avant-garde* was eliminated" (83).

This passage seems particularly important given the intensity of arguments over the use of theory in Afro-American studies during the late eighties. Although the differences between their individual positions should not be underestimated, Norman Harris, Barbara Christian, and Joyce A. Joyce all criticize the post-*Chant* theorists for imposing an inappropriate (continental, academic, Eurocentric) vocabulary on Afro-American materials, for ignoring the political circumstances conditioning Afro-American literature, and (although Christian would certainly not endorse this extension) failing to accept blackness as an "essence." Related to these substantial issues are a cluster of criticisms focusing on the theorists' styles, which are widely perceived as expressions of indifference to, or contempt for, the largely nonacademic Afro-American community. Although it frequently remains implicit—at least in print—this criticism is often accompanied by a corollary belief that the theorists, the most influential of whom are based at Ivy League institutions, have created a kind of literary Tuskeegee Machine, supported by the power of mainstream literary institutions such as *Critical Inquiry* and the *New York Times Book Review.*

An attentive reading of the theoretical work, however, suggests that these attacks are directed against "straw men" whose positions are only distantly related to those actually professed by Gates or Stepto, to cite two of the most prominent cases. For example, the oft-reiterated idea that Stepto and Gates seek to uproot literature from its social/cultural/political grounding clashes sharply with their actual practice. Both Gates and Stepto emphasize that the rhetorical and linguistic structures that characterize "black texts" derive from the specific historical circumstances of Afro-Americans in a world shaped by racist discourses. Far from denying the relationship between literary and political discourses, both Stepto and Gates understand linguistic structures as part of a larger context grounded in actively oppressive political institutions. When Gates identifies "signifyin(g)" as the crucial Afro-American rhetorical strategy, he does so with an awareness that this masked, but still subversive, form of parody reflects the practical, highly political experience of slaves forced to hide their "real" thoughts from masters who could well punish open expression with death. Gates's emphasis on the continued viability of "signifyin(g)," then, can justifiably be interpreted as a highly political, though appropriately masked, comment on the continuing presence of the slave-master power structure in contemporary American society. Similarly, Stepto's dialectic of ascent and immersion is inextricably intertwined with the political contexts connecting the experiences of fugitive slaves and contemporary black professionals, of students from the projects and their ancestors on the Mississippi delta.

An equally important cause of the breakdown in the dialogue between the sixties and the eighties (if we accept the generational construction of Houston Baker's "Generational Shifts and the Recent Criticism of Afro-American Literature") has been the failure of the theorists to draw explicit connections between their own formulations and those of Bullins, Kent, and, to a lesser extent, Neal. Stepto's "ascent and immersion" paradigm, for example, takes on new significance when juxtaposed with Bullins's definition of "Black dialectics." An awareness of "the *dialectic of change* and the *dialectic of experience*" (discussed more fully below) as interrelated elements present throughout the Afro-American intellectual tradition highlights both the political undertones of Stepto's paradigm and the complexity of its manifestation in particular texts or experiences.

Whatever the mutual distrust and divergences separating the various theoretical and political camps, however, it seems clear that any effective progressive agenda for the nineties, whether cultural or political, will require increased cooperation between races, genders, and classes. It seems vital that those sharing a serious interest in African-American culture join in constructing a usable tradition, one capable of providing theoretical insights adequate to the needs of particular struggles. For, as hooks, Cornel West, and Manning Marable emphasize, any movement that proceeds without adequate analytical tools opens itself to easy attack and defeat. In *Prophetic Fragments,* West suggests that a sophisticated understanding of postmodern theory reinforces values compatible with those of the traditional African-American communities described by hooks: "Postmodernism was the unique American version of avant-gardist revolt against Establishment high art (i.e., modernism) in the name of subversion, transgression, rupture, discontinuity, and, above all, freedom from political, social, and cultural hierarchical traditions." Emphasizing culture as a fundamental aspect of any resistance movement, West continues:

"this American postmodern revolt highlighted the redemptive function of art, called for the integration of art into everyday life, and attacked the institutional forms that preserved the autonomy of art" and concludes that the "enmeshing of art into everyday life called into question this hegemony and revived the emancipatory potential of art" (168). Or, as hooks comments in a self-interview conducted in January 1990, "Cultural production can and does play a healing role in people's lives. It can be a catalyst for them to begin the project of self-recovery" (225).

In the introduction to his Foucauldian project *The American Evasion of Philosophy: A Genealogy of Pragmatism,* West emphasizes that the point of a sophisticated theoretical critique grounded in an awareness of and dialogue with the broader community is its contribution to the "intellectual calling to administer to a confused populace caught in the whirlwinds of societal crisis, the cross fires of ideological polemics, and the storms of class, racial, and gender conflicts" (5). This suggests the continuing relevance of the most politically committed and intellectually adventurous writing of the Black Arts Movement to our contemporary struggles; the "confused populace," "whirlwinds of societal crisis," "cross fires of ideological polemics," and "storms of class, racial, and gender conflicts" were very much present in the sixties and seventies. Although its practical impact was limited by the sexism, homophobia, and romanticism characteristic of the sixties (not just of black culture), Ron Karenga's call for a revolutionary art retains much of its power today:

> Tradition teaches us, Leopold Senghor tells us, that all African art has at least three characteristics: that is, it is functional, collective and committing or committed. Since this is traditionally valid, it stands to reason that we should attempt to use it as the foundation for a rational construction to meet our present day needs. . . . [Art] must be functional, that is *useful,* as we cannot accept the false doctrine of "art for art's sake." All art reflects the value system from which it comes. So what, then, is the use of art— our art, Black art? Black art must expose the enemy, praise the people, and support the revolution. (32)

Although Karenga's critique would no doubt benefit from a postmodern understanding of the limitations of concepts such as "validity" or "rationality," his underlying impulse does not differ substantially from that of hooks, West, Marable, or even, ironically, from that of Ralph Ellison, a favorite target of cultural nationalist polemics, who once wrote: "Art by its nature *is* social. . . . Once introduced into society, the work of art begins to pulsate with those meanings, emotions, ideas brought to it by its audience and over which the artist has but limited control. . . . If it is to be more than dream, the work of art must simultaneously evoke images of reality and give them formal organization. And it must, since the individual's emotions are formed in society, shape them into socially meaningful patterns" (*Shadow* 55). Similarly, Bullins's vision of black culture as a source not only of inspiration and insight but also as part of a practical economic agenda remains vital. As Bullins told Marvin X, the Black Arts Movement sought to create institutions that would provide "a medium for communication to raise the consciousness throughout the nation for Black artistic, political, and cultural consciousness. It would keep a hell of a lot of people working. . . . And it would be an institution for the Black people in America who are a nation within a nation" (*New Plays* x).

Whatever their differences, Karenga, Bullins, West, Marable, and hooks all share an interest in the uses of intellectual and cultural insights in effecting political change. Although each would define key terms—"enemy," "praise," "revolution"—differently, none would reject their importance. This is precisely the situation that calls most clearly for a renewed dialogue concerning the facts and implications of recent African-American history. In the remainder of this chapter, I will examine the ways in which detailed examination of five writers active during the Black Arts Movement—Adrienne Kennedy, Ed Bullins, Etheridge Knight, Henry Dumas, and Audre Lorde—provides insight into the actual complexity and diversity of an era in African-American history that deserves—and in studies such as William Van Deburg's *New Day in Babylon: The Black Power Movement in American Culture* is beginning to receive—renewed attention as a source of insight into what Marable calls "the crisis of color and democracy." Although Adrienne Kennedy is not usually categorized as a Black Arts Movement writer, her plays, especially *Funnyhouse of a Negro,* help clarify the forces that propelled many black intellectuals out of the interracial cultural mainstream of the early sixties and into various forms of nationalist commitment. Complementing and illustrating the theory of "Black dialectics," Bullins's plays provide useful insights for those seeking to envision new responses to American life in all its (at least seemingly) anti-ideological complexity and confusion. Resisting limiting categorizations even as he sounds a populist call celebrating the equal importance of "the Poem, the Poet, and the People," Etheridge Knight suggests ways of reconceptualizing the apparent conflict between the poet/singers celebrated in *Chant of Saints* and the "aesthetic warriors" of the Black Arts Movement. Anticipating the "gospel impulse" discussed in chapter 9, Henry Dumas intimates a poetic voice that draws on a broad range of multicultural traditions to support a nationalist agenda grounded in and primarily concerned with changing the specific circumstances of African-American life. Finally, Audre Lorde, whose later work emphasizes the interrelationship between cultural politics on the domestic and global levels, critiques the patriarchal and homophobic attitudes that played a large role in the demise of the movement that nurtured her own early work.

Adrienne Kennedy and the Impasse of the Avant-Garde

In his 1969 essay "Nationalism Vs PimpArt," Amiri Baraka articulates a distrust of postmodernist Euro-American theater that became a leitmotif of Black Arts Movement theatrical manifestos: "The largest creation, the most exacting manifestation of Euro-American (white) creative motif is, right now, Viet-Nam. An Absurd White-Comedy. The Ethos (characteristic life-style) of Euro-America is death, about death, and/or dead, or the worship of. Beckett is the prize winner cause he tell about it so cool" (126). Although several of Beckett's plays can be accurately read as antitotalitarian statements, there is nonetheless an underlying truth in Baraka's hyperbolic attack. Typifying the avant-garde literary scene that embraced Baraka's "deathly" volumes *Preface to a Twenty-Volume Suicide Note* and *The Dead Lecturer,* Beckett's work, like that of many (post)modern Euro-American writers, returns almost obsessively to themes of death and psychological paralysis. Certainly, for most writers associated with the Black Arts Movement, it seemed clear that the avant-garde literary culture of the late fifties and early sixties showed little serious interest in the values of Afro-American expression presented in George Kent's essay "Langston Hughes and Afro-American Folk and Cultural Tradition": "the values of *is-ness, somebodyness,* and *as-if-ness.* To focus one's vision of is-ness exclusively on alienation and death would seem, at least superficially, to frustrate the impulses toward somebodyness—the desire to 'get up off your knees and be somebody'—and as-if-ness—the celebration of the pains of life as if they could easily be transformed into joys" (Kent 53-55).

Adrienne Kennedy's play *Funnyhouse of a Negro,* first produced at Edward Albee's Circle-in-the-Square workshop in 1962, shares numerous (post)modernist concerns. The consciousness of Sarah, Kennedy's protagonist, returns obsessively to the death of her father, a death that may have occurred only in her imagination. In turn, her father is repeatedly accused of destroying her mother. Perhaps inevitably, Sarah can find no exit from this necrophilic funhouse save through her own death, presumably by suicide. This focus on death, however, does not mean that Kennedy's work rejects Kent's criteria.

Rather, *Funnyhouse of a Negro* indicts the avant-garde consciousness it reflects. Focusing on the "is-ness" of a woman whose life has been shaped largely by her immersion in Euro-American culture, Kennedy implies that the cost of such immersion has been the destruction of both her sense of "somebody-ness" and her connection with the Afro-American tradition that makes "as-if-ness" possible. The distortion of historical relationships—expressed through the relationship between the protagonist and her parents—lies at the root of Sarah's losses, which involve both her racial and her sexual heritage. She is as isolated from other women, particularly her mother, as she is from other blacks. Devoid of contact with any reality outside her own consciousness, Sarah cannot tap the psychological and communal resources needed for surviving, much less transcending, the nightmarish funhouse world in which it may ultimately prove impossible to distinguish between a Beckett play and the latest newsreels from Vietnam, El Salvador, South Africa, Rwanda, or Bosnia. Far from repudiating Kent's aesthetic, *Funnyhouse of a Negro* reinforces its basic implications. Only by maintaining or recovering the sense of connection embodied in the folk tradition will it be possible to recover the psychological and communal resources needed to resist the nightmare.

From this perspective, Kennedy's play can be seen as a direct, if peculiarly postmodern, manifestation of one of the basic elements of the Afro-American folk tradition: call and response. Grounded in the traditions of the folk preacher and the blues singer, the call and response dynamic in many ways stands directly opposed to the (post)-modernist aesthetic, which focuses on alienated, isolated individuals such as the protagonist of *Funnyhouse of a Negro*. Writers such as Beckett, Thomas Pynchon, and John Ashbery, while they differ in many ways, have developed techniques designed to explore the linguistic, psychological, or philosophical richness of the isolated consciousness. Frequently, they view the "audience" as a problematic abstraction that may amount to nothing more than a fleeting idea in the isolated psyche. In contrast, the call-and-response form derives its power primarily from the artist's ability to establish contact with a real audience that actively contributes to the creation and impact of the artistic work. Without an "amen" from the congregation, the sermon—or the song, novel, poem, or play—is reduced to so much sound and fury. If the audience affirms the validity of the call, however, the leader can then draw on the combined energies of self and community. In relation to *Funnyhouse of a Negro*, call and response offers a way of overcoming individual isolation since the communal response to a cry of alienation in effect denies that the alienation is entirely an individual experience. Shared pain becomes a source of strength. As Kent wrote in his essay on Langston Hughes, reaching out to the black community allows the folk-based artist to share the hope embodied in the principle of as-if-ness: "Choosing the life of the black folk was also a way of choosing himself, a way of possessing himself through the rhythms and traditions of black people. His choice enabled him to allow for prevailing ideologies without being smothered by them" (56).

The dramatic effectiveness of *Funnyhouse of a Negro* derives primarily from the ability of its picture of Sarah's fragmented is-ness to elicit an "amen" from the theatrical congregation. The success of Kennedy's call can be explained in relation to Kent's discussion of the principle of is-ness. Kent argues that the successful presentation of is-ness involves three basic elements: the need to present the conflicting and contradictory poles of a single situation, character, or theme; the need to give each pole of the contradiction truthful representation; and the need to present the contradictions in a way that leads the viewer to accept both, saying, "It be's that way." The strange postmodern quality of Kennedy's call—not all that different from the surrealistic quality of Robert Johnson's "Crossroads" or Howlin' Wolf's "Killing Floor"—should not obscure the fact that it does almost exactly what Kent suggests. *Funnyhouse of a Negro* presents a highly convincing representation of the contradictions faced by the Afro-American community that, since the midsixties, has experienced the psychological impact of Euro-American attitudes with increasing intensity.

It is important not to simplify the folk attitude by locking it into archaic or nostalgic forms. As Kent noted, Hughes, the folk artist par excellence, "always seems current with the newer forces that arise with each decade" (74). Not surprisingly, the new forces unleashed in the era of "integration" called forth what at first seem radically new forms. Anticipating the ritual drama of the Black Arts Movement—plays such as Baraka's *Madheart* and *Great Goodness of Life* and Bullins's *The Electronic Nigger*—*Funnyhouse of a Negro* can be seen as a pioneering work in the folk tradition Kent delineates. To restate the point in terms of Bullins's theory of black dialectics—which I find almost entirely compatible with Kent's folk theory—Kennedy advances the "dialectic of experience" that, according to Bullins, "heighten[s] the dreadful white reality of being a modern Black captive and victim" and "is traceable to oral literatures of Africa" (*New Lafayette* 4). As anyone who has interacted extensively with black students at majority white universities such as my own is all too aware, it does continue to be the way Kennedy describes it.

If what I am suggesting concerning the implicit call-and-response dynamic in *Funnyhouse of a Negro* is true, it makes sense to examine actual responses to the play. A brief survey of critical response—and I am aware of the problems involved with viewing written response as indicative of anything other than a narrow slice of opinion—suggests that, while Kennedy's technique generated some debate, there was almost no disagreement over her central thematic statements. In part because Kennedy began her career with productions in the off- and off-off-Broadway theaters (such as the Circle in the Square and La Mama) that helped bring (post)modernist theater to an American audience, most critics have understood her techniques primarily in relation to those of white predecessors. Margaret Wilkerson, for example, calls her style "surrealistic" (163); Kimberly Benston calls it "expressionistic" (235-37); Genevieve Fabre, "symbolist" (122); Lorraine Brown sees Beckett and Genet as her crucial dramatic ancestors; I would add Ionesco. In light of this largely justifiable tendency in stylistic criticism, it hardly seems surprising to find critics aware of the African and Afro-American dimensions of Kennedy's style somewhat on the defensive. For example, Paul Carter Harrison who—along with James Hatch in his marvelously titled and important essay "Speak to Me in Those Old Words, You Know, Those La-La Words, Those Tung-Tung Sounds"—has been instrumental in drawing attention to the African analogues of Kennedy's techniques, began his discussion of "A Rat's Mass" with the statement that Kennedy's "dramaturgical style, while showing much excellence, tends to obscure the content of her work. Miss Kennedy's penchant for abstract forms tends to make her profoundly inquisitive introspections seem locked up in the ambiguity of too many voices talking at once, a fragmented soul" (*Drama* 216).

Although Harrison's view of Kennedy as part of the "Nommo" and "Kuntu" traditions of Afro-American theater is convincing, I would disagree with some of the implications of his comment on her style. Far from obscuring the content of her work, Kennedy's (post)modernist style can be seen as the precise instrument for communicating the reality of "too many voices talking at once, a fragmented soul." Again, a brief survey of commentary on *Funnyhouse of a Negro* reveals no evidence that Kennedy failed to communicate her themes clearly enough to elicit the necessary audience response. Wilkerson finds the center of *Funnyhouse of a Negro* in the portrayal of "internalized social and cultural forces" (164); Brown in the "the struggle of all women in a world which not only mocks and rejects Blackness but femaleness as well" (86); Rosemary Curb in "the nagging voices of [a] warring consciousness" and the themes of "imprisonment, powerlessness, and death" (188); Robert Tener in the "quest for a stable and unified self-image" (1); Harrison himself in the "acquaintance with oppression that is germane to the existence of black people everywhere" (217). Approaching the play from a variety of backgrounds and critical premises, all agree that *Funnyhouse of a Negro* reveals the fragmentation of the protagonist's consciousness, focuses on the racial and cultural sources of the fragmentation, and implies the need for a more unified sense of self.

Further, the critical response suggests that Kennedy's success derives from her ability to express "the conflicting and contradictory qualities" (Kent 53) of Sarah's situation. Kennedy's statement on her aesthetic concern with conflict echoes Kent's terminology almost exactly: "I struggled for a long time to write plays—as typified by *Funny House*—in which the person is in conflict with their inner forces, with the conflicting sides to their personality, which I found to be my own particular, greatest conflict. . . . It was an attempt to articulate that— your inner conflicts" (47). From *Funnyhouse of a Negro* through *The Owl Answers* to the brilliant, if largely unknown, 1976 play *A Movie Star Has to Star in Black and White,* Kennedy has continued to rework the theme of the tension between Afro- and Euro-American heritage and culture. Not surprisingly, her portrait of her characters' sometimes contradictory is-ness employs a mixture of Afro- and Euro-American forms. The resulting strangeness provides a bridge between the postmodernist and folk aesthetics. As Benston notes, "The further the plays move into the symbolic realm, the nearer they come to the world of the audience" (240). The same could be said of many of the finest works of the folk tradition from the Brer Rabbit tales to the hallucinogenic funk fables of George Clinton.

Combining realistic and expressionistic techniques, Kennedy expresses the contradictions of Sarah's is-ness in a way that brings the significance of her fragmentation home to the audience. Beginning with the opening stage directions, Kennedy stresses the obsession with death that Baraka sees as characteristic of the Euro-American avant-garde. "Great black ravens," traditional symbols of death, fly about the stage; the faces of the characters "possess a hard expressionless quality and a stillness as in the fact of death"; there is a "monumental bed resembling an ebony tomb"; even the curtain is "ghastly white, a material that brings to mind the interior of a cheap casket" (253). In addition, Kennedy's staging emphasizes the unresolved contradictions in Sarah's consciousness. The use of black/white imagery in the stage directions points to the unresolved contradictions that distort each color: "the rest of the stage is in strong *unnatural* blackness. . . . The quality of the white light is *unreal* and ugly" (253; emphasis added). The contrast between wild kinky black hair and either straightened hair or bald heads—introduced when a ghostly figure with wild straight black hair appears before the audience carrying a bald head even before the raising of the curtain—reinforces the idea of racial dichotomy. Kennedy notes that the central image of the play derived from her memory of an amusement park funhouse in Cleveland that had two giant white figures with bobbing heads outside the door. This powerful emblem of the dilemma of the Afro-American individual attempting to enter the mainstream of Euro-American society recurs in the form of the Landlady and Raymond, who at the end of the play stand outside Sarah's consciousness and comment dispassionately on her suicide. From start to end, *Funnyhouse of a Negro* focuses on an "is-ness" in which contradiction cannot be evaded or denied.

Within this structural arc, increasingly intricate internal divisions keep Sarah from realizing her somebody-ness. With the possible exceptions of Sarah and her ambiguous "mother"—who may be nothing more than another aspect of Sarah's fragmented memory—the characters are carefully paired with one another. One pair—the Landlady and Raymond/Funnyman—seems to represent something outside the protagonist's purely subjective consciousness, suggesting the split between internal and external "reality." The other two pairs—Queen Victoria and the Duchess of Hapsburg and Patrice Lumumba and Jesus Christ—represent splits within Sarah's mind. The following dialogue between Victoria and the Duchess, which typifies the verbal echoing and repetition permeating the play, emphasizes their linked identity:

> Victoria: He is my father. I am tied to the black Negro. He came when I was a child in the south, before I was born he haunted my conception, diseased my birth.
> Duchess: Killed my mother.
> Victoria: My mother was the light. She was the lightest one. She looked like a white woman.
> Duchess: We are tied to him. (254)

Similarly, Jesus' speeches make it clear that when "he" rails against Lumumba, he is in fact striking out at an aspect of himself: "I am going to Africa and kill this black man named Patrice Lumumba. Why? Because all my life I believed my Holy Father to be God, but now I know that my father is a black man" (269). Both pairs of characters represent aspects of Sarah's fragmented sense of self; she is male and female, black and white. The extent of her fragmentation is emphasized by the fact that each character suffers from a variety of internal splits; most wear masks and Lumumba actually has a split running down the middle of his face.

The inability of individuals or pairs to contact or communicate with one another reflects the protagonist's inability to accept the contradictions of her experience. Unable to embrace either her blackness or her femaleness, both of which might provide her with some access to the resources that enable those grounded in the folk tradition to survive seemingly incomprehensible situations, Sarah surrenders to the contemplation of her fragmentation. Like the solipsistic (post)modernist writer contemplating isolation, she dismisses external reality as a fantasy: "The characters are myself. . . . I know no places. That is I cannot believe in places. I find there are no places, only my funnyhouse." Her description of her situation sounds very much like a passage from Beckett: "The days are past when there are places and characters with connections with themes as in stories you pick up on the shelves of public libraries. Too, there is no theme. No statements" (257-58).

Kennedy traces Sarah's solipsistic attitude to her alienation from both her racial and her sexual heritages, an alienation that leads her to participate in the kind of imaginary or revisionist history that has frequently attracted (post)modernist writers. Although most critics accept the repeated assertions that Sarah's black father raped her lighter-skinned mother as statements of fact, the form of the play renders them problematic. They could as easily be seen as proof that she has rewritten history in a way that reflects her acceptance of Euro-American stereotypes. When the mother says "the wild black beast raped me and now my skull is shining," she restates a stereotype that has frequently been used by whites to obscure uncomfortable truths. The stereotype of the black beast obscures the historical reality that "miscegenation" originated primarily in the rape of black women by white men, especially slave owners. Because Sarah and her mother—or perhaps the maternal elements of Sarah's psyche—accept the myth of white purity that alienates them from their racial heritage, they are also forced to lie to one another concerning their experience as women. As Adrienne Rich comments in "Women and Honor: Some Notes on Lying": "In lying to others we end up lying to ourselves. We deny the importance of an event, or a person, and thus deprive ourselves of a part of our lives. Or we use one piece of the past or present to screen out another. Thus we lose faith even with our own lives" (188). Sarah suffers almost precisely such a loss of faith. The sense that the mother cannot be trusted emerges through other figures in Sarah's mindscape, most notably the "large dark faceless man" who says he is "shaken by nightmares of my mother" and refers to the "bald crazy mother" who speaks to Sarah of a black male rapist and "black diseases" (262).

Throughout the play, Sarah remains almost entirely incapable of recognizing any reality beyond her fragmented mind. The climactic movement toward Sarah's suicide begins shortly after Jesus, reflecting the protagonist's attempt to flee her own blackness, announces his intention to kill Lumumba. The scene shifts immediately to a jungle that Kennedy's stage directions describe in images reminiscent of Eugene O'Neill's *The Emperor Jones:* "over the entire scene . . . the jungle has overgrown the chambers and all the other places with a violence and a dark brightness, a grim yellowness" (269). Although O'Neill's attitude toward the stereotype seems ambiguous, Kennedy uses the jungle to represent Sarah's distorted relationship to her heritage. As Lumumba, Jesus, the Duchess, and Victoria appear in the jungle, the distinctions between them collapse; Sarah's efforts to repudiate or simplify aspects of herself are doomed to failure. The characters speak one another's lines interchangeably. Images of "ebony masks," "black beasts," "wild beasts," "niggers of torment," and "black anguished faces" build in a rhythm emphasizing the presence of "too many voices speaking at once" in Sarah's head. The conclusion focuses on her attempt to embrace only the whiteness associated with the simplified version of the mother: "Then at once the room will grow bright and my mother will come toward me smiling while I stand before his face and bludgeon him with an ebony head" (271). The image stands as a precise summation of Sarah's tormented "is-ness."

As this investigation of *Funnyhouse of a Negro* suggests, Adrienne Kennedy is an extremely complex dramatist who can be adequately understood only by recognizing both the Euro- and Afro-American dimensions of her work. *Funnyhouse of a Negro* presents a mindscape in which nothing can be accepted as "real" in the normal sense of the word. Although it is necessary to recognize the similarity between this mindscape and the Beckett-influenced postmodernist theater of individual alienation, it is equally necessary to recognize its analogues in African dramatic forms with powerful communal meanings. Once this complexity is recognized, it becomes possible to see the focus on the alienated individual in Kennedy's work as a kind of ritual act with deep significance for larger communities, whether composed of Afro-Americans seeking to come to terms with the psychological impact of the white world or (post)modernists who, aware of the tendencies that led Baraka to identify Beckett with Vietnam, seek to reconceptualize the relationship between the artist, the audience, and the work of art. Finally, although she does not approach her material in the same way as Hughes, Kennedy is very much a part of the "folk tradition" Kent describes. Presenting a compelling picture of an "is-ness" fragmented by the inability to accept the Afro-American heritage, she implies the need for the "somebodyness" and "as-if-ness." In effect, *Funnyhouse of a Negro* offers a call that attains maximum aesthetic power only through the audience that, even while admitting that "it be's that way sometimes," responds by embracing the folk-based strength that Sarah never knows.

Bullins's Black Dialectics

A radical playwright in both the simple and the complex senses of the term, Ed Bullins consistently challenges the members of his audience to test their political and aesthetic beliefs against the multifaceted reality of daily life in the United States. Committed to a revolutionary black nationalist consciousness, he attacks both liberal and conservative politics as aspects of an oppressive context dominated by a white elite. Equally committed to the development of a radical alternative to Euro-American modernist aesthetics, he incorporates a wide range of cultural materials into assertively black performances. The clearest evidence of Bullins's radical sensibility, however, is his unwavering refusal to accept any dogma, white or black, traditional or revolutionary, without testing it against a multitude of perspectives and experiences. Throughout his career, Bullins has subjected the hypocrises and corruptions of Euro- and Afro-American culture to rigorous examination and reevaluation. Refusing to accept any distinctions between aesthetics and politics or between the concerns of the artist and those of the community, Bullins demands that his audience synthesize abstract perception and concrete experience. Providing a set of terms useful to understanding the development of these concerns in his own work, Bullins defines a constituting dialectic in the black theatrical movement that emerged in the midsixties: "This new thrust has two main branches—the *dialectic of change* and the *dialectic of experience*. The writers are attempting to answer questions concerning Black survival and future, one group through confronting the Black/white reality of America, the other, by heightening the dreadful white reality of being a modern Black captive and victim" (*New Lafayette* 4). The dialectic of change focuses attention on political problems demanding a specific form of action. The dialectic of experience focuses on a more "realistic" (though Bullins redefines the term to encompass aspects of reality frequently dismissed by programmatic realists), and sometimes harsh, picture of black life. Reflecting his awareness that by definition each dialectic is in constant tension with the other, Bullins directs his work in the dialectic of change to altering the audience's actual experience. Similarly, his work in the dialectic of experience, while rarely explicitly didactic, leads inexorably to recognition of the need for change.

Bullins's work in both dialectics repudiates the tradition of the Western theater, which, he says, "shies away from social, political, psychological or any disturbing (revolutionary) reforms." Asserting the central importance of non-Western references, Bullins catalogs the "elements that make up the alphabet of the secret language used in Black theater," among them the blues, dance, African religion and mysticism, "familial nationalism," myth-science, vodun ritual-ceremony, and "nigger street styles." Despite the commitment to an Afro-American continuum evident in the construction and content of his plays, Bullins by no means repudiates all elements of the Euro-American tradition. Even as he criticizes Brechtian epic theater, Bullins employs aspects of Brecht's dramatic rhetoric, designed to alienate the audience from received modes of perceiving theatrical, and by extension political, events. It is less important to catalog Bullins's allusions to William Shakespeare, O'Neill, Camus, or Genet than to recognize his use of their devices alongside those of Baraka, Wole Soyinka, and Derek A. Walcott in the service of "Black artistic, political, and cultural consciousness" (*New Lafayette* 4).

Most of Bullins's work in the dialectic of change, which he calls "protest writing" when addressed to a Euro-American audience and "Black revolutionary writing" when addressed to an Afro-American audience, takes the form of the short satiric or agitprop plays produced to support the Black Panthers' agenda during the Black Arts Movement. Frequently intended for street performance, these plays aim to attract a crowd and communicate an incisive message as rapidly as possible. Fundamental to Baraka's ritual theater and Bullins's *Black Revolutionary Commercials*, this strategy developed out of the black nationalist movement in cities such as New York, Detroit, Chicago, San Francisco, and Newark. Reflecting the need to avoid unplanned confrontations with police, the performances described in Bullins's influential *Short Statement on Street Theater* concentrate on establishing contact with groups unlikely to enter a theater, especially black working people and individuals living on the margins of society—gang members, junkies, prostitutes, street people. Recognizing the impact of the media on American consciousness, Bullins frequently parodies media techniques, satirizing political advertising in *The American Flag Ritual* and "selling" positive black revolutionary images in *A Street Play*. Somewhat longer, though equally direct, *Death List*, which can be performed by a troupe moving through neighborhood streets, alerts the community to "enemies of the Black People," from Vernon Jordan to Whitney Young. Considered out of their performance context, many of these pieces seem simplistic or didactic, but their intent is to realize Bullins's desire that "each individual in the crowd should have his sense of reality confronted, his consciousness assaulted" (*Statement*). Because the "accidental" street audience comes into contact with the play in a "normal" frame of mind, Bullins creates deliberately hyperbolic images to dislocate that mind-set in a very short period of time.

When writing revolutionary plays for performance in traditional theaters, Bullins tempers his rhetoric considerably. To be sure, *Dialect Determinism*, a warning against trivializing the revolutionary impulse of Malcolm X, and *The Gentleman Caller,* a satiric attack on the master-slave mentality of black-white economic interaction, both resemble the street plays in their insistence on revolutionary change. *Dialect Determinism* climaxes with the killing of a black "enemy," while *The Gentleman Caller* ends with a formulaic call for the rise of the "Black nation that will survive, conquer and rule" (*Theme* 380). The difference between these plays and the street theater lies not in their messages but in Bullins's way of involving the audience. Recognizing the different needs of an audience willing to seek out his work in the theater but frequently educated by the dominant culture, Bullins involves it in a Brechtian analytic process leading to what seem, from a black nationalist perspective, relatively unambiguous political perceptions. Rather than asserting the messages at the start of the plays, therefore, he develops satiric settings before stripping away the masks and distortions imposed by the audience's normal frame of reference on its recognition of his revolutionary message.

Along with Baraka, Kennedy, Marvin X, Sonia Sanchez, and others, Bullins helped make the dialectic of change an important cultural force at the height of the black power movement, but his most substantial achievements involve the dialectic of experience. Ranging from his impressionistic gallery plays and politically resonant problem plays to the intricately interconnected Twentieth-Century Cycle, Bullins's work in this dialectic reveals a profound skepticism regarding revolutionary ideals that have not been tested against the actual contradictions of Afro-American experience. *Street Sounds,* parts of which were later incorporated into *House Party,* represents Bullins's adaptation of the gallery approach pioneered by poets such as Robert Browning (*The Ring and the Book*), Edgar Lee Masters (*Spoon River Anthology,* 1915), Melvin B. Tolson (*Harlem Gallery,* 1969), Gwendolyn Brooks (*A Street in Bronzeville,* 1945) and Langston Hughes ("Montage of a Dream Deferred," 1951). Montaging a series of thirty- to ninety-second monologues, Bullins suggests the tensions common to the experience of seemingly disparate elements of the Afro-American community. Superficially, the characters can be divided into categories such as politicians (Harlem Politician, Black Student), hustlers (Dope Seller, The Thief), artists (Black Revolutionary Artist, Black Writer), street people (Fried Brains, Corner Brother), working people (Errand Boy, Workin' Man), and women (The Loved One, The Virgin, Harlem Mother). None of the categories, however, survives careful examination; individual women could be placed in every other category; the Black Revolutionary Artist combines politics and art; the Harlem Politician, politics and crime. To a large extent, all types ultimately amount to variations on several social and psychological themes, which render the surface distinctions far less important than they initially appear.

Although their particular responses vary considerably, each character in *Street Sounds* confronts the decaying community described by the Old-timer: "They changin' things, you know? Freeways comin' through tearin' up the old neighborhood. Buildings goin' down, and not bein' put up again. Abandoned houses that are boarded up, the homes of winos, junkies and rats, catchin' fire and never bein' fixed up" (*Theme* 170). As a result, many share the Workin' Man's feeling of being "trapped inside of ourselves, inside our experience" (160). Throughout the play, Bullins portrays a deep feeling of racial inferiority that results in male obsession with white women (Slightly Confused Negro, The Explainer) and a casual willingness to exploit or attack other blacks (The Thief, The Doubter, Young West Indian Revolutionary Poet). Attempting to salvage some sense of freedom or self-worth, or simply to find momentary release from the struggle, individuals turn to art, sex, politics, or drugs, but the weight of their context pressures each toward the psychological collapse of Fried Brains, the hypocritical delusion of the Non-Ideological Nigger, or the unfounded self-glorification of The Genius. Even when individuals embrace political causes, Bullins remains skeptical. The Theorist, The Rapper, and The Liar—who ironically echoes Bullins's aesthetic when he declares "Even when I lie, I lie truthfully. . . . I'm no stranger to experience" (158)—express ideological positions similar to those Bullins advocates in the dialectic of change. None, however, seems even marginally aware that his grand pronouncements have no impact on the experience of the black community. The Rapper's revolutionary call—"We are slaves now, this moment in time, brothers, but let this moment end with this breath and let us unite as fearless revolutionaries in the pursuit of world liberation!" (179)—comes between the entirely apolitical monologues of Waiting and Bewildered. Similarly, the Black Revolutionary Artist's endorsement of "a cosmic revolution that will liberate the highest potential of nationhood in the universe" (149) is followed by the Black Dee Jay's claim that "BLACK MEANS BUY!" (149). The sales pitch seems to have a great deal more power than the nationalist vision of the lives of the Soul Sister and the Corner Brother, whose monologues frame the Black Revolutionary Artist–Black Dee Jay sequence.

One of Bullins's characteristic "signatures" is the attribution of his own ideals to characters unwilling or unable to act or inspire others to act on them. Reflecting his belief that without action ideals have little value, Bullins structures *Street Sounds* to insist on the need for the connection. The opening monologue, delivered by a white "Pig," establishes a political context similar to the one that Bullins uses in the dialectic of change, within which the dialectic of experience proceeds. Reducing all blacks to a single type, the nigger, Pig wishes only to "beat his nigger ass good" (147). Although Bullins clearly perceives the police as a basic oppressive force in the ghetto, he does not concentrate on highlighting the audience's awareness of that point. Rather, by the end of the play he has made it clear that the Afro-American community in actuality beats its own ass. The absence of any other white character in the play reflects Bullins's focus on the nature of victimization as experienced within and perpetuated by the black community. The Harlem Mother monologue that closes the play concentrates almost entirely on details of experience. Although she presents no hyperbolic portraits of white oppressors, her memories of the impact on her family of economic exploitation, hunger, and government indifference carry more political power than does any abstraction. This by no means indicates Bullins's distaste for political analysis or a repudiation of the opening monologues; rather, it reflects his awareness that abstract principles signify little unless they are embedded in the experience first of the audience and, ultimately, of the community as a whole.

While Bullins consistently directs his work toward the Afro-American community, his work in the dialectic of experience inevitably involves the interaction of blacks and whites. *The Taking of Miss Janie,* perhaps his single most powerful play, focuses on a group of California college students, several of whom first appeared in *The Pig Pen.* In part a meditation on the heritage of the sixties civil rights movement, *The Taking of Miss Janie* revolves around the sexual and political tensions between and within racial groups. Although most of the characters are readily identifiable types—the stage directions identify Rick as a cultural nationalist, Janie as a California beach girl, Flossy as a "soul sister"—Bullins explores individual characters in depth, concentrating on their tendency to revert to stereotypical behavior patterns, especially when they assume rigid ideological or social roles. The central incident of the play—the "rape" of the white Janie by Monty, a black friend of long standing—provides a severely alienating image of this tendency to both black and white audiences. After committing a murder, which may or may not be real, when the half-mythic Jewish beatnik Mort Silberstein taunts him for his inability to separate his consciousness from Euro-American influences, Monty undresses Janie, who does not resist or cooperate, in a rape scene devoid of violence, love, anger, or physical desire. Unable to resist the pressures that make their traditional Western claim to individuality seem naive, both Janie and Monty seem resigned to live out a "fate" that in fact depends on their acquiescence. Monty accepts the role of the "black beast" who rapes and murders white people, while Janie plays the role of plantation mistress. While these intellectually articulate characters do not genuinely believe in the reality of their roles, their ironic attitude ultimately makes no difference. The roles govern their actions.

While the rape incident provides the frame for *The Taking of Miss Janie,* Monty and Janie exist in a gallery of characters whose collective inability to maintain individual integrity testifies to the larger dimensions of the problem. Rick and Len enact the classic argument between nationalism and eclecticism in the black political/intellectual world; Peggy tires of confronting the neuroses of black men and turns to lesbianism; "hip" white boy Lonnie moves from fad to fad, turning his contact with black culture to financial advantage in the music business; several couples drift aimlessly into interracial marriages. Alternating scenes in which characters interact and monologues in which individuals reflect on their future development, Bullins reveals his characters' inability to create an alternative to the "fate" within which they feel trapped. Although none demonstrates a fully developed ability to integrate ideals and experiences, several seem substantially less alienated than others. In many ways the least deluded, Peggy accepts both her lesbianism and her responsibility for her past actions. Her comment on the sixties articulates a basic aspect of Bullins's vision: "We all failed. Failed ourselves in that serious time known as the sixties. And by failing ourselves we also failed in the test of the times" (447). Her honesty and insight also have a positive impact on the black nationalist Rick, who during a conversation with Peggy abandons his grandiose rhetoric on the "devil's tricknology" (a phrase adopted from the Nation of Islam)—rhetoric that masks a deep hostility toward other blacks. Although he has previously attacked her as a lesbian "freak," Rick's final lines to Peggy suggest another aspect of Bullins's perspective: "Ya know, it be about what you make it anyway" (447). Any adequate response to *The Taking of Miss Janie* must take into account not only Peggy's survival strategy and Rick's nationalistic idealism but also Janie's willed naivete and the accuracy of Mort's claim that, despite his invocation of Mao, Malcolm X, and Franz Fanon, Monty is still on some levels "FREAKY FOR JESUS!" (449). Bullins presents no simple answers nor does he simply contemplate the wasteland. Rather, as in almost all of his work in both the dialectic of change and the dialectic of experience, he challenges his audience to make something out of the fragments and failures he portrays, to attain a perspective from which the dialectic of experience and the dialectic of change can be realized as one and the same.

Etheridge Knight's Poetic Populism

In the preface to *Born of a Woman,* Etheridge Knight endorses an aesthetic that balances the demands of "The Poet, the Poem, and the People" (xiv). The third term is crucial, providing a necessary reminder of the populist roots of black expression. A polished artisan, capable of exploiting both traditional Euro-American and experimental Afro-American (frequently musical) forms, Knight deserves recognition as a major voice in the poetic tradition of Langston Hughes and Gwendolyn Brooks, itself an extension of a community-centered sensibility extending back through W. E. B. Du Bois and Pauline Hopkins to Frederick Douglass and David Walker. Seen in historical perspective, Knight's work expresses both the political and cultural currents of black nationalism and readjusts the position of the black aesthetic movement in the populist tradition. Technically, Knight merges musical rhythms with traditional metrical devices, reflecting the assertion of an Afro-American cultural identity within a Euro-American context. Thematically, he denies that the figures of the singer, central to the aesthetic of *Chant of Saints,* and the warrior, central to the aesthetic of the Black Arts Movement, are or can be separate.

One in a long line of black writers to have discovered his vocation while in prison, Knight began writing under the encouragement of Gwendolyn Brooks. His artistic awakening coincided both with the critical dominance of the Black Arts Movement and with Brooks's evolution from a "universalist" to a black nationalist perspective. Black aestheticians such as Addison Gayle, Jr., insisted that the historical oppression of black people in the United States had created a situation in which Afro-American writers must commit themselves to the freedom of their people and reject Euro-American cultural traditions as a mark of independence. In its most extreme forms, the black aesthetic demanded that the Afro-American writer serve as another tool of the revolution, creating works that would inspire the masses of black people to commit themselves anew to political action. The artist must be a warrior first, a singer only second.

Reflecting this political and aesthetic climate, Knight's early work, while employing numerous poetic devices associated with Euro-American traditions, insists on a specifically black poetry. "On Universalism" dismisses the concept of the encompassing unity of humanity as a response to the oppression of the people:

> No universal laws
> Of human misery
> Create a common cause
> Or common history
> That ease black people's pains
> Nor break black people's chains.
>
> (*Poems from Prison* 25)

This, of course, echoes the black aesthetic's insistence upon the primacy of the People in all artistic endeavors.

Knight's aesthetic as reflected both in his metrics and his imagery, however, always balanced the demands of Poet, Poem, and People, granting equal attention to the aesthetic demands of the language and to the impulse toward self-expression. This synthetic approach raised questions from the beginning of Knight's career. Even while identifying *Poems from Prison* as a "major announcement," Haki R. Madhubuti (then writing as Don L. Lee) questioned the propriety of Knight's allusions to Euro-American culture. Rather than abandoning such allusions, Knight soon relinquished the emphasis on a separate black aesthetic. Even while altering his stance, however, he maintained a strong sense of the black populist heritage: "Our poetry will always speak mainly to black people, but I don't see it being as narrow in the 70s as it was in the 60s." Extending this argument, Knight proposed a version of universalism based on shared emotional experience, rather than specific images or forms: "My poetry is also important to white people because it invokes feelings. . . . The feelings are common, whether or not the situations that create the feelings are common. . . . I might feel fear in a small town in Iowa. You might be afraid if you get off the subway in Harlem. It's the same fear, but the situations are different." This widening of the definition of the People to include any reader capable of responding to Knight's emotional impulse in no way entails a movement away from populism. The lasting contribution of the black aesthetic to Knight's poetics lies precisely in his continuing commitment to the People: "I pay attention only to the people in the audience. If they don't dig it, then it ain't nothing no way" ("Answers" 151).

This commitment to the People, even when "it is lonely . . . and sometimes / THE PEOPLES can be a bitch" ("A Poem to Galway Kinnell" 95), defines Knight's poetic achievement. As the structure of *Born of a Woman* indicates, Knight approaches this commitment from a variety of perspectives. Part 1, titled "Inside-Out," focuses on Knight's awakening in prison and his dawning awareness of his relationship with an outside world. Part 2, "Outside-In," concentrates on his self-exploration—the Poet is one-third of Knight's aesthetic trinity—once released. Part 3, "All About—And Back Again," reemphasizes that, whatever his explorations, the Poet Knight ultimately returns to the base he finds in the People and expresses in the Poems.

The political poetry written concurrently with "On Universalism" attests to the complexity of Knight's practice. His eulogy "For Malcolm, A Year After," originally published in *Poems from Prison,* carefully manipulates metrical tensions and rhyme schemes to make its statement of support for the nationalist warrior. Knight begins with a bitter statement that he will stay within the Euro-American tradition for fear that any formal departure might bring in its wake a self-destructive emotional explosion:

> Compose for Red a proper verse;
> Adhere to foot and strict iamb;
> Control the burst of angry words
> Or they might boil and break the dam.
> Or they might boil and overflow
> And drench, drown me, drive me mad.
>
> (67)

Like much of Knight's work, this passage is characterized by intricate sound textures such as the drench/drown/drive sequence and the internal "r" sound of "proper verse," "Adhere," and "control the burst of angry words." Pointing to the poem's intellectual and emotional core, rhyme connects the form in the "iamb" and the anger in "dam," which Knight then inverts in "mad" to complete the conceptual sight-oriented off-rhyme: i am damn mad. He concludes the opening section by at once embracing and rejecting the "white" language in which he writes: "Make empty anglo tea lace words— / Make them dead white and dry bone bare" (67). The very words he molds into the "proper verse" embody the values of a literally murderous culture.

The second stanza emphasizes that while Knight uses Euro-

American cultural forms, he uses them to advance the political cause of black nationalism. Inverting the traditional conceit of the poem that lives eternally despite the death of the man, Knight writes that his poem, an artifact of the oppressive culture, will die, but its message, the message of Malcolm X, will live:

> Compose a verse for Malcolm man,
> And make it rime and make it prim.
> The verse will die—as all men do—
> But not the memory of him.
>
> (67)

The concluding triplet of the poem, implicitly parodying the standard couplet form, further emphasizes the revolutionary emotion inspired by both the life and death of Malcolm X:

> Death might come singing sweet like C
> Or knocking like the old folk say
> The Moon and stars may pass away,
> But not the anger of that day.
>
> (67)

While Knight the singer works within traditional forms, his vision is insistently that of the nationalist warrior.

Most of the poems in "Inside-Out" echo this intense anger. Knight portrays Hard Rock, lobotomized, serving as a symbol of contemporary "slavery:" "The fears of the years, like a biting whip / Had cut deep bloody grooves / Across our backs" (4). He writes of his own isolation from his family in "The Idea of Ancestry," an isolation that leads him back to prison. Ironically juxtaposing his statement with the largely traditional forms in the first section, he concludes in "A Poem for Black Relocation Centers" with the portrait of Flukum who "couldn't stand the strain. Flukum / who wanted inner and outer order" (21) and who meets an uncomprehending death in Vietnam. Clearly, the poems in "Inside-Out" point to the necessity of a vision of the world going beyond the simple recognition of victimization.

"Outside-In" reflects both Knight's concern with the Poet's personal struggle to attain this vision and his determination to generate forms, many of them reflecting the Afro-American musical tradition, which adequately express this vision. Both a cry of personal agony and a demonstration of Knight's ability to shape his poem out of the materials of both Euro- and Afro-American culture, "The Violent Space" stands among the most powerful lyrics of recent decades. Mingling allusions to the Garden of Eden and the folklore of black Mississippi, Knight begins:

Exchange in greed the ungraceful signs. Thrust
The thick notes between green apple breasts.
Then the shadow of the devil descends,
The violent space cries and angel eyes,
Large and dark, retreat in innocence and in ice.
(Run sister run—the Bugga man comes!)

(26)

The intricate interplay of sound (large-dark; the repeated "in" sound that stresses the entrapment of innocence) and rhyme (cries-eyes-ice that implies the freezing of the emotions and tears) is set against the fear of the inchoate "Bugga man." The Bugga man image recurs throughout the poem; even the Poet's mystic chant is an insufficient response:

Well, shit, lil sis, here we are:
You and I and this poem.
And what should I do? should I squat
In the dust and make strange markings on the ground?
Shall I cant a spell to drive the demon away?
(Run sister run—the Bugga man comes!)

(26)

Finally, the Poet invokes the authority and strength of the black spiritual tradition, but that too fails to repulse the demon:

"O Mary don't you weep don't you moan"
O Mary shake your butt to the violent juke,
Absorb the demon puke and watch the white eyes pop,
(Run sister run—the Bugga man comes!)

(27)

The demon, now clearly associated with the white culture that passively supports the agony, undercuts the black source of strength. The Poet, unable to make his connection with the Person he loves, is isolated:

I am not bold. I cannot yet take hold of the demon
And lift his weight from your black belly.
So I grab the air and sing my song.
(But the air cannot hold my singing long.)

(27)

Clearly, isolated singing is an insufficient response to the situation of individuals victimized by an oppressive culture. Knight once again implies the need for the warrior to act when the song fades or erupts.

Not all of Knight's explorations in "Outside-In" lead to such stark confrontations. He has never been simply the Poet of the victim. Knight's musical experiments with toasts ("Dark Prophecy: I Sing of Shine"), blues ("A Poem for Myself"), and African percussive rhythms ("Ilu the Talking Drum") involve a wide range of emotional experiences, including that of remembered and discovered love in the jazz poem "For Eric Dolphy." Several of his jazz poems employ irregular but insistent rhythmical patterns and repetitions in the place of a basic Euro-American meter. "Another Poem for Me" typifies this practice:

> what now
> what now dumb nigger damn near dead
> what now
> now that you won't dance
> behind the pale white doors of death
> what now   is   to be
> to be what you wanna be
> what you spozed to be
> or what white / america wants you to be.
>
> (51)

The tension between the "what now" and the "to be" phrases moves the poem rhythmically and thematically, insisting that the Poet must not remain a victim but must shape his own being. Jazz, ultimately, aids the Poet in the necessary journey back into himself.

In the poems of "All About—And Back Again," these explorations and experiments merge in Knight's mature poetic voice. "I and Your Eyes" exemplifies the music and the concerns of this voice. The "And I . . . your eyes" pattern forms a rhythmic base, derived more from jazz than from traditional metrics:

> And I   and your eyes
> Draw round about a ring of gold
> And shout their sparks of fire
> And I   and your eyes
> Hold untold tales and conspire
> With moon and sun to shake my soul.
>
> (94)

Using the pause between the two repeated phrases, Knight creates a tension, a sense of separation leading toward the connection embodied by the imagery. As he expresses the separation and pain of love, he departs from the ground rhythm, leaving an emptiness in the sound of the poem:

```
Then I
Could stand alone        the pain
Of flesh      alone      the time and space
And steel     alone      but I am shaken.
It has taken
                         your eyes
To move this stone.
```

The traditional use of rhyme to emphasize crucial thematic points reinforces the jazz devices. This is the voice of an accomplished singer.

Along with this technical maturity, the poems in "All About—And Back Again" reveal a commensurate maturity of vision. Just as "I and Your Eyes" combines the control of traditional devices with jazz techniques, "We Free Singers Be" insists on the importance of both the warrior embodying the values of the black aesthetic movement and the singer, reflecting the evolutionary emphasis of *Chant of Saints*. The poem's title implies this. "We" gives the sense of group identity, the nationalist perspective, the People. "Free" provides an internal rhyme, demonstrating Knight's use of Euro-American traditions in a way that renders it indistinguishable from the authenticity of his individual, clearly black, voice, and establishes the political emphasis on liberation. "Singers" invokes the emphasis on the artist, the *Chant of Saints* orientation toward the Poet. "Be," the third rhyme word invoking the verbal play, the mock-excess of black oral tradition, provides the fulcrum for both the thematic and rhythmic movement of the poem.

Knight opens the poem with contrasting pastoral and military images of the "free singers":

```
We free singers be
sometimes swimming in the music
like porpoises playing in the sea.
We free singers be
come agitators at times, be
come eagles circling the sun
hurling stones at hunters.
```
                    (99)

They are at once porpoises swimming in music and eagles challenging the predators. "Be," which ends four lines, serves both as a statement of what they are and as the first term of what they will become. The rhythmic tension between the "we free singers be" phrase and the "become" phrases mirrors the tension between their aspirations—the drive to connect the singer and the warrior—and the specific circumstance in which they must become one or the other.

Throughout the poem Knight alternates the warrior and the singer images. He intersperses a number of memories: of days "of the raging fires when I clenched my teeth in my sleep and refused to speak"—the days of the warriors; and of days "when children held our hands and danced around us in circles"—the days of the singers (99). The circle imagery connected with the children echoes the circle imagery connected with the warrior eagles. No matter what the momentary manifestation, both the singer and the warrior coexist in the individual at all times. The function of the singer is in large part to be a visionary:

> We free singers be
> voyagers
> and sing of cities
> with straight streets
> and mountains piercing the moon—
> and rivers that never run dry.
>
> (99)

But even the visionary cannot afford to forget the reality of conflict:

> Remember, oh, do you remember
> the snow
> falling
> on broadway
> and the soldiers marching
> thru the icy streets
> with blood on their coat sleeves.
>
> (99)

The fact, one with which Knight began the poem, and with which he ends it, is simply that each individual must be both: "We Free singers be, baby, / We free singers be" (99). Ultimately, Knight says, the warriors of the black aesthetic and the singers of the *Chant* merge in the individual striving for the freedom of the Poet and the People.

Dumas: Nationalism and Multicultural Mythology

> they broke us like limbs from trees
> and carved Europe upon our
> African masks and made puppets
>
> —"The Puppets Have a New *King*"

lift up! and read the sky
written in the tongue of your ancestors.
It is yours, claim it.

—"Black Star Line"

Articulating a postmodernist nationalism with profound implications for writers throughout the multiculture, the works of Henry
Dumas testify to an aesthetic complexity too frequently ignored or
repressed in historical accounts of the Black Arts Movement. Often
dismissed as a polemical and philosophically naive expression of
black nationalism, the highly political writing associated with the
Black Arts Movement incorporated an implicitly postmodernist critique of cultural mythology parallel to, and as sophisticated as, that
carried out by more explicitly philosophical writers such as Michael
Harper, Jay Wright, Rita Dove, and Christopher Gilbert. Aware of the
multiplicity of mythologies available to conscious American writers,
Dumas treats myth not as an expression of "universal" (or "Black")
essence but as part of the process through which the individual constructs his/her relationship to an inevitably political world. Constructing an alternative poetic genealogy of use to all multicultural
poets, Dumas turns away from the (static, literary, alienated, academic) modernism of T. S. Eliot toward the (fluid, musical, recon-
structive, populist) modernism of Langston Hughes.

The adjectives associated with Eliot and Hughes, of course, reflect
a particular construction of modernism grounded in Dumas's own
cultural and personal situation. The simple dichotomies no more reflect the actual complexities of Euro-American modernism than David Perkins's condescending (and all too typical) dismissal of Hughes
in his *History of Modern Poetry* recognizes the complexities of Afro-
American expression. Unlike most Euro-American academics, however, Dumas is aware of the relationship between his construction
and his situation. For Dumas, the repudiation of Euro-American mythology is a first step toward reestablishing contact with the Afrocentric traditions capable of nurturing the psychological integrity vital
to multicultural communication.

Numerous references and allusions attest to Dumas's awareness of
the varied uses of myth in Euro-American modernist texts. Like Eliot,
Pound, and Joyce, Dumas juxtaposes diverse mythologies: Christian
(the crucifixion images in "Rose Jungle" and "The Zebra Goes Wild
Where the Sidewalk Ends"); Greek (both versions of "Somnus" and
"Kef 43"); Taoist (the Saba beginning "Tao was the first priest"); as
well as those associated with Africa, including several different types
of Islam. Frequently, Dumas's treatment of such myths directly in-

vokes Euro-American modernist texts. The association of the images of the train and the "green stinging worm" (*Ark* 51) in Dumas's story "A Boll of Roses" specifically echoes the conclusion of James Joyce's "A Painful Case." A more complex revoicing of Joycean motifs occurs in the "Somnus" poems, in which Dumas focuses his attention on the ways in which Euro-American myths can alienate the individual from the reality of his/her situation. Imaging Ulysses as an "indifferent pirate" (*Ebony* 24), Dumas condemns the black lotus-eater's uncritical acceptance of Euro-American mythology, the "memories of their genesis / that transfix and electrocute me" (25). A similar politicizing of modernist motifs occurs in "Harlem Gulp," the imagery and rhythm of which recall Wallace Stevens's "Thirteen Ways of Looking at a Blackbird": "like squawking blackbirds / pecking / mites in the circle of sun" (33). Like Stevens, Dumas uses the image to emphasize the relativity of perception. But whereas Stevens evokes the psychological and metaphysical implications of the image, Dumas casts it in racially resonant terms:

> we tremble off snow
> like black pearls
> trapped
> in the white cerebellum
> we glisten out of reach.
>
> (33)

Even as he acknowledges the validity of Stevens's relativistic mythology, Dumas insists on the political reality that has created, at least for the present, an unbridgeable gap between Afro- and Euro-American apprehensions of that relativity.

The majority of Dumas's frequent allusions to Eliot—his primary source of Euro-American modernist references—are associated with similar revisions. The opening lines of "Ikef 4" echo the imagery of desiccation from part 5 of *The Waste Land*: "when we needed rain / dust came" (115); the image of god as "a drunk fisherman" evokes Eliot's fisher king. Dumas's harshest treatment of Euro-American modernism, the story "Will the Circle Be Unbroken?" revoices Eliot's use of the circle as an emblem of a lost unity, associated with the classical past and inaccessible to the inhabitants of his wasteland. What Eliot images as the pervasive fate of contemporary humanity, however, Dumas sees as a malaise specific to Euro-American culture. Representing the whites encroaching upon the ritual ground of the black club as "three ghosts, like chaff blown from a wasteland" (*Ark* 113), Dumas counteracts Eliot's image of the fallen walls of the unreal cities by envisioning black music as the source of mythic rebirth:

"He is blowing. Magwa's hands. Reverence of skin. Under the single voices is the child of a woman, black. They are building back the wall, crumbling under the disturbance" (114).

Where Eliot presents Euro-American mythology as the source of value—an alternative to, as he phrased it in his essay "Ulysses, Order, and Myth," the "immense panorama of futility and anarchy which is contemporary history"—Dumas consistently identifies those myths as the *source* of the futility that must be counteracted through the recuperation of the repressed, or forgotten, myths of the *Afro*-American past (177). It is not surprising, therefore, that many of Dumas's poems center on the myths encoded in African words, the "unknown tongues and clefs" (*Ebony* 113). Anticipating Audre Lorde's *The Black Unicorn*, "Emoyeni, Place of the Winds," "Kef 4," and "Ikef 11" require the reader to engage African mythological systems in order to derive even a provisional meaning. The absence of *Waste Land*–style explanatory notes at once resists the academic quality of Eliot's erudition and emphasizes the distance between most readers and the African myths. This does not mean that Africa must *remain* distant. In fact, several African myths recovered by the Black Arts Movement have passed into common currency in the decades since Dumas's death, most notably those surrounding Shango, God of the spirit. Anticipating the approach to mythic identity in rap/funk records such as Afrika Bambaata's *Shango Funk Theology* (1984) and X Clan's *To The East, Blackwards* (1990), Dumas's poem "Funk" reads: "The great god Shango in the African sea / reached down with palm oil and oozed out me" (*Ebony* 86).

The link between Dumas's poetry and the music of the streets is by no means incidental. Dumas clearly understood that music—gospel, blues, jazz, or funk—would play a crucial role in recovery of the African mythological heritage. Section 9 of "Genesis on an Endless Mosaic" images music as the path to a blackness associated with past and future, but alienated in the present:

> dictation in gestures transposed to music
> starting and ending in the black beyond
> metamorphosis, said the preacher
> is starting under the sign of the cross
> wings, dreamed I are what we early lost.

(63)

Acknowledging Christianity as both mark of oppression and potential source of transformation, Dumas identifies gospel music—particularly that of his favorite group, the Swan Silvertone Singers—as a path to Africa in "Kef 25":

the swan silvertone singers
pulled chords of blue and purple
like the velvet robe of king Nkoko
sounding in their sounding
of gut and Benin strut.

(107)

Balancing his allusions to Eliot, Stevens, and other Euro-American modernists are Dumas's allusions to Hughes's treatment of myth and music. The "Mosaic" poems derive directly from Hughes's "Montage of a Dream Deferred," while "Island within Island" builds on the concluding section of Hughes's modernist epic. The deepest bond between Hughes and Dumas, however, relates not to specific echoes but to the two poets' choice of a readily accessible voice to articulate the deepest myths of Afro-American culture. Dumas's "Son of Msippi" is a powerful expression of what Robert Stepto calls "ascent," the drive to rise "Up / from the river of pain" (15). "Root Song" is an equally powerful expression of what Stepto calls "immersion," the drive to return to communal roots, which Dumas sees as grounded in the "African soil [which] nourished my spirit" (19).

What differentiates Dumas's "modernism" most clearly from that of his Euro-American antecedents—the Joyce who described the mythological impoverishment underlying the paralysis of his *Dubliners* would be the closest parallel—is his recognition of the practical imperatives of mythological awareness. Providing realistic and accessible images of the attempt to revive the African "king . . . fossilized in our brains" ("Saba: The Lost Diadem," *Ebony* 124), Dumas's short stories continually assert the need for, and possibility of, bringing myth to life, and life to myth. In "Ark of Bones," the protagonist Headeye leads the narrator to an awareness of the physical suffering—the experience of the countless black victims of white racism—which gives meaning to Afro-American Christianity. Paralleling what I discuss in chapter 9 as the "gospel impulse," Dumas presents the "call of the Lord" as an immersion in black experience, a way of bringing the fossilized African mythology back to life. And *lived myth*, rather than myth conceived in abstract or literary terms, is the primary concern of Dumas's fiction. In "Echo Tree," "Will the Circle Be Unbroken?" "Devil Bird," and "The Voice," Dumas focuses repeatedly on a basic theme: that the type of myth one lives depends on *choice*, not conscious choices focusing explicitly on mythological issues, but the daily choices that define the values by which one lives. Attempting to inspire an *actual* transformation of Afro-American life, Dumas poses a choice between two groups of values, associated—

in the specific circumstances confronting the majority of the Afro-American community—with different sets of myths: the values of presence, relation, and respect associated with African mythologies or the corrupt values of individuality, abstraction, and pride enforced by uncritical acceptance of the myths of Europe. Ultimately, the creation of myths capable of inspiring the Afro-American community cannot be separated from the willingness, the courage to live out the implications of the African myths. At the conclusion of the "Saba" beginning "we weep that our heroes have died / in our memories," Dumas negotiates the mythological challenge of "the devils / who came in Jesus ships from Europe." Celebrating the Afro-American myths that provided the driving impulse of the Black Arts Movement, Dumas concludes the "Saba" by celebrating a *lived* immersion that is powered by, and empowers, ascent:

> a people cannot create the real hero
> until they create the real hero
> not by mirrors or masks or muscles
> but by men the soil is nourished
> and one day
> we will not weep but sing him
> up.
>
> (*Ebony* 130)

Audre Lorde's Woman-Centered Process

As James Miller, David Lionel Smith, and Sondra Richards observed when participating in the panel "Understanding the Second Black Renaissance" at a 1993 conference on the sixties held at the University of Wisconsin, one of the most glaring deficiencies in understanding the Black Arts Movement involves the general failure to acknowledge the presence and importance of black women writers other than Gwendolyn Brooks. Although critics of the seventies and eighties accurately identified the sexism of major black aestheticians, few observed that novels written during the movement, often by writers who took an active part, already articulated most of the concerns fundamental to the later critiques. Alice Walker's *The Third Life of Grange Copeland* and *Meridian,* Paule Marshall's *The Chosen Place, the Timeless People,* and Toni Cade Bambara's *The Salt Eaters* are only a few of many possible examples. Similarly, although she published much of her early work with Dudley Randall's Broadside Press, probably the most important publishing house of the period, Audre Lorde is rarely discussed in relation to the movement. Rather, like Walker,

Marshall, Bambara, and June Jordan, her work is typically subsumed in a critical narrative focusing on the emergence of African-American women's writing. Although there are good reasons for viewing her in such a context, a recognition of Lorde's early poetry as part of a dialogue with other currents of the Black Arts Movement broadens our understanding both of her own poetic voice and of the complex lessons to be learned from the sixties.

Lorde introduces *Chosen Poems, Old and New,* which includes most of the work published during and shortly after the height of the Black Arts Movement, with a statement that accurately reflects the complexity of her early career: "Here are the words of some of the women I have been, am being still, will come to be. The time surrounding each poem is an unspoken image" (iii). As Lorde's introductory statement implies, she resists pressures toward ideological rigidity, committing herself instead to the discovery of individual processes while recognizing that each provisional self is inevitably conditioned by the unstated and elusive premises of its historical context. In line with this emphasis, Lorde's early work explores the limits and possibilities of various identities, traditional and innovative. The question she poses in "Change of Season" strikes near the core of her sensibility: "Am I to be cursed forever with becoming / somebody else on the way to myself?" (40). All views of Lorde exclusively in relation to any single context—lesbian, feminist, or black nationalist—radically oversimplify her voice, which also has roots in Romantic and modernist sensibilities.

Lorde shares a great deal with poets such as Gwendolyn Brooks and Adrienne Rich who, like Lorde, have passed through several distinct phases of development. All three gradually developed an awareness that the political and the personal aspects of experience, while not identical, cannot be separated. Like those of Brooks and Rich, Lorde's poems of the fifties concentrate on "universal" themes such as the destruction of childhood innocence by an oppressive environment. Lorde never abandoned these concerns, but, beginning in the midsixties, she began to emphasize the relationship of personal problems to more specific social and political forces. Rather than imitating her better-known contemporaries, Lorde has worked toward a synthesis of Brooks's and Rich's emphases on the racial and sexual dimensions of these larger forces, steadfastly refusing to elevate one concern over the other. She begins "Revolution Is One Form of Social Change" with an allusion to Malcolm X's question: "What does a racist call a black Ph.D.?" The answer is "nigger." Lorde pursues the implications of the question, concluding:

when he's finished
off the big ones
he'll just change
to sex
which is
after all
where it all began.

(68)

Refusing to participate in the divisiveness discussed by Angela Davis in *Women, Race, and Class* (1981), Lorde, like other contemporary Afro-American writers such as Toni Morrison and David Bradley, recognizes the necessity of confronting racial and gender oppression simultaneously.

Lorde's confrontation focuses on several crucial issues. First, she insists on the reality of the emotions, many of them violent and painful, generated by racial and gender oppression. Second, she observes that the violence of the culture inevitably infects each individual, including herself. Frequently this generates a defensive retreat into rigid categories that, in the interest of a specious protection of self, circumscribe individual processes and distort communication. Finally, she recognizes that individuals frequently transmit this historically conditioned rigidity and defensiveness to their children, denying the children's growth and perpetuating the forces that generate the entire vicious cycle. Ultimately, Lorde insists that any hope for the future demands an acceptance of processes that nurture the self and the children.

Although, as many feminist critics have recognized, Lorde shares many of these concerns with her contemporaries, her poetry also reveals affinities with Romantic and modernist poets, most notably T. S. Eliot, William Wordsworth, and Walt Whitman. Eliot, who at first glance seems profoundly incompatible with Lorde's radical sensibility, nevertheless anticipated her use of myth as a mirror for contemporary experience. Ironically, Lorde's explorations of African and matriarchal mythologies in poems such as "The Winds of Orisha" and "To Marie, in Flight," as well as in the much more extensive mythic investigations of *The Black Unicorn,* can be seen as applications of Eliot's method to specific circumstances he never anticipated. Lorde draws more directly on the Wordsworthian motif of childhood as the emblem of higher wisdom destroyed by socially conditioned experience in poems such as "Now That I Am Forever with Child," "What My Child Learns of the Sea," and "A Child Shall Lead"—which echoes Wordsworth's "Ode: Intimations of Immortality" in its concluding lines: "And I am grown / past knowledge." Similarly, "Rites of Passage" provides an image of fathers "dying / back to the freedom of wise children" (19). For Lorde at this stage, the hope for rebirth rests on an essentially romantic dedication to the universal innocence that precedes the consciousness of patriarchal power.

As she developed, however, Lorde yoked Wordsworth's celebration of childhood to a vision of personal and social growth that recalls Whitman's exhortation to "destroy the teacher" ("Song of Myself," section 47). Like Whitman, Lorde refuses to provide simple answers, and instead offers her own development as a model for inspiration and criticism. Lorde's poem "Mentor" echoes Whitman's vision of unique individual processes interacting for mutual benefit: "I sing this for beacon now / lighting us home / each to our separate house" (67). This recognition recurs in "Relevant Is Different Points on the Circle," in which Lorde asks to be blessed with "my children's growing rebellion." She then extends her imagination to the Native American heritage, attempting to generate a synthesis reflecting her knowledge that "This is a country where other people live" (55). Although her poetry frequently resembles Whitman's, Lorde never simply imitates him. Her poems, especially after 1969, express political rage much more intensely than Whitman's ever did. Placing her commitment to process in the context of a racist, patriarchal society, Lorde insists in the closing lines of "Teacher" that poetic visions, however idealistic, must contribute to social transformation or else become part of the oppressive machinery: "Promise corrupts / what it does not invent" (54).

Lorde incorporates these affinities and influences in a poetic voice, very much a part of the Black Arts Movement, that alternates between social didacticism ("Blackstudies," "Cables to Rage or I've Been Talking on This Street Corner a Hell of a Long Time") and conversational sympathy ("Martha," "To the Girl Who Lives in a Tree"). Nowhere is the impact of this essentially oral voice clearer than in her poems concerning children, especially, though not exclusively, the female children of Afro-American mothers. In her poems of the fifties and early sixties, as in her later autobiography *Zami*, Lorde focuses on her childhood and the ambiguity of her relationship with her mother. Gradually, she turns to her own role as mother. Ultimately, Lorde seeks to contribute to the development of a liberating tradition that she images in "Generation" as a bridge purchased "with our mother's bloody gold." Resisting the temptation to provide ideological manifestos that oversimplify history, Lorde refuses to romanticize the maternal tradition. In "Story Books on a Kitchen Table," for example, the persona confronts her mother's refusal to share her personal experience. In place of her pain, the mother offers fairy tales, "where white witches rule." Lorde's description of the mother's attempt to force her daughter into an "ill-fitting harness of despair" emphasizes the failure of the dominant tradition to provide any mythology capable of clarifying the experience of black women. Even in her meditation on "the vanished mother / of a Black girl," however, Lorde identifies the potential for a tradition that encourages rather than denies growth. Following an image of her mother's "womb of pain," the persona invokes a regenerative rage: "anger reconceived me" (35). Other early poems, notably "Father, Son, and Holy Ghost," trace the mother's pain to its source in the patriarchal desire to "redefine each of our shapes." Adding to the unavoidable tension of Afro-American life, this sexual oppression generates the black mother's desire to protect her daughter by shielding her from reality. Nevertheless, Lorde clearly rejects all such attempts that condemn the daughters to the internal conflict described in "Prologue":

> whatever my mother thought would mean survival
> made her try to beat me whiter every day
> and even now the color of her bleached ambition
> still forks throughout my words.

> (59)

The following lines, however, reveal Lorde's complex awareness that the very impulses she rejects also contribute to her ability to interact with the new generation of children: "but I survived / and didn't I survive confirmed / to teach my children where her errors lay" (59). Summing up this ambivalence in "The Woman Thing," Lorde sees both acquiescence to the dehumanization of women and an indestructible strength born of suffering in the heritage of Afro-American women: "the woman thing my mother taught me / bakes off its covering of snow / like a rising blackening sun" (14).

"Black Mother Woman," originally published in *From a Land Where Other People Live* (which deserves recognition as a crucial volume in articulating the critique of the Black Arts Movement's limitations), marks Lorde's symbolic transition from daughter to mother. After noting her mother's "deceitful longings" (52) and "myths of little worth" (52), the persona presents herself to her mother as "a dark temple where your true spirit rises" (53). As resurrected Black Mother Woman, she vows to provide her own children a source of strength without denying them their own explorations. Nevertheless, the possibility of failure, personal and social, haunts Lorde in her role as mother. "To My Daughter the Junkie on a Train" conjures up the "nightmare of all sleeping mothers" and demands that, however weary from their own struggles, the mothers find strength to support the suffering children. Without this support—without access to tradition—the children will inevitably be infected by the violence of the culture. Recognizing both the threatening and the liberating potentials of maternal tradition—a theme in black women's writing discussed brilliantly in Missy Dehn Kubitschek's *Claiming the Heritage*—Lorde both hopes and fears that her children will "use my legends to shape their own language." Specifically, she imagines that they will "discard my most ancient nightmares / where the fallen gods became demon / instead of dust" (80). Lorde's ambivalence involves, on the one hand, her fear that the children may discard the entire nightmare. If they do so, they will not recognize the demonic nature of the fallen gods, implicitly rejecting their mother's pain. If, however, the children discard the nightmare *at the place where* the gods are becoming demons, they will see *only* the demonic aspect of their adversary. Unable to dismiss the fallen gods/demons as insubstantial dust, the children will remain subject to their power, eventually succumbing to the rage and despair that lead the persona in the poem to the verge of suicide.

Against these pressures and fears, Lorde constructs rituals of resistance and courage. In "New York City," she repudiates the impulse to shield her children from the city's brutality:

> I submit my children
> to the harshness and growing cold to the brutalizations
> which if survived
> will teach them strength
> or an understanding of how strength is gotten.
>
> (74)

Significantly, she seeks to provide her children with an image of a mother in the *process* of becoming rather than as a fait accompli. Lorde realizes that submitting the children to "ritual scarifications" places each mother under an absolute obligation to love them "above all others save [herself]" (74). Furthermore, it obliges her to repudiate the fallen gods unambiguously. In "Sacrifice," the persona seeks to "pull down statues of rocks from their high places" and refuses "to sleep / even one night in houses of marble" (94). The outcome of these rituals—which ultimately demand the sacrifice of personal desire—remains uncertain. What is certain is that the experiences of Lorde, of her mother, and of the battered women portrayed in "Need: A Choral of Black Women's Voices" must not be denied. Only when the pain and the anger find full acceptance, internal and external, will women, and others among the dispossessed, be free to ac-

cept their mothers, their daughters, their potential selves, and ultimately their fathers and brothers and lovers. Only then will Lorde's
words, from a poem entitled "Now," assume meaning in a way that
broadens our access to community and ancestors:

> Woman power
> is
> Black power
> is
> Human power
> is
> always feeling.
>
> (88)

If we respond to the fullness of Lorde's highly individual Afro-
American lesbian feminist maternal voice, *Chosen Poems* provides a
chart of the processes, political and personal, necessary to change
her dream—resonant with those of the Black Arts Movement and of
the long tradition of black women's writing—into a reality that could
nurture the children it now mocks and destroys.

6

Black Blues in the City:
The Voices of Gwendolyn Brooks

▲ ▲ ▲ ▲

When Stephen Henderson claims that the sonnet form "literally baffles" the "explosive words" of Claude McKay's poetry (20), he sounds a keynote for discussions of the relationship of Black writers to Euro-American cultural traditions. When George Kent compares the impact of Gwendolyn Brooks's *In the Mecca* with that of Richard Wright's *Native Son* because of the way it draws on "the varying depths of Black blues in the city" (36), he provides a similar point of departure for discussions of the relationship of Black writers to Afro-American cultural traditions. Although such statements are valuable as stimulants for discussion, they must ultimately be judged by their contribution to our understanding of poetic voices not easily pigeonholed: voices with the power and the range of Amiri Baraka, Rita Dove, Robert Hayden, Audre Lorde, or Gwendolyn Brooks.

The first of the group to receive widespread acclaim, Brooks has been honored as a "mainstream" American poet, a "new" Black poet, and a foremother of a younger generation of writers. While critics as diverse as Kent, Haki Madhubuti (Don Lee), and Dan Jaffe have worn themselves out arguing with one another's premises, they have rarely had harsh words for Brooks's poetry. How important are the critical debates? Does Jaffe's claim that Brooks is accessible to readers from the white suburbs in any way violate Madhubuti's celebration of her special relevance to the Black community? Does Brooks's statement that "I know now that I am essentially an African" in any way preclude her continued employment of the traditional techniques she mastered under the guidance of Inez Cunningham Stark (*Report* 45)?

This chapter examines Brooks's relationship to two poetic traditions with an emphasis on her prosody. The first section will focus on Brooks's relationship to Euro-American poetic traditions: her use of conventional forms and modernist techniques. The second section will consider her relationship to the Black tradition: her use of the blues as direct reference and underlying attitude. The final section— which was originally written nearly a decade after the first two (a fact visible in the shift away from the capitalization of "Black")—will examine how her prosodic mastery contributes to her vision of the Black blues of the city, of survival and love in the midst of pain.

Brooks and Euro-American Prosody

Kent defends Brooks's use of white forms on the basis of her "intuitive feel" for the appropriate form and her ability to avoid the "rigidity" that he sees as a part of the English formal tradition. Certainly Brooks avoids "rigidity" in employing traditional stanzaic forms and metrical techniques to deal with the common material of Black life. But Brooks's practice should be understood in relation to the general loosening of the sonnet's traditional structural limitations that had already been carried out in the early twentieth century by such poets as E. A. Robinson, Robert Frost, and e. e. cummings. As Harvey Gross demonstrates, the "intuitive feel for form" is the prime requirement of any poet, white or Black, working within any poetic tradition. The crucial issue concerns Brooks's ability to exploit the possibilities of the forms with which she chooses to work.

A list of some of Brooks's poems in traditional forms indicates her thorough familiarity with Euro-American traditions and suggests that her "explosive words" lose little of their power because of the association. Indeed, the sonnet form provides the vehicle for many of her most effective works (the "Gay Chaps at the Bar" sequence, the "Children of the Poor" series, and powerful individual poems such as "the rites for Cousin Vit" and "The Egg Boiler"). Although her success with the form has been less consistent, Brooks has also used the ballad stanza repeatedly ("Of De Witt Williams on His Way to Lincoln Cemetery" and "The Last Quatrain of the Ballad of Emmett Till"). She uses both terza rima ("Kitchenette Building") and individual tercets (poem X of "The Womanhood" in *Annie Allen*) effectively. Although no poem is written entirely in couplets, Brooks frequently uses them within individual poems, often to emphasize final lines ("the independent man" and "obituary"). Perhaps the most "exotic" of Brooks's traditional forms is the modified seven-line rhyme royal stanza of "The Anniad." In addition to using these stanzas in individual poems, Brooks frequently mixes different stanzas in the same poem. For example, "Old Laughter" contains both ballad stanzas and tercets. Later poems such as *In the Mecca,* while basically free verse, sometimes use traditional stanzaic patterns for specific effects. "The Ballad of Edie Barrow" in *In the Mecca* and the couplet of the concluding section of *Riot* are examples.

Within each of these traditional forms, Brooks claims the modern prerogative of freely varying individual foot and line length. "The old-marrieds" in *A Street in Bronzeville* (the first poem in Brooks's first volume) demonstrates her metrical freedom. The basic meter of the poem is iambic hexameter, but scansion shows that only one line conforms perfectly to the pattern:

> x / x / x / x / x / x x /
> But in the crowding darkness not a word did they say,
>
> x x / x / x / x / x / x / x /
> Though the pretty-coated birds had piped so lightly all the day.
>
> x / x / x / x x x / x / /
> And he had seen the lovers in the little side-streets.
>
> x / x / x / x / x / x /
> And she had heard the morning stories clogged with sweets.
>
> x x / x / x / x x x / / x x /
> It was quite a time for loving. It was midnight. It was May.
>
> x x x / x / x / x / x x /
> But in the crowding darkness not a word did they say.

(Blacks 19)

There is certainly nothing revolutionary about the prosody, but its variations on the metrical base are quietly effective. The substitutions of anapests for iambs in the final feet of the first and last lines emphasize the pause, the silent quality of the old-marrieds' life. The spondee in the final foot of line three stresses the pressing environment, the side-streets of Bronzeville that control the emotional tone of their life. The use of pyrrhic feet creates a lightness of rhythm matching the temporary romantic thoughts of line five. Even line four, the one line that scans as unbroken iambic hexameter, is varied by the tonal quality of "clogged," which slows the reader slightly, a rhythmic effect appropriate to the meaning of the word.

Or consider the first six lines of the sonnet "the rites for Cousin Vit":

> / x x / / / x / x /
> Carried her unprotesting out the door.
>
> / / x / x / x x / / (/)
> Kicked back the casket-stand. But it can't hold her.
>
> x / x / x / x x x / (/)
> That stuff and satin aiming to enfold her,

<pre>
   x   /   x / x   /   x   /   x   /
The lid's contrition nor the bolts before.
   /   /   /   /   /   /   / x   /   x   /
Oh oh. Too much. Too much. Even now, surmise,
   x   / x x   x   /   /   /   /   /
She rises in the sunshine. There she goes.
</pre>

(125)

Within the bounds of a relatively strict form, Brooks takes a large risk in using three consecutive spondees at the beginning of line five. The heavy stress, which is one of Brooks's typical "signatures," perfectly expresses the agonized sense of constriction straining to break free. Similarly, the use of eleven, rather than ten, syllable lines in lines two and three suggests the expansive urge that lies at the poem's center.

Brooks manipulates rhyme with extraordinary effectiveness in both "tight" and "free" forms. The rhyme schemes of the five sonnets of "The Children of the Poor" series demonstrate Brooks's ability to vary forms within one overall structural pattern. Each of the sonnets is divided in an octave-sestet pattern that serves both formal and thematic purposes. Each octave follows an abba abba rhyme scheme, establishing the basic unity of the series both as a thematic construct and as a structural entity. The sestets, however, follow rhyme schemes of ccddee, cdcdee, cdcdee, cddcee, and cddece, underlining the diversity of the individual experience within the general framework.

Brooks's comment on the off-rhyme sonnet sequence "Gay Chaps at the Bar" indicates her awareness of the significance of varieties of rhyme. She composed the poems as "a sonnet sequence in off-rhyme, because I felt it was an off-rhyme situation—I did think of that. I first wrote the one sonnet [sonnet one of the sequence] without thinking of extensions ... then I said, there are other things to say about what's going on at the front and all, and I'll write more poems ... and I felt it would be good to have them all in the same form, because it would serve my purposes throughout" (*Report* 156).

The closeness of the end rhymes varies throughout the sequence, always reflecting the degree to which the persona has managed to come to terms with the jarring experience that surrounds him. Consider the end couplets of the sonnets "my dreams, my works, must wait till after hell":

> My taste will not have turned insensitive
> To honey and bread old purity could love;

(*Blacks* 66)

"God works in a mysterious way":

> Step forth in splendor, mortify our wolves.
> Or we assume a sovereignty ourselves;
>
> (72)

"love note II: flags":

> Like a sweet mournfulness, or like a dance.
> Or like the tender struggle of a fan;
>
> (74)

and the sestet of the series' final sonnet, "the progress":

> But inward grows a soberness, an awe,
> A fear, a deepening hollow through the cold.
> For even if we come out standing up
> How shall we smile, congratulate: and how
> Settle in chairs? Listen, listen. The step
> Of iron feet again. And again wild.
>
> (75)

In the first two examples, the speaker desperately attempts, in the one case optimistically and in the other pessimistically, to come to a clear apprehension of his situation. His resolve to maintain his ability to love despite the horror of war is extremely artificial, a fact Brooks underlines with the close juxtaposition and imperfect rhyming of "insensitive" and "love." In the second example, the speaker has been forced to confront the illusion-shattering power of war and demands that God prove his presence. His bitter rejection of all meaning, which can no more deal with the complexity of the experience than the simple resolve of "my dreams," is emphasized by the proximity and imperfect rhyme of "wolves" and "ourselves." In neither case does Brooks endorse the persona's attitude with the synthetic technical device of an exact rhyme. Rather she draws our attention to their inadequacy. "Love note II," the penultimate sonnet, presents a more experienced persona, who has resolved to love in spite of a full recognition of the horrors of war. The rhyming of "dance" and "fan" is appropriate. The sound value of "dan" and "fan" is almost exact, indicating Brooks's tacit acceptance of the resolve. But the final sound (-ce) is missing from the final rhyme, reminding the reader that the resolve, as the persona realizes, is somewhat strained and artificial. The final sonnet, "the progress," abandons the couplet altogether in order to stress the continuing emotionally disruptive power of the war despite its increasing distance in time. The rhyme of "cold" and "wild" reflects Brooks's final statement on the nature of war and stresses the inability of the mind to come to terms adequately with the radically apocalyptic experience.

Brooks's relationship to white "modernist" traditions is more difficult to assess than her use of traditional "strict" forms. She has acknowledged that she has studied and been influenced by the work of modernists such as Eliot, Pound, cummings, and Joyce. Kent lists irony, imagery, sensitivity to the musical phrase, and free verse as areas of modernist influence on Brooks's poetry. Merely glancing through her work reveals the obvious use of irony (light irony in "Hattie Scott" and "Maxie Allen" and a more pointed irony in "A Bronzeville Mother Loiters in Mississippi. Meanwhile, a Mississippi Mother Burns Bacon."), and condensed imagery ("Negro Hero" and "The Anniad"). But Brooks's use of musical phrase (which I take to mean cadence in the modernist sense) bears close examination and reveals the extent of her control over modernist devices.

There is an unmistakable and appropriate cadence to Mrs. Sallie's observation of St. Julia and Prophet Williams in *In the Mecca:*

<pre>
      x / x / x
      And Mrs. Sallie

     x / x / x /   x / x /
     all innocent of saints and signatures

      /   x   x /   x / x   x /
     nods and consents, content to endorse

      /   x x /   x (x) x /   x   /
     Lord as an incense and a vintage. Speaks

     x / x   / x   x   x (x) / / x
     to Prophet Williams, young beyond St. Julia,

      x   /   x   / x   / x   /   x   /
     and rich with Bible, pimples, pout: who reeks

     x   /   x   x x / x / x   /   x
     with lust for his disciple, is an engine

     x   / x   /   / x   x   / x /
     of candid steel hugging combustibles.

      x   /   x   / x / x x
     His wife she was a skeleton.

      x   /   x   / x /
     His wife she was a bone

       /   x   x
     (Kinswomen!

       /   x   x
     Kinswomen!)

     / x / x /
     Ida died alone.
</pre>

(408)

The passage begins in a fairly standard blank verse line as Sallie observes St. Julia's defensive religious raptures. (Almost all of the attitudes held by characters in *In the Mecca* serve as defenses against confronting the harshness of ghetto reality.) But as the focus shifts mentally to Prophet Williams, the rhythm begins to break down, the sounds become harsher. Where the vowel sounds in the section associated with St. Julia are mostly broad *a*'s or *o*'s, the vowel sounds associated with Prophet Williams are jumbled with a tendency toward the guttural *u*'s of "hugging combustibles." The focus shifts further, to Prophet Williams's dead wife Ida, destroyed by his personal "defense." The rhythm becomes chantlike, building to the anguished repeated cry of "Kinswomen" (the falling dactylic feet emphasize the futility of Ida's plea). The finality of "Ida died alone" (a headless iambic trimeter line, placing maximum stress on the key syllables "I", "died," and "lone") is lent an additional poignancy by the nearly "nursery-rhyme" effect of the internal rhyme of consecutive feet in "Ida died a-." The final syllable provides both metrical and thematic finality.

Even in this free verse, Brooks relies heavily on "traditional" devices such as internal rhyme and alliteration. The numerous sibilants of the section dealing with Mrs. Sallie unify lines 1-4 both thematically and formally. The *s* sound links "Sallie," "saints," "consent," and "incense," showing the progressive ratification of Julia's life. The internal rhyme of "consents" and "content" stresses the necessity of Julia's acquiescence to her withdrawal. In this passage, as elsewhere in Brooks's poetry, two metrical patterns recur frequently, providing a kind of poetic "signature" for her work. The first of these patterns is ////, or a large number of heavy stresses in close proximity. These heavy stresses are often used to emphasize concrete detail as in *In the Mecca,* or severe emotional strain, as in "the rites for Cousin Vit." The cumulative effect of these stresses is to create a feeling of extreme pressure and intensity in the reader's mind. The second signature pattern is xxx/, or a large number of syllables with no stress or only extremely light stresses. This general pattern, of course, is used by many poets to create a feeling of colloquial speech rhythms. The combination of this technique with heavily stressed passages, however, creates a unique feeling in Brooks's free verse. The alternation creates a feeling of an underlying tension, or uncertainty, matching Brooks's observations on the nature of Black urban life.

In the Mecca is typical of Brooks's tendency in her later work to employ free verse rather than traditional stanzaic forms. While Henderson would probably see this as her declaration of independence from the European tradition, at no time has she abandoned the venerable accentual patterns (and equally venerable variations) of the tradition. She remembers the lessons she mastered during the 1940s and 1950s and remains willing to use her knowledge whenever it contributes to her poetic effectiveness.

Brooks and the Blues

When in doubt, the unofficial critical truism concerning Black writing goes, say it comes from the blues. While most readers would agree in some sense with the basic idea, Henderson's introduction to *Understanding the New Black Poetry: Black Speech and Music as Poetic References* remains one of the most specific discussions of the relationships between Afro-American music and prosody. Henderson lists ten ways in which Black poets make use of their musical heritage, but the list can be reduced to four basic areas:

1. Employing specific lyrical or musical patterns.
2. Alluding to musicians or pieces of music.
3. Using the poem as a chart lending itself to improvisation.
4. Referring to an attitude toward experience traditionally associated with the blues.

The basic musical pattern associated with the blues is the twelve-bar, three-line structure. The first line states the situation; the second line restates the first line; and the third line functions as a comment or expansion. A typical example is Big Bill Broonzy's "Hollerin' the Blues": "Yes, I'm settin on this old stump, baby, got a worried mind. / Yes, I'm settin on this stump, baby, I've got a worried mind. / Yeah, I'm gonna find my baby, Lord, or lose my life tryin." Langston Hughes, who worked both as a lyricist and a poet and pioneered the acceptance of the blues in the Black poetic establishment, frequently worked with this basic pattern. Both of the actual blues (musical compositions) included in *The Langston Hughes Reader* follow the AAB pattern, as do all five poems titled "blues" in Hughes's *Selected Poems.* Similarly, the two poems titled "blues" in Henderson's anthology follow Hughes's lead. So it is apparent that actual lyrical patterns do play a role in the Black poetic tradition. But is it a central role? And does it help us understand Brooks?

Only one of Brooks's poems, "Queen of the Blues," attempts to create a blues feeling through the use of lines that could actually be blues lyrics in the classic sense. It is instructive to note that Brooks does not allow the lyrics to stand on their own. Instead, following Hughes's practice in "The Weary Blues" and anticipating later works such as Sherley Anne Williams's celebration of Bessie Smith in *Some One Sweet Angel Chile,* she establishes a context within which a character in the poem sings the blues. Although Brooks breaks her stanzas into seven, eight, or nine lines in order to manipulate emphasis by visually isolating words for the reader (such as "Kitchens" in the example below), they obviously conform to the basic AAB pattern. To anyone familiar with the classic blues, Brooks's lines immediately evoke echoes of musical settings. When one attempts to scan them in traditional terms, however, a tension becomes obvious between the accents that would result from a reading of the lines as printed poetry and the accents that one "hears" as a result of subjective memories of the music evoked by the poem. In the following stanza of Brooks's poem, "straight" scansion is indicated by the traditional / and x markings while the musical accent is indicated by ø:

> x   x   ø   x x   ø x
> I was good to my daddy.
>
> ø   /   /   x   ø
> Gave him all my dough.
>
> / / /   x   ø x   x   ø x
> I say, I was good to my daddy.
>
> / ø   x   / x x   ø
> I gave him all of my dough.
>
> /   ø x   x   /   /
> Scrubbed hard in them white folk's
>
> ø   x
> Kitchens
>
> x   x   ø   x   / x
> Till my knees was rusty
>
> /   ø
> And so.

$$(58)$$

While all of the musical accents fall on syllables that also bear spoken accents, there are a great number of normal accents that are musically unimportant. In the actual performance the singer would quite probably place minor accents on most, but not all, of the normally accented syllables. It is apparent that there is a significant gap between the emphasis of the musical blues and their poetic recreation.

There are, however, traditional sanctions for an "expanded" form of the basic blues pattern. Mississippi John Hurt's "Stack O'Lee Blues," for example, mixes three-, four-, and five-line stanzas and never employs the AAB form. Many of Bessie Smith's blues have more in common structurally with the traditional English ballad than they do with the classic blues ("Midnight Blues" is one of many examples). Archie Shepp has mixed jazz and blues forms in "Money Blues," which retains a basic three-part structure but can be reduced to an AAB pattern only through extreme imaginative overreaching.

So the blues can be legitimately extended beyond a strict formal definition. But this observation would indicate that almost any of Brooks's poems could be considered a "blues" in the extended sense. While probably accurate, this gives us almost no help in determining the specific function of the Black musical tradition in her prosody.

Similarly, Brooks's allusions to musicians and songs from the Black musical heritage do little to explain the presence of the "blues feeling" in her poetry. She often uses these allusions to differentiate her Black characters' attitudes and environments from those of the surrounding white society, as in these lines from "The Sundays of Satin-Legs Smith":

> The Lonesome Blues, the Long-Lost Blues, I Want A
> Big Fat Mama. Down these sore avenues
> Comes no Saint-Saens, no piquant elusive Grieg,
> And not Tschaikovsky's wayward eloquence
> And not the shapely tender drift of Brahms.
> But could he love them? Since a man must bring
> To music what his mother spanked him for
> When he was two: bits of forgotten hate,
> Devotion: whether or not his mattress hurts.
>
> (45–46)

But there is little difference between the use of musical allusion in those blank verse lines and in these free verse lines from *Riot:*

> The young men run.
> They will not steal Bing Crosby but will steal
> Melvin Van Peebles who made Lillie
> a thing of Zampoughi a thing of red wiggles and trebles
> (and I know there are twenty wire stalks sticking out of her head
> as her underfed haunches jerk jazz).
>
> (473)

It appears that mere allusion functions thematically rather than technically and that it can be adapted to forms with their roots in any tradition with equal, if different, effect.

Perhaps the most useful suggestion Henderson offers is that the blues can be evoked by the poet's relationship to a general attitude toward experience. But even this suggestion poses difficulties and forces one to attempt to determine the actual meaning of the blues tradition in Black experience. Ralph Ellison, writing on Wright's *Black Boy,* which, significantly, can be considered a "blues" in neither the formal nor the allusive sense, defines the blues as "an impulse to keep the painful details and episodes of a brutal experience alive in one's aching consciousness, to finger its jagged grain, and to transcend it, not by the consolation of philosophy but by squeezing from it a near-tragic, near-comic lyricism" (*Shadow* 78). Langston Hughes, whose writings on the blues Ellison probably knew, is in basic agreement when he writes: "Sad as Blues may be, there's almost always something humorous about them—even if it's the kind of humor that laughs to keep from crying" (*Reader* 160).

These kinds of tragicomic situations dealing with the painful details of experience are quite common in Brooks's poetry. From the first poem in *A Street in Bronzeville*, "the old-marrieds," through the individual vignettes of *In the Mecca*, Brooks's primary concern is precisely coming to terms with the pain of a harsh reality, the attempt to overcome helplessness and confusion. The following lines from *In the Mecca* echo the "bluesy" feeling of the early sections of *Black Boy* that inspired Ellison's definition:

> Emmett and Cap and Casey
> are skin wiped over bones
> for lack of chub and chocolate
> and ice cream cones,
> for lack of English muffins
> and boysenberry jam.
> What shall their redeemer be?
> Greens and hocks of ham.
> For each his greens and hock of ham
> And a spoon of sweet potato.
>
> (*Blacks* 414)

This resigned lyrical attitude toward experience, however, came under heavy attack from some critics associated with the Black Arts Movement. While praising the lasting beauty of the blues, Ron Karenga asserted that "the blues are invalid; for they teach resignation, in a word acceptance of reality—and we have come to change reality" (36). Baraka, conversely, presented a strong defense of the blues tradition in his essay "The Changing Same (R&B and New Black Music)." Presenting an "organic" theory of Black music, Baraka argues that "the songs, the music, changed as the people did." The blues, Baraka continues, "is, it seems, the deepest expression of memory. Experience re/feeling. It is the racial memory. . . . The Blues (impulse) lyric (song) is ever descriptive of a plane of evolution, a direction" (115). The specific content of the blues, in this scheme, is a function of a fluid reality rather than a determinant of attitude, making them much more adaptable to a militant Black perspective.

Brooks's later poems support Baraka's contention. Without sacrificing any of her characteristic lyrical emphasis on painful past experience, she has put an increasingly greater emphasis on Black pride and assertion. Her 1975 poem "The Boy Died in My Alley" typifies her perspective. A Black youth has been murdered in the alley behind the speaker's home. When asked by a policeman if she heard the shot that killed him, the speaker's first reaction is a feeling of historical inevitability and resignation:

> The Shot that killed him yes I heard
> as I heard the Thousand shots before;
> careening tinnily down the nights
> across my years and arteries.

When pressed further by the policeman's questions, however, the speaker begins to recognize her own involvement in the youth's death, an involvement stemming from exactly the passive attitude Karenga associates with the blues tradition:

> I have always heard him deal with death
> I have always heard the shout, the volley.
> I have closed my heart-ears late and early
> And I have killed him ever.
>
> I joined the Wild and killed him
> with knowledgeable unknowing.

But the act of realization is also an act of dissociation from the passivity of the tradition. At the poem's climax the speaker perceives the essential bond linking all Black people, while maintaining the lyrical blues attitude toward the immediate generative experience:

> He cried not only "Father!"
> But "Mother!
> Sister!
> Brother!"
> The cry climbed up the alley
> It went up to the wind.
> It hung upon the heaven
> for a long
> stretch-strain of Moment.

The final lines quietly endorse the blues's confrontation of the past painful experience, but at the same time hold the promise of the transformation hinted at in the immediately preceding lines. Implicitly they promise that the insight derived from the blues can be transformed into a direct form of resistance: "The red floor of my alley / is a special speech to me" (*Beckonings* 5–6).

In addition to demonstrating the possibilities for further constructive development of the blues tradition, "The Boy Died in My Alley"
illustrates Brooks's continuing ability to exploit the potential of Euro-
American poetic techniques. The diction and vocabulary are standard English and the rhythm is based on the iambic foot with the
numerous anapestic and spondaic interpolations that mark Brooks's
poetic signature. But the feeling and message (while certainly "universal" in their implications) are unmistakably Black. The poem, like
Gwendolyn Brooks, transcends easy categorization and demonstrates
that the ultimate importance of any tradition, Black or white, is in its
contribution to the tenor of the individual poetic voice.

Perhaps Brooks best states her own position in her tribute to Paul
Robeson, whose name is inextricably associated with both the Black
heritage (through his rendition of numerous spirituals) and the
white tradition (through his performances in plays by Shakespeare
and O'Neill). Brooks recognizes that Robeson's art, too, transcends
categorization. Even when functioning in the traditionally resigned
blues form, Robeson's is

> The adult Voice
> forgoing Rolling River,
> forgoing tearful tale of bale and barge
> and other symptoms of an old despond.

He takes the core of the Black tradition and transforms it into

> Warning, in music-words
> devout and large
> that we are each other's
> harvest . . .
>
> we are each other's
> magnitude and bond.
>   (*Blacks* 496)

Love in the Warpland

While the subject of these lines is Paul Robeson, it as easily, and as
accurately, could have been Gwendolyn Brooks. Even as she envisions
the harvest of black love, Brooks uses her mastery of poetic forms
to mirror the uncertainties of characters or personae who embrace
conventional attitudes to defend themselves against internal and external chaos. Whatever form she chooses, Brooks consistently focuses
on the struggle of people to find and express love, usually associated

with the family, in the midst of a hostile environment. In constructing their defenses and seeking love, they often experience a disfiguring pain. Brooks devotes much of her energy to defining and responding to the elusive forces, variously psychological and social, which inflict this pain. Increasingly in her later poetry, Brooks traces the pain to political sources and expands her concept of the family to encompass all black people. Even while speaking of the social situation of blacks in a voice crafted primarily for blacks, however, Brooks maintains the complex awareness of the multiple perspectives relevant to any given experience. Her ultimate concern is to encourage every individual, black or white, to "conduct your blooming in the noise and whip of the whirlwind" (456).

A deep concern with the everyday circumstances of black people living within the whirlwind characterizes many of Brooks's most popular poems. From the early "Of De Witt Williams on His Way to Lincoln Cemetery" and "A Song in the Front Yard," through the "The Life of Lincoln West" and "Sammy Chester Leaves 'Godspell' and Visits UPWARD BOUND on a Lake Forest Lawn, Bringing West Afrika," she focuses on characters whose experiences merge the idiosyncratic and the typical. She frequently draws on black musical forms to underscore the communal resonance of a character's outwardly undistinguished life. By tying the refrain of "Swing Low, Sweet Chariot" to the repeated phrase "Plain black boy," Brooks transforms De Witt Williams into an Everyman figure. Brooks describes his personal search for love in the poolrooms and dance halls, but stresses the representative quality of his experience by starting and ending the poem with the musical allusion.

"We Real Cool," perhaps Brooks's single best-known poem, subjects a similarly representative experience to an intricate technical and thematic scrutiny, at once loving and critical. The poem is only twenty-four words long, including eight repetitions of the word "we." It is suggestive that the subtitle of "We Real Cool" specifies the presence of only seven pool players at the "Golden Shovel" (331). The eighth "we" suggests that poet and reader share, on some level, the desperation of the group-voice that Brooks transmits. The final sentence, "We / die soon," restates the carpe diem motif in the vernacular of Chicago's South Side.

On one level, "We Real Cool" appears simply to catalog the experiences of a group of dropouts content to "sing sin" in all available forms. An intricate ambiguity enters into the poem, however, revolving around the question of how to accent the word "we," which ends every line except the last one, providing the beat for the poem's jazz rhythm. Brooks has said that she intended that the "we" *not* be accented. Read in this way, the poem takes on a slightly distant and ironic tone, emphasizing the artificiality of the group identity that involves the characters in activities offering early death as the only release from pain. Conversely, the poem can be read with a strong accent on each "we," affirming the group identity. Although the experience still ends with early death, the pool players metamorphose into defiant heroes determined to resist the alienating environment. Their confrontation with experience is felt, if not articulated, as existentially pure. Neither pool players, poet, nor reader can be *sure* which stress is valid.

Brooks crafts the poem, however, to hint at an underlying coherence in the defiance. The intricate internal rhyme scheme echoes the sound of nearly every word. Not only do the first seven lines end with "we," but the penultimate words of each line in each stanza also rhyme (cool/school, late/straight, sin/gin, June/soon). In addition, the alliterated consonant of the last line of each stanza is repeated in the first line of the next stanza (Left/lurk, Strike/sin, gin/June) and the first words of each line in the middle two stanzas are connected through consonance (Lurk/strike, Sing/thin). The one exception to this suggestive texture of sound is the word "Die," which introduces both a new vowel and a new consonant into the final line, breaking the rhythm and subjecting the performance to ironic revaluation. Ultimately, the power of the poem derives from the tension between the celebratory and the ironic perspectives on the lives of the plain black boys struggling for a sense of connection.

A similar struggle informs many of Brooks's poems in more traditional forms, including "The Mother," a powerful exploration of the impact of an abortion on the woman who has chosen to have it. Brooks states that the mother "decides that *she,* rather than her world, will kill her children" (*Report* 184). Within the poem itself, however, the motivations remain unclear. Although the poem's position in Brooks's first book, *A Street in Bronzeville,* suggests that the persona is black, the poem neither supports nor denies a racial identification. Along with the standard English syntax and diction, this suggests that "The Mother," like poems such as "The Egg Boiler," "Callie Ford," and "A Light and Diplomatic Bird," was designed to speak directly of an emotional, rather than a social, experience, and to be as accessible to whites as to blacks. Recreating the anguished perspective of a persona unsure whether she is victim or victimizer, Brooks directs her readers' attention to the complex emotions of her potential Everywoman.

"The Mother" centers on the persona's alternating desire to take and to evade responsibility for the abortion. Resorting to ambiguous grammatical structures, the persona repeatedly qualifies her acceptance with "if" clauses ("If I sinned," "If I stole your births"). She refers to the lives of the children as matters of fate ("Your luck") and backs away from admitting that a death has taken place by claiming that the children "were never made" (22). Her use of the second person pronoun to refer to herself in the first stanza reveals her desire to distance herself from her present pain. This attempt, however, fails. The opening line undercuts the evasion with the reality of memory: "Abortions will not let you forget" (21). At the start of the second stanza, the pressure of memory forces the persona to shift to the more honest first person pronoun. A sequence of spondees referring to the children ("damp small pulps," "dim killed children," "dim dears") interrupts the lightly stressed anapestic-iambic meter that dominates the first stanza. The concrete images of "scurrying off ghosts" and "devouring" children with loving gazes gain power when contrasted with the dimness of the mother's life and perceptions. Similarly, the first stanza's end-stopped couplets, reflecting the persona's simplistic attempt to recapture an irrevocably lost mother-child relationship through an act of imagination, give way to the intricate enjambment and complex rhyme scheme of the second stanza, which highlight the mother's inability to find rest.

The rhyme scheme—and Brooks rivals Robert Frost and W. B. Yeats in her ability to employ various types of rhyme for thematic impact—underscores the persona's struggle to come to terms with her action. The rhymes in the first stanza insist on her self-doubt, contrasting images of tenderness and physical substance with those of brutality and insubstantiality (forget/get, hair/air, beat/sweet). The internal rhyme of "never," repeated four times, and "remember," "workers," and "singers" further stresses the element of loss. In the second stanza, Brooks provides no rhymes for the end words "children" in line 11 and "deliberate" in line 21. This device draws attention to the persona's failure to answer the crucial questions of whether her children did in fact exist and of whether her own actions were in fact deliberate (and perhaps criminal). The last seven lines of the stanza end with hard *d* sounds as the persona struggles to forge her conflicting thoughts into a unified perspective. If Brooks offers coherence, though, it is emotional rather than intellectual. Fittingly, the *d* rhymes and off-rhymes focus on physical and emotional pain (dead/instead/made/afraid/said/died/cried). Brooks provides no easy answer to the anguished question: "How is the truth to be told?" (22). The persona's concluding cry of "I loved you / All" rings with desperation. It is futile but it is not a lie. To call "The Mother" an anti-abortion poem distorts its impact. Clearly portraying the devastating effects of the persona's action, it by no means condemns her or lacks sympathy. Like many of Brooks's characters, the mother is a person whose desire to love far outstrips her ability to cope with her circumstances and serves primarily to heighten her sensitivity to pain.

Perhaps the most significant change in Brooks's poetry following her nationalist conversion involves her analysis of the origins of this pervasive pain. Rather than attributing the suffering to some unavoidable psychological condition, Brooks's later poetry indicts social institutions for their role in its perpetuation. The poems in her first two volumes frequently portray characters incapable of articulating the origins of their pain. Although the absence of any father in "The Mother" suggests sociological forces leading to the abortion, such analysis is purely speculative. The only certainty is that the mother, the persona of the sonnet sequence "The Children of the Poor," and the speaker in the brilliant sonnet "My Dreams, My Works, Must Wait Till after Hell" share the fear that their pain will render them insensitive to love. The final poem of *Annie Allen,* "Men of Careful Turns," intimates that the defenders of a society that refuses to admit its full humanity bear responsibility for reducing the powerless to "grotesque toys" (*Blacks* 140). Despite this implicit accusation, however, Brooks perceives no "magic" capable of remedying the situation. She concludes the volume on a note of irresolution typical of her early period: "We are lost, must / Wizard a track through our own screaming weed" (140). The track, at this stage, remains spiritual rather than political.

Beyond the Warpland: Images of Black Heroism

Although the early volumes include occasional poems concerning articulate political participants such as "Negro Hero," Brooks's later work frequently centers on specific black political heroes such as Malcolm X, Paul Robeson, John Killens, and Don Lee. Since the early sixties, a growing anger informs poems as diverse as the ironic "The Chicago *Defender* Sends a Man to Little Rock," the near-baroque "The Lovers of the Poor," the imagistically intricate "Riders to the Blood-Red Wrath," and the satiric "Riot." This anger originates in Brooks's perception that the social structures of white society value material possessions and abstract ideas of prestige more highly than individual human beings. The anger culminates in her brilliant narrative poem *In the Mecca,* concerning the death of a young girl in a Chicago housing project, and in the three sermons on the "Warpland."

The "Warpland" poems mark Brooks's departure from the traditions of Euro-American poetry and thought represented by T. S. Eliot's *The Waste Land*. The sequence typifies her post-1967 poetry, in which she abandons traditional stanzaic forms, applying her technical expertise to a relatively colloquial free verse. This technical shift parallels her rejection of the philosophical premises of Euro-American culture. Brooks refuses to accept the inevitability of cultural decay, arguing that the "waste" of Eliot's vision exists primarily because of our "warped" perceptions. Seeing white society as the embodiment of these distortions, Brooks embraces her blackness as a potential counterbalancing force. The first "Sermon on the Warpland" opens with Ron Karenga's black nationalist credo: "The fact that we are black is our ultimate reality" (451). Clearly, in Brooks's view, blackness is not simply a physical fact; it is primarily a metaphor for the possibility of love. As her poem "Two Dedications" indicates, Brooks sees the Euro-American tradition represented by the Chicago Picasso as inhumanly cold, mingling guilt and innocence, meaningfulness and meaninglessness, almost randomly. This contrasts sharply with her inspirational image of the Wall of Respect on the South Side. To Brooks, true art assumes meaning from the people who interact with it. The Wall helps to redefine black reality, rendering the "dispossession beakless" (445). Rather than contemplating the site of destruction, the politically aware black art Brooks embraces should inspire the black community to face its pain and renew determination to remove its sources. The final "Sermon on the Warpland" concludes with the image of a black phoenix rising from the ashes of the Chicago riot. No longer content to accept the unresolved suffering of "The Mother," Brooks forges a black nationalist politics and poetics of love.

Although her political vision influences every aspect of her work, Brooks maintains a strong sense of enduring individual pain and is aware that nationalism offers no simple panacea. "The Blackstone Rangers," a poem concerning one of the most powerful Chicago street gangs, rejects as simplistic the argument, occasionally advanced by writers associated with the Black Arts Movement, that no important distinction exists between the personal and the political experience. Specifically, Brooks doubts the corollary that politically desirable activity will inevitably increase the person's ability to love. Dividing "The Blackstone Rangers" into three segments—"As Seen by Disciplines," "The Leaders," and "Gang Girls: A Rangerette"— Brooks stresses the tension between perspectives. After rejecting the sociological-penal perspective of part 1, she remains suspended between the uncomprehending affirmation of the Rangers as a kind of government-in-exile in part 2 and the recognition of a young black woman's continuing pain in part 3.

Brooks undercuts the description of the Rangers as "sores in the city / that do not want to heal" ("As Seen by Disciplines" 446) through the use of off-rhyme and a jazz rhythm reminiscent of "We Real Cool." The disciplines, both academic and corrective, fail to perceive any coherence in the Rangers' experience. Correct in their assumption that the Rangers do not want to "heal" themselves, the disciplines fail to perceive the gang's strong desire to "heal" the sick society. Brooks suggests an essential coherence in the Rangers' experience through the sound texture of part 1. Several of the sound patterns echoing through the brief stanza point to a shared response to pain (there/thirty/ready, raw/sore/corner). Similarly, the accent cluster on "Black, raw, ready" (446) draws attention to the pain and potential power of the Rangers. The descriptive voice of the disciplines, however, provides only relatively weak end rhymes (are/corner, ready/city), testifying to the inability of the distanced, presumably white, observers to comprehend the experiences they describe. The shifting, distinctively black, jazz rhythm further emphasizes the distance between the voices of observers and participants. Significantly, the voice of the disciplines finds no rhyme at all for its denial of the Rangers' desire to "heal."

The denial contrasts sharply with the tempered affirmation of the voice in part two that emphasizes the leaders' desire to "cancel, cure, and curry" (447). Again, internal rhymes and sound echoes suffuse the section. In the first stanza, the voice generates thematically significant rhymes, connecting Ranger leader *"Bop"* (whose name draws attention to the jazz rhythm, which is even more intricate, though less obvious, in this section than in part 1) and the militant black leader *"Rap"* Brown, both nationalists whose "country is a Nation on no *map*" (447). "Bop" and "Rap," of course, do not rhyme perfectly, attesting to Brooks's awareness of gang leaders' limitations. Her image of the leaders as "Bungled trophies" further reinforces her ambivalence. The only full rhyme in the final two stanzas of the section is the repeated "night." The leaders, canceling the racist association of darkness with evil, "translate" the image of blackness into a "monstrous pearl or grace" (448). The section affirms the Blackstone Rangers' struggle; it does not pretend to comprehend fully the emotional texture of their lives.

Certain that the leaders possess the power to cancel the disfiguring images of the disciplines, Brooks remains unsure of their ability to create an alternate environment where love can blossom. Mary Ann, the "Gang Girl" of part 3, shares much of the individual pain of the characters of Brooks's early poetry despite her involvement with the Rangers. "A rose in a whiskey glass" (449), she continues to live with the knowledge that her "laboring lover" risks the same sudden death as the pool players of "We Real Cool." Forced to suppress a part of her awareness—she knows not to ask where her lover got the diamond he gives her—she remains emotionally removed even while making love. In place of fully realized love, she accepts "The props and niceties of non-loneliness" (450). The final line of the poem emphasizes the ambiguity of both Mary Ann's situation and Brooks's perspective. Recommending acceptance of "the rhymes of Leaning," the line responds to the previous stanza's question concerning whether love will have a "gleaning." The full rhyme paradoxically suggests acceptance of off-rhyme, of love consummated leaning against an alley wall, without expectation of safety or resolution. Given the political tension created by the juxtaposition of the disciplines and the leaders, the "Gang Girl" can hope to find no sanctuary beyond the reach of the whirlwind. Her desperate love, the more moving for its precariousness, provides the only near-adequate response to the pain that Brooks continues to see as the primary fact of life.

7

Blues for T. S. Eliot and Langston Hughes: Melvin B. Tolson's Afro-Modernist Aesthetic

▲ ▲ ▲ ▲

Contemplating the "bifacial nature" of Hideho Heights's poetry, Melvin B. Tolson provides an appropriate image of the tension in his own work between "the racial ballad in the public domain / and the private poem in the modern vein" (145). Throughout *Harlem Gallery*, Tolson's two faces, as elusive and inseparable as those of Hideho and the Curator, or Mister Starks and John Laugart, gaze toward a re-vision of aesthetic perspectives that have typically been seen as incompatible. Confronting a cultural context that assumes and at times enforces the reality of racial (black-white) and aesthetic (popular art–high culture) distinctions, Tolson reveals the false dichotomies as at best simplistic and at worst destructive. Just as he grants the Black Boy and White Boy of "Psi" and "Omega" distinct social identities while revealing the profound similarity of their psychological situations, so Tolson acknowledges the existence of a community-oriented oral aesthetic developed primarily by Afro-American artists and an individually oriented visual aesthetic developed primarily by Euro-American modernists. Ultimately Tolson demonstrates the potential power of an aesthetic synthesis by creating *Harlem Gallery*, a complex Afro-Modernist blues that signifies, sometimes with irony, sometimes with sympathy, on the words of George Herbert and T. S. Eliot as well as those of Langston Hughes and W. E. B. Du Bois. Through the juxtaposition of diverse aesthetic sensibilities and his own synthetic prosody, Tolson attempts to develop an audience willing to support or participate in the creation of an art capable of resisting the false dichotomies permeating the aesthetic and political context.

Visual and Musical Aesthetics

Although rarely discussed, the perceived dichotomy between oral and visual aesthetics constitutes a basic element of the sometimes acerbic arguments over the relative merits of Afro- and Euro-American poetry. Emphasizing Eliot's and Ezra Pound's attempts to "undermine the inherent consecutiveness of language, frustrate the reader's normal expectation of a sequence and force him to perceive the elements of the poem as juxtaposed in space rather than unrolling in time" (10), Joseph Frank argues the centrality of "spatial form" in Euro-American modernism. Similarly, Hugh Kenner in the "Space-Craft" chapter of *The Pound Era* argues that the growing affinity between writing and painting in the nineteenth century created a cultural matrix in which visual artists such as Picasso and Henri Gaudier-Brzeska exerted a decisive influence on modernist literary aesthetics. Even Harvey Gross in *Sound and Form in Modern Poetry,* a sensitive study of the music of Euro-American modernist poetry, observes that imagism developed an aesthetic in which "the poem's appearance on the page constitutes its chief prosodic feature" (105). Highlighting the radical difference in Afro-American discourse, Stephen Henderson directly contradicts these visually oriented premises when he contends that, in analyzing Afro-American poetry, "the central problem is the printed page" (30). Most analysts of Afro-American expression, including Amiri Baraka, Eugene Redmond, Sherley Anne Williams, and Houston Baker, would agree with Henderson's assertion that black poetry "derives its form from two basic sources, Black speech and Black music" (30–31). However undesirable or unnecessary, the divergence of Euro- and Afro-American aesthetic assumptions seems an unquestionable fact of modern literary politics.

Ironically, Pound's original statement of the principles of imagism provides theoretical justification for both aesthetic emphases:

1. Direct treatment of the "thing," whether subjective or objective.
2. To use absolutely no word that does not contribute to the presentation.
3. As regarding rhythm: to compose in the sequence of the musical phrase, not in sequence of a metronome. (36)

Especially given the absence of any explicit mention of the visual arts, Pound's invocation of musical rhythm would seem to suggest an underlying compatibility between imagism and Afro-American aesthetics, both of which developed at least in part as reactions against what were perceived as imposed and inappropriate aesthetic conventions. The historical divergence of the impulses, however, can be traced to the impact of Pound's subsequent definition of the image as "that which presents an intellectual and emotional complex in an instant of time" (37). This separation of perception from temporal flow, while profoundly compatible with Eliot's attempt to "transmute the time world of history into the timeless world of myth" (Frank 60; Gross 105), militates against the exploitation of music, which explores the dynamic relationship between an ever-changing sequence of intellectual and emotional complexes. As a result of this profound difference in temporal perception, Euro-American modernists seeking non-European poetic sources gravitated toward Asia and the ideographic emphasis of Pound's translation of Ernest Fenallosa's "The Chinese Written Character as a Medium for Poetry"; when they looked to Africa they were more likely to be interested in visual arts such as masks than in polyrhythmic musical styles. Conversely, Afro-American poets generally concentrated on absorbing musical influences such as the jazz suites of Duke Ellington. Despite the accuracy of Ralph Ellison's observation that "at least as early as T.S. Eliot's creation of a new aesthetic for poetry through the artful juxtapositioning of earlier styles, Louis Armstrong, way down the river in New Orleans, was working out a similar technique for jazz" (*Shadow* 225), the difference in source materials rendered the shared aesthetic invisible to most observers.

One major result of the failure to recognize the underlying similarity of Afro- and Euro-American aesthetic impulses has been an extensive misunderstanding of the difference in performance dynamics in each tradition. Euro-American modernist poems such as Pound's "In a Station of the Metro," Wallace Stevens's "Thirteen Ways of Looking at a Blackbird," and Eliot's *The Waste Land* support Richard Poirier's definition of modernist performance as "an exercise of power, a very curious one. Curious because it is at first so furiously self-consultive, so even narcissistic, and later so eager for publicity, love and historical dimension. Out of an accumulating of secretive acts emerges at last a form that presumes to compete with reality itself for control of the minds exposed to it" (87). An aspect of modernist consciousness in a rapidly changing context, such a performance style seems deeply suspect from an Afro-American perspective. From Du Bois's analysis of "double consciousness" in *The Souls of Black Folk* through Franz Fanon's similar discussion in "The Negro and Language," the black intellectual tradition treats as politically suspect all external attempts to control the individual apprehension of reality. Observing the historical connection between Euro-American expressive conventions and white political domination, Afro-American poets—drawing on the examples of folk artists and singers generally ignored by Euro-American aestheticians—embrace a performance tradition that seeks to forge a communal response to assaults on black integrity. In the alternative call-and-response tradition, described by Baraka, Ben Sidran, and Robert Farris Thompson, the performer derives aesthetic power not from secretive acts of perception intended to "control the minds exposed to it" but from his/her ability to elicit an affirmation from the audience, which in effect assumes the role of a collaborator in the performance. As Harold Scheub observes, this communal dynamic entails a conception of the image that emphasizes the connection rather than the difference between the artist's and the audience's senses of reality: "Images are felt actions or sets of actions evoked in the imaginations of the members of an audience by verbal and nonverbal elements arranged and controlled by the performer, requiring a common experience by both artist and audience" ("Oral" 71). The continual testing of artistic perception against audience response, immersed in the flow of time, eliminates much of the potential for cultural domination involved in the performance tradition derived from Pound's definition of the image.

The aesthetic divergence described above is by no means inevitable or all-encompassing. From a perspective outside the historical context that has in fact eliminated almost all such perspectives, poems such as Hughes's "Ennui" or "Be-Bop Boys" fulfill Pound's criteria for imagism as thoroughly as "In a Station of the Metro" or H. D.'s "Sea-Rose," which in turn support their visual images with a verbal music at times recalling the shifting phrasings of a Coleman Hawkins solo. Similarly, Stevens's "The Idea of Order at Key West" can be approached as an intriguing Euro-American adaptation of the call-and-response dynamic, while Hughes's "Montage of a Dream Deferred" derives its form from visual arts such as murals and film as well as from Ellington's suites and Charlie Parker's be-bop improvisations. Only rarely, however, did the Euro-American modernists, or their subsequent critics, reveal any real awareness of the rich Afro-American tradition or recognize any important similarity between their own work and that of Tolson, Hughes, or Sterling Brown. Sadly, the multiple failures of perception involved in this chapter of literary history testify all too clearly to the pervasive influences of the cultural and aesthetic dichotomies Tolson confronts in *Harlem Gallery*.

Harlem Gallery

Tolson's explicit awareness of both the oral and visual aesthetics provided a nearly unique foundation for his search for a synthetic sensibility. His M.A. thesis, "The Harlem Group of Negro Writers," identifies Hughes's adaptation of Afro-American music to mainstream American prosody as a significant aesthetic development. At the same time, Tolson was developing his interest in visual aesthetics in the sections of Harlem portraits titled "Chiaroscuros," "Silhouettes," "Etchings," and "Pastels" in *A Gallery of Harlem Portraits*. Although this early version of *Harlem Gallery* invokes visual forms, its prosody is grounded almost entirely on the oral aesthetic. Frustrated by the lack of response to the manuscript and sensing the underlying aesthetic tension, Tolson began an extensive study of the Euro-American modernists that eventually provided major elements of the prosodic synthesis of *Harlem Gallery:* "I stashed the manuscript in my trunk for twenty years. At the end of that time I had read and absorbed the techniques of Eliot, Pound, Yeats, Baudelaire, Pasternak and, I believe, all the great Moderns. God only knows how many 'little magazines' I studied and how much textual analysis of the New Critics" (Hill 195). During this period, Tolson complemented his academic inquiries into the Afro- and Euro-American prosodic traditions by experimenting with various combinations of visual and musical prosody in poems such as "Dark Symphony," "African China," "E. & O.E.," and the two "Do" sections of *Libretto for the Republic of Liberia*, which anticipate the merger of typographical/visual and oral/musical techniques in *Harlem Gallery*.

After an introductory sequence ("Alpha" through "Epsilon") devoted to the Curator's (and to a large extent Tolson's) view of art as an organic outgrowth of specific social and psychological circumstances, Tolson devotes the bulk of *Harlem Gallery* ("Zeta" through "Chi") to an examination of the characters and settings associated with particular aesthetic orientations and performance styles. Among the most important characters are the ironic modernist painter John Laugart, the "People's Poet" Hideho Heights, and the complex poet-composer Mister Starks. Serving as backdrops for the Curator's interaction with these characters and their works of art, the actual Gallery and the musically dynamic Zulu Club serve as physical emblems of the social reality of the visual/oral dichotomy. After testing his characters' aesthetic approaches against their concrete experiences, Tolson returns to theoretical issues in two final poems ("Psi" and "Omega") that reiterate the insufficiency of both the aesthetic dichotomies and the racial dichotomies on which they are based.

Tolson's treatment of the visual aesthetic in *Harlem Gallery* honors the performance of artists relying on their individual perceptions while recognizing their potentially fatal alienation. Both the Curator in "Zeta" and Starks in *Harlem Vignettes* present Laugart, creator of the satirical painting *Black Bourgeoisie,* as an artist comparable to the great satirists of the Western tradition, most notably the French lithographer Daumier. Drawing an additional analogy between Laugart and Picasso, the Curator describes the distinctly modernist style of *Black Bourgeoisie:*

> colors detonating
> fog signals on a railroad track,
> lights and shadows rhythming
> fog images in a negative pack.
>
> (38)

Laugart's willingness to delve into obscurity and to confront the Regents of the Gallery with their babbitry reflects his aloof contempt for his context. Even as the power of *Black Bourgeoisie* tempts the Curator to cry "Eureka," however, Tolson expresses deep reservations concerning the adequacy of Laugart's aesthetic. Laugart's disgust over the corruption of the black middle class also severs his contact with the energizing elements of the Harlem community. Speaking with the "undated voice of a poet" (38), his face "haply black and mute" (39), Laugart withdraws into the timeless world of high modernist aesthetics. A final emblem of the isolation that both lends power to and limits the range of his art, Laugart's murder, witnessed only by a "Hamletian rat," ironically asserts the reality of the context from which he withdrew. In addition, Laugart's modernist performance fails to exert any real power over that context. When Guy Delaporte, a major target of the satire of *Black Bourgeoisie,* resists the message of the painting in "Kappa," the Curator expresses his disappointment in a way that implies the need for a synthesis of visual and oral aesthetics: "On its shakedown cruise, / the 'Black Bourgeoisie' runs aground / on the bars of the Harlem blues" (66). The blues humor of the Harlem bars resists the harsh irony of Laugart's vision, intimating the need for an aesthetic approach uniting individual perception and communal response.

If modernist visual art risks losing its power through isolation from the community, the musical art Tolson considers in *Harlem Gallery* encounters equally serious problems because of its immersion in that community. In "Eta" music elicits a strong response from Dipsy Muse, an "average" Harlemite whose "blue-devils' pockets" (43) identify him with the music on the jukebox. Attesting to the shared experience of singer and audience, Dipsy and his wife participate directly in the blues experience when they confront one another in the Elite Chitterling Shop. Watching their angry encounter, Nkomo observes that, like his own African heritage, the blues resist the traditions of the American mainstream: "That rebel jukebox! Hear the ghetto's dark guffaws / that defy Manhattan's Bible Belt Aeons / separate my native veld and your peaks of philosophy" (48). African traditions shape this resistance by encouraging active audience participation in the artistic performance. Listening to the performance in the fixed form of the record, however, Dipsy and his wife have no conscious sense of participation in the aesthetic process. If the "ambivalence of the classic blues" (43) provides even momentary transcendence in "Eta," the transcendence is experienced not by the members of the "blues community" but by the Curator and Nkomo, who contemplate the musical/experiential performance in much the way they encounter Laugart's painting, as a source for speculation and observation. Wailing "from everlasting to everlasting" (43), the recorded performance occupies a position midway between the isolated timelessness of the visual aesthetic and the participatory immediacy of the oral aesthetic.

The choice of music as a medium, of course, does not dictate that an artist commit him/herself to the call-and-response dynamic. As composer/conductor of the Harlem Symphony Orchestra, Starks works in a distinctly modernist mode, although he had earlier mastered an Afro-American style. Abandoning the communal focus of his million-selling boogie-woogie record "Pot-Belly Papa," Starks turns to complex orchestral works such as "Black Orchid Suite," which earn him the title "piano-modernist / of the Harlem Renaissance" (104). Basing his magnum opus on his memory of the dancer Black Orchid's willingness to "sell" her favors to Delaporte (105), Starks transmutes the blues experience into a statement that he describes in terms recalling Du Bois's "Essay toward an Autobiography of a Race Concept," *Dusk of Dawn:*

> the "Black Orchid Suite"—
> sunrise on the summit
> between
> sunset and sunset.
>
> (113)

Despite the fact that the suite, unlike Laugart's *Black Bourgeoisie,* celebrates as well as satirizes the Afro-American community, Starks fails to elicit strong responses from either the community as a whole or his orchestra. The root of his problem lies not in lack of insight or choice of medium but in an inability to repudiate the aesthetic dichotomies permeating the American context. The pressure he feels to "Put the notes on the staff, Black Boy" (131) is in part a pressure to abandon the improvisational Afro-American tradition in favor of the individual control of modernist performance. Unable to totally dismiss the cultural definitions of racial inferiority implicit in this aesthetic pressure, Starks adopts a form that alienates him from the audience whose experience he addresses.

Tolson's portrait of Starks's murderer Crazy Cain emphasizes the destructiveness of the psychological and aesthetic contradictions created by American racial dichotomies. The murder is directly motivated by aesthetic issues with their roots in the "black-white" split. Starks fires Cain from the symphony because he disrupts the orchestral format, which demands that the individual performer subordinate his/her voice to those of the composer and conductor, the "real" performers in modernist terms. Significantly, Cain's disruptiveness reflects his inability to fully internalize the dichotomies, to control his ambivalence concerning his mixed aesthetic and racial heritage. On the one hand, an "Eliotic vein of surrender" (115) characterizes Cain's style; on the other, "His Negro tradition bitched the night" (115). Reduced to a function of American racial dichotomies, the contemporary Cain lives up to his name by murdering his aesthetic brothers. Caused as much by Starks's inability to communicate with Cain as by Cain's internal division, the tragedy testifies clearly to the very real damage inflicted by the belief in dichotomies with no inherent validity.

Turning from musicians torn between Euro- and Afro-American aesthetics, Tolson considers the oral aesthetic that involves both artist and audience in the creation of the work. Fresh from a jam session "with the blues a-percolatin in my head" (69), Hideho greets the Curator with an explicit challenge to the visual aesthetic: "In the beginning was the Word . . . not the Brush!" (68). He then provides a sample of his performance style, significantly choosing an explicitly musical theme. His celebration of Louis Armstrong as a heroic figure able to resist all forms of white domination relies on allusions familiar to the average Harlem resident: Bessie Smith, W. C. Handy, Storyville, the drug scene that has destroyed so many black musicians, the biblical politics that transform Armstrong's jazz into a superior version of Gabriel's call on Judgment Day. Yet, in the Gallery, even this assertively Afro-American statement seems afflicted with the isolation Tolson associates with modernist performance. Without a responsive audience, Hideho can only "rhetorize in the grand style / of a Doctor Faustus in the dilapidated Harlem Opera House" (69).

Only in the extended treatment of the Zulu Club in "Xi" does Tolson express the vitality of the Afro-American performance dynamic in its most basic form. Hideho's reading of "The Birth of John Henry" inspires comment, applause, and additional performances from the audience: a blues from piano player Frog Legs Lux and a contemporary bad man tale from Joshua Nitze. Each of these performances in turn elicits additional responses. Closely resembling the tale-telling dynamic portrayed in Zora Neale Hurston's *Mules and Men*, the presence of the actual performer at the Zulu Club calls forth an active response from audience members such as Dipsy Muse, who had sat in a mute stupor while listening to the jukebox at the Elite Chitterling Shop. When Hideho begins to recite, Dipsy's exclamation of "Great God A'Mighty" (80) provides the initial spur for the performance. Energized by this immediate response to his call, Hideho responds to the calls implicit in his audience's personal responses. When his storm imagery stirs Wafer Waite's memory of a Texas tornado, Wafer breaks in with a question that both challenges and acknowledges the validity of Hideho's performance: "Didn't John Henry's Ma and Pa / get no warning?" (81). Drawing on a rhetorical strategy familiar to his audience, Hideho answers with an abbreviated tall tale: "Brother / the tornado alarm became / tongue-tied" (81). Resuming the story with a stanza emphasizing the infant hero's prodigious drinking ability, Hideho solidifies his link with the drinkers in the club, leading to a high point of the communal collaboration: "the poet and the audience one, / each gears itself to please" (84). When, at the height of this energetic exchange, "The creative impulse in the Zulu Club / leaps from Hideho's lips to Frog Legs' fingers" (83), the Curator feels a sense of awe over the primal link between communal art and religion: "*Witness to a miracle*—I muse—*the birth of a blues*" (83).

Just as he points out the limitations of the visual aesthetic, however, Tolson recognizes the potential problems of a call-and-response dynamic. If either artist or audience possesses the power to coerce response, call and response can be reduced from a kinetic process to an empty form. In "Xi," Tolson follows his celebration of Hideho's performance with a satire on the subsequent performance of racketeer Black Diamond, who learned his aesthetic theory from the Curator without absorbing any of its social implications (87). When Black Diamond quotes Hideho's "Flophouse Blues" he does so not as an acknowledgment of shared experience but because he wishes to have "His ego lionized / in the first, second, and third person" (87). Basing his performance on a power derived from fear rather than insight, Black Diamond distorts the call-and-response dynamic by repeatedly claiming a position of hierarchical superiority over the "little guys" for whom he purports concern. Unaware of the profound violation of the oral aesthetic implied by this self-elevation, Black Diamond forces his audience, reduced to symbolic anonymity, to fulfill the form of response:

> Tom, Dick and Harry,
> pigmied by the ghetto Robin Hood
> (unconscious *now* as a basking shark),
> catch the cue, double up like U-bridle irons inverted, and
> let loose
> geysers of guffaws.
>
> (89)

In addition, Tolson perceives that the original call may be distorted or even directly contradicted as the response spreads through the audience. The heroic call of "The Birth of John Henry," originally intended as an emblem of Afro-American resistance to Euro-American psychological domination, devolves into a typically Euro-American critical argument. Following the original phase of the performance in which Hideho's poem summons Frog Legs's and Nitze's folk-oriented affirmations, the Zulu Club wits draw one another into an acerbic debate over the symbolism of Dolph Peeler's "Ode to the South." Because the audience exists in a context conditioned by both Afro- and Euro- American traditions, any form of aesthetic energy inevitably encounters implicit resistance from individuals conditioned to deny its validity. The fragmentation of the audience in the Zulu Club subverts the communal energies released by Hideho's oral performance. Ironically, Hideho descends into modernist alienation by the end of "Xi," in large part because of the epic drinking he celebrates as part of his strategy for eliciting audience response. The image of a slobbering, sobbing Hideho that closes the section underscores Tolson's awareness that even an artist committed to an alternative vision may become an ironic emblem of modernist alienation. Unable to overcome "the white magic of John Barleycorn" (92), Hideho remains very much time bound as he issues a despairing call to an audience unaware of its internal contradictions: "My *people, my* people,— / they know not what they do" (92).

Toward an Afro-Modernist Prosody

Although he perceives the limitations of both visual and oral aesthetics, Tolson repudiates neither. Rather, he seeks a form of expression combining individual and communal performances, distanced irony, and empathetic blues humor. Expressed most strongly in Tolson's choice of prosodic devices, the synthesis is intimated in his portraits of Starks and Hideho. After considering visual and oral forms, Tolson turns his attention increasingly to written poetry in the later stages of *Harlem Gallery*. The four poems leading up to the final repudiation of dichotomies in "Psi" and "Omega" all focus on literary performances: "Tau" and "Epsilon" on Starks's *Harlem Vignettes;* "Phi" on Hideho's "The Sea-Turtle and the Shark"; and "Chi" on Hideho's "E. & O.E." Each mediates between Euro- and Afro-American performance styles, forcing the reader to reconsider the "opposed" images of Starks and Hideho. Although no poem succeeds totally, each intimates important aspects of the synthesis implied by the Afro-modernist prosody of *Harlem Gallery*.

In *Harlem Vignettes,* which bears an obvious resemblance to Tolson's early poems published under the title *A Gallery of Harlem Portraits,* Starks acknowledges his own ambivalence toward the aesthetic dichotomies that condition both music and poetry: "My talent was an uptown whore: my wit a Downtown pimp" (112). Although the title page of the manuscript bears an inscription reading "I should have followed—perhaps—*Des Imagistes*" (111) and the poems reveal a distinctly modernist sensibility in their use of obscure allusions and ironic humor, the manuscript clearly reveals Starks's desire to move beyond the purely modernist performance of the "volume of imagistic verse" he had published in his youth. Incorporating the emotional and intellectual complexes of various instants of time in a narrative structure that allows for greater contextual understanding than is common in Euro-American imagism, Starks echoes many of Tolson's insights into the nature of the aesthetic dichotomy. On the one hand, his critiques of Laugart's modernist isolation (127) and Cain's cultural fragmentation (115–16) complement the ironic self-knowledge of his self-portrait (112–23). On the other, the narrative of his meeting with mobster Dutch Schultz, like the Black Diamond segment of "Xi," reveals an awareness of the distorting impact of power on the call-and-response dynamic. Moving beyond a simple description of the problem, Starks's response to a mobster's henchman's attempt to force response identifies an important Afro-Modernist aesthetic strategy. Performing in a context where he lacks social power, Starks improvises his "Rhapsody in Black and White," a parody of Gershwin's "Tin Pan Alley blues classic" (131), as ironic commentary on the "Derby" who "wanted to be Caruso" (129) despite a total lack of sympathy for the oral aesthetic. Starks's aesthetic strategy in this scene seems specifically modernist in its use of an irony based on the implicit juxtapositions of sensibilities evoked through allusion. At the same time, it employs the Afro-American strategy of signifying on the white "call" in a superficially responsive but profoundly subversive manner. Ultimately, however, *Harlem Vignettes,* like Starks's orchestral performances, fails to reach a communal audience. As a result, it contributes to the alienation that eventuates in Starks's death. The poet's final call is expressed neither to himself nor to an audience but through "the performance of the Angelus Funeral Home" (134). Starks's intricate modernism, even when tempered by a direct use of Afro-American forms, offers no real alternative to the wasteland it describes.

Hideho's Zulu Club performance of "The Sea-Turtle and the Shark" places the ironic strategy of "Rhapsody in Black and White" in relief against an actual audience. Thinking of the critical argument over "Ode to the South" that followed his performance of "The Birth of John Henry," Hideho indirectly solicits the Curator's help in responding to Peeler's "bunkum session on the Negro" (138). Conscious of his role as catalyst and audience/collaborator, the Curator mouths provocative "cliches" while Hideho carries out a "self-consultation" more typical of Euro-American modernism than his own public performance style. Like "Rhapsody in Black and White," "The Sea-Turtle and the Shark" signifies on white cultural power in an ironic allusive manner. Accepting Peeler's image of racial relations as an animalistic struggle in which the symbolic white (the serpent) devours the symbolic black (the frog or pig depending on whether one follows the text of "Xi" or "Phi"), Hideho transforms the story into a statement of ultimate black triumph with the image of the turtle gnawing its way out of the belly of the shark that has swallowed it. Stunned by this uncharacteristically bitter literary irony from the "People's Poet," the Zulu Club audience, unable to provide its normal collective affirmation, feels itself "tied neck and heels by a poetic analogy" (142). By mixing performance modes and basing his recited poem on individually rather than communally generated images, Hideho sacrifices some of the immediate energy of the call-and-response dynamic but gains some of the shocking originality of the modernist mode.

He by no means, however, surrenders all response. In fact, he communicates on a deep level with at least two members of his audience: the Curator and the Jamaican bartender. Even as they reflect Hideho's ability to exercise a "modernist" power over individual perception, these responses contribute to the development of a synthetic mode of call and response. Their shared reaction to Hideho's complex performance transforms the Curator and bartender into a community for which the ironic image becomes part of an expanded image pool available for use in subsequent performances. Although it is possible to view the curator's response—"I knew his helm was in line with his keel / as an artist's helm should be" (141)—as a characteristically theoretical appreciation, the bartender's intense affirmation—"God knows, Hideho, you got the lowdown" (142)—makes it clear that the performance, unlike those modernist performances oriented toward a "timeless world," leads the audience toward reengagement with the concrete context distorted by Peeler's "Ode." The bartender, who gives no indication of a special literary talent or interest, responds to Hideho's signifying through ironic allusion. Extending Hideho's repudiation of Peeler's image of the black man as pig, the bartender claims literary precedence for Claude McKay, whose repudiation of the black/hog equation in "If We Must Die" was ironically and without attribution quoted by Churchill as inspiration for Jamaica's English oppressors during the Nazi bombing. The success of Hideho's performance, however, is limited by the fact that the majority of his audience, which he has never before allowed a glimpse through "the cellar door / of his art" (143), seems unable to step outside the dichotomies that assume the incompatibility of populist and modernist, Euro- and Afro-American expression.

Focusing on "E. & O.E.," Hideho's poem "in the modern idiom" (146), "Chi" emphasizes the connection between the political and aesthetic dichotomies that force Hideho to repress half his poetic "split identity" (145). Contrasting sharply with his racial ballads in the public domain, "E. & O.E." is "self-consultive" in precisely the modernist sense described by Poirier. Hideho's individual fears—"not Hamlet's . . . not Simon Legree's" (145)—inspire his "private poem in the modern vein," which he hopes will win him literary immortality. Again, Tolson's treatment of Hideho's modernism parallels Poirier's observation concerning the drive for "historical dimension" in modernist performance. Articulating aesthetic doubts and frustrations remarkably similar to those felt by Laugart and Starks, Hideho employs a densely allusive modernist style even further removed from the oral aesthetic than "The Sea-Turtle and the Shark," which considers issues familiar to the communal discourse of the Zulu Club. Posed like Eliot's *Waste Land* "'twixt fragments of requiems and stones of decay" (149), "E. & O.E." relies primarily on visual rather than musical prosodic devices and is directed toward an audience of reflective individuals rather than active participants.

In general Hideho's public poems belong to the "epic" mode, which, according to Northrop Frye, "makes some attempt to preserve the convention of recitation and a listening audience" (248).

"E. & O.E.," on the other hand, clearly belongs to Frye's "lyric" mode in which "the poet, like the ironic writer, turns his back on his audience" (272). As Frye notes, Pound's theories—at least as developed in the Euro-American modernist tradition—are "lyric-centered theories" (272). Although he shows no awareness of the racial implications of his perception, Frye identifies the intersection of racial and aesthetic politics when he observes that "the most admired and advanced poets of the twentieth century are chiefly those who have most fully mastered the elusive, meditative, resonant, centripetal word-magic of the emancipated lyrical rhythm" (273). Despite Frye's contention that the lyric mode draws extensively on musical rhythm, it is clear that his conception of both music and lyric performance was derived without knowledge of Afro-American materials or traditions. For Frye, music remains the creation of individuals rather than communities. The definitions of achievement used to admit poets into the anthologies Hideho seeks to enter effectively exclude modern poets working in the epic mode. Although Frye discusses the mode only in relation to pre-twentieth-century poetry, it clearly forms the foundation of almost all of the work in the aesthetic tradition to which both Hideho and Tolson, in part, belong.

Given this aesthetic context, Hideho faces an unresolvable conflict. To achieve immortality, he must write in forms acceptable to the Euro-American critical establishment. Even though he finds aspects of these forms congenial, he realizes that to accept them is at least partially to repudiate his connection with his community. As the only audience for Hideho's performances in each mode, the Curator recognizes the tragic dimensions of the dilemma. Although Hideho's talent transcends the perceived dichotomies, he lives in a context where "the Color line, as well as the Party line, / splits an artist's identity" (147). Contemplating this distortion of aesthetic process by forces in both the black and white communities, the Curator laments

> the white and not-white dichotomy,
> the Afro-American dilemma in the arts—
> the dialectic of
> to be or not to be
> a Negro.

(146)

The brilliance of Hideho's performance in "E. & O.E.," which assumes a power over the Curator's perception of reality at least as profound as the power granted Hideho by the Zulu Club audience of "The Birth of John Henry," stems from his ability to address the existential (to be or not to be) and racial (to be or not to be a Negro) dilemmas with a single gesture. The final stanza, which overwhelms the Curator's professed "unbelief," articulates Hideho's decision *not* to articulate his modernist sense of alienation and despair:

> I do not shake
> the Wailing Wall of Earth—
> nor quake
> the Gethsemane
> of Sea—nor tear
> the Big Top
> of Sky
> with Lear's prayer
> or Barabas' curse, or Job's cry.
>
> (151)

Ironically signifying on the words and heroes of the masters he seeks to join in the anthologies of world literature, Hideho determines both to go on living and to go on living and speaking in his black voice.

Tolson, of course, articulates both the despair and the refusal to despair, again testifying to his synthetic sensibility. Acknowledging the power inherent in both performance modes, he intimates the possibility of an Afro-modernist aesthetic capable of transcending or obliterating the false dichotomies. The Curator's description of his own response to "E. & O.E." calls for the creation of a context in which artists can work without constant pressure to deny aspects of their sensibility for the comfort of audiences conditioned to accept simplifying dichotomies. Juxtaposing a variety of performance styles, Tolson subverts the authority of any single approach. *Harlem Gallery* incorporates elements of epic and lyric, visual and oral, modernist and populist traditions. It makes little sense to attribute any particular element of Tolson's performance to any particular tradition. His point is precisely that the dichotomies, whether racial or aesthetic, are insufficient and destructive; any artist or audience member who takes them seriously inevitably limits his/her perception of and interaction with reality.

The resolution of the issues that the characters in *Harlem Gallery* find almost entirely intractable involves Tolson's own aesthetic choices. Throughout the volume, he demonstrates his mastery of a wide range of aesthetic approaches and prosodic devices. Each major character speaks or writes in a distinctive voice with specific prosodic signatures appropriate to her/his immediate needs. In "The Birth of John Henry," Tolson (through Hideho) employs the ballad stanza with its alternating lines of iambic tetrameter and iambic trimeter and its abcb rhyme scheme. The opening stanza of the poem demonstrates Tolson's ease with traditional prosody:

> x   /   /   / x x   / x /
> The night John Henry is born an ax
>
> x /   x   /   x /
> of lightning splits the sky
>
> x x /   x   x /   x   /   x   /
> and a hammer of thunder pounds the earth,
>
> x   x / x   x /   x   /
> and the eagles and panthers cry!

(81)

The substitution of anapests for iambs, a common prosodic device used by Byron and Poe in poems intended for recitation, strengthens the narrative drive by accelerating the rhythm. In addition the "sky-cry" rhyme alludes to one of the classic blues images ("the sky was crying"), unobtrusively drawing the audience into a communal frame of reference. Adopting an alternative prosody suitable to the written format of the post-imagist *Harlem Vignettes,* Starks writes in a free verse reminiscent of Edgar Lee Masters. Relying on line breaks, clusters of accented syllables, and sound echoes for poetic effect, Starks varies his prosody only slightly from one vignette to the next. In accord with his broader poetic talent, Hideho varies his prosody substantially from poem to poem. Despite a predominantly iambic metrical base, for example, "E. & O.E." clearly belongs to the visual aesthetic tradition in which, as Gross comments, "typography, not sound, controls the rhythms" (105). At any rate, Tolson recognizes that any prosodic device may be appropriate depending on the particular audience, medium, or context.

The prosody of *Harlem Gallery* implicitly repudiates any belief in the inherent incompatibility of the visual and oral aesthetics the characters usually keep separate. Tolson's use of shape and rhyme, devices associated with the visual and oral aesthetics respectively, reinforces the poem's vision of a synthetic sensibility. Tolson establishes his spatial prosody in "Alpha," centering each line on the page. A device maintained throughout the poem, this typography creates a visual analogue for Tolson's thematic emphasis on balance. By using this centering even in sections attributed to Hideho and Starks, Tolson maintains a presence throughout *Harlem Gallery,* silently occupying the territory "where / curator and creator / meet" (170) and establishing links between even the most diverse aesthetic stances. In addition to setting the general spatial prosody, "Alpha" demonstrates Tolson's use of visual prosody for special effects. Recalling the thematically resonant shapes of George Herbert's "concrete poetry," the final stanza of "Alpha" takes the shape of the elusive "I," which is its central thematic concern:

> Although the gaffing "Tò tí" of the Gadfly girds
> the I-ness of my humanness and Negroness,
> the clockbird's
> jackass laughter
> in sun, in rain
> at dusk of dawn
> mixes with the pepper bird's reveille in my brain,
> where the plain is twilled and the twilled is plain.
>
> (20)

Reflecting the synthesis of visual and musical prosody in *Harlem Gallery,* the closing couplet underscores the thematic implications of the stanza's shape. The "brain-plain" rhyme resolves the "human-Negro" dilemma by combining the communal African-based self (the pepper bird in the brain) and the ironic modernist "I."

Throughout *Harlem Gallery,* Tolson uses couplets (though usually not in the metrically identical lines of "Alpha") to suggest thematic connections that he then revises in an ongoing process of individual and communal call and response. Placing couplets at the end of only two poems—"Alpha" and the bitterly ironic "Nu"—Tolson implicitly subverts their traditional use for thematic resolution. Rather, he presents all resolutions as strictly provisional. Connections such as those implied by the "plain-brain" (20) rhyme in "Alpha" or the "mouth-South" rhyme in "Psi" (154) emerge as momentary points of reference but are quickly withdrawn or revised. Frequently, subsequent use of a rhyme sound from a couplet explicitly redefines the provisional resolution, as in the following stanza from "Phi":

```
          x  /  x  /
       Beneath the sun

 x  x     /    x   / x x / x /
 as he clutched the bars of a barracoon

       x /    x   /
       beneath the moon

  x  x  /   x   /   /   /
  of a blind and deaf-mute Sky

 x   /   /   /  x /  x  x
 my forebears heard a Cameroon
```

/ x   x /   x   x   x   /   /   / x   /
chief, in the language of the King James Bible, cry,

x / x /   x   /   x   /
"O Absalom, my son, my son!"

(135)

The stanza is a virtuosic prosodic performance, drawing on both visual and oral techniques. The couplet rhyming "barracoon" and "moon" stresses the slave's alienation. Almost immediately, however, Tolson redefines the tentative resolution with the rhyme of "Cameroon," directing attention to the African heritage that belies the New World definition of blacks as slaves. The off-rhymes of "sun" and "son" with "moon-barracoon-Cameroon" emphasize the underlying tension, as does Tolson's manipulation of the iambic-anapestic metrical base to create thematically significant clusters of stressed syllables. The clusters on "deaf-mute Sky," "forebears heard," and "King James Bible" suggest the Euro-American attack on the African sense of an animate universe implied by the capitalization of "Sky." It seems particularly significant that the African's alienation involves the destruction of aural/oral connections; the deafness of the Sky cuts off the call and response between human beings and the world they live in, a basic modernist dilemma. Similarly, the allusion to the biblical Absalom both reflects the shift in Afro-American religious sensibility from spirit (the sun) to Jesus (the son) and invokes Faulkner's literary meditation on the absurdity and destructiveness of America's racial dichotomies.

Distrusting all resolutions, questioning all definitions, Tolson commits himself to an artistic process that envisions a world in which the artist can express all sides of his/her sensibility, whether in the Zulu Club, the Gallery, or the anthologies of world literature. The problem with such a commitment, as for all synthetic artists, is that most actual audiences continue to perceive art in a frame of mind conditioned by belief in the reality of the dichotomies. Only a small segment of the modernist/Euro-American/visual arts audience understands the populist/Afro-American/oral aesthetic as a serious encounter with the central problems of contemporary consciousness. Conversely, most audience members who are aware of black cultural traditions view the modernist tradition as irrelevant to Afro-American concerns. The question then becomes: how can the artist conscious of aesthetic and social interrelationship, actual or potential, help create an audience not bound to the dichotomies? In *Harlem Gallery*, Tolson suggests that if the artist can establish contact with the members of a particular audience through the use of techniques and themes already familiar to it, then he/she can use that contact to initiate the audience into new aesthetic and social experiences. In theory, Tolson's mastery of irony and Euro-American modernist aesthetics should enable him to communicate something of the blues sensibility to an audience comfortable with the performances of Pound and Eliot. His familiarity with call and response and the details of Afro-American experience should enable him to communicate the value of the high modernist tradition to an audience that associates it primarily with an oppressive social system. To date, this approach has attained at best limited success. Most readers of the Euro-American modernists simply ignore Tolson while most members of the Afro-American audience prefer music to literature and, on the occasions when they turn to poetry, respond more readily to the relatively direct calls of Hughes or Gwendolyn Brooks. A blues irony, which Tolson would certainly have recognized, adheres to the situation. Public and private, racial and modern, Tolson's Afro-modernist blues suite remains ironically enmeshed in the dichotomies it so eloquently and thoroughly discredits.

PART 3

PLAYING THE CHANGES:
GOSPEL, BLUES, JAZZ

▲ ▲ ▲ ▲

8

Bigger's Blues: *Native Son* and the Articulation of Afro-American Modernism

▲ ▲ ▲ ▲

There will be time to murder and create.

—"The Love Song of J. Alfred Prufrock"

The problems are fragmentation, alienation, sense-making: the shoring up of fragments against our ruins; what to make of a diminished thing. Timothy Reiss and Michel Foucault, indispensable genealogists of the "modern," have identified the European origins of these crucial twentieth-century concerns in pre-Enlightenment challenges to the medieval worldview. Social, scientific, technological, and theological innovations shape new discourses that in turn generate new insights, in a process Henry Adams labeled the "law of acceleration." One of the earliest Euro-American texts framed in self-consciously modernist terms, *The Education of Henry Adams* was published in 1909, six years after W. E. B. Du Bois's *The Souls of Black Folk*. Du Bois's absence from most discussions of the central aesthetic, intellectual, and cultural issues raised in Euro-American modernism helps explain both the continuing invisibility of Afro-American modernism as a literary movement and the marginalization or simplification of Langston Hughes's "Montage of a Dream Deferred," Zora Neale Hurston's *Moses, Man of the Mountain,* and, crucially, *Native Son.*

Although most of Adams's insights had been anticipated by Melville, Henry James, William James, and Emily Dickinson, the publication of *The Education of Henry Adams* serves as a convenient marker for the beginning of modernism as a self-conscious element of literary discourse in the United States. Recognizing the complex continental history behind this relatively late emergence, critics such as Hugh Kenner, Malcolm Bradbury and James McFarlane, and Frederick Karl quite properly orient their investigations of Ezra Pound, T. S. Eliot, William Faulkner, and other recognized modernists toward the continental figures and movements that influenced their work. Even the emerging histories of "alternative modernisms"—such as those of Cyrena Pondrum, Sandra Gilbert, Susan Stanford Friedman, Susan Gubar, and Shari Benstock—share this Eurocentric focus. Certainly it would be remiss to discuss Eliot without reference to symbolism, H. D. without reference to Freud, Faulkner without reference to Joyce.

Nonetheless, such approaches create and perpetuate significant lacunae by excluding or marginalizing texts and traditions that cannot adequately be articulated in vocabularies derived from Baudelaire, Freud, Nietzsche, or Joyce. Calling for a historicized view of modernism, Lillian S. Robinson and Lise Vogel's germinal essay "Modernism and History" (1971) addresses the limitations of the traditional New Critical view of modernism as a movement committed to "esthetic inviolability" (28). Robinson and Vogel argue that such an approach both reflects and furthers the politically problematic tendency of modernism "to intensify isolation. It forces the work of art, the artist, the critic, and the audience outside of history. Modernism denies us the possibility of understanding ourselves as *agents* in the material world, for all has been removed to an abstract world of ideas, where interactions can be minimized or emptied of meaning and real consequences" (45). Since the publication of "Modernism and History," the New Critical approach to modernism has been substantially revised in response to a variety of challenges posed by "postmodernists," many of whom adapt the premises of politically aware theorists such as Bertolt Brecht and Mikhail Bakhtin. Similarly, poststructuralist theory questions the foundations of all oppositional thinking, including the assertion of a division between aesthetics and politics. It seems unlikely that either Robinson or Vogel—who are aware of their scholarship as part of a kinetic process grounded in the particular historical circumstances of the moment of composition—would today be quite so categorical in their political repudiation of modernism.

If much has changed since 1971, much has remained the same. Despite sensitive revisions of "canonical" modernism—particularly Frederick Karl's *Modern and Modernism*—Robinson and Vogel's comment on the Euro- and phallocentrism of modernism as traditionally defined in academia retains its cogency: "To be conscious of race, class, or sex with respect to high culture is to be conscious, first of all, of exclusion" (29). This remains particularly clear in relation to Afro-American literature. Even as they challenge the hegemony of traditional discourse, many feminist and postmodernist critics—even some who grant attention to individual Afro-American texts or writers—show only a passing acquaintance with the complexity of the cultural traditions informing Afro-American writing.

By considering *Native Son*—usually viewed as a realistic protest novel (whether ideological or existential)—specifically in the matrix of Euro-American modernism, this chapter seeks to reclaim access to a modernist tradition compatible with the communal, kinetic, and political (though usually not ideological) imperatives of the Afro-American blues tradition. Several Afro-American critics—most notably Toni Morrison, Houston Baker, Ralph Ellison, Henry Louis Gates, and Robert Stepto—have identified points of connection between Euro-American theoretical discourse and Afro-American vernacular expression. None is entirely comfortable with Wright's position in that dialogue or, more generally, in the Afro-American literary tradition. Each evinces some discomfort with *Native Son* and prefers to focus on *Black Boy*. In addition to suggesting a revised sense of the modernist movement, approaching *Native Son* as a modernist text helps reassert its position as a central, if problematical, Afro-American text. Standing at the crossroads (to use the term Baker adapts from Robert Johnson, after Johnson had adapted it from the black and unknown bards who preceded him in the New World and the Old) where Afro- and Euro-American traditions intersect, Wright focuses his treatment of fragmentation, alienation, and sense-making on his most powerfully resonant figure of exclusion: Bigger Thomas.

In part because he can articulate his experience fully neither in Afro- nor Euro-American terms—an inability that connects him profoundly with his creator—Bigger has too frequently been undervalued by even Wright's most insightful critics. In the midst of a moving celebration of *Black Boy,* for example, Ellison criticizes Wright for forcing "into Bigger's consciousness concepts and ideas which his intellect could not formulate" (100). Commenting on Bigger's limitations, Ellison wrote: "Wright could imagine Bigger, but Bigger could not possibly imagine Richard Wright. Wright saw to that" (*Shadow* 121–22). Stepto, whose book *From behind the Veil* follows Ellison in placing *Black Boy* at the center of Wright's canon, pursues the implications of Ellison's critique further, connecting Bigger's limitations with Wright's own. In "I Thought I Knew These People: Richard Wright and the Afro-American Literary Tradition," Stepto observes that "Wright's refusal to partake of the essential intra-racial rituals which the situation demanded suggests that he was either unaware of, or simply refused to participate in, those viable modes of speech represented in history by the preacher and orator and in letters by the articulate hero" (197). Stepto is certainly correct in identifying the central issue as "Wright's idea of the hero." Where Stepto accords Bigger a "sub-heroic posture" (207), however, I would suggest the phrase "pre-heroic posture." Thwarted in his attempts to achieve what Stepto calls ascent—the passage from oppression to a limited freedom based on the attainment of Euro-American literacy—Bigger provides a compelling figure of the internal dynamics of what Stepto calls the "symbolic South" (*Veil* 167). Ironically, it is Bigger's very sense of alienation from Afro-American community that makes him such a powerful figure for the part of that community which has not achieved the ascent. While I would agree with Stepto that Wright's sense of alienation places him in "the mainstream of American letters" (*Chant* 207), a close reading of *Native Son* in relation to the concerns of the modernist current of that mainstream suggests the ways in which his articulation of that alienation places him in the blues-based mainstream of Afro-American letters. Listening carefully to Bigger Thomas's inarticulate blues, we can more easily perceive the modernist blues novel inside the realist protest novel and envision a crossroads meeting of Bigger Thomas with Samuel Beckett, Toni Morrison, or Bertolt Brecht.

Afro-American Culture and the Discourse of Modernism

At least since Du Bois produced *The Souls of Black Folk,* Afro-American culture has explicitly addressed the central concerns of modernism: fragmentation, alienation, sense-making. Du Bois's description of "double consciousness" emphasizes one particular experience of the fragmented world, an experience that alienates the individual from both the disintegrating community and a secure sense of self. According to Du Bois, the Afro-American experiences "a world which yields him no true self-consciousness, but only lets him see himself through the revelation of the other world. It is a peculiar sensation, this double-consciousness, this sense of always looking at one's self through the eyes of others" (364). Contemporary critics such as Stepto and Henry Louis Gates address the ways in which this fragmented worldview gives rise to "double" or "multiple" modes of sense-making. Gates's analysis of the Afro-American practice of signifying complements Stepto's sense of distinct types of "literacy" associated with specific situations within American society. Like Charles W. Chesnutt, Zora Neale Hurston, and Ellison, these critics recognize Afro-American expressive practices as intricate adjustments to a world fragmented by the communal experience of slavery and racial oppression. Understood from a Du Boisean perspective, then, the central problem confronted by Afro-American culture closely resembles that confronted by mainstream modernism: the alienated individual experiences a profound sense of psychological and cultural disorientation in a world characterized by an accelerating rate of change; he or she subsequently attempts to regain some sense of coherence. The primary difference between Afro- and Euro-American responses to this dilemma can be seen in the tendency of many Euro-American modernists to experience their situation as individual and, to some extent, ahistorical, while Afro-American modernists generally perceive a communal dilemma deriving from historical and political forces. This association of racial experience with the modernist sensibility is not limited to Afro-American writers. As Thadious Davis and Eric Sundquist have demonstrated, for example, William Faulkner's use of modernist techniques—in particular, fragmented narrative perspectives—can be traced to his perception of the black-white division of his native Mississippi as well as to his awareness of continental modernist literature.

Despite the general unawareness of Du Boisean double consciousness in discussions of modernism, both traditional and revisionist critics have understood modernism as a pervasive cultural dislocation affecting the quality of life not just for artists but also for those unaware of the historical origins and philosophical implications of their own situations. Paul Fussell's *The Great War and Modern Memory* and Samuel Hynes's *The Auden Generation* identify World War I as the culmination of a long historical process that led to a widespread perception of the world as a moral and psychological "waste land." The postwar malaise seems to have been felt most acutely in urban settings, where the impact of technological advances had been accelerating for nearly a century. The first two major Afro-American literary movements of the century were centered in cities: New York during the Harlem Renaissance of the twenties and, as Robert Bone has convincingly argued, Chicago during an equally significant but less publicized Chicago Renaissance that included Wright and lasted from the midthirties through the early fifties. It seems particularly noteworthy that one of the major contrasts between the early Harlem Renaissance, particularly as described in Alain Locke's "The New Negro," and the Chicago Renaissance lies in the increasing awareness of the city not as promised land but as an unreal wasteland that destroys blacks in particularly vicious ways.

If we align our perspective with that of Bigger Thomas, this urban wasteland can be seen as a disorienting texture of competing discourses of equivalent significance. Literary modernism, whatever its particular form, takes its place alongside a number of other discourses, including those of film, advertising, and journalism. Each of these discourses has been viewed as a signal index of the modern world; each excludes Afro-American participation almost entirely. Roland Marchand's *Advertising the American Dream: Making Way for Modernity, 1920–1940* discusses advertising professionals as self-described "apostles of modernity" who saw themselves both responding to and shaping cultural realities as profoundly important as those addressed by Eliot. Competing styles of advertising—as Joyce realized when he placed advertising salesman Leopold Bloom at the center of his epic novel—reflect concerns over the relationship of artist/advertiser to material and audience that parallel those of more traditional artists such as Stephen Dedalus. In *Ulysses* and in Dos Passos's *U.S.A.*, advertising provides a fascinating focal point for examination of the relationship between "high" and "popular" discourses. From Bigger Thomas's viewpoint, however, the claims put forward in the advertising journal *Printers' Ink* are not qualitatively different from those advanced in *Des Imagistes*. The same critique can be applied to Bigger's relationship with practically every other mainstream discourse, whether or not it is immediately available to him in his corner of the wasteland.

Wright's presentation of a variety of these discourses—advertising, journalistic, cinematic, legal, aesthetic, Marxist—continually emphasizes Bigger's exclusion. Some of the exclusions are self-evident. The journalistic discourse pictured in *Native Son* contributes directly to Bigger's death. In addition to discovering Mary's body in the furnace, the journalists—and in his presentation Wright was, as Keneth Kinnamon has demonstrated, accurately reporting the actions of the Chicago press during the Nixon case, which provided the background for the novel—convict Bigger of rape in the absence of any evidence and prior to his trial. Although Bigger hopes momentarily that his acts of rebellion will force the newspapers to "carry the story, *his* story" (188), his continuing exclusion is made clear in the newspaper clipping that tacitly endorses the Jackson, Mississippi, journalist who labels Bigger a "trouble-making nigger" (239). It hardly seems surprising that a large percentage of references to newspapers in *Native Son* associate journalism with the bloody head of Mary Dalton (79, 100, and many others). Together, Mary's head and the journalistic discourse assure Bigger's death.

Wright presents the movies and advertising in similar terms. Although Bigger looks to the movies for escape from the circumstances of his life (12, 24), the movies he sees in *Native Son* simply reiterate his exclusion. *Trader Horn* is a Tarzan-style movie that presents blacks in stereotypical images: "naked . . . whirling in wild dances" (29); *The Gay Woman* presents equally stereotypical images of upper-class white life. Similarly, the two advertisements Bigger sees early in the "Fear" section combine mockery and direct attack. When he encounters the first—a campaign poster for Buckley, the state's attorney who prosecutes his case—Bigger is aware of a "huge colored poster" showing a "white face" (11). Despite his limited knowledge of the white world, Bigger clearly recognizes the mockery of the slogan "if you break the law, you can't win" (11). Shortly thereafter Bigger and Gus see a skywriting plane "so far away that at times the strong glare of the sun blanked it from sight" (14). When they are able to decipher the words, the message—"Use Speed Gasoline" (15)—has little relevance to their lives. In each case, Wright presents a discourse that either mocks or excludes Afro-American experience. When they involve blacks at all—as in the poster advertising *Trader Horn* (25) or the newspaper photo of Bigger with his "teeth bared in a snarl" (285)—the discourses perpetuate stereotypical images. Boris Max comments on the significance of these exclusions when he observes: "How constantly and overwhelmingly the advertisements, radios, newspapers and movies play upon us! But in thinking of them remember that to many they are tokens of mockery. These bright colors may fill our hearts with elation, but to many they are daily taunts. Imagine a man walking amid such a scene, a part of it, and yet knowing that it is *not* for him!" (332).

Although Max directs his comments primarily toward popular discourses, his observation is equally applicable to aesthetic and political discourse. When he first enters the Dalton house, Bigger encounters "several paintings whose nature he tried to make out" (39). Failing to do so, in part because he has been excluded from the cultural heritage of nonrepresentational modernist art, Bigger experiences a rapidly increasing sense of alienation: "strange objects challenged him; and he was feeling angry and uncomfortable" (39). Wright does not, however, use this scene to endorse the "social realist" aesthetic that had emerged after the suppression of technical experimentation following the Soviet "Silver Age." In *How "Bigger" Was Born*, Wright implies that by the time he began writing *Native Son* the Communist party leadership had lost all sense of the deconstructive implications of Marx. As a result, Wright felt a strong pressure to simplify his presentation of Bigger, in effect to exclude aspects of his experience: "How could I create such complex and wide schemes of associational thought and feeling, such filigreed webs of dreams and politics, without being mistaken for a 'smuggler of reaction'?" (22). For the moment, it is sufficient to emphasize that, like the popular discourses, the leading aesthetic discourses of the thirties excluded important aspects of Bigger's—and Wright's—experience. Nonetheless, the very attempt to include the discourses, or more precisely fragments of these discourses, in the text of *Native Son* highlights Wright's close relationship to a modernism grounded—though Wright would almost certainly not have thought of his work in these terms—in the blues.

The Modernism of *Native Son*

Wright's interest in modernism, well established by the time he wrote *Native Son,* is thoroughly documented. Although his earliest reading focused on American realists and naturalists, he developed a serious interest in the modernist avant-garde soon after he moved to Chicago in the late twenties. By 1935 he was discussing Eliot, Joyce, and Stein with members of the John Reed and South Side Writers' Clubs. He continued these discussions with Ralph Ellison—later to be recognized as an Afro-American modernist—whom he met after moving to New York in the late thirties. Writing in the Federal Writers' Project publication *New York Panorama,* Wright observed in obviously self-referential terms that "Joyce's *Ulysses* influenced some of the Negro writers, and even the gospel of Gertrude Stein claimed a number of Negro adherents" (143). More importantly, Wright had experimented extensively with modernist techniques in the fiction and poetry he had written prior to *Native Son. Lawd Today,* written during the midthirties but published only after Wright's death, is a conscious rewriting of *Ulysses.* Filled with direct allusions to Joyce and Eliot, the novel employs a mythic parallel and multiple styles to catalog one day in the life of a black Chicago postal worker. *Uncle Tom's Children,* Wright's first published book, intentionally recalls *Dubliners;* the final story, "Bright and Morning Star," ends with a direct revoicing of the conclusion of Joyce's "The Dead." In *American Hunger,* Wright describes the aesthetic approach of *Uncle Tom's Children* and his thirties poetry in terms reminiscent of Eliot's "objective correlative": "My purpose was to capture a physical state or movement that carried a strong subjective impression. . . . If I could fasten the mind of the reader upon words so firmly that he would forget words and be conscious only of his response, I felt that I would be in sight of knowing how to write narrative" (22).

Compared with the obvious modernism of Wright's earlier works, *Native Son* appears superficially to be a traditional narrative, especially in formal terms. To dismiss its modernism entirely, however, is to risk repressing a central element of Wright's literary genealogy, and thereby to perpetuate the identification of modernism with a specific set of techniques. Perhaps the clearest mark of *Native Son*'s modernism is Wright's presentation of Chicago as an Afro-American version of Eliot's "unreal city." Echoing Eliot and Carl Sandburg (another Chicago-based writer who saw no necessary contradiction between populist politics and modernist aesthetics), *How "Bigger" Was Born* emphasizes the unresolved tensions of the "fabulous city in which Bigger lived, an indescribable city, huge, roaring, dirty, noisy, raw, stark, brutal; a city of extremes: torrid summers and sub-zero winters, white people and black people, the English language and strange tongues, foreign born and native born, scabby poverty and gaudy luxury, high idealism and hard cynicism!" (28). In his introduction to St. Clair Drake and Horace Cayton's study of Chicago, *Black Metropolis,* Wright elaborates on this "fatal division of being, a war of impulses" he shared with many other black migrants in Chicago: "in the great iron city, that impersonal, mechanical city, amid the steam, the smoke, the snowy winds, the blistering suns; there in that self-conscious city, that city so deadly dramatic and stimulating, we caught whispers of the meanings that life could have, and we were pushed and pounded by facts much too big for us" (xvii).

While most critics stress the naturalistic quality of the treatment of the city in *Native Son,* Wright tempers his naturalism with a modernist subtext emphasizing the city's psychological impact. Bigger Thomas experiences the city as an entity that is at once living and dead: "There were many empty buildings and black windows, like blind eyes, buildings like skeletons" (147), and "They stopped in front of a tall, snow-covered building whose many windows gaped blackly, like the eye-sockets of empty skulls" (195). Recalling the modernist genealogy linking Poe, Baudelaire, and the "Circe" section of *Ulysses,* Wright presents the city as an objective correlative for Bigger's psychological state. The burned-out buildings of the black belt serve as a particularly effective objective correlative for Bigger's situation. Not only do they impose a constant reminder of the wasteland, they also recall the racially specific history that excludes Bigger from even the shared experience of fragmentation. Entering one of the collapsing buildings, Bigger sees "walls almost like those of the Dalton home. . . . That was the way most houses on the South Side were, ornate, old, stinking; homes once of rich white people, now inhabited by Negroes or standing dark and empty with yawning black windows" (155). What from a Euro-American perspective could serve as an emblem of the decay of a once-proud tradition is, from an Afro-American perspective, simply another reminder of the continuity of racial exclusion.

It is hardly surprising that Bigger experiences this wasteland in surrealistic terms. Several of Wright's descriptions present the city as a psychic landscape of the type associated with the "meta-physical picaresque," a genre that, as Monique Chefdor has demonstrated, unifies apparently distinct strains of modernism. As Bigger crosses the threshold of the ornate old building with Bessie, the shift in the imagery describing his perception reflects his growing sense of absolute exclusion: "He looked up and down the street, past ghostly lamps that shed a long series of faintly shimmering cones of yellow against the snowy night. He took her to the front entrance which gave into a vast pool of inky silence. He brought out the flashlight and focused the round spot on a rickety stairway leading upward into a still blacker darkness" (155). The image of the "inky silence" preceding the existential blackness in which he will kill Bessie seems particularly significant given Bigger's exclusion from written discourse. After the murder, Wright emphasizes Bigger's previous experiences of perceptual dislocation, his sense of inhabiting a world where even fundamental laws of physics fail to provide a coherent framework for perception: "never had he felt a sense of wholeness. Sometimes, in his room or on the sidewalk, the world seemed to him a strange labyrinth even when the streets were straight and the walls were square; a chaos which made him feel that something in him should be able to understand it, divide it, focus it" (203–4).

The murders of Mary and Bessie bring this long-standing sense of dislocation to a climax. Bigger senses that his violence is inextricably linked to the city in which he lives; each murder is accompanied by a redefinition of Bigger's sense of what the city means. Immediately after realizing that Mary is dead, Bigger experiences the city—imaged as a totally white presence—as an absolute determinant of his actions: "The reality of the room fell from him; the vast city of white people that sprawled outside took its place" (75). Having crossed the threshold into the metaphysical darkness of the ornate old building, however, his sense of the city undergoes a profound transformation. Immediately before he kills Bessie, he experiences a moment in which "the city did not exist" (199). Torn between these extremes— experiencing a tension of a sort basic to the modernist sensibility— Bigger gradually realizes that the question is not whether or not the city exists; rather it is what his own consciousness *makes* of the city. Associating the city with the whiteness of the fallen snow, Bigger— like many modernist criminal-artist-metaphysical picaros—begins to explore his own sense-making process: "The snow had stopped falling and the city, white, still, was a vast stretch of roof-tops and sky. He had been thinking about it for hours here in the dark and now there it was, all white, still. But what he had thought about it had made it real with a reality it did not have now in the daylight. When lying in the dark thinking of it, it seemed to have something which left it when it was looked at" (204).

This ever-changing wasteland exerts a profoundly fragmenting impact on Bigger's consciousness. In *How "Bigger" Was Born,* Wright echoes Du Bois's analysis of double consciousness when he traces the Afro-American sense of fragmentation to the existence of "two worlds, the white world and the black world." The split is as much psychological as political, because "the very tissue of [Afro-Americans'] consciousness received its tone and timbre from the striving of that dominant civilization." Aggravating the racially specific problems for Bigger is the fact that even the dominant civilization had come to perceive itself as a wasteland. Wright observes that Bigger is a "product of a dislocated society; he is a dispossessed and disinherited man; he is all of this, and he lives amid the greatest possible plenty on earth and he is looking and feeling for a way out" (19). Although Wright purses the implications of this observation in specifically political terms, the description would serve as well for Eliot's J. Alfred Prufrock. Like his modernist contemporaries, Bigger experiences a profound sense of entrapment emanating from a confusion of subjective and objective that subverts his sense of self. Just as the city assumes an organic quality, other people repeatedly lose their human solidity, casting Bigger adrift in a world of semianimate barriers. Mary and Jan seem "two vast white looming walls" (59). When he is captured, Bigger looks out at "a circle of white faces; but he was outside of them, behind his curtain, his wall" (228). In this context, the similarity between the modernist malaise and Du Boisean double consciousness seems clear. Both alienate the individual from any unified sensibility. Throughout *Native Son,* Bigger feels his own fragmentation: "He was divided and pulled against himself" (21); "There were two Biggers" (214). Such division seems the inevitable response to a context in which every word, every symbol possess at least two—and frequently many more—possible meanings. The cross of the preachers and the cross of the Ku Klux Klan dissolve into one another in Bigger's fragmented consciousness (287). Although he lacks words to express his sense of this fragmentation—and in this he is more a modernist artist/hero than the inarticulate victim described by Ellison—Bigger is acutely aware of his own lack of wholeness: "never in all his life, with this black skin of his, had the two worlds, thought and feeling, will and mind, aspiration and satisfaction, been together; never had he felt a sense of wholeness" (203–4). As he prepares for death, Bigger's apprehension of his fragmentation takes the form of an intensely solipsistic speculation that would not be out of place in a Beckett mindscape: "If he were nothing, if this were all, then why could not he die without hesitancy? Who and what was he to feel the agony of a wonder so intensely that it amounted to fear? Why was this strange impulse always throbbing in him when there was nothing outside of him to meet it and explain it? Who or what had traced this restless design in him? Why was this eternal reaching for something that was not there? Why this black gulf between him and the world: warm red blood here and cold blue sky there, and never a wholeness, a oneness, a meeting of the two?" (350–51).

Bigger's internal response to his fragmentation, like those of "metaphysical picaros" from Leopold Bloom to Ellison's invisible man and Tyrone Slothrop of *Gravity's Rainbow,* passes through several distinct phases. Gradually, Bigger's initial disorientation gives way to an exhilarating sense of himself as questing hero, which in turn disintegrates into a solipsistic sense of total meaninglessness, differing from the original situation because previously Bigger had been unaware of even the possibility of meaning. The final stage of Bigger's metaphysical wandering, explicitly recalling Eliot's "The Love Song of J. Alfred Prufrock," involves a direct confrontation with the association of criminal and artist in the modernist sensibility, an extended meditation on what it means "to murder and create."

At the outset of *Native Son,* Bigger embodies, to use Wright's phrase from *How "Bigger" Was Born,* "a hot and whirling vortex of undisciplined and unchannelized impulses" (18). His perception oscillates wildly between extreme subjectivity and extreme objectivity: "The sharp precision of the world of steel and stone dissolved into blurred waves. He blinked and the world grew hard again, mechanical, distinct" (14). Similar feelings of being cast adrift in a discontinuous world recur throughout the novel. Confronting the journalists in the Dalton basement, Bigger feels that "events were like the details of a tortured dream, happening without cause. At times it seemed that he could not quite remember what had gone before and what it was he was expecting to come" (169). Paralyzed by this Dostoyevskian "deadlock of impulses" that renders him "unable to rise to the land of the living" (83), Bigger experiences himself as a cipher, surrendering all sense of control to the mechanical world around him: "He was not driving; he was simply sitting and floating along smoothly through darkness" (67).

This feeling of ease, of course, collapses almost immediately, leaving Bigger with only the darkness. His growing awareness of alienation, however, marks the beginning of a significant new stage of Bigger's metaphysical journey. Whereas in the "Fear" section Bigger seems unaware of the relationship between external and internal experience, in "Flight" he senses the importance of sense-making processes to the construction of reality. This recognition begins as a vague desire to resist being defined by the discourses that surround him. In a sequence of passages recalling Pound's imagist principle of "direct presentation of the 'thing,' whether subjective or objective," Bigger "wished that he could be an idea in their minds" (110). At several points, he immerses himself directly in a level of experience that strips away the verbal discourse—the Eliotic "babble of voices" (184)—that surrounds him: "The world of sound fell abruptly away from him and a vast picture appeared before his eyes, a picture teeming with so much meaning that he could not react to it all at once" (116). Bigger enters this new realm of experience with a feeling of exhilaration grounded on an unfamiliar sense of his own significance: "he held within the embrace of his bowels the swing of planets through space" (151).

This sense of liberation from external discourses, however, generates its own countermovement, plunging Bigger into solipsistic isolation. An extreme, and dangerous, separation from the external social realities that condition his consciousness accompanies Bigger's growing awareness of the world of images: "He had been so deeply taken up with his own thoughts that he did not know if he had actually heard anything or had imagined it" (162). As the external forces reassert their power, Bigger struggles to maintain a grasp on his internal reality, which Wright images increasingly in terms of total isolation. Staring into the airshaft of the old ornate building, Bigger projects his sense of desolation: "He looked downward and saw nothing but black darkness into which now and then a few flakes of white floated from the sky" (196). Again, the description suggests Beckett. Echoing the Faulkner of *The Sound and the Fury,* Wright associates this landscape with Bigger's experience of a meaninglessness that he feels all the more intensely for his dawning sense of his own significance: "Outside in the cold night the wind moaned and died down, like an idiot in an icy black pit" (200).

As his treatment of Bigger's subsequent metaphysical wandering demonstrates, however, Wright does not simply abandon his metaphysical picaro to a wasteland "signifying nothing." Rather, Wright emphasizes Bigger's attempt to wrest meaning from his isolation. The final section of *Native Son* can be seen as a gloss on the line from "The Love Song of J. Alfred Prufrock" that provides the epigraph for this chapter: "There will be time to murder and create." Wright alludes directly to Eliot's line several times, first near the start of the "Flight" section—"He had murdered and had created a new life for himself" (90)—and again near its end—"He had committed murder twice and had created a new world for himself" (204–5). Both claims, however, are premature, based on the momentary exhilaration associated with Bigger's discovery of his own significance. When the power of the external world is reasserted in the capture scene, Bigger's sense of creative power vanishes almost entirely. At the beginning of the "Fate" section, Bigger is back in a wasteland where even the murders lack meaning. Recalling Eliot's ironic treatment of rebirth imagery in *The Waste Land*, Wright underlines Bigger's despair: "He had reached out and killed and had not solved anything, so why not reach inward and kill that which had duped him? This feeling sprang up of itself, organically, automatically; like the rotted hull of a seed forming the soil in which it should grow again" (234).

Faced with this dead end, Bigger gradually recaptures the perception that had first emerged during the early stages of his metaphysical quest. Confronted by the babble of voices in his jail cell, he focuses on the relatively unmediated images that resist or redefine the excluding discourses: "there appeared before him a vast black silent void and the images of the preacher swam in that void, grew large and powerful; familiar images which his mother had given him when he was a child at her knee; images which in turn aroused impulses long dormant, impulses that he had suppressed and sought to shunt from his life. They were images which had once given him a reason for living, had explained the world. Now they sprawled before his eyes and seized his emotions in a spell of awe and wonder" (241). Anticipating the blues emphasis that emerges in the final section of the novel, this reimmersion in images inspires Bigger to recapitulate the earlier stages of his picaresque journey. Recalling the "sense of exclusion that was as cold as a block of ice," Bigger reiterates his awareness of the insufficiency of external discourse: "To those who wanted to kill him he was not human, not included in that picture of Creation." This in turn allows him to recapture his sense of potential creativity, now phrased with an increased awareness of the power of the external world: "that was why he had killed it. To live, he had created a new world for himself, and for that he was to die" (242). This more complex apprehension of the connection between murder and creation drives Bigger back into himself: "He lived in a thin, hard core of consciousness" (305). At this stage, he is aware of his solipsism as a conscious choice, a final stage of the Beckettesque metaphysical journey toward confrontation with his own death: "To accustom his mind to death as much as possible, he made all the world beyond his cell a vast grey land where neither night nor day was, peopled by strange men and women whom he could not understand" (349). Nor—and this is very much to the point in regard to the alienation of both Wright and Bigger—could they understand him.

Sense-Making and the Form of *Native Son*

In part because of Ellison's influential description of Bigger as "a near sub-human indictment of white oppression" (121), Bigger's sense-making process—the crucial element that connects him with the modernist artist-outsiders—has attracted little attention. Wright contributed substantially to this oversight by constantly reiterating Bigger's inarticulateness. The following passage typifies Wright's comments on Bigger: "Though he could not have put it into words, he felt that . . ." (235). Similarly, in *How "Bigger" Was Born*, Wright explicitly denies that Bigger possesses any capacity that might be construed as artistic: "Bigger did not offer in his life any articulate verbal explanations" (26). Wright offers this comment in part as justification of his decision to "fall back upon his own feelings as a guide" in the presentation of Bigger, implicitly seconding Ellison's emphasis on the distance between creator and character. Nonetheless, a deep connection exists between Bigger's struggles to articulate, and perhaps communicate, his experience, and Wright's analogous struggles, which are reflected in the formal irresolution of *Native Son*. Both Wright and Bigger inhabit a world that offers no vocabulary capable of expressing the particular Afro-American experience of the modernist situation. Nonetheless, both struggle to articulate their experience despite profound problems regarding their relationship to their audiences, both real and potential. Although Bigger and Wright share strong doubts concerning the validity and utility of Afro-American vernacular traditions, both emerge from *Native Son* as blues artists of profound, if ironically tinged, power.

Wright identifies several environmental and psychological causes for Bigger's inarticulateness, reinforcing the view of Bigger as lacking in essential human resources. Wright traces Bigger's alienation to an environmentally determined repression of thought and feeling. Bigger's refusal to acknowledge the emotional reality of his family's suffering is presented as a self-protective strategy grounded in his feeling "that they were suffering and that he was powerless to help them. He knew that the moment he allowed himself to feel to its fullness how they lived, the shame and misery of their lives, he would be swept out of himself with fear and despair" (9). Similarly, his feeling of impotence in the face of vast environmental pressures stunts his intellectual perception: "But what could he do? Each time he asked

himself that question his mind hit a blank wall and he stopped thinking" (11). Bigger's repression of the reality of his own experience,
which would in any case preclude a comprehensive articulation, is
reinforced by external factors throughout *Native Son.* Both whites
and blacks encourage, and enforce, Bigger's repressed silence. The
Mississippi newspaper editor exemplifies white attitudes when he observes that the effectiveness of the southern system rests on "regulat-
ing [blacks'] speech and actions" (240). Even the relatively sympathetic Boris Max contributes to the problem when he tells Bigger,
"You won't have to say anything here" (265) and later informs the
court that "he does not wish to testify here" (279). Similarly, Bigger's
family—imaged as "inarticulate and unconscious" (91)—and friends
discourage his attempts at articulation. When Bigger begins to question the social structure of Chicago, Gus dismisses his words: "Aw,
nigger, quit thinking about it. You'll go nuts" (17). As both politically and psychologically oriented critics have emphasized, Bigger's
environment places crushing pressure on the development of his
perceptions.

In addition to the environmental factors, *Native Son* suggests a
more elusive aspect of the problem of articulation. Beginning with
the opening pages of *How "Bigger" Was Born,* Wright intimates a basic
inability of language to communicate experience. Focusing on his
own problems as a writer trying to articulate Bigger's experience,
Wright reveals a profound connection with the character incapable
of offering "articulate verbal expressions." Three times within the
first two pages, Wright describes his frustration over an inability to
articulate his own process: "Always there is something that is just beyond the tip of the tongue that could explain it all"; "the author is
eager to explain. But the moment he makes the attempt his words
falter"; "he is left peering with eager dismay back into the dim
reaches of his own incommunicable life" (1–2). That almost all modernist writers experience a similar frustration is precisely the point:
Bigger Thomas's struggle to render his experience in words is only
more extreme than—not qualitatively different from—that which
led Yeats to create the private language of *Mythologies* or Joyce to write
Finnegans Wake.

The problem lies not only with the environment but with the difficulty of articulation per se, a difficulty that lies near the foundation
of postmodernist literature and poststructuralist theory. The situation for Wright was particularly problematic given the obvious inadequacy of Euro-American discourses for the expression of Afro-
American experience. That Bigger Thomas senses this makes his
struggle for articulation all the more significant. At the start of the

novel, Bigger shapes his expression in such a way as to repress feeling. When Mary questions him at the Kitchen Shack, Bigger "groped for neutral words, words that would convey information but not indicate any shade of his own feelings" (63). In part because his attempts to exert even such limited control over his expression fail, Bigger occasionally arrives at startlingly clear insights into the nature of discourse. Contemplating the social segregation that breeds double consciousness, Bigger realizes that the white power structure conditions all discourse. "As long as he and his black folks did not go beyond certain limits, there was no need to fear that white force. But whether they feared it or not, each and every day of their lives they lived with it; even when words did not sound its name, they acknowledged its reality" (97). After the murders, Bigger's sense of the "white force" that frustrates his attempts at articulation focuses as much on the inadequacy of the forms of discourse as on external oppressive forces. This sense intervenes when he is confronted by Buckley: "he could never tell why he had killed. It was not that he did not really want to tell, but the telling of it would have involved an explanation of his entire life" (261–62). A similar despair over the inadequacy of language, coupled with a haunting intimation of an alternative discourse, recurs when Bigger speaks with Max: "he knew that the moment he tried to put his feelings into words, his tongue would not move. . . . He wondered wistfully if there was not a set of words which he had in common with others, words which would evoke in others a sense of the same fire that smoldered in him" (308–9).

The search for such words—Bigger's desire "to say something to ease the swelling in his chest" (38)—exerts a profound influence on both the thematic content and the formal structure of *Native Son*. Bigger tells his story, or attempts to tell his story, repeatedly, at first for reasons of self-defense but increasingly in order to address his sense of fragmentation. His first response upon realizing that Mary is dead focuses on the necessity of articulation: "He had to construct a case for 'them'" (75). While self-defense remains an important element of Bigger's later attempts to shape his story, he soon recognizes articulation as a potentially more active form of resistance designed to subvert dominant discourses: "They wanted him to draw the picture and he would draw it like he wanted it. He was trembling with excitement. In the past had they not always drawn the picture for him? He could tell them anything he wanted and what could they do about it?" (135). After his imprisonment, Bigger moves even farther toward the modernist concept of art as salvation. Struggling for a mode of articulation entirely free of the dominant discourses, he envisions "a vast configuration of images and symbols whose magic and power could lift him up and make him live so intensely that the dread of being black and unequal would be forgotten" (234).

Alongside this developing sense of the significance of articulation, Wright portrays what amounts to an aesthetic evolution in Bigger's craft. When he first attempts to tell his story, Bigger's approach is almost entirely realistic: "He went over the story again, fastening every detail firmly in his mind" (108). This emphasis on the concrete entails a belief in the story as fixed form: "he would have to go into details and he would try to fasten hard in his mind the words he spoke so that he could repeat them a thousand times, if necessary" (131). Such an emphasis on precise rendition of external facts, however, fails to address the actual complexity of Bigger's situation. Soon, he realizes that any adequate articulation must take into account the subjective as well as the objective. Questioned by Buckley, he "wondered how he could link up his bare actions with what he had felt; but his words came out flat and dull. White men were looking at him waiting for his words, and all the feelings of his body vanished, just as they had when he was in the car between Jan and Mary" (263). During the final stage of Bigger's metaphysical journey, after his conviction renders the utilitarian purposes of articulation nearly irrelevant, Wright highlights the increasing subjectivity of Bigger's approach to articulation: "In him again, imperiously, was the desire to talk, to tell; his hands were lifted in mid-air and when he spoke he tried to charge into the tone of his words what he *himself* wanted to hear, what *he* needed" (354–55).

Although his awareness of the subjective element of sense- making increases greatly, Bigger never values articulation simply as solipsistic monologue. In large part because his story-telling process originates in the need for self-defense, Bigger is acutely aware of his audiences, shaping distinct versions of his story for Peggy (109), Bessie (120, 192), Britten and Mr. Dalton (143), Buckley (260), and Max (296). Even during his trial, when it becomes apparent that his story will not save his life, Bigger continues to perceive audience as a vital element of articulation. Examining the connection between subjective and external realities—"How could he find out if this feeling of his was true, if others had it?"—Bigger defines his sense of wholeness, of adequate articulation, in terms of contact: "in the touch, response of recognition, there would be union, identity; there would be a supporting oneness, a wholeness which had been denied him all his life" (307). As his execution nears, Bigger finds it difficult to maintain any belief in the possibility of such contact: "Why this black gulf between him and the world: warm red blood here and cold blue sky there, and never a wholeness, a oneness, a meeting of the two?" (351). Despite his alienation from Max and his feeling that "What he wanted to say was stronger in him when he was alone" (352), Bigger attempts to combine subjective intensity and external contact in his final conversation with Max.

The failure of Bigger's attempt to communicate with Max—"He could not talk" (353)—underscores the insufficiency of modernist discourses for the articulation of Afro-American experience. The failure results most immediately from Max's inability to recognize the seriousness of Bigger's gesture: "Max did not know, had no suspicion of what he wanted, of what he was trying to say" (353). Reflecting the limitations of the Marxist analysis presented in the "Guilt of the Nation" speech, which reduces Bigger to a victimized "symbol, a test symbol" (324), Max shows little sense of the complexity of Bigger's consciousness, responding only with "a casual look, devoid of the deeper awareness that Bigger sought" (353). More importantly, Max's failure to respond increases Bigger's sense of exclusion from the entire world of Euro-American discourse: "Was there any way to break down this wall of isolation? Distractedly, he gazed about the cell, trying to remember where he had heard words that would help him. He could recall none. He had lived outside of the lives of men. Their modes of communication, their symbols and images, had been denied him" (353).

This sense of exclusion points to a profoundly significant connection between the "inarticulate" Bigger Thomas and the eloquent Richard Wright, a connection readily discernible in the formal characteristics of *Native Son*. Both character and author engage in serious attempts to articulate the connection between subjective and objective experience to the multiple, and frequently threatening, audiences of the fragmented modernist world. Wright's description of Bigger's momentary insight serves as an emblem of his own attempts to communicate: "What was the use of running away? He ought to stop right here in the middle of the sidewalk and shout out what this was. It was so wrong that surely all the black people round him would do something about it; so wrong that all the white people would stop and listen" (211). Thematically, Wright emphasizes that the difficulty of realizing this vision drives Bigger Thomas toward an anguished solipsism (although, as I shall demonstrate, this is not Bigger's final position). In its superficially traditional narrative voice that conceals a multitude of unresolved modernist tensions—most notably that between Bigger as character/subject and Wright as objective narrator— *Native Son* suggests that, even as he attempted to shout out the truth, Wright sensed the inevitable frustration of his own attempts.

Like Bigger's, Wright's attempts at articulation took place in the context of the historical exclusion of Afro-Americans from the Euro-American "modes of communication," the "symbols and images" of the dominant discourses. Like the Joyce who employed a different style for each chapter of *Ulysses* or the Pound who assumed innumerable voices in the *Cantos,* Wright responded to the problem in a distinctly modernist way. Summarizing the critical consensus concerning the defining characteristics of modernist form, Richardo Quinones lists

> a determination to look at events from radically shifting points of view, the close juxtaposition of references from different areas of experience (the lofty as well as the banal, the Dionysian as well as the Apollonian), the evolution of character types whose register is complex enough to contain these rapidly shifting emotional, imagistic and lexical changes, and finally the location of this complex of emotional interrelations in a setting that is decidedly cosmopolitan (and polyglot), urban, industrial, and even technological. (7–8)

Some of these elements are immediately obvious in *Native Son.* However, the critical failure to recognize Bigger as a character type of sufficient complexity has combined with Wright's use of realistic techniques—a superficially consistent third-person limited point of view and an emphasis on concrete external details—to obscure the fact that *Native Son* incorporates a modernist form reflecting Wright's "determination to look at events from radically shifting points of view." Nonetheless, the text is filled with competing—and essentially unresolved—perspectives. The fact that many of these violate the realistic surface of the novel—the simultaneous presence of family, friends, lawyer, prosecutor, friends of the victim in Bigger's prison cell is the clearest example—can be traced to the modernist impulses at work in Wright's sensibility. The same principle holds in relation to the lengthy speeches that dominate the "Fate" section. Rather than simple failures of judgment, these speeches represent Wright's attempt to incorporate the range of discourses conditioning Bigger's experience. Max's voice competes with Buckley's; the newspapers propagate the voice of the Ku Klux Klan; a multitude of voices echoes in Bigger's head. Wright offers no more trustworthy center for interpretation than his Euro-American modernist contemporaries.

Bigger's Blues

Recognizing the modernist dimension of *Native Son* leads to the question of why Wright chose not to employ an obviously modernist form such as that of *Lawd Today.* One of the least discussed scenes in

Native Son—that centering on the figure of the screaming prisoner who commands Bigger's attention before being straitjacketed and removed from the cell block—suggests an interesting approach to this issue. Adding to the montage of voices in "Fear," the prisoner—clearly a voice from the margins of American society—introduces the type of articulate black perspective absent from the rest of the text. His summary of conditions on the South Side, cataloging crowded living conditions, poor-quality food, exploitative prices, poor schooling and medical care, parallels that offered by Max in his defense of Bigger. Yet when the man screams obsessively about the loss of papers concerning these white crimes he threatens to "publish . . . to the whole world" (291), he is rejected as "balmy" by both white captors and black prisoners. "Turning and twisting in the white men's hands," he is "trying desperately to free himself" (290).

In many ways, the crazy prisoner can be seen as Wright's representation of himself in *Native Son*. Despite his essentially accurate insights into the nature of Afro-American experience, his listeners misapprehend or simply dismiss his words. His failure results both from his blackness and from his refusal to separate intellectual insight and emotional intensity. Conditioned by the inadequacy of existing discourses—an inadequacy against which both Euro- and Afro-American modernists rebelled—his audience is unable to respond to the underlying power of his insights: "Bigger watched, fascinated, fearful. He had the sensation that the man was too emotionally wrought up over whatever it was that he had lost. Yet the man's emotions seemed real; they affected him, compelling sympathy" (291). The form, rather than the content, of the prisoner's words subverts the communication he desires. If my suggestion that the prisoner provides an image of Wright's aesthetic situation—screaming out to an uncomprehending audience in a multilevel prison—is accurate, then it seems particularly significant that he is imaged as Bigger's double: "He was about Bigger's size. Bigger had the queer feeling that his own exhaustion formed a hair-line upon which his feelings were poised" (291). Clearly, this suggests a potential connection between Bigger and his more articulate counterpart. But so long as the prisoner articulates his emotional and intellectual insights in a disjunctive manner, there seems little possibility of real contact between the two.

The relevance of this passage to Wright's rejection of modernist form in *Native Son* seems clear. To employ a modernist form would have been to relinquish the possibility of an audience, of the contact that Wright consistently images as crucial to full articulation. Speaking from the margins of Euro-American discourse, Wright could not risk further marginalization. Like Bigger Thomas, who begins to articulate his experience as a matter of self-defense, Wright could not afford—as a matter of practical survival in an intensely racist culture—to assume a solipsistic stance and declare the audience unreal, irrelevant.

As a result, he was forced to confront a recurring—and still unresolved—problem concerning the relationship between the modernist artist and his or her audience. The most common Euro-American response to the problem has been incisively presented in Charles Baxter's essay "Assaulting the Audience in Modernism," which argues that for the modernist artist "the consumer of art becomes the adversary, no matter what his or her class may be" (275). Baxter traces this adversarial attitude to an attempt "to restore the artist's authority" (276). In its typical modernist forms, this elevation of artistic sovereignty encourages the solipsistic stance that Wright, in large part because of his racial experience, found untenable. Unwilling to surrender either his modernist sensibility or his determination to reach a real audience, Wright found himself marginalized.

Wright was not entirely devoid of modernist allies. During the early thirties many of the young English writers discussed in Samuel Hynes's *The Auden Generation* envisioned a leftist modernism. Elsewhere, John Dos Passos, William Carlos Williams, and Bertolt Brecht shared Wright's desire to create a voice capable of integrating modernist technique and social commitment. Responding to the influential, if formally conservative, leftist critic Georg Lukács, Brecht asserted that realism had developed as an expression of bourgeois society and that a modernism grounded in vernacular forms was the inevitable, if not yet fully developed, voice of the forces that would ultimately lead to the emergence of a dominant proletariat: "Reality changes: in order to represent it, modes of representation must change" (83). For Brecht, this dictated the development of a leftist modernism that would be popular in the sense that it would be "intelligible to the broad masses, adopting and enriching their forms of expression, assuming their stand-point, confirming and correcting it" (80–81). There is no evidence, however, that Wright was familiar with Brecht's theoretical writing, which attained widespread circulation in English only after World War II. Even if he had known it, it is likely that Wright would have experienced it as yet another form of European discourse that took Afro-American experience insufficiently into account. Still, the general parallel between Wright and Brecht is instructive. Both writers take the audience much more seriously than the majority of their Anglo-American modernist contemporaries; both resist the leftist repudiation of modernist techniques;

both turn to vernacular expression—popular or folk culture—as a means of resolving their aesthetic dilemmas.

Where Brecht openly embraced popular forms, however, Wright felt a deep sense of ambivalence. Although he occasionally wrote blues poetry ("Red Clay Blues," "The FB Eye Blues"), Wright never settled on a clear attitude toward Afro-American vernacular music. Perhaps his most famous rejection of the tradition occurs in *Black Boy:* "after the habit of reflection had been born in me, I used to mull over the strange absence of real kindness in Negroes, how unstable was our tenderness, how lacking in genuine passion we were, how void of great hope, how timid our joy, how bare our traditions. . . . I brooded upon the cultural barrenness of black life" (33). Ellison and Stepto have discussed at length the paradoxical irrelevance of the passage to the "blues life" presented in the text. The importance of the passage lies not in what it says about Afro-American culture but in what it says about the depth of Wright's feeling of exclusion. Although Wright demonstrates a greater appreciation of vernacular expression elsewhere, the underlying ambivalence articulated in *Black Boy* remains a consistent thread in his thought. His essay "Blueprint for Negro Writing" presents folk expression as the strongest existing expression of "the collective sense of Negro life in America" (41), even as Wright emphasizes the limitations of its implicitly nationalistic political stance. Similarly, Wright's ambivalence toward vernacular forms can be seen in his description of Bigger Thomas, who is described in *How "Bigger" Was Born* as "a Negro nationalist in a vague sense" but "not nationalist enough to feel the need of religion or the folk culture of his own people" (25).

Even Wright's appreciations of folk culture reflect a somewhat simplified sense of Afro-American vernacular aesthetics, particularly in regard to music. Wright's foreword to Paul Oliver's *Blues Fell This Morning,* for example, presents the blues as a form of cultural compensation that excludes major areas of experience. Interpreting the blues as a response to an oppressive racist system that had systematically "nullified" African forms of expression, Wright describes its limitations: "a vocabulary terser than Basic English, shorn of all hyperbole, purged of metaphysical implications, wedded to a frankly atheistic vision of life, and excluding almost all references to nature and her various moods" (viii). Even Wright's most moving description of the blues, included in *Twelve Million Black Voices,* emphasizes images of stasis rather than kinetic process: "The ridiculousness and sublimity of love are captured in our blues, those sad-happy songs that laugh and weep all in one breath, those mockingly tender utterances of a folk imprisoned in steel and stone" (128). Comparing these descriptions with the richly metaphysical and distinctly hyperbolic lyrics of Robert Johnson's "Stones in My Passway," "Hellhound on My Trail," and "Me and the Devil Blues" or the natural meditation of Bessie Smith's "Backwater Blues" reveals the limitations of Wright's perspective. Deeply grounded in an essentially religious sensibility—Johnson speaks of damnation, *not* atheism—the blues (as Ellison, Greil Marcus in *Mystery Train,* Jon Michael Spencer in *Blues and Evil,* and Lawrence Levine in *Black Culture and Black Consciousness* have demonstrated) directly address a wide range of metaphysical concerns, though certainly not in the vocabulary of Euro-American theological discourse.

Wright's misapprehension of the connection between the blues and gospel, which complement one another to form the kind of comprehensive worldview he finds absent, in turn generates the second major limitation in his view of vernacular aesthetics. Both in the foreword to Oliver's book and in the text of *Native Son,* Wright presents black music as essentially passive. Anticipating Ron Karenga's 1960s repudiation of the blues as an "invalid" form expressing "resignation" (36), Wright associates the blues with "renounced rebellious impulses," emphasizing the form's "passivity, almost masochistic in quality" (ix). This description sounds the keynote of the treatment of Afro-American vernacular culture in *Native Son.* For Bigger, folk music does not even offer momentary compensation for or escape from oppression. When his mother sings, "the song irked him" (9); when Mary Dalton sings "Swing Low, Sweet Chariot" (66), he feels the song as a direct mockery. Bigger's alienation reflects Wright's view of folk expression as politically passive. Listening to a church congregation singing "Steal Away," Bigger thinks that "the music sang of surrender, resignation" (215). The self-demeaning interaction of Reverend Hammond and his mother with the whites in Bigger's jail cell reinforces such attitudes.

There are several problems with Wright's presentation of folk aesthetics. Despite his sensitivity to the ironies and ambiguities of modernist writing, Wright seems almost entirely deaf to the double meanings of Afro-American song. From Du Bois and Zora Neale Hurston to the present, Afro-American critics have been acutely aware that the experience of double consciousness had shaped an expressive tradition in which a self-protective surface acceptable to white listeners masked subversive, frequently political, meanings discernible primarily to black listeners. Thus "Steal Away" and "Swing Low" can be heard either as purely religious songs expressing a passive yearning for eternal salvation or as implicitly political messages calling on slaves to escape from their bondage. Such double messages—ex-

ploited by Paul Laurence Dunbar in his "Ante-Bellum Sermon" and
James Weldon Johnson in "Let My People Go"—highlight the potential for resistance of the Afro-American church, a potential tapped
very effectively by Martin Luther King, Jr., and the Southern Christian Leadership Conference. Grounded in the intense sense of community created in the Afro-American church, this political potential
makes the exclusion of "damned" blues singers even more significant. Not only are they excluded from the dominant white world,
they also feel excluded from the vital core of the Afro-American
community.

Yet—and this touches on the underlying sources of the blues
power in *Native Son*—this exclusion is more apparent than real. On
the one hand, the blues, like all forms of Afro-American secular music, derive their aesthetic and formal characteristics directly from sacred forms such as the spirituals and gospel. As Amiri Baraka observes in *Blues People,* the AAB form of the classic blues stanza
encodes the call-and-response dynamic common to slave spirituals,
modern gospel music, and work songs. The significance of this form
lies in its ability to connect individual and communal experience. In
the early forms, the leader of the congregation or work group would
sing a line, which would be repeated by the members of the group,
who should be understood as collaborators rather than an "audience" in the Euro-American sense. Given the validation of the response, the leader then comments on the issue or experience raised
in the initial call. Since many of the "call" lines are grounded in the
communal experiences expressed in earlier songs, the call-and-
response dynamic validates the individual, who is able to articulate
his or her experience in communally valid forms even in a world
at best indifferent and at worst openly hostile to such efforts. Transformed into the individual AAB form of the blues, the call-
and-response dynamic both encodes the possibility of communal-
individual contact—precisely the aspect of articulation Wright found
modernist discourse unable to accommodate—and emphasizes an
intensely alienated experience of reality. This profound feeling of
exclusion juxtaposed with the sense of a lost former world where
things had not yet fallen apart marks the crossroads where the blues
and modernism meet in the Afro-American tradition.

This suggests why, despite Wright's personal ambivalence, his work
has consistently inspired some of the deepest insights into the literary use of the blues. Wright does not speak *about* the blues; he speaks
the blues. Both the definition of the blues advanced in the introduction to *Blues Fell This Morning*—"All blues are a lusty, lyrical realism
charged with taut sensibility" (xi)—and the previously quoted pas-

sage from *Twelve Million Black Voices* pale beside Ellison's classic description of the blues as "an impulse to keep the painful details and episodes of a brutal experience alive in one's aching consciousness, to finger its jagged grain, and to transcend it, not by the consolation of philosophy but by squeezing from it a near-tragic, near-comic lyricism. As a form, the blues is an autobiographical chronicle of personal catastrophe expressed lyrically" (*Shadow* 90). Combined with Ellison's often-reiterated awareness of the metaphysical density and paradoxical imagery of blues performance, this description of Wright's *Black Boy* provides a much more satisfactory approach to Afro-American vernacular aesthetics than anything Wright ever *consciously* articulated. Nor is it surprising to find that the most significant extension of Ellison's definition—that included in Houston Baker's *Blues, Ideology, and Afro-American Literature: A Vernacular Theory*—relies heavily on Wright (as well as on Ellison). Articulating the impact of economic forces on Afro-American aesthetics in the vocabulary of poststructuralist literary theory, Baker uses "The Man Who Lived Underground" to discuss the way in which Wright employs the *difference* between Euro- and Afro-American discourse to generate a powerful sense of "the vision and feeling of a *black blues life*" (147).

While Ellison, Baker, and Stepto (who presents *Black Boy* as both a response to previous Afro-American expression and a call for subsequent writers) all recognize Wright's importance to the tradition of blues literature, it seems curious that none focus their discussions on *Native Son*. Nonetheless, *Native Son* remains for many readers, including myself, Wright's most profound vision of the black blues life, combining Ellison's sense of vernacular aesthetics with Baker's awareness of the ideology of language. It is precisely Wright's discomfort with both folk and modernist discourses that accounts for the blues power of his novel. The intensity of *Native Son,* its implicit call, derives from its indirect articulation of exclusion, of an experience which by its very nature cannot be rendered directly. Bigger Thomas's inability to sound a call *is* his call; his despair of envisioning a response *is* his response to the alienation of the Afro-American community in the modernist wasteland.

Despite, or perhaps because of, Bigger's sense of exclusion from the Afro-American community, *Native Son* portrays him as a truly representative figure, a leader whose call attracts the validation of a strong communal response, though neither leader nor congregation is aware of the ritual Wright unconsciously articulates. Bigger repeatedly senses his connection with other blacks. In one sequence of fewer than ten pages, Wright establishes the underlying blues experience Bigger shares with the other black characters. Wright introduces the sequence with Bigger's meditation on this common experience, which includes the sense of alienation from the black community, which keeps him from articulating his thoughts, in the form of a blues call: "Each person lived in one room and had a little world of his own. He hated this room and all the people in it, including himself. Why did he and his folks have to live like this? What had they ever done? Perhaps they had not done anything. Maybe they had to live this way precisely because none of them in all their lives had ever done anything, right or wrong, that mattered much" (90). He sees his own sense of exclusion reflected in his brother: "Looking at Buddy and thinking of Jan and Mr. Dalton, he saw in Buddy a certain stillness, an isolation, meaninglessness" (92). Although he cannot openly acknowledge the blues link, Bigger knows that his friend Gus shares many of his feelings: "he knew Gus, as he knew himself, and he knew that one of them might fail through fear at the decisive moment" (98). Despite his alienation from women, Bigger perceives the shared weariness of his mother and sister: "though [Vera's] face was smaller and smoother than his mother's the beginning of the same tiredness was already there" (92).

The association of the blues life with black women provides an important blues subtext of *Native Son*. A major theme in Baker's exploration of blues expression concerns the way in which economic oppression distorts relationships between black men and black women, both of whom are trapped in a discourse that all but precludes deep contact. As many feminist critics have demonstrated, a deep current of misogyny runs through Wright's work. Yet *Native Son* demonstrates at least a subliminal awareness of the nature of the problem. Bigger and Bessie's entire relationship is predicated on money: the money needed to buy the whiskey that Bigger in effect exchanges for sex. While Bigger does nothing to challenge or alter these relationships, Wright does not simply endorse the underlying sexist power structure. In a passage that culminates in Bigger's acknowledgment that Bessie likes him because "he gave her money for drinks," Wright suggests that such forces condition the life of the entire Afro-American community. Ironically, Bigger's refusal to respond to Bessie's suggestion that he articulate his experience sparks one of Wright's clearest articulations of the blues experience: "Her voice had come in a whisper, a whisper he had heard many times when she wanted something badly. It brought him to a full sense of her life, what he had been thinking and feeling when he had placed his hand upon her shoulder." Bigger explicitly associates his internal response to Bessie's whispered call with his earlier awareness of his family's suffering: "The same deep realization he had had that morning at home at the breakfast table while watching Vera and Buddy and his mother came back to him; only it was Bessie he was looking at now and seeing how blind she was. He felt the narrow orbit of her life" (118). Which is, of course, the narrow orbit of his own. Shortly before her death, Bessie articulates her own sense of exclusion in a long blues moan beginning, "All my life's been full of hard trouble. If I wasn't hungry, I was sick. And if I wasn't sick, I was in trouble" (194). Although he has previously arrived at similar perceptions, Bigger has no vocabulary capable of providing a response, of creating a space in which he and Bessie could acknowledge the depth of their shared blues life.

Despite his feeling of being "alone, profoundly, inescapably" (264), Bigger repeatedly feels a desire for the affirmation encoded in the call-and-response dynamic. His thoughts in the prison cell reflect both his personal anguish and his creator's dissatisfaction with the solipsistic tendencies of modernist aesthetics: "why did not he hear resounding echoes of his feelings in the hearts of others? There were times when he did hear echoes, but always they were couched in tones which, living as a Negro, he could not answer or accept" (264). As Bigger becomes more aware of his situation, his desire for a response to his call increases: "he wondered wistfully if there was not a set of words which he had in common with others, words which would evoke in others a sense of the same fire that smoldered in him" (308–9).

Bigger attempts to break through the encompassing silence three times in "Fate," once with his family and twice with Boris Max. When his family visits him in the prison cell, he responds to their suffering with the defiant compassion typical of the blues attitude: "he tried to think of words that would defy [the whites], words that would let them know that he had a world and life of his own in spite of them. And at the same time he wanted those words to stop the tears of his mother and sister, to quiet and soothe the anger of his brother" (252). This desire translates into an awareness of his actual bonds with the Afro-American community: "No matter how much he would long for them to forget him, they would not be able to. His family was a part of him, not only in blood, but in spirit" (254). Bigger's failure to articulate these feelings—to sound a call—reflects Wright's limited apprehension of the Afro-American vernacular tradition. Immediately after the intensely significant embrace of the Thomas family, which takes place under the eyes of the whites in the cell, Bigger's mother begins to grovel before the Daltons, echoing the self-demeaning religious passivity Wright has previously attributed to Reverend Hammond. Wright's conscious sense of the limitations of black folk culture precludes the possibility of any positive image of call and response between Bigger and his family.

Bigger's two attempts to tell his story to Max (298–300, 352–59) are not successful. Despairing over his feeling of exclusion from the black community, Bigger turns to a white audience just as Wright sought some response from his white contemporaries, whether modernist or Communist. Partially because Max fails to apprehend the complexity of Bigger's humanity and partially because of the inadequacy of the available discourse, both attempts collapse. In the final pages of *Native Son,* Bigger comes close to an adequate articulation of his experience. But the articulation receives no response. Max withdraws, abandoning Bigger to the modernist solipsism that has been the undercurrent of his experience throughout: "Bigger's voice died; he was listening to the echoes of his words in his own mind" (335).

Reflecting the "near-tragic, near-comic lyricism" Ellison identified as the core of "Richard Wright's Blues," Bigger's response to his own call takes the form of the haunting laughter that echoes through the final pages of the novel. After Max's refusal to respond to the intensity of his call becomes clear, "Bigger laughed." When Max, typically unfamiliar with the Afro-American vernacular tradition, reacts with surprise, Bigger explains, "I ain't going to cry" (358). The final image of Bigger reiterates the blues resonance of his situation: "Then he smiled a faint wry, bitter smile. He heard the ring of steel against steel as a far door clanged shut" (359). Bigger is most certainly, to use Langston Hughes's classic definition of the blues, "laughing to keep from crying." Yet the laughter—much bleaker than either Hughes's or Ellison's, sharing the solipsistic intensity of Samuel Beckett, the tormented isolation of Robert Johnson—is neither Bigger's nor Wright's alone. It echoes throughout *Native Son.* From the time Bigger leaves his family in their apartment until he reaches the Daltons, there are at least a dozen references to laughter. Bigger laughs. Gus laughs. Jack and G. H. laugh. Doc laughs. After an outburst of blues laughter, Bigger says, "I laughed so hard I cried" (35). Incorporating Afro- and Euro-American sensibilities, establishing and repudiating bonds, feeling excluded from them all, *Native Son* resounds with a painful blues laughter, echoing through a modernist wasteland that may or may not resound in response.

9

James Baldwin:
Politics and the Gospel Impulse

▲ ▲ ▲ ▲

By the end of his life, James Baldwin had fallen out of intellectual fashion. The primary reason lies in his unflagging concern with the possibility of salvation, a term nearly meaningless in the vocabularies of late twentieth-century intellectual culture. Never really leaving the Harlem storefront churches where he preached as a teenager, Baldwin developed what I am calling the *gospel impulse* into an intensely idiosyncratic existentialist politics that, for a fleeting moment during the sixties, resulted in his designation as "official Negro spokesman," a role he both understood and, at least in retrospect, profoundly hated. Like the gospel music he loved, Baldwin evolved along with the surrounding culture, developing new styles, testing new vocabularies in response to new manifestations of ancient problems. Like gospel, Baldwin consistently asserted the ultimately moral connection of political and cultural experience, a connection capable of empowering both self and community. Grounded in a profoundly black refusal to accept the categories underlying Euro-American thought and institutions, Baldwin's gospel vision demands a complex understanding of the ever-changing demands of the moment as the precondition for the moral—which for him was to say political—salvation of blacks and whites, men and women, Asians and Native Americans, heterosexuals and homosexuals.

As the moving funeral testimony of Toni Morrison and Amiri Baraka demonstrates, Baldwin's voice was heard, and loved. We cannot, if we are even dimly conversant with American cultural and intellectual history, deny Baldwin his importance or his impact. We can, however, deny him our attention. And, despite the tributes that came in from every corner of the intellectual and political world following his death, this is what we have done. For fashions change; the New Criticism and individualist existentialism of the fifties give way to the activist existentialism and cultural nationalism of the sixties that in turn metamorphose into the academic deconstruction of the eighties. And it does not seem surprising that the poststructuralist critique of the limitations of "essentialist" terms such as "self" and "truth" (in fact if not in theory) has resurrected an ironic sensibility that renders Baldwin's moral seriousness and his political activisim nearly incomprehensible to literary intellectuals. As the debate over the Paul de Man case develops, it seems increasingly clear that, despite the dissenting voice of founding figure Jacques Derrida, academic deconstruction in the United States remains a quintessentially *theoretical* movement acutely uncomfortable with its own position in the political world. Baldwin would certainly not have us pass judgment on de Man or the theorists; he understood all too well that we create demons when we are afraid of examining our own spirit. Further he understood that we need access to all parts of our selves—and to as many cultural resources as possible whether black, white, red, or yellow in origin—if we are to survive the attacks that *will* come. Rather than condemning de Man then, it is sufficient, at present, to observe that the same academic world that seems unable to resolve the meaning of his youthful flirtation with fascism plays a major role in the institutional context in which Baldwin has been effectively marginalized.

Wright, Baldwin, and Cultural Politics

Never forgetting his experience growing up on the streets of Harlem, Baldwin realized the danger of losing his grounding in Afro-American premises concerning the inseparability of politics and culture and the interdependence of self and community. As analysts from W. E. B. Du Bois to Cornel West and bell hooks have continually asserted: in African and Afro-American life, culture *is* politics and politics *is* culture. To the extent that any political agenda embraces a broad spectrum of the black community, it must be grounded in the institutions and forms of expression that connect the community: most particularly the churches and bars where black people gather with minimal white mediation; and the various forms of music, sacred and secular, that articulate the shared perceptions developed in those gatherings. While most Afro-American writers would endorse this perception in some form, its implications have not always been clear. Baldwin's celebrated clash with Richard Wright serves as a disquieting illustration of the ways in which the *perceived* conflict of aesthetic and political visions can create very real problems for writers seeking to transcend the dichotomies.

The general contours of the Baldwin-Wright clash were established during the debate over the "avant-garde" in late nineteenth- and early twentieth-century Europe. Originating in the rebellion against what was widely perceived as an increasingly decadent bourgeois culture, the concept of the avant-garde developed distinct, and functionally antagonistic, meanings in "political" and "aesthetic" discourse. On one side, artists inspired by Baudelaire, Strindberg, or Nietzsche (to highlight a few of many possible genealogies) attempted to re(dis)cover truths suppressed by bourgeois conventions. Believing that popular forms such as the realistic novel or the melodrama perpetuated corrupt and superficial consciousness, avant-garde artists frequently assumed antagonistic stances toward the communities in which they lived. Although there were notable exceptions, the avant-garde artists most influential in the Anglo-American world saw *all* political and economic activity as part of the corruption. To the extent that they were politically active—T. S. Eliot, who declared himself a "monarchist" in politics, and Ezra Pound, who supported the Italian fascists, are the most celebrated cases—they generally upheld conservative or reactionary programs, which they associated with the "universal" values lost in the modern world.

Developing contemporaneously with the aesthetic avant-garde, the political avant-garde interpreted bourgeois corruption from diametrically opposed philosophical premises. Strongly influenced by the Marxist vision of cultural institutions as manifestations of the dominant mode of production (to reduce a complex argument to a central premise), the political avant-garde argued that cultural forms would improve only after the power structure had been changed. This perspective typically dismisses avant-garde art as the self-indulgent expression of a leisure class insufficiently aware of its position of privilege within a capitalist economic structure. Significantly, this dismissal emanated from political avant-gardes on both the Left and the Right; Lenin, Hitler, and Mussolini shared a deep distrust of art that explicitly challenged traditional forms.

When Wright embarked on his literary career in association with the John Reed Club of Chicago during the thirties, the conflict between political and aesthetic conceptions of the avant-garde had developed into a major source of tension in the American Left. Echoing the dominant aesthetic theory of official Soviet culture (at least after the "Silver Age" of the twenties), many prominent American leftists, especially those associated with the Communist party, endorsed "social realism"; Mike Gold's literary column for the *Daily Worker* was the most influential forum for the discussion of social realism in the American context. Concerned primarily with the creation of inspirational heroes for the masses, social realism relied almost exclusively on the realistic and melodramatic forms of nineteenth-century middle-brow fiction. Attracted by Trotsky's insightful literary criticism and repelled by the fascist exploitation of romantic aesthetics—both Hitler and Mussolini were adept at using popular culture to advance their political agendas—some American leftists argued that realism in fact had originated as an expression of the individualism fundamental to the interests of the rising middle class during the seventeenth and eighteenth centuries, an argument brilliantly elaborated in Ian Watt's *The Rise of the Novel*. These "leftist modernists" concluded that social realism inadvertently reinforced the value structure of capitalist society inasmuch as it elevated the individual hero, whatever his or her ostensible values, over the mass struggle. This debate assumed classic form in the clash between Georg Lukács, who defended the use of traditional aesthetics in association with radical themes, and Bertolt Brecht, who argued that new, truly modern art forms must be developed for the expression of new consciousness. Both in his drama and in his theoretical writing, Brecht emphasized the importance of folk or popular forms as sources for a radical avant-garde art. Because popular forms generally express little explicit interest in theoretical issues—which is *not* to say that they lack theoretical implications—the Brechtian position suggests a useful approach for Afro-American artists concerned with changing political and economic conditions but unwilling—ultimately unable—to accept the opposition of politics and culture that became a dominant aspect of the discourse framing the Wright-Baldwin debate.

Brecht, however, remained largely unknown in the United States until after World War II. As a result, Afro-American writers wishing to participate in public discourse were forced to choose between an aesthetic avant-garde committed to a conservative ideology and an aesthetically conservative political avant-garde committed, at least rhetorically, to the struggle against racism. The choice, however unsatisfactory, was obvious. Wright, whose first novel *Lawd Today* (not published until the sixties) revoices Joyce's *Ulysses*, began his career under the sponsorship of a left wing whose cultural representatives either repudiated or were unaware of the holistic premises of Afro-American expression. Because Wright wrote for the *Daily Worker* and *New Masses*, it was widely assumed that he accepted the elevation of political over aesthetic discourse. Although his 1937 *New Masses* essay "Blueprint for Negro Writing" asserts the unity of Afro-American politics and culture, very few of the original readers of *Native Son* seem to have understood the essay's implications. As a result, Wright's novel was received as a political document. Both supporters and detractors responded to its ideology first and its aesthetics later, if at all. Arguments raged, in black newspapers as well as mainstream intellectual journals, over the political significance of Bigger Thomas. Bourgeois apologists, whether politically or culturally oriented, dismissed the book as pure propaganda. Similarly, numerous black bourgeois readers, including W. E. B. Du Bois, saw the book as a distortion of Afro-American life. Many leftists celebrated it as a telling attack on corrupt American institutions, a black voicing of John Steinbeck's *The Grapes of Wrath,* which had been published the previous year. Some leftists, however, including Gold, were acutely uncomfortable with *Native Son,* correctly perceiving that Wright had identified a serious inadequacy in the leftist interpretation of Bigger's experience; Communist lawyer Boris Max's defense of Bigger in fact marginalizes crucial elements of his specifically black experience in order to present him as a symbol of the oppressed proletariat of all races. As a result, such critics gave the book only lukewarm praise. Despite these hesitations, however, Wright came to be seen as synonymous with "protest literature." Not until Donald Gibson's 1969 essay "Wright's Invisible Native Son" did the complexity of Bigger's consciousness—the implicit assertion of the Afro-American challenge to the political-cultural dichotomy of the earlier debate—receive adequate attention.

Unintentionally contributing to the polarization of the debate over aesthetics and politics, Baldwin's essay "Everybody's Protest Novel" played a crucial role in establishing the image of Wright as an exclusively political novelist. Readers seeking a black spokesman for the "aesthetic" position seized on Baldwin's criticism of Wright as vindication of the "New Critical" principles developed from Eliot's essays by southern conservatives such as Allen Tate, Cleanth Brooks, and Robert Penn Warren (who later repudiated the implicit racism of his earlier position). Concentrating on formal structures rather than content or context, many New Critics marginalized political, and especially progressive, concerns. From the leftist perspective, of course, such formalism is itself a political statement in support of the status quo. When Baldwin's first novel *Go Tell It on the Mountain* received enthusiastic praise from conservative academic critics, the intent was in part, and at times explicitly, to marginalize Wright's political concerns. Just as the original readers of *Native Son* simplified the work to accommodate their ideology, Baldwin's aesthetic defenders ignored major political elements of his novel. For example, as I will demonstrate more fully below, Baldwin's treatment of John Grimes's biological father, Richard—and it is hard not to hear the name as a tribute to the lost father Wright—emphasizes that political forces permeate every element of black experience. Highly intelligent and culturally aware, Richard struggles to transcend the limitations imposed on black aspiration in the pre-*Brown* era through a rigorous program of cultural self-education. Despite his intelligence and determination, however, Richard maintains a naive innocence concerning the possibility of escaping, even provisionally, from political reality. Only after he is arrested on suspicion of a robbery he did not commit is Richard forced to recognize that his political context defines him, whatever his accomplishments, as simply another "nigger." Unable to reconcile this imposed definition with his drive for cultural transcendence, he despairs and commits suicide.

In retrospect, this clearly belies the idea of a simple opposition between Baldwin's "art" and Wright's "propaganda." Whatever the underlying connection between *Native Son* and *Go Tell It on the Mountain*, however, Wright and Baldwin (along with Ralph Ellison) were *perceived* as representatives of starkly opposed sensibilities. Implicitly accepting the divisions that had distorted reception of his own previous work, Wright read "Everybody's Protest Novel" as a vicious attack from a younger writer to whom he had given intellectual and financial support. Baldwin's apparently sincere surprise over Wright's anger suggests that he intended both essay and novel as part of an ongoing discussion of how to balance interdependent values (politics and aesthetics) in a context that views them as separate categories. The fact that discussions of Afro-American fiction continued until quite recently to phrase the relationship between "art" and "protest" in antagonistic terms demonstrates the immense influence of this seemingly unnecessary quarrel *within* the Afro-American community.

Anticipating the current situation in Afro-American studies, the Wright case demonstrates how Baldwin's cultural presence has from the beginning been mediated by narrow understandings of the relationship between culture and politics. It is only necessary to juxtapose Eldridge Cleaver's rejection of Baldwin as an affront to black masculinity with Trudier Harris's presentation of Baldwin as a spokesman for black patriarchy to understand the potential absurdity of the situation. Similarly, Ishmael Reed's signifying on Baldwin as a great writer "within the framework of Judeo-Christian culture" reflects a profound misapprehension of Baldwin's relation to Afro-American culture, which long ago developed techniques for employing a Judeo-Christian vocabulary without violating the integrity of black experience. It is perhaps not surprising that Baldwin's blackness has never been clearer than in his rejection. For if Baldwin's sensibility allowed him to speak, to *signify,* in any number of "white" vocabularies, it also rendered it impossible for him to abandon what he saw as the most important premises of black life. One of the premises most commonly misapprehended in interracial discussions concerns Baldwin's approach to racial identity as metaphorical. As he wrote in *The Fire Next Time,* racial identity is a construct predicated on specific attitudes, *choices.* Racial

> tensions are rooted in the very same depths as those from which love springs, or murder. The white man's unadmitted—and apparently, to him, unspeakable—private fears and longings are projected onto the Negro. The only way he can be released from the Negro's tyrannical power over him is to consent, in effect, to become black himself, to become a part of that suffering and dancing country that he now watches wistfully from the heights of his lonely power and, armed with spiritual traveller's checks, visits surreptitiously, after dark. (*Price* 375)

These words ring as true in the late eighties as they did in the sixties, strongly intimating the value of a serious reconsideration of both the development and continuity of Baldwin's vision.

The Gospel Impulse

Despite the attacks of Cleaver, Reed, and others, Baldwin's work asserts an unmistakably *black* vision, a process of encountering the world grounded in Afro-American history and values. Not surprisingly, given both the complex influence of African culture and the relative autonomy of black musicians (as opposed to writers), this sensibility has received its fullest expression in Afro-American music. Although an analytical vocabulary inevitably creates the illusion of difference where relationship is crucial, this sensibility can be understood as an interaction of blues, jazz, and gospel impulses, which recombine and evolve in later forms such as funk, rap, and soul. Blues and jazz have long been recognized as crucial to black writers from Langston Hughes and Zora Neale Hurston to Ralph Ellison and Toni Morrison. Inspired largely by Ellison's brilliant essays, the influence of jazz and blues on literature has come to be seen in terms not of specific forms but of *impulses,* processes capable of generating and expressing powerful insights grounded in, but not limited to, Afro-American experience (which Ellison, like Baldwin, understands as part of a dialectic with Euro-American history and processes). Ellison provides classic definitions of both the blues and jazz impulses. Presenting the blues as a way of defending one's experience against external attack, Ellison describes "an impulse to keep the painful details

and episodes of a brutal experience alive in one's aching consciousness, to finger its jagged grain, and to transcend it, not by the consolation of philosophy but by squeezing from it a near-tragic, near-
comic lyricism" (*Shadow* 78). Extending the integrity wrested from
the blues process, the jazz impulse focuses on realizing the relational
possibilities of the self, of expanding consciousness through a process of continual improvisation. If the blues assume their deepest significance when they elicit the recognition of individuals within the
community (the listener-participants), jazz challenges the potential
limitations inherent in the blues process, which may resist perceptions that are not already familiar, defining them as external distortions. Again, Ellison provides the classic articulation of the jazz impulse: "true jazz is an art of individual assertion within and against
the group. Each true jazz moment (as distinct from the uninspired
commercial performance) springs from a contest in which each artist
challenges all the rest; each solo flight, or improvisation, represents
(like the successive canvases of a painter) a definition of his identity:
as individual, as member of the collectivity and as a link in the chain
of tradition" (234).

Baldwin's brilliant novella "Sonny's Blues," as numerous readers
have recognized, is a classic expression of the blues and jazz impulses. A recovering addict and jazz pianist, the title character has
nearly succumbed to "brutal experience." When Sonny returns to
the nightclub that provides a ritual ground for the Afro-American
community, Baldwin emphasizes that his triumph, his ability to articulate his identity, is grounded firmly in the blues. Although Sonny
fears "drowning"—reaching a point of perception that receives no
response—his fellow musicians and audience hear, understand, and
respond to his "autobiographical chronicle of personal catastrophe"
assuring him that "deep water ain't drowning." Even though the brutal world remains real—Baldwin reiterates the line "it can come
again"—Sonny accepts the challenge of his own identity, a challenge
that in turn transforms the community whose strength informed his
journey. Responding to Sonny's response, his narrator/brother is finally able to write his own blues, to release the emotion blocked by
his choice of a "white" identity predicated on the illusion of safety.

What has been less frequently recognized is the equal importance,
in Afro-American culture generally and in "Sonny's Blues" specifically, of the gospel impulse informing both blues and jazz. Because
it developed in the black church—the institutional space farthest removed from the attention and mediation of whites—gospel music
has provided the Afro-American community with a forum for developing appropriate articulations of its experience with relative auton-

omy. Ironically, the failure of the music industry to effectively market gospel to whites has helped gospel maintain a black perspective with fewer ambiguities than forms such as the blues or soul, which have been forced to devote substantial energy to negotiating mainstream economic institutions. Asserting a vision grounded in West African philosophical values—Robert Farris Thompson's brilliant work *Flash of the Spirit* details the shared rhythms of African and Afro-American thought—gospel music refuses to accept, though it has always felt the effects of, the oppositional structures of the Euro-American analytical tradition. Gospel contains the clearest traces—and the usage is consistent with the Derridean concept of an always partial echo of an unrecapturable original itself traced with earlier, and partial, intertexts—of an African sensibility that, while not an absolute alternative to the Euro-American context that has unquestionably influenced its specific form, certainly keeps alive the concept of difference from and within the white world.

Although not conceived as a philosophical position—recall Ellison's assertion that the blues do *not* provide the consolations of philosophy—this distance from the unstated premises of Euro-American discourse enables the black church to resist white institutions that unconsciously attack the foundations of Afro-American integrity by separating politics from culture, self from community. Extending the values of African—and other oral—cultures, gospel focuses insistently on the *now,* apprehended as a rhythm connecting past with future. To participate fully in the moment—to feel the presence of the Lord, the gospel spirit, soul—demands a consciousness transcending the divisions of intellect, emotion, and body, of self and other. When it is real, when the spirit moves, gospel music absolutely cannot be a *performance* in the Euro-American sense defined by Richard Poirier as "an exercise of power, a very curious one. Curious because it is at first so furiously self-consultive, so even narcissistic, and later so eager for publicity, love, and historical dimension. Out of an accumulation of secretive acts emerges at last a form that presumes to compete with reality itself for control of the minds exposed to it" (45). Public from its inception, the gospel performance values collaboration over control. The power of a good gospel performance rests on the gathering of energies, the focusing of processes, that unify God, singer, and congregation in a communal improvisation on the theme of the blues. As much as any Afro-American text, "Sonny's Blues" acknowledges the grounding of the blues-jazz process in the gospel impulse. Baldwin connects the experience of the gospel street singers with those of Sonny and his narrator/brother: "As the singing filled the air the watching, listening faces underwent a change, the eyes focusing on something within; the music seemed to soothe a poison out of them" (*Going* 111). "Sonny's Blues" concludes with an epiphany in which Baldwin's narrator rediscovers his symbolic blackness, breaking through the barriers, grounded in his acceptance of white institutions, which have separated him from his brother and his own emotional life. Baldwin casts this final call and response specifically in a gospel vocabulary: "Then [Sonny] put [the drink] back on top of the piano. For me, then, as they began to play again, it glowed and shook above my brother's head like the very cup of trembling" (122).

This sense of gospel as the source of alternative premises, as an entry into the fullness of life that provides the energy for all moral and political action, helps explain why gospel, although clearly grounded in Afro-American experience, by no means limits consciousness; it is compatible both with the secular realism of the blues impulse and the synthetic multiculturalism of the jazz impulse. In addition, it is important not to confuse the gospel impulse with the *ritual* of Afro-American churches that, as Baldwin cautioned in *Go Tell It on the Mountain* and *The Amen Corner,* can be corrupted by personal hypocrisy in the service of institutional power. Recognizing this dynamic, Baldwin articulated the gospel impulse in vocabularies that are not narrowly religious. For Baldwin, and again his closest relatives are the numerous Afro-American musicians who show little patience with attempts to establish strict taxonomies of "jazz," "blues," or "funk," the constituting sensibility is of far greater importance than its specific form; insistence on specific forms of articulation is in itself a profound violation of the gospel impulse. Baldwin's interest in existentialist thought, considered from this perspective, parallels John Coltrane's interest in Asian religion; each employs "non-black" vocabularies in concert with, rather than in opposition to, the gospel impulse. Perceiving the deep connection between *presence* as understood in gospel and Hindu terms, Coltrane created complex musical textures such as "India" and "Om" that speak to Gyorgy Ligeti or Pierre Boulez in terms close enough to their own to command the composers' most serious levels of attention without compromising his ability to play the deep, and deeply political, blues of "Alabama," written in response to the Birmingham church bombings.

Baldwin developed the expansive implications of the gospel impulse as a vision of universal salvation, a primary source of the tension that led some black nationalists to dismiss him as a "great white writer." The irony lies in the fact that it was precisely the knowledge of how the constructs of Euro-American thought—call them the devil or tar baby—deform even the finest impulses (including those of whites who, Baldwin knew, rarely *mean* harm) that protected Baldwin and the gospel church from simply inverting binary racist thought structures. Perhaps it is not so ironic that it was just such simplistic inversion—which leaves the foundation of Euro-American oppression unchallenged—that created the sexism and elitism that doomed the Black Arts Movement. Maintaining his clear-eyed perception that most whites didn't act much like they were interested in being saved—which is to say in living a moral life—Baldwin nonetheless refused to create demons, to simplify the other in a way that would inevitably force him to simplify himself. Like Malcolm after his return from Mecca—and like the Afro-American women who have been in actuality as well as in stereotype a nurturing presence in American culture despite everything that whites, and at times black men, have said and done—Baldwin insisted that only full commitment to telling, and acting on, the truth could make us all, black and white, male and female, straight and gay, free. The gospel impulse—its refusal to accept oppositional thought, its complex sense of presence, its belief in salvation—sounds in Baldwin's voice no matter what his particular vocabulary at a particular moment. This is the quality of his voice that is unmistakably *black* and unmistakably his own, just as those of Aretha Franklin, Sam Cooke, Amina Claudine Myers, or Sister Rosetta Tharpe are black and individual, whether they are singing gospel, blues, or pop standards. While Baldwin's body and perhaps his mind left the gospel church, his voice and spirit lingered.

Baldwin's Fiction

As he examined the relationship of consciousness and context over four decades, Baldwin revoiced two basic themes grounded in the gospel impulse: the full responsibility of the individual, understood as part of a larger community and tradition, for his or her moral identity, and the inadequacy of received definitions, particularly those derived from Euro-American oppositional thought, as a basis for self-knowledge or social action. The introductory essay in *Notes of a Native Son* sounds the leitmotif of Baldwin's intellectual position: "I think all theories are suspect, that the finest principles may have to be modified, or may even be pulverized by the demands of life, and that one must find, therefore, one's own moral center and move through the world hoping that this center will guide one aright" (6). This insistence informs the deconstructive understanding of race—paradoxically, a profoundly black understanding—that links the various stages of Baldwin's career. Long before poststructuralism questioned their authority in American intellectual life, Baldwin identified the uncritical acceptance of binary thought structures as the source of a wide range of problems. Anticipating Gates's, Baker's, and Stepto's extensions of academic deconstruction, Baldwin recognized that any real challenge to the groundless authority asserted by such binary structures must embrace not only abstract philosophical positions but also the institutional settings where they are propagated.

Attempting to work through the relationship of consciousness and context, Baldwin's novels present images of this complex dynamic. His most powerful novels—*Go Tell It on the Mountain* (1953), *Another Country* (1962), and *Just above My Head* (1979)—portray a series of evasive and simplifying definitions built into religious, economic, and educational institutions. Reflecting the pervasive influence of binary thought structures, these definitions—all of which can be quickly dismissed as "essentialist"—nonetheless control the social perception of difference, which is perceived as *absence* of relationship, thus reinforcing the solipsistic tendencies of "white" life. Baldwin knew, for example, that we construct our ideas of blackness and whiteness, that race is not an essence. Recognizing the contingency of race, however, by no means negates its reality and power. For Baldwin also understood that we construct our images of ourselves, the images that direct our social interactions, in accord with ideas of blackness and whiteness available in our contexts. This conceptually simple, but practically intractable, process provides the mechanism by which race—a relatively unimportant *concept* in gospel religion, democratic politics, or existential philosophy—exerts so much control over individual experience. Granted an immense unconscious authority, these concepts *seem* to constitute "human nature," to embody inevitable limits of experience. While sympathizing with the difficulty of distancing self from context without simultaneously denying experience (again understood in relational rather than essentialist terms), Baldwin insists that acquiescing to the definitions inevitably results in self-hatred and social immorality. The individual incapable of accepting his or her existential complexity embraces the illusion of certainty offered by institutions that assume responsibility for moral decisions.

This cycle of institutional pressure encouraging existential evasion ensuring further institutional corruption recurs in each of Baldwin's novels. Responding to larger changes in the contexts of Afro-American experience from the forties to the eighties, Baldwin examined the relationship between consciousness and context from several perspectives. His first novel, *Go Tell It on the Mountain*, employs a tightly focused Jamesian form to explore the developing awareness of the adolescent protagonist John Grimes. Written during the early years of the civil rights movement, *Go Tell It on the Mountain* focuses on the internal dynamic of Afro-American experience, presenting the gospel impulse in a voice accessible to white readers. The novel focuses on the consciousness of the young protagonist as he begins to develop an awareness of his context. As more Afro-Americans began entering previously segregated areas of Euro-American culture during the fifties, Baldwin gravitated toward the relatively loosely structured Dreiserian mode in *Another Country,* placing a greater degree of emphasis on the power of context. Baldwin's treatment of a wide range of characters from diverse backgrounds implies that nuances of individual response must be understood in relation to larger forces limiting the individual ability to realize the values of the gospel impulse. Synthesizing his earlier forms and insights, *Just above My Head* can be read as a meditation on the value and contradictions of the political movements whose concerns were clearly being removed from the national agenda by 1980. Consciousness and context are presented in a more intricate relationship as Baldwin's characters strive to articulate the implications of their experience to, and with, their communities.

Baldwin's gospel process parallels William Blake's vision of morality as a movement from innocence through experience to a higher innocence. Beginning with an unaware innocence, individuals—especially those who conceive of their individuality in Euro-American terms—inevitably enter the deadening and murderous world of experience, the world of limiting definitions. Those who attempt to deny the world and remain children perish alongside those who cynically submit to the cruelty of the context for imagined personal benefit. Only those who plunge into experience, recognize its cruelty, and resolve to forge an aware innocence—to feel the gospel spirit—can hope to survive morally. Specifically, Baldwin urges families to pass on a sense of the higher innocence to their children by refusing to simplify—either sentimentally or cynically—the truth of experience. This painful honesty makes love possible despite the inevitability of pain and isolation. It provides the only hope, however desperate, for individual or political rejuvenation. To a large extent, Baldwin's career develops in accord with the Blakean pattern, which can be seen as an English voicing of the gospel impulse. John Grimes begins his passage from innocence to experience in *Go Tell It on the Mountain;* Rufus Scott, Ida Scott, and Vivaldo Moore struggle to survive experience in *Another Country,* which intimates the need for the higher innocence. *Just above My Head,* with its middle-aged narrator and his teenaged children, portrays the entire process of finding and communicating the processes needed to conceive, and perhaps realize, the higher innocence.

Go Tell It on the Mountain examines the gospel impulse in its actual social context. Centered on the struggle of John Grimes, clearly modeled on Baldwin's own younger self, to come to terms with his tyrannical preacher father, the novel appears to have a highly individualistic focus. On a more important level, however, it concerns the ways in which Afro-Americans confront, and defend themselves against, the binary structures of Euro-American thought. The structure of the novel, supported by its thematic focus on the tension between "temple" and "street," first presents and then critiques the apparent oppositions. Of the three major sections of *Go Tell It on the Mountain*, the first and third focus directly on John, apparently as an individual in the Jamesian, Euro-American sense. The long middle section, "The Prayers of the Saints," a Faulknerian excavation of history, traces the origins of John's struggle to the experience of his elders. Together, the prayers assert the power of context, portraying the great migration of blacks from South to North, from rural to urban settings. Far from bringing true freedom, the movement reveals the underlying continuity of Afro-American historical experience, a continuity grounded in the persistence of Euro-American constructions of reality. As John's mother, Elizabeth, recognizes: "There was not, after all, a great difference between the world of the North and that of the South which she had fled; there was only this difference: the North promised more. And this similarity: what it promised it did not give, and what it gave, at length and grudgingly with one hand, it took back with the other" (163). Even in his most individualistic phase, Baldwin is acutely aware of institutional power. The origins of John's particular struggle against the power of limiting definitions, of Baldwin's struggle to free his consciousness from the limitations of religious rituals that deny the gospel impulse, lie in their historical impact on his elders.

Similarly, Baldwin's treatment of Elizabeth's relationship with John's biological father emphasizes the power of context over consciousness. Richard's suicide destroys Elizabeth's chance for obtaining a greater degree of freedom. She is not, however, simply a victim. Implicitly accepting the opposition of personal and political experience, she contributes to its destructive impact. Fearing that Richard will be unable to cope with the responsibility of a family, she fails to tell him of her pregnancy. Far from protecting him, this evasion contributes to his destruction by allowing Richard to view his situation as purely personal; in effect, it severs his real connection with the gospel sense of the self-in-relation. Elizabeth's own choice, conditioned by the evasive society in which she lives, combines with the racist legal system to circumscribe her possibilities. Forced to care for her infant son, she marries Gabriel, thus establishing the terms for John's subsequent struggle.

Seen in relation to John, Gabriel seems one of the most despicable hypocrites in American literature. Seen in relation to his own history in "The Prayers of the Saints," however, he seems victimized by the institutional context of his youth. In turn, he victimizes his family by attempting to force them into narrowly defined roles. The roots of Gabriel's character lie in the "temple-street" dichotomy of his southern childhood, a dichotomy that Baldwin thoroughly deconstructs. Encouraged by his religious mother to deny his sensuality, Gabriel undergoes a conversion experience, becomes a preacher, and defines himself entirely in "temple" terms. As a result, he enters a loveless asexual marriage with his mother's friend Deborah, herself a victim of the oppositional psychology (both racist and sexist)—enforced by blacks as well as whites—which condemns *her* after she has been brutally raped by a group of whites. Eventually, Gabriel's repressed street self breaks out and he fathers an illegitimate son. Again attempting to deny his sensuality, Gabriel refuses to acknowledge this son, Royal. Like John's half-brother Roy, Royal immerses himself in the street life Gabriel denies; he dies in a barroom brawl. Gabriel fears that Roy will share Royal's fate, but his attempt to crush his second son's street self merely strengthens the resulting rebellion. Faced with the guilt of Royal's death and the sense of impending doom concerning Roy, Gabriel retreats into a solipsism that makes a mockery of the gospel impulse he theoretically represents.

Against this backdrop, John's conversion raises a basic question that recurs in each of Baldwin's novels: can an individual hope to break the cycle of evasion that shapes his/her personal and social context? In John's case, the problem takes on added ambiguity, since he remains ignorant of many of the events shaping his life, including those involving his own birth. By framing the prayers with John's conversion, Baldwin stresses the connection between past and present, a connection that can oppress or liberate. The complex irony of "The Threshing Floor" section allows informed readings of John's conversion as either a surrender to evasion or as a movement toward the responsibility implicit in the gospel impulse. Forced to reconstruct his identity as he lies transfixed on the floor of the temple, John progresses from a sense of profound isolation, centering on his recognition of Gabriel's hypocrisy, to a gospel vision of the dispossessed with whom he shares his agony and his potential. John's vision of the multitude, whose suffering and voice merge with his own, recalls the process through which the blues obliterate both the safety and the isolation of imposed definitions. Near the end of his vision, John explicitly rejects the separation of opposites, of street and temple, white and black: "The light and the darkness had kissed each other, and were married now, forever, in the life and the vision of John's soul" (204). Returning to his immediate context, John responds not to the call of Gabriel but to that of Elisha, a slightly older friend with whom he had previously engaged in a sexually suggestive wrestling match reminiscent of D. H. Lawrence's critique of gender roles in *Women in Love*. John's salvation, then, may bring him closer to an acceptance of his own sensuality, to a self-definition encompassing both temple and street. Baldwin ends the novel with the emergence of the newly "saved" John onto the streets of Harlem. John's fate hinges on his ability to realize the higher innocence suggested by his implicitly political vision of the dispossessed—Baldwin describes them as the "armies of the darkness"—rather than submitting to the experiences that have destroyed and deformed the consciousness of the saints.

Written at the height of Baldwin's public prominence, *Another Country* reframes his exploration of the gospel impulse in relation to increasing Afro-American participation in newly "integrated" areas of American life. Exploring the actual significance of the belief in universal salvation so vital to Martin Luther King's interracial coalition, Baldwin employs a loosely structured naturalistic form, emphasizing the diverse forms of innocence and experience in American society. The three major sections of *Another Country* progress generally from despair to renewed hope, but no single consciousness or plot line provides a frame similar to that in *Go Tell It on the Mountain*. Rather, the novel's structural coherence derives from the informing gospel impulse, the moral concerns present in each of the plots.

Casting a Melvillean shadow over the novel is the black jazz musician Rufus Scott, whose fate cautions against uncritical celebration of the "success" of the civil rights movement. Unable to forge the innocence necessary for love in a context that repudiates the relationship at every turn, Rufus destroys both himself and his white southern lover, Leona. Although highly aware of the dynamics of black music in the secular world—his consciousness closely resembles Sonny's—Rufus fails to maintain his grounding in the gospel vision. Once he has accepted the premises of white life, he loses his belief in salvation and commits suicide. Struggling to overcome the internalized racial and sexual definitions that destroyed Rufus, Rufus's sister Ida, an aspiring singer, and his friend Vivaldo Moore, an aspiring white writer, seek a higher innocence capable of countering Ida's sense of the world as a "whorehouse." Baldwin developlops the prostitution theme—which encompasses both institutional forces and individual consciousness—in relation to three couples: Ida and Vivaldo, bisexual actor Eric Jones and his French lover Yves, and the white couple Richard and Cass Silenski. Cumulatively, Baldwin's portraits suggest that the problems of the civil rights movement were grounded in a general failure to understand the ways in which integration worked to destroy the gospel impulse.

The major achievement of *Another Country*, Baldwin's portrait of Rufus testifies to a moral insight and raw artistic power reminiscent of Dreiser, Wright, and Emile Zola. Forgoing the formal control and emotional restraint of his earlier novels, Baldwin opens the novel with an image of Rufus who "had fallen so low, that he scarcely had the energy to be angry" (9). Both an exceptional case and a representative figure—he might well serve as an emblem for political energy in the Reagan era—Rufus embodies the seething anger and hopeless isolation rendering Baldwin's United States, even at the height of the movement's perceived success, a landscape of nightmare. Experiencing his own situation as unbearable, Rufus meditates on the fate of a city tormented by an agony like his own: "He remembered to what excesses, into what traps and nightmares, his loneliness had driven him; and he wondered where such a violent emptiness might drive an entire city" (56). Baldwin emphasizes the political implications of Rufus's situation while reiterating that his specific fate originates in his own moral failure with Leona. Where Gabriel Grimes remained insulated from his immorality by arrogance and pride, Rufus feels the full extent of his self-enforced damnation. Like blues people such as Robert Johnson and Bessie Smith, Rufus's alienation is not that of the atheist but that of the damned; his failure assumes meaning in relation to the gospel impulse. Ironically and belatedly, his destitution clarifies his awareness of the ways in which Euro-American binary definitions have contributed to his destruction.

Wandering the streets of Manhattan, Rufus feels beyond human contact. Desperately in need of love, he believes his past actions render him unfit for even minimal compassion. His abuse of Leona, who as white woman represents both the "other" and the focal point of the most obvious social definitions circumscribing his—and her— life, accounts for his original estrangement. The community of his family and friends, like Rufus himself, fails to understand soon enough that his abuse of Leona combines rebellion against and acceptance of the role dictated by racial and sexual definitions. Separated from the psychological source of his art—to the extent that it remains true to the gospel impulse, jazz resists oppositional definitions—Rufus descends into a paranoia reinforced by the racist context. Once on the street, he begins to recognize not only his immediate but also his long-term acceptance of destructive definitions. Thinking back on a brief homosexual affair with Eric, Rufus regrets having treated his friend with contempt. Having rejected the other in Eric and Leona, Rufus realizes he has rejected himself. Unable to reconnect, unable to conceive of a challenge to the destructive institutions, Rufus kills himself.

Revoiced in Vivaldo, Richard, Cass, and Ida, Baldwin's comprehensive portrayal of moral failure provides the thematic center of *Another Country*. Given the general optimism of the early sixties, it is particularly significant that Baldwin's attempt to image salvation seems entirely unconvincing. Baldwin concludes the novel with an almost Edenic image of the reunion of Yves and Eric, an image of a separatist community that seems particularly naive seen retrospectively from the age of AIDS. Even within the novel, the most convincing of the narrative lines deny the possibility of simple dissociation from institutional pressures. The intensity of Rufus's pain and the intricacy of Ida and Vivaldo's struggle overshadow Eric and Yves's problematic innocence. Purely individual solutions, like purely individual consciousness, change little. Reflecting on their interracial love in terms applicable to American culture on a much more general level, Ida tells Vivaldo, "Our being together doesn't change the world." Ida's later question, "how can you say you loved Rufus when there was so much about him you didn't want to know?" could easily provide the epitaph for the United States in the seventies and eighties (227).

In *Just above My Head*, which has received little serious critical attention, Baldwin responds to the collapse of both integrationist and nationalist phases of the movement by reasserting the gospel impulse as the necessary foundation for renewed activity. Although he employed elements of the black nationalist vocabulary in *Tell Me How Long the Train's Been Gone* and *If Beale Street Could Talk*, Baldwin realized that the simple inversion of racist hierarchies characteristic of some parts of the black power and Black Arts movements reiterated the fundamental mistake of the integrationist movement. Attempting to reclaim the power of the gospel impulse, Baldwin cautions against superficial ideological interpretations of the Afro-American apprehension of, and response to, oppression. In *Just above My Head*, Baldwin creates a narrator, Hall Montana, capable of articulating the psychological subtleties of *Go Tell It on the Mountain*, the social insights of *Another Country*, and the political anger of *Tell Me How Long the Train's Been Gone*. Like other observer-participants in

American literature, such as Nick Carraway in *The Great Gatsby* and Jack Burden in *All the King's Men,* Hall tells both his own story and that of a public figure, in this case his brother Arthur, a gospel singer who has died two years prior to the start of the novel. In part Baldwin's reflection on his own celebrity, *Just above My Head* echoes countless motifs from his earlier writings. Though not precisely self-reflexive, *Just above My Head* takes on added richness when juxtaposed with Baldwin's treatment of the church in *Go Tell It on the Mountain;* of homosexuality in *Giovanni's Room;* of music and brotherhood in "Sonny's Blues"; of the civil rights movement in *Blues for Mister Charlie;* of the Nation of Islam in *The Fire Next Time* and *No Name in the Street;* and the intermingling of family love and world politics in *If Beale Street Could Talk.* Baldwin's reconsideration of his own artistic history, which is at once private like Hall's and public like Arthur's, emphasizes the need for continual reexamination of the place of the gospel impulse in the process leading to a higher innocence.

Hall's resolve to understand the political and existential meaning of Arthur's experience originates in his desire to answer honestly his children's questions concerning Arthur. Refusing to protect their original innocence—an attempt he knows would fail—Hall seeks both to free himself from the despair of experience and to discover a mature innocence he can pass on to the younger generation. Perhaps the finest summation of Baldwin's gospel politics, Hall's meditation on the gospel impulse bears quotation at length:

> To overhaul a history, or to attempt to redeem it—which effort may or may not justify it—is not at all the same thing as the descent one must make in order to excavate a history. To be forced to excavate a history is, also, to repudiate the concept of history, and the vocabulary in which history is written; for the written history is, and must be, merely the vocabulary of power, and power is history's most seductively attired false witness.
>
> And yet, the attempt, more the necessity, to excavate a history, to find out the truth about oneself! is motivated by the need to have the power to force others to recognize your presence, your right to be here. The disputed passage will remain disputed so long as you do not have the authority of the right-of-way—so long, that is, as your passage can be disputed: the document promising safe passage can always be revoked. Power clears the passage, swiftly: but the paradox here is that power, rooted in history, is also, the mockery and the repudiation of history. The power to define the other seals one's definition of one's self. . . .
>
> Perhaps, then, after all, we have no idea of what history is: or are in flight from the demon we have summoned. Perhaps history is not to be found in mirrors but in our repudiations: perhaps, the other is ourselves. . . .

Our history is each other. That is our only guide. One thing is absolutely certain: one can repudiate, or despise, no one's history without repudiating and despising one's own. Perhaps that is what the gospel singer is singing. (428)

Baldwin's portrayal of Hall's courage and Arthur's experience illustrates the liberating potential of the gospel politics implicit in this passage. If an individual such as Hall can counteract the pressures militating against personal responsibility, Baldwin implies, he or she may be able to exert a positive influence on relatively small social groups such as families and churches, which in turn may affect the larger political process. Nevertheless, Baldwin refuses to encourage simplistic optimism. Rather than focusing narrowly on Hall's individual process, he emphasizes the aspects of the political context that make his success atypical. Although Hall begins with his immediate family history, his excavation involves the Korean War, the civil rights movement, the rise of Malcolm X, and the role of advertising in American culture. Hall's relationships with his family and close friends provide a Jamesian frame for the Dreiserian events of the novel, somewhat as John's conversion frames the historical "Prayer of the Saints" in *Go Tell It on the Mountain*. *Just above My Head*, however, leaves no ambiguity concerning the individual's ability to free himself or herself from history. Only a conscious decision to accept the pain and guilt of past political failures promises any real hope for love, for the higher innocence. Baldwin reiterates that, while the desire for safety is understandable, all safety is illusion. Pain inevitably returns; only a firm grasp of the gospel impulse—accepting the full complexity of the moment, living out the interrelationship of self and community, politics and culture—makes survival possible.

Like *Go Tell It on the Mountain*, *Just above My Head* provides clear warnings against attempting to maintain innocence through simplistic self-definition. Like *Another Country*, it provides an unflinching vision of the brutality such simplification creates. Julia Miller, like the young Baldwin, undergoes a salvation experience and embarks on a career as a child evangelist. Encouraged by her parents, friends of the Montanas who rely on their daughter for economic support, she assumes a sanctimonious attitude that she uses to manipulate her elders. Arthur's parents deplore the indulgence of Julia, unambiguously rejecting the idea that her religious vocation absolves her of responsibility for the "naughty" street side of her personality. Ultimately, and in great pain, Julia confronts this truth. After her mother's death, she discovers that her father, Joel, views her primarily as an economic and sexual object. His desire to exploit her earning potential even when she says she has lost her vocation reflects his underlying contempt for the gospel spirit. This contempt leads to the incestuous rape that destroys Julia's remaining innocence and drives her to life as a prostitute in New Orleans. Eventually, Julia recovers from this brutalization—a clear expression of the gospel belief in salvation—but her example provides a clear warning to Arthur against confusing his vocation as a gospel singer with a transcendence of human fallibility.

A gifted gospel singer as a teenager, Arthur rises to stardom as the "emperor of soul." Arthur's success, however, is of less importance than the broader context that renders the idea of success nearly meaningless. The experiences of the members of Arthur's first gospel group, the Trumpets of Zion, reveal how the very context that celebrates Arthur accepts the murders—symbolic and real—of those whose experiences he articulates. Peanut, Arthur's companion on the road, vanishes into the Alabama night following a civil rights rally, presumably murdered by whites seeking to enforce the separation of gospel "culture" from political action. Equally devastating, though less direct, is the political context's impact on Red, another member of the Trumpets, who turns to drugs in an attempt to escape the Harlem streets. Even Hall finds himself an unwilling accomplice when he is drafted and sent to Korea. Powerless to alter the political structure, Hall can at least challenge the pervasive refusal to recognize its substructure; he tells Arthur that the American military spreads not freedom but repudiation through the Third World.

Building on the gospel refusal of oppositional thought, Arthur's power as a singer derives from his ability to combine the reality of street and temple, communicating sexual pain in his gospel songs and spiritual aspiration in his blues. Yet this power does not provide him with sufficient strength to overcome the isolation he shares with Rufus Scott. The expectation of loss periodically overpowers his determination to communicate, severing his sense of his own voice as part of a larger community. Attempting to survive by rededicating himself—and he oscillates between thinking of that self in Euro- and Afro-American terms—to sexual relationships, Arthur drives himself past the limits of physical and psychological endurance. He dies in the basement bathroom of a London pub after a lovers' quarrel. Concluding Arthur's life with an image of isolation, Baldwin emphasizes the power of the limiting definitions to destroy even the most aware consciousness.

Arthur's death inspires Hall's quest for the higher innocence, which, with the support of Julia and Arthur's piano player and lover Jimmy, he passes on to the younger generation. This higher innocence involves both individual consciousness and political commitment, requiring the mutual support of individuals willing to excavate their own histories. This support expresses itself in the call-and-response dynamic basic to the gospel, blues, and jazz impulses. Baldwin's image of this dynamic begins with the call of a leader who expresses his own experience through the vehicle of a traditional song, a call originating in the communal history that traces all later stages. This call provides a communal context for exploration of the "individual" emotion. If the community, as it exists in the present, recognizes and shares the experience evoked by the call, it responds with another phrase, again usually traditional, communicating the sense of validation and acceptance that enables the leader to go on exploring the implications, including the political implications, of the material. Implicitly the process enables both individual and community to define themselves, to validate their experiences, in opposition to dominant social forces. If the experience of isolation is shared, it is no longer the same type of isolation that brought Rufus to his death. In *Just above My Head,* the call and response rests on a rigorous excavation requiring individual silence, courage, and honesty expressed through social presence, acceptance, and love. Expressed in the interactions between Arthur and his audiences, between Hall and his children, between Baldwin and his readers, this call and response provides a realistic image of the higher innocence possible in opposition to the simplifying definitions of a murderous context.

Gospel Politics in *The Fire Next Time*

If *Just above My Head* marks the point of maximum resolution in Baldwin's exploration of the gospel impulse, *The Fire Next Time,* which assumes a more obvious importance in light of the Los Angeles rebellion/conflagration of 1992, marks the point of maximum tension. Because the quarrel with Wright had established Baldwin, however simplistically, as spokesman for the "aesthetic"—as opposed to "propagandistic"—tradition of Afro-American expression, the uncompromising anger of *The Fire Next Time* attracted an unusual degree of attention. No subsequent work of nonfiction by an Afro-American writer—with the problematic exception of *Roots*—has exerted anything approaching a similar impact on public discourse. In our time, when aggressive statements of black anger are beginning to reemerge in public discourse—witness the demonstrations on college campuses and the street-level rage articulated by rap musicians such as Ice T, Boogie Down Productions, Sistah Souljah, and Public Enemy—Baldwin's prophetic voice offers important insights into the nature of the problems that have all too frequently subverted effective cooperation between the white Left and the black community since the sixties. Perhaps the most crucial of these problems was the failure of the white Left to comprehend the significance of the gospel impulse in Afro-American culture; the most obvious result of this failure was the common assumption that blacks supported "integration," which was understood primarily as a movement of blacks into the mainstream of white society. *The Fire Next Time* reveals the inadequacy, indeed the destructiveness, of such crucial equivocations. Read today, when "political" readers rarely possess even a passing familiarity with Baldwin's novels, it seems particularly important that white readers approach *The Fire Next Time* not as a source of fashionable slogans but for an understanding of the gospel impulse that must inform any effective interracial coalition.

The titles and epigraphs of *The Fire Next Time* unambiguously ground Baldwin's politics in the gospel vision. The titles of the major sections—"My Dungeon Shook" and "Down at the Cross"—refer directly to Afro-American revoicings of the Judeo-Christian tradition. Like the title of the book as a whole, "My Dungeon Shook" invokes the militant Old Testament tradition that promises the ultimate, if not necessarily imminent, destruction of the oppressors. Addressing his nephew, Baldwin writes: "You come from a long line of great poets, some of the greatest poets since Homer. One of them said, 'The very time I thought I was lost, My dungeon shook and my chains fell off'" (*Price* 336). Similarly, Baldwin concludes his book with a phrase that would echo through discussions of the riots in Watts, Newark, and Detroit: "If we do not now dare everything, the fulfillment of that prophecy, recreated from the Bible in song by a slave, is upon us: 'God gave Noah the rainbow sign, No more water, the fire next time!'" (379).

Reflecting a more complex sense of the relationship between Afro-American and Judeo-Christian iconography, the phrase "Down at the Cross"—also derived from a gospel hymn—emphasizes that substituting religion for action (rather than integrating religion and action) perpetuates oppressive institutions and psychology. Examining his experience as a child evangelist, Baldwin reiterates the central theme of *Go Tell It on the Mountain:* that "religion," as the term is typically understood in American discourse, is synonymous with "safety." And, for Baldwin, to believe in safety is to accept a "white" identity. Tracing the origins of this acceptance—which violates the fundamental premise of the gospel impulse—to European colonialism, Baldwin notes that, from the beginning of the encounter of Africa and Europe, religious and political discourses were profoundly, if not openly, connected: "The spreading of the Gospel, regardless of the motives or the integrity or the heroism of some of the missionaries, was an absolutely indispensable justification for the planting of the flag" (351).

Even as he acknowledges the corruption of the church as institution, Baldwin recognizes the potential power implicit in the connection between individual and community within the black church. Acknowledging that he has never really disengaged himself from the "visceral" excitement of the gospel church, Baldwin describes a dynamic of great interest to anyone seeking to motivate large segments of the black community to political action: "I have never seen anything to equal the fire and excitement that sometimes, without warning, fill a church, causing the church, as Leadbelly and so many others have testified, to 'rock.' Nothing that has happened to me since equals the power and the glory that I sometimes felt when, in the middle of a sermon, I knew that I was somehow, by some miracle, really carrying, as they said, 'the Word'—when the church and I were one" (345–46). It is of the utmost importance that the white Left understand the dynamic generating this communal power. Leader and community define one another in relation to the shared historical understandings encoded in the songs and the form of their expression. This is most definitely *not* a situation in which a leader of superior insight defines and directs the community. On the most immediate political level, this means that the implications of the gospel impulse are not integrationist, at least as the term is usually understood. To the extent that the black church provides a resource for constructive action, it is because it affirms racial experience and resists Euro-American thought structures. Therefore, white political agendas that, implicitly or explicitly, assume that blacks wish to enter the white institutional world as it now exists may receive a certain degree of support from those seeking "safety." Such agendas will not, however, tap the energies of the church as effectively as Afro-American preacher politicians—Jesse Jackson is only the most recent example—who understand the complexity of the dynamic.

The Fire Next Time intimates a political-cultural movement consistent with the gospel impulse. If, as a result of Baldwin's awareness of institutional corruption, this vision is not religious in any simple sense, neither is it ideological. Baldwin identifies the contradictions inherent in the most prominent agendas present in the racial discourse of the early sixties, which might be labeled in general terms integrationist and separatist. Following the introductory letter ("My Dungeon Shook") that sounds his central themes—the need to resist white thought structures and the power of love—Baldwin divides the lengthy central section ("Down at the Cross") into three parts. The first, focusing on Baldwin's experience in Harlem churches, critiques the premises of integrationist politics; the second, focusing on Elijah Muhammad and the Nation of Islam, critiques separatism. After examining these ideologies—and the fact that they are publicly perceived in an oppositional manner is part of the problem—Baldwin focuses the final section on his vision of a gospel politics.

Emphasizing the ways in which white thought structures—the separation of religion and politics, the urge for safety—frequently render the church ineffectual in responding to the realities of black life, the first section of "Down at the Cross" directly, and repeatedly, addresses the misunderstandings inherent in most white progressive rhetoric, then and now: "There appears to be a vast amount of confusion on this point, but I do not know many Negroes who are eager to be 'accepted' by white people, still less to be loved by them; they, the blacks, simply don't wish to be beaten over the head by the whites every instant of our brief passage on this planet" (340). While this statement is most certainly consistent with the goals of the *desegregation* movement of the fifties, it resists the unstated premises of the integrationist agenda that, as Manning Marable notes, had effectively replaced desegregation as a central way of phrasing the progressive racial agenda by the midsixties. Addressing "the reality which lies behind the words *acceptance* and *integration*," Baldwin cautions his nephew: "There is no reason for you to try to become like white people and there is no basis whatever for their impertinent assumption that *they* must accept *you*. The really terrible thing, old buddy, is that *you* must accept *them*" (335).

The second section of "Down at the Cross" presents an equally uncompromising rejection of the Nation of Islam's separatist ideology, which Baldwin views as a simple inversion that fails to challenge the oppositional structure of Euro-American thought. Summarizing the Nation's "white devil" theology, Baldwin observes that "the dream, the sentiment is old; only the color is new" (357). Specifically, Baldwin identifies the unstated political motivations linking the Nation of Islam's theology with the racist assumptions of white Christianity: "it had been designed for the same purpose; namely, the sanctification of power" (353). Repudiating any ideology that perpetuates oppositional thought, Baldwin explicitly rejects separatism: "The glorification of one race and the consequent debasement of another— or others—always has been and always will be a recipe for murder" (369). Although he insists on the reality of the historical events and emotional responses that attract many young blacks to the Nation of Islam, Baldwin contends that in both philosophical and practical terms, its agenda is a "fantasy" (365), doomed to failure. His observations concerning the subordination of women reinforce his sense that the Nation has simply exchanged "black" for "white" while accepting the oppositional thought structures that elevate male over female, straight over gay, mind over feeling, and aesthetics over politics (or vice versa). Sadly—since Baldwin senses a tremendous potential energy in Elijah Muhammad and values his ability to transform the lives of junkies and criminals—the Nation of Islam has, ironically, repeated "the European error" (377).

As he shifts attention from the inadequacy of existing ideologies to his own vision, Baldwin underlines the single most important premise of his thought: "It is so simple a fact and one that is so hard, apparently, to grasp: *Whoever debases others is debasing himself*" (369). In the final section of "Down at the Cross," Baldwin envisions a gospel politics grounded firmly in the refusal to debase self or other. This vision celebrates the central elements of the gospel impulse: the refusal to accept oppositional thinking; the complex sense of presence as interrelationship (of politics and culture, self and individual, history and the present); and the belief in universal salvation predicated on the power of love. In "My Dungeon Shook," Baldwin associates the destruction of Afro-Americans individually and collectively with the uncritical acceptance of white thought structures: "it was intended that you should perish in the ghetto, perish by never being allowed to go behind the white man's definitions, by never being allowed to spell your proper name" (336). Underlining the political implications of this observation in "Down at the Cross," Baldwin argues that "the power of the white world is threatened whenever a black man refuses to accept the white world's definitions" (362).

Because it resists the categorization that excludes certain types of information as irrelevant, such refusal demands a more complex sense of *presence* than is normally incorporated in political analysis; Baldwin italicizes the word repeatedly in *The Fire Next Time*. Whether describing the budding sexuality of girls in Harlem, the similarity in the language used by pimps and preachers, or the face of Elijah Muhammad, Baldwin emphasizes the connection between seemingly contradictory qualities. Oxymoron is as basic to his politics as it is to his style. Yet, Baldwin observes, because they internalize oppositional thinking, most individuals deny their own complexity: "such a person interposes between himself and reality nothing less than a labyrinth of attitudes. And these attitudes, furthermore, though the person is usually unaware of it (is unaware of so much!), are historical and public attitudes. They do not relate to the present any more than they relate to the person" (350). Insisting on the inadequacy of any political approach that does not take the actual complexity into account, Baldwin insists on the profound connection between what are frequently viewed as separate discourses: "It can be objected that I am speaking of political freedom in spiritual terms, but the political institutions of any nation are always menaced and are ultimately controlled by the spiritual state of that nation" (371). Emphasizing that simplification of reality inevitably perpetuates destructive patterns, Baldwin writes: "We are controlled here by our confusion, far more than we know, and the American dream has therefore become something much more closely resembling a nightmare, on the private, domestic, and international levels. Privately, we cannot stand our lives and dare not examine them; domestically, we take no responsibility for (and no pride in) what goes on in our country; and, internationally, for many millions of people, we are an unmitigated disaster" (371–72). Given the increasing fragmentation of public discourse, on the Left as on the Right, it is hardly surprising to find that *The Fire Next Time* presents a litany of specific observations that remain as relevant in the wake of the Los Angeles uprising as they were in 1962. Baldwin's observations concerning the baffled response of white liberals to expressions of black rage, and the ways Western hypocrisy destroys the possibility of constructive interaction with what we persist in calling the "Third World," to cite only two examples, remain disturbingly accurate. Even more disturbing as a summation of the political psychology of the eighties is his observation that "white Americans are not simply unwilling to effect these changes; they are, in the main, so slothful have they become, unable to envision them" (370).

Despite, or perhaps because, of this complex realistic perception of the problem—both realism and complexity are fundamental to the gospel impulse—Baldwin maintains a belief in the possibility of change, of salvation: "I think that people can be better than that, and I know that people can be better than they are. We are capable of bearing a great burden, once we discover that the burden is reality and arrive where reality is" (372). The foundation of Baldwin's hope is his belief in the power of a tough, realistic "Love [that] takes off the masks that we fear we cannot live without and know we cannot live within. I use the word 'love' here not merely in the personal sense but as a state of being, or a state of grace—not in the infantile American sense of being made happy but in the tough and universal sense of quest and daring and growth" (375). Relating this vision of love directly to the tangled reality and potential of the Afro-American church, Baldwin celebrates the impulse rather than the institution: "If the concept of God has any validity or any use, it can only be to make us larger, freer, and more loving. If God cannot do this, then it is time we got rid of Him" (352).

This love—the God who, Baldwin states explicitly, can be apprehended only by those willing to "divorce [themselves] from all the prohibitions, crimes, and hypocrisies of the Christian church"—has long been fundamental to the Afro-American community. As Baldwin tells his nephew, "if we had not loved each other none of us would have survived" (335). As the Afro-American tradition has always known, this love is at once personal and political. Without an awareness of the reality of power, Baldwin writes, love is meaningless, for "power *is* real and many things, including, very often, love, cannot be achieved without it" (364). In *The Fire Next Time*, as in "Sonny's Blues," Baldwin identifies music as the clearest articulation of black love. Even in the confusion created by the internalization of white definitions, Baldwin observes, the black community—"pimps, whores, racketeers, church members, and children"—at times realized "a freedom that was close to love," a freedom articulated most powerfully in black music, whatever its specific form: "This is the freedom that one hears in some gospel songs, for example, and in jazz. In all jazz, and especially in the blues" (349). Applying this "cultural" vision to the specific political context of his time, Baldwin articulates the political imperative of the gospel impulse in terms clearly relevant to our own: "And if the word *integration* means anything, this is what it means: that we, with love, shall force our brothers to see themselves as they are, to cease fleeing from reality and begin to change it" (336).

Awareness of this process will not directly alter the divisive institutions that would destroy the gospel impulse. Without an awareness of the process, however, any political movement is doomed to oversimplify and distort the internal dynamic of Afro-American culture, which is to say Afro-American politics. For the most part, attempts to forge interracial coalitions have been based on contact between white individuals and a small part of the Afro-American community. The most common approaches emphasize the importance of the black avant-garde—the educated elite capable of translating between white and black vocabularies—or the proletariat conceived primarily in secular economic terms. Recognition of the pervasive influence and significance of the gospel impulse, however, suggests strongly that such limited approaches, based on a belief in the reality of categories with little relevance to the actual dynamic of Afro-American culture, are doomed to fail. At times, gospel politics will seem, from a Euro-American perspective, overly passive, unwilling to engage in necessary struggles. But it should be clearly understood that such disengagement is not a failure of courage but a determination to leave tar baby be, not to enter into situations—liberal, conservative, or radical—that consciously or unconsciously deny the premises of Afro-American culture. And perhaps Baldwin's most profound legacy lies in his belief that gospel politics must be a realistic politics of love, of connection. The "leadership" of such a movement does not *control* its direction; rather it provides a context in which the energies of gospel, blues, and jazz (which is to say of soul and rap and funk) can be focused on resisting the powers that would destroy the spirit. As Baldwin writes, "The man who tells the story isn't *making up* a story. He's listening to us, and can only give back, to us, what he hears: from us" (*Head* 494). To enter into this process, to attempt to realize the gospel vision of a freedom at once individual and communal, cultural and political, we must above all *hear* other voices. If Baldwin had been a larger presence in public discourse of the eighties it would have been much more difficult to have ignored AIDS. As Baldwin knew, and as those who turned away from the crisis have inevitably and painfully learned, the fate of the other can never be divorced from the fate of the self. If Baldwin were a larger presence in our public discourse today, we would be less likely to ignore or distort the voices of the streets, whether the mingling of celebration and political anger in the raps of Queen Latifah, Kid Frost, and Ice Cube or the Judeo-Christian, but by no means white, gospel testimony of Shirley Caeser, the L.A. Mass Choir, or the Canton Spirituals. If, in the future, we return our attention to Baldwin, to the voices of the streets, perhaps we can begin to give substance to the vision of a gospel politics sounded in the final passage of *The Fire Next Time:* "Everything now, we must assume, is in our hands; we have no right to assume otherwise. If we—and now I mean the relatively conscious whites and relatively conscious blacks, who must, like lovers, insist on, or create, the consciousness of others—do not falter in our duty now, we may be able, handful that we are, to end the racial nightmare, and achieve our country, and change the history of the world" (*Price* 379). If we should choose to deny this call, to withhold our response—and responding with rhetoric without action is the most insidious of denials—then, as Baldwin knew in 1963 and as we should know today, the fire will return.

10

Leon Forrest and the AACM:
The Jazz Impulse and
the Chicago Renaissance

▲ ▲ ▲ ▲

Leon Forrest's hometown of Chicago is in many ways the most paradoxical of American cities. By many measures the most segregated major American city (W. Wilson), Chicago nonetheless nurtured some of the most challenging, multiculturally inclusive black artists of the 1960s, 1970s, and 1980s. Influenced by the interracial political and cultural exchanges of what Robert Bone has labeled the "Chicago Renaissance" (1935–50), Chicago-based writers and musicians have felt little sense of contradiction between the vernacular and "high art" traditions of European- and African-American culture. Like Gwendolyn Brooks—whose life and work represent crucial links between the Chicago Renaissance and the generation of black Chicago artists who began working in the sixties and seventies—Forrest and contemporaries such as Clarence Major draw much of their power from the juxtaposition of European-American modernist and African-American musical traditions. Like founder and spiritual leader Muhal Richard Abrams, musicians affiliated with the Association for the Advancement of Creative Musicians (AACM) (Anthony Braxton, Roscoe Mitchell, Amina Claudine Myers) combine European modernist approaches to composition with their multifaceted African-American musical heritage to transcend limiting categorizations based on race or genre.

Theoretically engaging and emotionally compelling, their works offer crucial insights into the relationship between culture and liberation, understood in psychological, spiritual, or institutional terms. Brooks's dedication to community-based arts programs, particularly following her "conversion" to a black nationalist perspective during the sixties, made her one of the South Side's best-loved elders. Similarly, the AACM drew inspiration from, and shaped its agenda in response to, the community activism centered on the Coordinating Council of Community Organizations (Radano, "Classics"). Although Forrest was never a member of the Nation of Islam, he worked on the staff of the Nation's newspaper *Muhummad Speaks* from 1969 through 1973. Sharing the fundamental African-American sense of art as a "functional" aspect of everyday life, post-Renaissance Chicago artists consistently resist the academic tendency to divorce cultural production from political or spiritual awareness.

Outside of relatively small communities of intellectuals and artists, however, neither the writers nor the musicians have attained widespread recognition. Despite its marvelous live performances and fascinating revoicings of "accessible" classics such as Bob Marley's "No Woman No Cry" and Jimi Hendrix's "Purple Haze," the Art Ensemble of Chicago (whose members include AACM members Mitchell, Lester Bowie, Malachi Favors, and Joseph Jarman) receives much less attention (and sells many fewer albums) than Ornette Coleman or the World Saxophone Quartet, who share many AACM concerns. Although he shares both thematic and stylistic concerns with successful black novelists such as John Wideman or his former editor Toni Morrison, Forrest's work remains relatively unknown. In the context of American cultural economics, this lack of popular recognition perpetuates itself. Many of the best AACM recordings—including the vast majority of those produced prior to Abrams's move to New York in 1976—remain unavailable. Despite the support of Morrison and Saul Bellow, who wrote a glowing statement for the cover of *The Bloodworth Orphans,* Forrest's original publisher, Random House, allowed all three of his novels to go out of print prior to their reissue by Another Chicago Press in the late eighties. Only a historically significant "rescue" by Norton, which has no realistic hope of short-term financial gain, kept Forrest's Joycean (in both size and, in numerous passages, brilliance) *Divine Days* from going out of print when original publisher Another Chicago Press encountered paralyzing difficulties.

In the remainder of this chapter, I will argue that the art and experience of Leon Forrest and the AACM musicians highlight the difficulties faced by artists responding to W. E. B. Du Bois's call for African-Americans to merge the fragments of their "double consciousness" into "a better and truer self" incorporating African and European traditions. After surveying the main currents of the Chicago Renaissance as they provided the setting in which Forrest and the AACM began to work, I will delineate some of the connections between the explicitly multicultural "jazz impulse" (which parallels important currents of European-American modernism) and the specifically black (and implicitly Afrocentric) "gospel impulse" in African-American culture. Finally, I shall provide a brief demonstration of how the jazz/modernism/gospel nexus comes together in Forrest's powerful narrative voice that—like Abrams's *Levels and Degrees of Light*, Mitchell's "Noonah," or Myers's "African Blues"—clearly deserves a stronger response than it has yet received.

The Chicago Renaissance

One of the most important revisions of twentieth-century Afro-American cultural history focuses on the significance of Chicago between the midthirties and the midfifties. Prior to the publication of Robert Bone's germinal essay "Richard Wright and the Chicago Renaissance" (1986), constructions of Afro-American literary history typically identified the Harlem Renaissance of the twenties and the Black Arts Movement of the sixties as primary points of reference. Whether phrased in terms of the "School of Wright" or of "protest literature," criticism of the intervening decades focused almost obsessively on Richard Wright. In turn, criticism of Afro-American literature of the fifties frequently posited a simple reaction against Wright. In such frameworks, Wright becomes a writer of sociology, a naturalist with leftist inflections; Baldwin and Ellison appear as champions of a nonracial "universalism"; black women writers are marginalized (Hurston) or distorted (Ann Petry as naturalist, the early Brooks as universalist). Perhaps the most important implication of Bones's revision concerns the long-term influence of this simplifying critical discourse. The "sociological" approach to Afro-American literature, like its deracinated "universalist" double, established an interpretive framework—reflected in both academic criticism and the mass media—that continues to undervalue the work of artists who cannot be reduced to familiar categories.

Providing an alternative to such narrow constructions, Bone's identification of a Chicago Renaissance contributes to the construction of a cultural history in which the synthetic sensibilities and reception difficulties of Forrest and the AACM are at least comprehensible. Bone asserts that between 1935 and 1950 Chicago had all of the elements of the Harlem Renaissance with the exception of an effective publicist such as Alain Locke. Listing the Chicago-based writers (Wright, Brooks, Margaret Walker, Frank Marshall Davis, William Attaway, Theodore Ward, Arna Bontemps, Marita Bonner) who created a body of work as rich as that emanating from Harlem in the twenties, Bone details the importance of migration, patronage, academic institutions, and publishing outlets. In exploring the significance of the Chicago Renaissance, it is useful, if somewhat artificial, to focus first on developments within the African-American community and then on the interaction of this community with white Chicago.

The Chicago Renaissance originated in the massive migration of Afro-Americans from the rural South to Chicago that began just before World War I and continued throughout the thirties and forties. Inspired in part by the crusading journalism of Robert Abbott in the *Chicago Defender* (which also published the work of black writers such as Langston Hughes who did not participate directly in the Renaissance), the migration was significant in economic, political, and cultural terms. Black workers moving to the South Side brought with them cultural traditions that shaped some of the most important subsequent developments in American vernacular culture. Transplanted from Mississippi and Arkansas by Muddy Waters, Howlin' Wolf, and others, the Delta blues strongly influenced black secular music and rock and roll, which was in its inception interracial, but rapidly came to be marketed primarily by and for whites. Similarly, the sacred traditions of the southern black church rapidly developed into the polished gospel music of Clara Ward, Roberta Martin, and Mahalia Jackson, which in turn contributed to the vocal styles fundamental to fifties rhythm and blues and sixties soul music. Alongside these musical developments arose literary organizations exemplified by the South Side Writers group, which the Mississippi-born Wright helped organize in 1936 (Fabre, *Quest* 128). As interracial cultural contact declined during the fifties and sixties, these specifically African-American cultural resources provided a supportive context for the development of second-generation Chicago artists such as Forrest, whose family came to Chicago from Mississippi (the paternal side) and New Orleans (the maternal side).

Several significant forums for interracial cultural and political interaction complemented these developments within the black community. As Berndt Ostendorf and William Howland Kenney note in their investigations of Chicago jazz of the twenties, pre-Renaissance Chicago had provided a setting in which white musicians could absorb at least the superficial aspects of Afro-American musical aesthetics. Of greater lasting importance, however, was the patronage provided black artists and intellectuals by the Julius Rosenwald Fund. Noting the shift away from the individual patronage characteristic of the Harlem Renaissance, Bone details the importance of the fund as a source of economic support for black writers and scholars, especially after Edwin Embree assumed its directorship in 1928. Relying on the advice of an interracial board of trustees including Charles S. Johnson, Embree used the fund's fellowship program to support Wright, Bontemps, Attaway, Walker, Horace Cayton, St. Clair Drake, E. Franklin Frazier, and Katherine Dunham. The fund's support of non-Chicago writers such as Ralph Ellison, Zora Neale Hurston, Langston Hughes, Robert Hayden, and, later, James Baldwin underscored the significance of the Chicago Renaissance in the general development of Afro-American culture of the thirties and forties.

Most of the writers supported by the Rosenwald Fund were directly involved in organizations that encouraged interracial contact. Wright viewed the John Reed Clubs, sponsored by the Communist Party of the United States, as a vital source of support for black writers attempting to overcome their cultural isolation. The Illinois branch of the Federal Writers' Project provided both financial support and a forum for contact between black and white writers. While a great deal of the interracial cultural activity took place on the political Left, even relatively conservative cultural organizations supported interracial communication during the Renaissance. Based in Chicago, Harriet Monroe's influential *Poetry* magazine published the work of black poets, most notably Langston Hughes, alongside that of T. S. Eliot and Carl Sandburg. One of *Poetry*'s patrons and a prominent member of Chicago's social scene, Inez Cunningham Stark conducted a poetry workshop for aspiring South Side poets, which culminated in a competition won by the young Gwendolyn Brooks.

The most significant institutional interaction between black and white intellectuals during the Renaissance, however, centered on the University of Chicago Sociology Department. Developed under the guidance of Robert Park, the "Chicago School" of sociology viewed cities as settings for the development of new, more advanced forms of culture. Delineating a race relations cycle progressing from contact and conflict to accommodation and assimilation, Park envisioned America as a "melting pot" that would eventually generate a "raceless" society (Matthews; Ross; Bone 455–56). Part of Park's attempt to realize this vision involved direct support for black intellectuals, most importantly Charles Johnson, St. Clair Drake, and Horace Cayton (Ross 439). As chair of the Sociology Department at Fisk University, Johnson extended the influence of his former teacher into the Afro-American academic world. Equally significant, however, was the research carried out by Cayton and Drake as graduate students at Chicago. Investigating the South Side from a Parkian perspective, Cayton and Drake published their findings as *Black Metropolis*, which includes an important preface by Wright.

Reflecting the interaction of sociological and cultural perspectives, *Black Metropolis* and Wright's novel *Native Son* played crucial roles in encouraging sociological approaches to Afro-American culture. Focused on the broad social significance rather than the individual nuances of Afro-American experience, the sociological approach encouraged interpretations of black culture as "protests" intended to engage and rectify social "problems." Despite the Parkian commitment to increased interracial contact, the widespread acceptance of such approaches (which were rarely applied to white artists) ironically contributed to the growing intellectual and social segregation that helped bring the Chicago Renaissance to an end in the fifties. Despite the use of quantitative evidence generated by Chicago school researchers in support of liberal policy agendas beginning in the forties, the application of sociological methods to cultural criticism allowed white readers and critics to underestimate both the individuality and the complexity of Afro-American cultural expression. Neither Forrest's fiction nor the AACM's music responds well to interpretations emphasizing "problem" or "protest."

The legacy of the Chicago Renaissance, then, is mixed. On the one hand, it encouraged an explosion of creative and intellectual activity by Afro-Americans that has few parallels. For young blacks such as Brooks, Forrest, Abrams, and Mitchell, the Renaissance provided a stimulating environment that allowed them to respond with equal intensity to the black community as a distinct reality and to the surrounding white community. At the same time, however, the Chicago Renaissance established the sociological premises that would discourage the development of an interracial audience willing to engage the full complexity of the resulting work.

After the Renaissance

By the middle of the fifties, the Chicago Renaissance had clearly come to an end. Whatever the critical misapprehensions of their work, Ellison and Baldwin signaled new concerns in Afro-American literature. Afro-American music was entering a period of rapid transition. Influenced strongly by the electric blues emanating from Chicago's Chess Studios, rock and roll emerged as a focal point of American popular music. Transforming American musical traditions without regard to racial or generic distinctions, Ray Charles, Sam Cooke, and others created the blues/gospel hybrid that would eventually be labeled "soul." Most directly relevant to the development of the AACM, early fifties jazz underscores the cultural dilemma facing post-Renaissance Chicago artists. Long perceived as an example of white exploitation of black musical forms, big band jazz attracted few young black musicians during the forties, although several, including Charlie Parker, served apprenticeships with big bands. Developed as a radical alternative to white jazz, be-bop was increasingly perceived as an African-American "art" music requiring great technical virtuosity and theoretical knowledge, but no longer deeply embedded in the life of the black community. In response, jazz musicians such as Miles Davis, Ornette Coleman, and John Coltrane established the contours of the multifaceted "free jazz" movement, which includes most AACM work.

Politically, several significant national developments deeply influenced Chicago's young black artists. The southern civil rights movement created a new sense of optimism regarding the possibility of racial progress. Whether viewed in terms of *desegregation*—the removal of barriers excluding blacks from full participation in public life—or of *integration*—the realization of a Parkian vision of assimilation—the movement encouraged community-based political activity. Ronald Radano has demonstrated convincingly that the AACM drew its inspiration and institutional structure directly from community organizations founded in Chicago during the late fifties and early sixties: the Coordinating Council of Community Organizations, the Chicago Freedom Movement, Operation Breadbasket, People United to Save Humanity, and the local offices of the Student Non-Violent Coordinating Committee and the Southern Christian Leadership Conference.

Despite the general optimism, however, several cross-currents anticipated the de facto cultural segregation that undercut the development of an audience prepared to respond to the new generation of musicians and writers. Under the guidance of Elijah Muhammad, the Nation of Islam articulated its black separatist agenda from a South Side base. Particularly after the emergence of New York–based Malcolm X as a charismatic national leader, the Nation exerted a strong influence not just on its members but on the growing number of young northern blacks for whom the promise of the civil rights movement increasingly appeared to be a lie. Although Forrest never seriously considered joining the Nation (which did not require the staff of *Muhammad Speaks* to be members), he was obviously aware of its mythology and agenda. Equally important was a shift in tone within the civil rights movement during the midsixties. The black liberation theologian James Cone describes Malcolm's perspective during the fifties and early sixties as a vision of America as "nightmare" in contrast to Martin Luther King, Jr.'s, vision of the American "dream." Extending his analysis to the midsixties, Cone emphasizes the increasing similarity between Malcolm and Martin's visions. After his journey to Mecca, Malcolm returned with a much broader vision of the possibility of human community. Confronting Vietnam and domestic violence, King increasingly emphasized the nightmarish reality rather than the visionary possibilities.

Nowhere was the connection between these visions clearer than in Chicago. King's experience in Chicago—specifically his unsuccessful campaign to desegregate housing—marks a major turning point in the civil rights movement. The shift of attention from the South to the urban North—which brought the movement to the communities of the northern liberals who had supported the earlier stages—brought the reality of northern segregation (both physical and cultural/intellectual) into sharp focus. When the residents of the white working-class suburb of Cicero met King's march with taunts and violence, it became clear to many young blacks—especially in Chicago—that the dream was far from realization. The increasing prominence of black militant organizations in the community both reflected and contributed to the growing separation between black and white communities, especially outside the middle classes.

So, although their visions of human and artistic possibility had been shaped in a world where interracial communication seemed a possibility if not yet a reality, black Chicago artists who began work during the sixties found themselves in an almost entirely African-American context. Although the members of the AACM were highly aware of the works of European and European-American composers such as Stravinsky, Bartok, Dvorak, Stockhausen, and Cage, they had almost no direct contact with white composers in the Chicago area. As Radano and John Litweiler observe, their activities were based almost exclusively on the South Side. The most important academic institution for the younger generation was not the University of Chicago but Wilson Junior College, where Forrest and musicians such as Mitchell, Jarman, Favors, Henry Threadgill, and Anthony Braxton studied between 1955 and the founding of the AACM in 1965.

Despite these tensions, neither the AACM musicians nor Forrest express any sense of contradiction regarding their use of European- and African-American cultural traditions. In large part, this reflects their understanding of the relationship between the modernist and traditionalist currents of European-American aesthetics. Avant-garde composers such as Schoenberg, Webern, and Cage interest Abrams, Jarman, and Mitchell in large part because they reject nineteenth-century compositional practices. Much modernist composition reflects a widespread dissatisfaction with the hierarchical implications of harmonic structure, which (at least in the new constructions of musical history) required that all musical elements be subordinated to a tonal center, conceived in terms of "tonic" and "dominant" elements. The serial composers' rebellion against traditional harmony paralleled Miles Davis's movement away from scale-based be-bop improvisation to the melodic emphasis of modal jazz. Similarly, explorations of "folk" music as the base of "high art" composition conducted by Stravinsky, Bartok, and Ives could be seen as analogous to the African-American composers' revoicings of blues and gospel. Significantly, each of these composers evinced a serious interest in African-American music, both as vernacular "material" and as a source of insight into the relationship between compositional structure and improvisational freedom. Rather than representing an antagonistic alien influence, then, European-American modernism provided many AACM musicians with access to alternative perspectives on shared aesthetic problems.

Similarly, as his incisive comments on William Faulkner, Ralph Ellison, and James Joyce indicate, Forrest draws freely on European, European-American, and African-American cultural resources. Honoring the memory of Lucille Montgomery, a black teacher who encouraged his development by insisting that Forrest read Langston Hughes and Du Bois alongside the European-American classics, Forrest asserts a "complex, varied, Black/white" perspective as the foundation necessary to respond to the "ancestral imperative" and to "forge the intellectual tools to free our people" ("Light" 29). This sense of a shared cultural project was of immense importance to post-Renaissance Chicago writers and musicians. Performing under various names including Abrams's germinal Experimental Band and the Art Ensemble of Chicago, AACM members have made major contributions to the American compositional and improvisational traditions. Among the musicians who have contributed to what Art Ensemble of Chicago member Joseph Jarman (echoing New England Conservatory faculty member and influential jazz critic Gunther Schuller) called "third stream music with a heavy jazz bias" (Litweiler 173) are Roscoe Mitchell, Lester Bowie, Malachi Favors (all of the Art Ensemble), Henry Threadgill, Amina Claudine Myers, and Anthony Braxton. Movements associated either directly or indirectly with the AACM developed in St. Louis (the Black Arts Group), Detroit (Strata), New York (Collective Black Artists), and, more recently, New Haven, where composer-pianist Anthony Davis occupies a position in some ways analogous to Abrams's in Chicago (Giddins, *Riding* 193). Significantly, each of these cities also supported the work of broadly conscious writers including Eugene Redmond and Henry Dumas (St. Louis) and Robert Hayden (Detroit).

In addition to their interest in European-American modernism, most of the musicians affiliated with these groups resist attempts to draw distinctions between forms of black music. Articulating the sensibility behind the Art Ensemble's use of the phrase "Great Black Music Ancient to Future," Mitchell observes that when he was growing up in Chicago "music wasn't divided into categories the way it is now, with one age group listening to this and the next age group listening to that, and so on. I liked what my parents liked—Nat Cole and other pop singers, as well as Charlie Parker and Lester Young. You were exposed to all kinds of music on the radio in those days, and when you became a musician, it was just a matter of deciding what kind of music you wanted to play" (F. Davis 180). Recalling his early career as a writer, Forrest emphasizes a similar access to multiple sources of inspiration: "I listened almost religiously to all kinds of Black music, while I was writing and incorporating every sound I could set my ear to into my fiction including of course the spiritual incantation of 'A Love Supreme' by 'Trane" ("Light" 31).

Critical descriptions of both AACM music and Forrest's fiction tend to foreground the modernist, rather than the vernacular, dimensions of the work. Perhaps the best musicological analysis of the AACM (and free jazz generally) is that of Ekkehard Jost, who describes "a movement in all directions, toward all aspects of world music. This could become possible only when the formal, tonal and rhythmic canons of traditional jazz were overthrown, and it has led not only to incorporating musical elements of the Third World, but equally to adapting the materials and creative ideas of the European avant garde" (175). Attributing the distinctiveness of the AACM specifically to "geographical location" (163), Jost identifies a number of concerns involving the fundamental elements and relationships of the art form, which are analogous to those explored in Forrest's fiction. Jost specifies the AACM concern with the relationship between individual (solo) voice and its collective setting (168); a tendency to emphasize the texture or tone color of local events (168); and the belief that each of these events assumes meaning "not as an isolated occurrence sufficient unto itself" but from "a dialectical relationship to the music around it" (171). Similarly, John Litweiler frames his discussion of the AACM in terms that recall Forrest's investigation of the fundamental mystery of the artist's voice. For Litweiler, the most intriguing dimension of AACM music is "the tension of sounds in the free space of silence" (176). Identifying the underlying aesthetic assumptions of the Art Ensemble of Chicago as an outgrowth of "modern American selectivism," Gary Giddins sees the core of the group's structural practice in "contrasting tableaux or accumulated details assembled around a single motif; in each case, a large-scale work is constructed of fragments" (*Rhythm-a-ning* 196). Jost sounds a similar theme when he describes several of the most important AACM works as "multi-thematic suites, or pieces in which one or more melodic models serve as the contents of a collective or 'group memory' improvisation" (171). No literary critic has provided a better description of the structures of *There Is a Tree More Ancient than Eden, The Bloodworth Orphans,* or *Two Wings to Veil My Face.*

Jazz, Afrocentric Spirituality, and the Gospel Impulse

What distinguishes both Forrest's fiction and the AACM's music most clearly from European-American modernism is their underlying spiritual vision. Where many AACM members articulate their spirituality in Afrocentric or mystical terms, however, Forrest draws his vocabulary directly from the gospel church. The difference is more apparent than real. Many AACM members trace their musical roots directly to the gospel church: Braxton sang in a gospel chorus; Leroy Jenkins learned to play violin in church; Malachi Favors is the son of a preacher. Similarly, Forrest's perspective on the gospel church, particularly as it involves the black preacher, clearly emphasizes an encompassing spiritual vision that moves far beyond the confines of most European-American popular religion.

For the AACM, as Radano suggests, modernism (understood as a reaction against hierarchical aesthetics), rhythm-centered experimental technique (understood as a reaction against the tyranny of harmony), and a serious interest in spirituality express the same basic concern. Mitchell makes the connection between technique and spiritual vision explicit when he says "Cats that play bop are more concerned with things like chords and changes rather than spirits. . . . In free music you are dependent on the spirits because you don't want to fool with those chords" (Radano, "Classics" 90). Similarly, Abrams explains the AACM emphasis on process in spiritual terms: "Change is synonymous with any conception of the deity" (Litweiler 198). In an often-cited comment on the impact of the AACM on his own life, Art Ensemble member Joseph Jarman describes what amounts to a conversion: "Until I had the first meeting with Richard Abrams, I was like all the rest of the hip ghetto niggers; I was cool, I took dope, I smoked pot, etc. I did not *care* for the life that I had been given. In having the chance to work in the Experimental Band with Richard and the other musicians there, I found the first something with meaning/reason for doing. That band and the people there was the *most* important thing that ever happened to me" (Jost 164). AACM member Alvin Fielder echoes Jarman when he comments simply that the AACM "was like a church—it *was* my church" (Radano, "Classics" 83).

Generally recognized as the spiritual center of the AACM, Abrams sums up the communal function of the organization: "if the AACM is anything, it's a very excellent idea. It's not so much what is or isn't done, it's the idea and what it could mean to different groups, depending on their energy. The idea: to pool our energies to a common cause" (Litweiler 196). It is hardly surprising that some of the most powerful AACM music—Abrams's *Levels and Degrees of Light* and Myers's gospel-inflected "African Blues" from *Amina Claudine Myers Salutes Bessie Smith*—expresses spiritual experience. In contrast to this spiritual emphasis, European-American modernism, as Timothy Reiss observes, has been predicated largely on a repudiation of theological, essentialist, or transcendental ideas. This characteristic divergence of European- and African-American worldviews may well account for the difficulties both the AACM and Forrest have experienced in obtaining a serious hearing from the white avant-garde in spite of large areas of shared concern.

These issues coalesce around the changing significance of the "jazz impulse" in African-American aesthetics. Ralph Ellison, the most insightful and influential theorist of the relationship between African-American music and literature, defines the jazz impulse as a way of defining/creating the self in relation to community and tradition. Applicable to any form of cultural expression, jazz provides a way for new ideas, new *vision,* to enter the tradition. As many artists and critics have observed, almost all successful jazz is grounded in what Ellison calls the "blues impulse." Before one can hope to create a meaningful new vision of individual or communal identity, the artist must acknowledge the full complexity of his/her experience. (For Ellison's definitions of these impulses, see chapter 9.) Although the blues impulse is based on intensely individual feelings, these feelings, for most blues artists, can be traced in part to the brutal racist context experienced in some form by almost all blacks. Substituting the less "philosophical" term "affirmation" for what Ellison calls the "transcendence" derived from the blues confrontation, Albert Murray emphasizes that, especially when his/her call elicits a response from a community that confirms a shared experience, the blues artist becomes "an agent of affirmation and continuity in the face of adversity" (*Stomping* 38). Both the individual expression and the affirmative, and self-affirming, response of the community are crucial to the blues dynamic. Seen in relation to the blues impulse, the jazz impulse provides a way of exploring implications, of realizing the relational possibilities of the self, and of expanding consciousness (of self and community) through a process of continual improvisation.

What has been less clearly recognized in discussions of African-American aesthetics is that both the blues and jazz impulses are grounded in the "gospel impulse" (see chapter 9). The foundations of African-American cultural expression lie in the call-and-response forms of the sacred tradition; in the twentieth century, the gospel church provides the institutional setting for the communal affirmation of individual experience. As Amiri Baraka notes in *Blues People,* both the call-and-response structure of the secular work songs and the AAB form of the classic blues can be traced to sacred forms that encode West African understandings of self, community, and spiritual energy. If the blues impulse can be described as a three-stage secular process—brutal experience, lyrical expression, affirmation— then the gospel impulse can be described in parallel terms derived from the sacred vocabularies of the African-American church: the burden, bearing witness, the vision of (universal) salvation. Bearing witness to his/her experience of the "burden," the gospel artist— possessed by a "Spirit" transcending human categorization—communicates a vision affirming the possibility of salvation for any person willing, as Forrest phrases it, to "change their name." Whether phrased as "burden" or "brutal experience," as "near-tragic, near-comic lyricism" or as "bearing witness," as existential "affirmation" or spiritual "vision," the blues/gospel process provides a foundation for the jazz artist's exploration of new possibilities for self and community.

The relationship of blues and gospel is not simply formal, however. As Greil Marcus notes in his discussion of Robert Johnson, most black blues artists bear witness to their brutal experience in a vocabulary derived from the black religious community, from which they feel excluded. Contrasting sharply with European-American modernist expressions of a world in which religion has been reduced to comforting delusion or oppressive institution, Johnson's songs express a theologically resonant *damnation,* not simply alienation. Many of his most powerful blues have explicitly religious titles: "Hellhound on My Trail," "Me and the Devil Blues," "Stones in My Passway," "If I Had Possession over Judgement Day."

Both the relational sense of self and the refusal to separate secular and sacred experience reflect what V. Y. Mudimbe refers to as a West African *gnosis.* In traditional West African thought, as Robert Farris Thompson demonstrates, human beings stand continually at the crossroads, negotiating the exchange of energies between spiritual and material spheres, between ancestors and descendants. Organizing this *gnosis* around the "orisha"—spirits associated with overlapping and interrelated energies that can be summoned in response to ever-changing circumstances—this Afrocentric sensibility contrasts sharply with Judeo-Christian traditions emphasizing the battle between God and Devil (seen as profoundly *different,* essentially binary, forms of energy) for possession of the *individual* human soul. Described in detail by Mudimbe, Thompson, bell hooks, and Patricia Hill Collins (who emphasizes the connections between Afrocentric and feminist epistemologies), this type of Afrocentrism also differs from the Nile Valley (priestly and at least implicitly patriarchal) Afrocentrism of Molefi Kete Asante, which frequently inverts existing binary structures to assert a relatively static vision of "African" civilization. Recognizing the Afrocentric dimensions of the gospel impulse is important for several reasons. Although some black religious singers—notably Bessie Jones and Bernice Johnson Reagon—are conscious of the African roots of the gospel tradition, many church members continue to view Africa through the European-American dichotomy of "pagan" and "Christian," thus creating the seeming paradox of a profoundly Afrocentric institution that openly repudiates Afrocentric phrasing.

Recognizing the underlying connection helps clarify the relationship of Forrest's aesthetics to those of the AACM. In part because of their emphasis on rhythm, AACM members frequently express the spiritual core of their vision in (West) Afrocentric terms. Perhaps because of the Nation of Islam's association of Africa with a binary mythology of black gods and white devils, Forrest emphasizes the specifically American practices of the gospel church. Like the early James Baldwin, who critiques binary myth-making (whether Christian or Muslim) in *The Fire Next Time,* Forrest articulates a profoundly Afrocentric cultural sensibility in a voice that insists on the "jazz" complexity of African-American experience. Commenting on the significance of Africa in the contemporary black church in Chicago, Forrest emphasizes the actual distance between American blacks and (one of) their ancestral homeland(s): "Yet how much the congregation knows of Africa is worthy of contemplation. More than likely, the thinking would go something like this: There are oppressed poverty-stricken people over there; they are black and we are black; they have been oppressed and so have we. Wherever the black man is in the world, he is catching hell. We came from Africa; therefore, we must help them. And it is in this sense that the black man here identifies with the heartaches over there" ("Souls" 133). However useful as a source of political or cultural motivation, this type of identification remains far too abstract to provide a base for the type of *transforming* voice Forrest seeks to create in his fiction.

Leon Forrest and Transformation

One of the most frequently used terms in Forrest's nonfiction, *transformation* is crucial to the jazz, blues, and gospel dimensions of his vision. In an important autobiographical essay titled "In the Light of the Likeness—Transformed," Forrest associates the "improvisational genius" of jazz with the "magical realism" of Latin American writers such as Gabriel Garcia Marquez and Isabel Allende. Commenting on his own multicultural heritage, Forrest emphasizes black music as a "source of personal or group survival" that enables African-Americans "to place a stamp of elegance and elan upon the reinvented mode." *"Reinvention,"* for Forrest, "has been the basic hallmark of the transformation" of black fiction exemplified by Ellison and Toni Morrison (31–32).

Although his own work is obviously oriented toward modernism and the jazz impulse, Forrest acknowledges its base in blues and gospel. He agrees with Ellison and Murray that a direct apprehension (rather than a theoretically mediated interpretation) of experience defines the blues impulse: "For the blues singer, personal, existential experience always outweighs handed-down wisdom" (33). Echoing Murray's observation that the purpose of the blues is to allow the singer to survive long enough to get the blues again, Forrest observes: "the worst thing that can happen to you, if you are a blues believer, is the loss of the blues. It is an eternal education. You lose the blues at the risk of losing your hold on existence" (33). Responding to Big Bill Broonzy's music as a process in which "each new carving [is] connected to the theme of the larger blues he's creating," Forrest emphasizes the jazz implications of the blues impulse, describing Broonzy's "shape-singing of his character's personae; transformed into something heightened and different" (22).

One of the most significant aspects of Forrest's perspective concerns his awareness of gospel, which has received little attention as a source of literary inspiration. Commenting on the "transformations" of Thomas A. Dorsey, widely recognized as the "father of gospel music," Forrest celebrates the former blues pianist's ability to "transform the refinements of the spiritual into a music that fitted the more angular needs of an awakening people, hungry-hearted for a dialogue in song which captured both their secular and their spiritual sense of life as agony and wonder" (26). In his discussion of call and response in Chicago's black churches, Forrest again emphasizes the irrelevance of binary constructions: "There is a place here for the commingling of the sexual and the spiritual" ("Souls" 130). Forrest describes the sermon form in terms paralleling AACM musical structures: "The structure of a black Baptist sermon is orchestrated, with highly associative links to group memory, the Bible, Afro-American folklore, Negro spirituals, secular blues phrases, politics, and personal testimonial" (131). Highlighting the jazz implications of such complex structures, Forrest celebrates the sermon as "the very source for reinvention and transformation of the self" ("Light" 23).

Describing his vocation as a writer, Forrest images the African-American novelist as a kind of jazz preacher: "he can go on to transform life into new life, even as he is transformed by his creation, as a preacher is transformed, as he seeks a collective transcendence" ("Light" 24). Forrest connects this vision directly with his own career when he describes how a visitation from the spirit of Mahalia Jackson helped him find his voice during a period when few of his "intellectual friends . . . cared for the life of the spirit" (33–34). Mahalia's presence helped focus Forrest's desire "to be a singer of the language—in the tradition of her majestic self and the Negro Preacher" (34). Turning his attention to his fiction, Forrest identifies the "Black church, the Negro spiritual, gospel music, sermons, the blues and jazz" as "both the railroad tracks and the wings for my imagination" (30).

However compelling this conceptual framework, Forrest has encountered many of the difficulties faced by the AACM in calling forth a broad-based response to his vision. On one level, this is an economic problem. Gary Giddins has detailed the problems faced by AACM members trying to make a living from their music (*Riding* 190–91). Lester Bowie recalls the early days of the AACM: "I and other players . . . enjoyed playing in free form, free fashion, but we would always play it for ourselves and never thought seriously about performing it in front of an audience. We knew that it was impossible to get hired at a club doing that" (Litweiler 186). Such real and pressing economic concerns reflect a related problem in contemporary African-American culture. As Forrest observes, the power of call-and-response aesthetics derives precisely from their realization in a communal context. The affirmations (and dissents) of the congregation—which in turn call forth responses from the preacher—express the dialectical relationship between improvisational vision and individual experience. Forrest describes the ideal: "A sermon is open-ended, allowing a preacher to expand new ideas or to cut out sections if they aren't working. The role of the congregation during a sermon is similar to that of a good audience at a jazz set—driving, responding, adding to the ever-rising level of emotion and intelligence. Ultimately, the preacher and the congregation reach one purifying moment and a furious catharsis is fulfilled" ("Souls" 131).

If this dynamic interaction is available to preachers and jazz musicians, it remains relatively abstract for novelists, who rarely engage in a direct call and response with an audience. Observing the reluctance of some middle-class blacks to accept the "marriage of blues and spiritual" ("Light" 26), Forrest questions whether call-and-response aesthetics are still capable of organizing the "cosmic consciousness of the race:" "If the preacher stood as the linkage and the oracle from Mississippi to St. Louis to Chicago, let us say, how much does the substance of his sermon now renew the sons and daughters of the great migrations—now unto the fifth and sixth generations" ("Light" 32). This troubled awareness of the changes experienced by the black community in northern cities—the fragmented urban world familiar to European-American modernism—lies behind Forrest's understanding of contemporary alienation (whether phrased in blues or existential terms) in relation to a spiritually resonant heritage that at times seems to be slipping away. However difficult it may be to elicit an affirmative response (and the absence of the response, as numerous jazz musicians and modernist writers have learned at great cost, may result in madness, addiction, or death), only a complex, realistic call offers any hope for meaningful transformation.

I would like to conclude by suggesting several approaches to Forrest's work in relation to the jazz impulse. Gayl Jones provides a valuable overview of the ways African-American novelists translate jazz into written forms:

> In literature jazz can affect the subject matter—the conceptual and symbolic functions of a text, translate directly into the jazz hero, or have stylistic implications. The writer's attempt to imply or reproduce musical rhythms can take the form of jazz-like flexibility and fluidity in prose rhythms (words, lines, paragraphs, the whole text), such as nonchronological syncopated order, pacing, or tempo. A sense of jazz—the jam session—can also emerge from an interplay of voices improvising on the basic themes or motifs of the text, in key words and phrases. Often seemingly nonlogical and associational, the jazz text is generally more complex and sophisticated than the blues text in its harmonies, rhythms, and surface structures. (*Liberating* 200)

In addition to using many of these devices, Forrest draws on jazz by treating the literary text as a form subject to revision in the manner of a jazz composition and mythology as a reflection of cultural psychology rather than a repository of universally applicable values. It should be emphasized that these approaches are analytical conventions; the real jazz richness of Forrest's voice is best experienced through direct response to the many passages in his novels that resemble the contextualized solos of AACM music. Among the most powerful of these are Nathaniel's meditation on the nightmare of history in chapter four of *There Is a Tree More Ancient than Eden* and Ironwood "Landlord" Rumble's solo (along with Nathaniel and Noah Grandberry's responses) in chapter eleven of *The Bloodworth Orphans.*

One of the major problems facing Forrest as a jazz writer involves the relatively "fixed" form of the literary text. Where musicians can vary their call in response to the changing contexts of performance, writers are usually limited to the original form of publication. This problem parallels that faced by jazz musicians who record their music, thereby transforming a single version of a piece into a "standard" point of reference. Although some musicians address this problem by recording multiple versions of the same song over an extended period of time, Langston Hughes's term "disc-tortion" (*Reader* 89) applies to both recorded music and literary forms. Highly aware of this problem, Hughes suggested one response when he published distinct versions of his modernist epic "Montage of a Dream Deferred." The version published in the 1958 *Langston Hughes Reader* is divided into five distinct sections, while the version published in *Selected Poems* the following year treats the entire poem as one large movement. In addition, the later version reorganizes smaller sections. For example, Hughes breaks the poem "Jam Session" (*Reader* 107–8) into three distinct lyrics, "Jam Session," "Be-Bop Boys," and "Tag" (*Selected* 246–47).

Adapting this approach to the novel form, Forrest significantly altered the 1973 text of *There Is a Tree More Ancient than Eden* when it was republished by Another Chicago Press in 1988. Published during a period when some of the most influential black writers—notably Baraka—were asserting relatively closed ideological visions that simplified cross-cultural experience, the first version of the novel concludes with an image of ongoing process that cannot be easily reduced to a political formulation: "i crumbled upon the floor rising and falling rising and falling and rising and falling" (163). Published during the later years of the Reagan presidency, the later version concludes with a new section, "Transformation," that places the first version's theme of ongoing process in an explicitly political context. An implicit response to the increasingly desperate realities of the black community, Pompey c.j. Browne's sermon in the final chapter of "Transformation" calls for a renewed response to Martin Luther King, Jr.'s, vision. Listening to Rev. Browne at "The Crossroads

Rooster Tavern," whose name combines African, blues, and gospel imagery, Nathaniel Witherspoon meditates on the preacher as a figure who "over the years, has himself become something of a transformation of Adam Clayton Powell, Martin Luther King, Leon Sullivan and Richard Pryor" (205). Although Rev. Browne is capable of beating a young black man to death when he discovers his transvestism (10), he sounds a necessary challenge to the community that is literally and figuratively at the crossroads: "Yet I hear Martin's voice still to fight on, crying forth in the wilderness; we feel like-a-shouting marching out of the wilderness demanding of the Lord remembrance: Honor, Honor unto the Dying Lamb of our learning lanterns—the frontier of the shrouded dream. Thank God Almighty I'm free at last; but free to uncover what freedom beyond the mountain top's metamorphosis? Is paradise without politics?" (213–14). As contextually aware jazz artist, Forrest knows that the question demands a much different response in 1988 than it would have in 1973.

Forrest's treatment of myth also reflects his commitment to envisioning new possibilities. In his influential essay on *Ulysses*, T. S. Eliot defined the "mythical method" as "a way of controlling, of ordering, of giving a shape and significance to the immense panorama of futility and anarchy which is contemporary history" ("Ulysses" 177). Resisting Eliot's elevation of myth over experience, both leftist (Bertolt Brecht) and Afro-American modernists (Zora Neale Hurston) view myth as a *part* of the perceptual system operating *within* the world. The shift in emphasis encourages a dialectical understanding of how experience leads to changes in the understanding of particular myths and of how choosing new myths for inspiration can change experience. Hurston's *Moses, Man of the Mountain* exemplifies the process. Although she acknowledges both the Judeo-Christian and Freudian interpretations of Moses, Hurston emphasizes his role as African conjure man, thereby encouraging black readers to develop a higher awareness of their African cultural heritage.

Reflecting Hurston's work in comparative anthropology with Franz Boas and Ruth Benedict at Columbia University, which culminated in her writings on African religions in Haiti (*Tell My Horse*) and New Orleans (*Mules and Men*), Moses is part political leader and part conjure man. Revoicing a familiar image from the spirituals, which frequently parallel the situation of the slaves with that of the Hebrews in Egypt, Hurston presents a Moses who experiences deep frustrations while attempting to shape an oppressed and demoralized people into a powerful, self-reliant nation. Unlike the biblical Moses, however, Hurston's Moses is not by birth a member of the community he leads out of bondage. Rather, he is a member of the Egyptian

nobility who is transformed first into a Hebrew and then into a Hebrew leader by the mythmaking powers of Miriam and Jethro. The
phrase "I AM WHAT I AM" reveals the importance of Hurston's confrontation with the inherently ambiguous substructure of cultural
mythology. Drawing on his profound knowledge of natural and su-
pernatural forces—from a West African spiritual perspective there is
no fundamental difference—Moses uses beliefs, as much as material
forces, to restructure political reality.

Anticipating Hurston's political positions of the fifties—which superficially appear "conservative"—*Moses, Man of the Mountain* suggests that the key to meaningful progress for African-Americans lies
in a belief in their own myth-making power rather than in protesting
their political situation. Sounding the jazz/modernist theme of the
isolation of the artist who redefines the mythology, and therefore the
reality, of a community, Hurston summons the rhythms of the gospel
preacher in her description of Moses as an artist who gradually assumes power over and responsibility for his own mythology. As Moses
contemplates the beauty and terror of self-creation, of transformation, Hurston describes his situation in terms that would certainly be
recognizable to Forrest and the musicians of the AACM:

> Moses had crossed over. He was not in Egypt. He had crossed over and
> now he was not an Egyptian. He had crossed over. The short sword at his
> thigh had a jewelled hilt but he had crossed over and so it was no longer
> the sign of high birth and power. He had crossed over, so he sat down on
> a rock near the seashore to rest himself. He had crossed over so he was
> not of the house of Pharaoh. He did not own a palace because he had
> crossed over. He did not have an Ethiopian Princess for a wife. He had
> crossed over. . . . The sun who was his friend and ancestor in Egypt was
> arrogant and bitter in Asia. He had crossed over. He felt as empty as a
> post hole for he was none of the things he once had been. He was a man
> sitting on a rock. He had crossed over. (104)

Forrest uses a similar mythic method in his treatment of Wallace D.
Fard, who is described in *The Autobiography of Malcolm X* as the mes-
senger who "had given to Elijah Muhammad Allah's message for the
black people who were the Lost-Found Nation of Islam here in this
wilderness North America" (161; for background on Fard, see Lincoln). Associating Fard with the organizing theme of the lost child,
Forrest approaches the "source" of the Nation of Islam's binary
mythology in a way that underscores his determination to decenter
simplifying myths.

Throughout *The Bloodworth Orphans,* Fard appears in myriad
forms, most of them associated with the African-American search for

origins. From his initial appearance in the "List of Characters" where he places newspaper advertisements in hopes of obtaining unwanted babies, Fard—under numerous names—is frequently mentioned but never unambiguously present. Forrest's treatment of Fard as a trickster figure in the tradition of Brer Rabbit or Rinehart from Ellison's *Invisible Man* emphasizes the inadequacy of any identity or spiritual vision based on an unambiguous myth of origins. Present only as a linguistic construct, the Fard of *The Bloodworth Orphans* can be called on to authorize any belief system. In the final chapter of *The Bloodworth Orphans,* Noah Grandberry describes Fard—transformed into Ford, perhaps in reference to one of the founders of white America's economic mythology—as an animal trapper, a curve-ball pitcher, and a conjure man who, in the tradition of Hurston's Moses, eludes all definition: "But I have never known anyone in my long life to eat one of those graveyarders and live to tell it (yet FORD, why old *Ford,* old centerpiece W.W.W., or W.F., could)" (322). Referring to the "character" explicitly as "mythical," Grandberry interprets "Ford's" association with the snake in accord with both the Christian myth of the snake as a sign of the devil and the West African myth of the snake as an emblem of the orisha Shango (himself a figure for the conjure man): "Oh, I've seen some wear the skin of that snake around their waists to conquer their foes. I remember when I met our foe, and particularly Your Foe, for the Second time, the mythical Reverend W.W.W. (or as I used to call him, upon a sterling occasion, W.A.D.) Ford, as he was then known, *why,* he was wearing one of *those* snakes about his waist" (322). Resolution of these meanings lies entirely in the responses of Grandberry's and Forrest's audiences. In contrast to both Eliot and the Nation of Islam, myth for Forrest represents a way of meditating on origins rather than a fixed point of reference for judging the chaos of contemporary experience.

The most rewarding experience of Forrest's fiction, however, is to be derived not from a general set of guidelines for reading but from the reader's open response to passages such as Rumble's solo, which revoices motifs from the spirituals (the motherless child), the *Odyssey* (the lost son), the Nation of Islam (the Lost-Found people), *Invisible Man* (the hospital setting as the equivalent of the Golden Day), Afro-American folklore (John Henry), and countless other sources. Like the musicians of the AACM, Forrest consistently strives to realize the underlying imperatives of the jazz, blues, and gospel impulses: to acknowledge the complexity of experience in a way that enables the individual and the community to realize change in accord with an encompassing spiritual vision. I would hope that by suggesting appropriate contexts for the reading of Forrest's fiction, this chapter will encourage the development of an audience willing to provide an affirmative response contributing to the release of the potentially liberating energies of our African- and European-American ancestors.

11

The Burden and the Binding Song: August Wilson's Neoclassical Jazz

▲ ▲ ▲ ▲

Jazz Coda: In the Tradition

The end is in the beginning and lies far ahead.

—Ralph Ellison, *Invisible Man*

For here there are warriors and saints. Here there is hope refreshing itself, quickening into life. Here there is a drumbeat fueled by the blood of Africa. And through it all there are the lessons, the wounds of history. There are always and only two trains running. There is life and there is death. Each of us rides them both. To live life with dignity, to celebrate and accept responsibility for your presence in the world is all that can be asked of anyone.

—August Wilson, *Two Trains Running*

Are you sure, sweetheart, that you want to be well?

—Toni Cade Bambara, *The Salt Eaters*

In *Two Trains Running*, August Wilson offers a healing vision, a jazz response to the call of black men and women bearing their burdens, singing their blues: Sterling with his gangsta rap; Risa with her self-scarred legs.

Remembering the sources: Aunt Ester, whose living spirit carries three centuries of jazz voices down the wind, who asks only that we throw our money in the river, let the devil be. That we *use* our past to envision our future.

The "we" is as limited and limiting as we believe.

August Wilson and Black Music

Playing the changes in a jazz voice grounded in gospel and the blues, Wilson revoices both African- and European-American expressive traditions in a heroic attempt to heal the wounds devastating individuals and communities as we near the end of the twentieth century. Highly aware of the tension between received notions of "universality" and the specific circumstances of African-American communities, Wilson crafts a vision closely related to the "neoclassical" jazz of Wynton Marsalis. As Paul Carter Harrison demonstrates, Wilson (like Marsalis) expresses a profound appreciation of black music as serious art. Both Wilson and Marsalis actively seek a broad audience for their work and emphasize the need for a mastery of their craft based on serious study and discipline. Wilson differs from Marsalis, however, in his awareness that, if it is to remain *functional*, the tradition must remain aware of, and responsive to, the changing circumstances of communities with little knowledge of, or interest in, "classical" aesthetics.

In her meditation on Thelonious Monk as a source of literary aesthetics, Wanda Coleman describes the "chilling" situation of African-American writers at the end of the 1980s: "To escape economic slavery the Black artist is forced to turn his/her back on Black heritage and adapt to White tastes/sensibilities in order to make money (in this case, money is synonymous with freedom but not power" (69). Coleman insists that conscious use of the jazz tradition provides the best foundation for a meaningful response to the crisis of African-American communal memory during the Reagan/Bush era: "By relegating Jazz (and the Jazz principle) to obscurity, the people who give birth to it are kept in a position of economic and cultural inferiority. And the *quality* of one's work has *nuthin'* to do with it." Coleman's conclusion that "to recognize is to empower" (74) echoes bell hooks's observations concerning the centrality of cultural expression to communal health: "there was in the traditional southern racially segregated black community a concern with racial uplift that continually promoted recognition of the need for artistic expressiveness and cultural production" (105). Recalling the Black Arts Movement focus on black audiences, hooks's statement contrasts with Alain Locke's belief in art as a means of changing white attitudes. Near the end of "The New Negro," Locke wrote: "The especially cultural recognition they [the artists and writers of the Harlem Renaissance] win should in turn prove the key to that revaluation of the Negro which must precede or accompany any considerable further betterment of race relationships" (15). Aware that masterworks such as *In-*

visible Man and *Song of Solomon* have failed to change conditions in poor black communities, hooks emphasizes African aesthetic traditions as a source of political and psychological resistance within those communities: "Art was seen as intrinsically serving a political function. Whatever African-Americans created in music, dance, poetry, painting, etc., it was regarded as testimony, bearing witness, challenging racist thinking which suggested that black folks were not fully human, were uncivilized, and that the measure of this was our collective failure to create 'great art'" (105).

As Coleman suggests, both approaches to the function of art are problematic. On one hand, it has become clear that individual black artists can attain financial and critical acceptance without generating any benefits for poor black communities. On the other, writers and, to a lesser extent, musicians who direct their work primarily to black audiences often have difficulty supporting themselves economically, which in turn limits their ability to support social change. Given this situation, one of the primary challenges facing highly "successful" writers such as Toni Morrison, Alice Walker, and Wilson is developing ways of using their positions of relative "freedom" (though not necessarily, as Coleman notes, of power) to locate new possibilities for themselves and for the communities they are forced, without concern for their individual preference, to "represent."

The dilemma of successful black artists was complicated by forces at work within the African-American community during the seventies and eighties. Even as writers (Morrison, Walker), critics (Gates, Houston Baker) and musicians (Prince, Michael Jackson) attained unprecedented levels of popular success, conditions in many African-American communities deteriorated seriously. Generated by the post–civil rights movement ability of black individuals to move out of the ghetto (W. Wilson) and by the polarization of wealth resulting from Reagan-era taxation policies (Phillips), this deterioration contributed to a growing physical separation between middle-class and poor black communities. This in turn intensified the cultural fragmentation of Afro-America. Where artists such as Duke Ellington or Ralph Ellison, both of whom enjoyed considerable mainstream recognition, could assume a shared base of cultural references with the larger black community—particularly those relating to the black church and the blues—contemporary black artists confront a more difficult situation.

The implications of this situation can be seen in the juxtaposition of two highly visible forms of eighties black cultural expression: the novels of Toni Morrison, Alice Walker, Gloria Naylor, and Terry McMillan; and rap music, particularly that created by young black men from poor urban communities. Although their differences are at least as striking as their similarities, black women's novels exemplify the potential of direct engagement with the cultural mainstream. Novels exploring African-American history; the specific circumstances of black women; and, increasingly, the problems of black professionals in middle-class America have attracted favorable attention within academia and the publishing industry. Despite their enthusiastic reception by educated blacks and whites, however, these novels are rarely read by younger blacks from poor economic backgrounds, especially young black men who have been denied even basic reading skills by underfunded and indifferent school systems (Kozol). Media stereotypes to the contrary, the lack of literacy does not indicate that young blacks have acquiesced in their dehumanization. Rather, they have developed innovative cultural forms, most notably rap, to express their rage against both the oppressive white system and what many perceive as the indifference of the black middle class; rappers such as N.W.A., Ice Cube, and Naughty by Nature ridicule what they see as irrelevant standards of "culture" and "decency," whether imposed by whites or privileged blacks. Perhaps the most disturbing signs of the fragmentation of African-American culture are the dehumanizing images of women in many raps. Reflecting the impact of economic forces, the fundamental division seems to follow class rather than gender lines, as evidenced by the relatively strong awareness of the specific situations of black women in the novels of John Edgar Wideman and Leon Forrest and the harsh sexuality in the raps of female rappers Choice and B.W.P. The fact that the rappers show no awareness of, rather than conscious contempt for, the work of the novelists emphasizes the historically unprecedented fragmentation of black audiences. The high level of white interest in and economic support for *both* the novelists and the rappers simply places a final ironic twist on the situation confronting artists such as Wilson who are determined to heal the wounds of the African-American community.

Functionality and the Jazz Impulse

Adding her voice to a critical tradition extending at least as far back as W. E. B. Du Bois's *The Souls of Black Folk*, Coleman suggests that overcoming the divisions within black America requires a high level of awareness of the connections between literary and oral traditions: "there was no effective way to discuss Black language without interjecting Black music" (68). As Paul Carter Harrison demonstrates, just such a sense of language-as-music and music-as-language characterizes August Wilson's "blues poetics." More specifically, Harrison views Wilson's drama as a variation on the "modal" jazz pioneered by Miles Davis during the fifties: "As an expressive strategy in blues and jazz improvisations, the modal distribution of related and nonrelated ideas often revivifies the familiar story with new illumination" (306).

Before Harrison's formulation can be usefully applied to Wilson's "healing song," it is helpful to examine several issues regarding the meaning of jazz in African-American culture. Despite significant differences in interpretive perspective, theorists such as hooks, Jon Michael Spencer, James Cone, Ellison, Amiri Baraka, Ben Sidran, and Robert Farris Thompson agree that throughout the African diaspora, cultural production is viewed in terms of *functionality;* rather than serving as a respite from or alternative to everyday reality, art is intricately involved with the daily lives of individuals and communities. Thompson's list of aesthetic practices linking diaspora communities culminates in "*songs and dances of social allusion* (music which, however danceable and 'swinging,' remorselessly contrasts social imperfections against implied criteria for perfect living)" (xiii). On occasion the social function may be obvious, as in Ben Sidran's description of the revolutionary implications of black music:

> each man developed his own "cry" and his own "personal sound." The development of "cries" was thus more than a stylization; it became the basis on which a group of individuals could join together, commit a social act, and remain individuals throughout, and this in the face of overt suppression. It has been suggested that the social act of music was at all times more than it seemed within the black culture. Further, to the extent the black man was involved with black music, he was involved with the black revolution. Black music was itself revolutionary, if only because it maintained a non-Western orientation in the realms of perception and communication. (14)

Although art may occasionally transmit a specifically political "message," the underlying meanings of functionality are more subtle and elusive. Reflecting the importance of the ancestors in West African societies, black music encodes memories of historical events and personal experiences omitted from or distorted by the written documentation of European-American cultural memory. As Coleman notes, "If one defines art as memory, then Black music (or music infused with/infected by blackness) gives me *my* memory" (78). Transmitting such memory to the present, music provides organizing rhythms for daily life. Whether "political"—as in the use of gospel music to provide organization, inspiration, and courage during the civil rights movement—or "personal"—as in the use of music in courtship—

black music helps maintain a sense of African difference within a hostile cultural context.

It should be emphasized that, especially within the jazz tradition, this assertion of difference does not entail a repudiation of European influences or traditions. Discussing the impact of African traditions on the Caribbean in terms applicable (to different degrees) to other New World multicultures, Antonio Benitez-Rojo highlights the coexistence—*not* the synthesis—of multiple decentered energies, including those European energies grounded in relatively rigid binary concepts. As hooks observes, jazz plays a central role in developing concepts of freedom appropriate to these energies. Revolutionary jazz, writes hooks, resists any attempt to reduce the complexity of African-American experience: "avant-garde jazz musicians, grappling with artistic expressivity that demanded experimentation, resisted restrictive mandates about their work, whether they were imposed by a white public saying their work was not really music or a black public which wanted to see more overt links between that work and political struggle" (109). Developing primarily in urban settings where blacks were forced into proximity with various cultural traditions, jazz plays a crucial role in opening the African-American tradition to new energies, including those associated with the European-American "masters." Since the beginning of the twentieth century, jazz has drawn on the European-American orchestral tradition and mainstream American popular music, as well as those forms reflecting the worldviews of poor black communities: the harsh realism of the blues and the visionary community of gospel music.

As I have discussed previously (see chapters 9 and 10 for complete discussions including Ellison's and Murray's definitions), Ellison's theoretical writings provide a useful vocabulary for conceptualizing this dynamic. Ellison defines the jazz impulse as a way of defining/creating the self in relation to community and tradition. Revoicing Ellison's classic definition of the jazz impulse, Coleman writes: "THE KEY/history + vision + craft = transcendence" (68). As Coleman's emphasis on "history" intimates, almost all successful jazz is grounded in what Ellison calls the "blues impulse." Before one can hope to create a functional new vision of individual or communal identity, the artist must acknowledge the full complexity of his/her experience. Both the individual expression and the affirmative, and self-affirming, response of the community described by Albert Murray are crucial to the blues dynamic. Seen in relation to the blues impulse, the jazz impulse provides a way of exploring implications, of realizing the relational possibilities of the self, and of expanding consciousness (of self and community) through a process of continual improvisation. Equally important to African-American musical aesthetics is the "gospel impulse" (see chapters 9 and 10), which centers on what Coleman's formulation refers to as "vision." If the blues impulse can be described as a three-stage secular process—brutal experience, lyrical expression, reaffirmation—then the gospel impulse can be described in parallel terms derived from the sacred vocabularies of the African-American church: the burden, bearing witness, the vision of (universal) salvation. To summarize, awareness of its blues and gospel roots highlights two central functions of the jazz impulse: *clarifying (blues) realities* and *envisioning (gospel) possibilities.* The most successful jazz performances articulate these issues in response to the specific historical context of the ever-changing moment.

Prior to the widespread integration of the black middle class into mainstream institutions, numerous jazz-oriented African-American artists—Miles Davis, Duke Ellington, Ralph Ellison, Billie Holiday, Gwendolyn Brooks—were able to forge styles commanding respect in both affluent European-American and relatively disadvantaged African-American settings. Their immaculate clothes, polished speech, proper manners, and understanding of European-American traditions were not intended, nor understood, as betrayals of the broader black community. The problem today facing Wilson, Marsalis, and Morrison, among others, derives from the fragmented context that, to a disturbing degree, forecloses the cultural space occupied by Ellington, Ellison, and Davis. Change, of course, is nothing new for jazz artists. Derived from the Yoruba concept of "itutu" or "the correct way you represent yourself to a human being" (Thompson 13) and parallel, as Murray notes, to Ernest Hemingway's "grace under pressure" (*Hero* 35–43), the idea of "cool" exemplified by Miles Davis places a central value on the ability to negotiate unpredictable, and uncontrollable, changes in social, economic, and political conditions.

Nevertheless, the specific conditions of the eighties and nineties present unique challenges for artists who desire to reach a broad audience within and beyond the black community. As noted above, black musicians and writers today confront a situation in which middle-class/academic/literary (and feminist-informed) and poor/street/oral (and often aggressively masculine) perspectives *appear* to be in open conflict with one another. Unlike Ellington and Brooks, who could address a privileged (and at that time almost exclusively white) audience for purposes of economic reward and "serious" critical attention without surrendering their connection with the larger black community (including those "organic intellectuals" who provide "serious" responses outside the network of formal cultural institutions), Wilson and Marsalis find themselves in a context where success with one group too often entails rejection by the other. With crucial differences in understanding and application, both have responded to the situation by creating what might be called a "neoclassical" voicing of the jazz impulse.

Wynton Marsalis and Neoclassicism

In part because of his award-winning recordings of trumpet concertos by Haydn, Mozart, and other European composers, Marsalis has been seen by both supporters and detractors as the leading figure in a "neoclassical" movement determined to "save" jazz from the perceived chaos of free jazz. Jazz drummer and critic Stanley Crouch articulates the values and intentions of the neoclassical movement in his provocative liner notes to Marsalis's jazz albums, especially *Black Codes from the Underground* (1985), *The Majesty of the Blues* (1989), the three volumes of *Soul Gestures in Southern Blue* (1991), and *Blue Interlude* (1992). Emphasizing the balance between composition and improvisation as a means of exploring the relationship between individual and community within the tradition, Crouch offers Marsalis as an exemplar of jazz as high art: "Wynton Marsalis continues to make even more explicit those human vistas of jazz that exemplify its ongoing revitalization. That revitalization calls upon the best of the art and reinterprets it with affection and adventure of the sort that corresponds to the serious listener's mood for a classic. Marsalis is quite successfully working at a vision in which there is an organic relationship between the power of the jazz pen and the members of his group" (*Interlude* 1).

Insisting on conscious understanding of tradition—whether European or African in origin—Crouch quotes Marsalis's belief that "in order to understand the meaning of an art form, you have to find out what the greatest artists have in common" (*Majesty* 6). Perhaps the single most important attribute of the greatest African-American artists for Marsalis is their repudiation of any contemporary manifestation of the "black codes" that deprived "chattels of anything other than what was necessary to maintain their positions as talking work animals" (*Codes* 4). Assuming a high humanist stance, Marsalis views his neoclassical aesthetic as an alternative to both racism and the vulgarization of contemporary culture:

> Black codes mean a lot of things. Anything that reduces potential, that pushes your taste down to an obvious, animal level. Anything that makes you think less significance is *more* enjoyable. Anything that keeps you on

the surface. The way they depict women in rock videos—black codes. People gobbling up junk food when they can afford something better— black codes. The argument that illiteracy is valid in a technological world—black codes. People who equate ignorance with soulfulness— definitely black codes. The overall quality of every true artist's work is a rebellion against black codes. (*Codes* 8)

Marsalis's neoclassicism should not be confused with an uncritical acceptance of European-American standards. Crouch emphasizes the importance of both blues-based African-American and classical European traditions to Marsalis's developing conception of great art:

> Marsalis arrived in jazz with both a technical fluidity that had little prece-dent and an acknowledged authority in European concert music that no jazz musician before him had ever possessed. At the same time the trum-peter was critical of his own jazz work and of the obstacles to learning how to play jazz. Coming from New Orleans, he was immersed in the blues tradition, but having grown up during the fusion era, he had no awareness of the importance of the blues to jazz. Though well schooled in harmony, he knew little about how to apply it during an improvisation, and worried over his ability to swing on the level of the art's masters, living or dead. But he was a man ready to endure the isolation and the feeling of impotence that are inevitable when one chooses to learn formi-dable amounts of information. (*Interlude* 1)

Drawing on his classical training to analyze the blues as a response to "the central chords of Western harmony," Marsalis shares Wanda Coleman's interest in Thelonious Monk as an artistic ancestor who both developed an innovative approach to composition and recog-nized that "the European approach was not sufficient for what he wanted to do" (*Majesty* 6). In his treatment of the jazz classics—exem-plified by his brilliantly humorous rendition of Monk's "Think of One"—Marsalis makes it clear that his neoclassicism cannot be re-duced to a preference for high-brow, European, or conventional "classical" music. Moreover, as Francis Davis argues, Marsalis's classi-cal albums have effectively exhausted the repertoire of interesting trumpet concertos (30).

Nor is Marsalis unaware of the links between the "classical jazz-men" and the African-American community. Recorded on Marsalis's *The Majesty of the Blues*, Crouch's jazz sermon "Premature Autopsies" invokes Ellington as Marsalis's stylistic ancestor, a profoundly intel-lectual figure "willing to face the majesty of their heritage and en-dure the slow, painful development of serious study." Celebrating the courage that allowed Ellington to overcome "the pain and the agony and the self-doubt and the disappointment" inherent in his attempt to articulate the "majesty he heard coming from the musicians of all hues and from all levels of training," Crouch concludes with a reminder that the roots of a functional African-American art lie in the continuing relationship between artist and community: "This noble sound, this thing of majesty, this art, so battered but so ready for battle, it just might lift you high enough in the understanding of human life to let you know in no uncertain terms why that marvelous Washingtonian, Edward Kennedy Ellington, NEVER came off the road" (*Majesty* 10).

Despite Crouch's eloquent promotion/defense of Marsalis, the broader critical reception of his work raises serious questions concerning Marsalis's adaptation of the Ellingtonian style. In a 1982 review, Greg Tate sounded what has become the leitmotif of attacks on the neoclassical movement: "Because jazz was once a music defined as much by brinkmanship—social and aesthetic—as by virtuosic refinement, the music's current hidebound swing toward bop and post-bop revivalism has to be seen as not only regenerative but reactionary" (45). Although Tate concludes the passage with the qualifier "but necessary," his use of the term "reactionary" implies that neoclassicism, at least indirectly, supports the neoconservative agenda of the Reagan/Bush administrations. Such criticism results in part from the willingness of Marsalis's most ardent defenders to support neoconservative attacks on cultural pluralism. An extreme example of the neoconservative construction of Marsalis's neoclassicism—unfortunately echoed in numerous mass media celebrations of the movement—can be found in Ted Gioia's *The Imperfect Art: Reflections on Jazz and Modern Culture*. Trivializing Gunther Schuller's analytical concern with the "third stream" synthesis of jazz and classical traditions, Gioia dismisses critics who "take [Marsalis] to task for not progressing beyond existing jazz conventions" (73). Gioia concludes with a nostalgic invocation of a (largely mythical) common language destroyed by a pluralism he constructs as hostile to civilized standards of excellence and moral values: "The abundance of schools and styles has led to the all but complete disappearance of a common language, a common set of standards, a shared notion of good and bad. In the absence of these things, the continued health of the art form lies in doubt. The benefits of pluralism threaten to collapse into the uncertainties of relativism" (74).

Blaming fragmentation on aesthetic exploration (rather than a hostile political and economic environment), Gioia laments "the collapse of the jazz world into countless schools and tendencies, each unable to communicate with those outside its own small world" (84). Gioia bases much of his argument on an almost entirely inaccurate image of the experimental jazz tradition as an "avant-garde" that "delights in lengthy solo performances by instruments once thought to be incapable of sustaining interest without a group" (77). Such a formulation strongly suggests that Gioia has not actually listened to the leading experimentalists of the past two decades: Murray, Muhal Richard Abrams, John Carter, Anthony Davis, Anthony Braxton, or the Art Ensemble of Chicago, all of whom combine composition and improvisation. Casting the neoclassicist as a rebel conducting "his lonely pursuit for form and order," Gioia concludes with a celebration of "musical perfection—almost Platonic in nature" (94) that echoes the neoconservative attribution of artistic excellence solely to the Greco-Roman tradition. The irony of this attitude in jazz criticism should be obvious. As John Gennart and McDonald Smith Moore have demonstrated in different contexts, during the 1910s and 1920s the classical tradition, strongly associated with Victorian constructions of morality, was continually invoked in attacks *against* what Gioia now celebrates as "classical jazz."

Inasmuch as criticism of Marsalis's neoclassicism focuses on the larger cultural debate, it is at least partially undeserved; Marsalis clearly has no wish to contribute to any form of neoconservatism that would adversely affect black communities. Nonetheless, his public statements at times seem to endorse neoconservative "cultural pathology" interpretations of inner-city problems. Commenting on the 1992 Los Angeles riot, Marsalis sympathized with the underlying frustration: "I've been hustled by the police. You grow up in this society as a black, you get that." His subsequent analysis, however, reveals the limits of Marsalis's identification with, and understanding of, street perspectives: "But the greatest menace in the black community is not the police. It's all these young black men who beat up old ladies and kids. Whenever you elevate hoodlums to heroes, you've got trouble. When you look at that looting, by blacks *and* whites, that wasn't a protest. They wanted TV sets" (quoted in Brady). Similarly, Marsalis's hostile generalizations concerning rap videos, which show little awareness of rap's organic intellectuals such as KRS-One of Boogie Down Productions, align him strongly, despite his claims to the contrary, with an "anti-street" perspective:

> My vibe has always been "down with the street and down with ignorance." But it takes me 10 years of going to different schools to touch maybe 10,000 kids. A music video will do that in five seconds . . . and it'll be someone holding his dick. These things have nothing to do with poverty. Louis Armstrong grew up impoverished. You wouldn't see him holding his dick in public. His statement wasn't "Well, I was a victim of prejudice, so screw everything in the world." That's not heroic. You didn't hear him say, "Well, I grew up in poverty, so I'm excused from this or that." A lot

of Afro-Americans think like I do. They're tired of seeing this garbage elevated and considered an Afro-American way. (quoted in Brady)

Presented without extensive contextual and historical qualification, such statements encourage neoconservative appropriation of Marsalis.

The language of the debate over neoconservatism recurs frequently in criticism of Marsalis's neoclassical approach. Francis Davis, for example, views neoclassicism as an attempt to impose "a rigid code of attitudes" on performers, showing "little tolerance for those who play by a looser set of rules" (29). Echoing Davis's suspicion that Wynton and his brother Branford "may be musical reactionaries who are fooling even themselves into believing they are radicals" (40), Carlos Figueroa contrasts David Murray's traditionalism with Marsalis's neoclassicism: "Murray goes about the business of being himself with a fervor and dedication truly worthy of the art form in which he has chosen to express his world view. Mention is made of this choice because it stands in stark contrast to the one made by many of his younger compatriots in the music who seem to be content with recapturing and recapitulating the sounds and stylings (both musical and sartorial) of their musical forebears" (4). Similarly, Gary Giddins acknowledges Marsalis's "complete instrumental mastery, reverence for the complexities of jazz improvisation, and sartorial elegance on the bandstand" but concludes that "Marsalis hasn't found his own voice" (158). Both Giddins and Figueroa insist on individual style as fundamental to the visionary function of jazz. Identifying David Murray as a leading *neo*classicist, Figueroa writes: "To be sure, Murray's music is solidly in the tradition; his approach has been to blaze a fresh trail through the woods as opposed to trodding a path already delineated" (6).

Even as Martin Williams emphasizes the dialectic between innovation and consolidation in the jazz tradition, he observes that Marsalis's reverence for standards has rarely been the hallmark of leading African-American jazz performers: "the most obviously outstanding young black players are (so far) doing nothing truly new. That has certainly never happened in jazz before: in the past, the kind of musical conservatism they represent has largely been the white man's burden" (46). Similarly, Ronald Radano emphasizes that the celebration of the neoclassical movement in cover stories in *Time* and *New York Times Magazine* threatens to repress the more visionary currents of jazz: "for its challengers in improvised, experimental music, it is often seen as a travesty of the flexibility that is said to characterize black music" (*Figurations* 272).

Perhaps the most cogent response to such criticism focuses not on the jazz artist's role as visionary, but on his/her relationship with the actual community/audience. Gary Giddins focuses on Marsalis's desire to broaden the audience for *both* neoclassical and experimental jazz: "Not unlike the popularizers of swing in the 1930s and soul in the 1950s, musicians such as Marsalis are needed to restore order, replenish melody, revitalize the beat, loot the tradition for whatever works, and *expand the audience*" (161). Caustically observing that "you know it's his ability to play that classical shit which gives him so-called legitimacy" and signifying on "how slick a hustle these brothers have pulled in mainstreaming their models for middle-American consumption," Greg Tate nevertheless recognizes that the real measure of the neoclassicists' success is not the content of their work but their still undemonstrated ability to make "sociocultural breakthroughs equal to the aesthetic ones of their mentors" (52). Responding to Marsalis both as potential inspiration and cautionary example, the remainder of this chapter will place August Wilson's plays in the forefront of a jazz-inflected movement to envision such breakthroughs.

Wilson, Universalism, and Jazz Neoclassicism

In literary criticism, the neoclassical discourse focuses largely on the concept of "universalism," the idea that certain themes, images, and techniques express fundamentally "human" concerns that transcend the limitations of any particular set of circumstances. The implications of this discourse, which consistently associates the "universals" with the specific experiences of white males of relatively privileged social standing, are by now a well-known story to scholars of African-American and women's literature. Within this institutionally sanctioned discourse only those black writers whose work can be presented in terms of the "universals"—Ellison is perhaps the most obvious example—receive "serious" (if extraordinarily narrow) attention and financial rewards. As early distrust of Ellison among the aggressively anti-universalist writers associated with the Black Arts Movement demonstrates, such success can create difficulties for a jazz writer seeking to engage in a call and response with the community.

As Wilson's plays demonstrate, however, visionary jazz cannot simply accept or reject "universalism." In an interview with Bill Moyers, Wilson expresses values reminiscent of Marsalis's neoclassicism: "I was writing about black America—the specifics of the play are about black America. But there is something larger at work. A painter, when asked to comment on his work, once said, 'I try to

explore in terms of the life I know best those things which are common to all culture.' So while the specifics of the play are black, the
commonalities of culture are larger realities in the play. You have
father-son conflict, you have husband-wife conflict—all these things
are universal" (177). Avoiding the trap revealed in Marsalis's comments on the Los Angeles disturbance, Wilson emphasizes the presence of "universal" values in black communities where neoconserva-
tives see only a pathological absence of culture. Emphasizing the
centrality of the blues to his understanding of universal truths, Wilson describes his own struggle against racist notions of universality:

> There was a nobility to the lives of blacks in America which I didn't always
> see. At that time I was living in a rooming house in Pittsburgh. After I
> discovered the blues, I began to look at the people in the house a little
> differently than I had before. I began to see a value in their lives that I
> simply hadn't seen before. I discovered a beauty and a nobility in their
> struggle to survive. I began to understand the fact that the avenues for
> participation in society were closed to these people and that their ambi-
> tions had been thwarted, whatever they may have been. The mere fact
> that they were still able to make this music was a testament to the resil-
> iency of their spirit.

When Moyers adds "which everyday life squashed," Wilson provides
the necessary corrective: "Attempted to squash because the spirit was
resilient and strong and still is" (169). In a tribute to Romare Bearden that emphasizes the depth of his own response to canvases such
as *Mill Hand's Lunch Bucket*, *The Piano Lesson* (which provided the title
for Wilson's play), and *Mr. Seth and Miss Bertha*, Wilson provides a
description of Bearden's work that applies equally well to his own
plays: "What I saw was black life presented on its own terms, on a
grand and epic scale, with all its richness and fullness, in a language
that was vibrant and which, made attendant to everyday life, en-
nobled it, affirmed its value, and exalted its presence. It was the art
of a large and generous spirit that defined not only the character of
black American life, but also its conscience" (*Bearden* 8).

Wilson's concerns parallel those of George Kent, whose essays on
Gwendolyn Brooks, Langston Hughes, and Ellison question simplistic understandings of "universalism." Seeking what he calls a "legiti-
mate universalism," Kent advances the idea of a "subjective correlative" as an alternative to the appropriation of T. S. Eliot's "objective
correlative" by academically powerful and politically conservative
New Critics. Focusing on Brooks's poetry, Kent rejects the idea of
"universalism" as "a reach for some preexisting Western universal to
be arrived at by reducing the tensions inherent in the black experience." Although such reduction might attract a white audience seek-

ing an accessible, comforting, or perhaps simply comprehensible image of black experience, it inevitably reduces the ability of art to address the tensions dividing African-American communities. Like Wilson, however, Kent emphasizes the presence of "universal" concerns *in black experience:* "universalism derives, instead, from complete projection of a situation or experience's *space* and *vibrations* (going down deep, not transcending). Even where a preexisting universal may be paraphrasable, the true roots of the poet's universalism are in her power of enforcing the illusion that the vibrations from the space her imagination has encircled are captured and focused with all the power and significance which the raw materials afforded" (112). The core of August Wilson's success lies precisely in his treatment of "universal" themes in relation to the particular and changing conditions of black life.

As Wilson has frequently observed, the fullest expression of black life at any time can be found in the community's music: "I listen to the music of the particular period that I'm working on. Inside the music are clues to what is happening with the people. I don't know that much about contemporary music, so if I were going to write a play set in 1980, I would go and listen to the music, particularly music that blacks are making, and find out what their ideas and attitudes are about the situation, and about the time in which they live" (Moyers 168). Wilson's preface to *Ma Rainey's Black Bottom* applies this approach to Chicago in 1927. Focusing on the great migration of blacks from the rural South to the urban North, Wilson emphasizes the play's concern with "their values, their attitudes, and particularly their music" (9). Defining the music of the twenties as "music that breathes and touches. That connects" (9), Wilson locates "universal" virtues in the music's response to potentially cataclysmic changes in the specific circumstances of black life: "The men and women who make this music have learned it from the narrow crooked streets of East St. Louis, or the streets of the city's South Side, and the Alabama or Mississippi roots have been strangled by the northern manners and customs of free men of definite and sincere worth" (10). Wilson concludes with a reminder of the importance of functionality to the "men for whom this music often lies at the forefront of their conscience and concerns. Thus they are laid open to be consumed by it: its warmth and redress, its braggadocio and roughly poignant comments, its vision and prayer, which would instruct and allow them to reconnect, to reassemble and gird up for the next battle in which they would be both victim and the ten thousand slain" (10).

If the musical power of Wilson's work derives from this profound sense of African-American music, its commercial success derives in large part from his equally sure knowledge of, and interest in, the concerns of "classical" American theater, particularly that of Eugene O'Neill. Wilson employs numerous themes and motifs familiar to theater audiences grounded in the O'Neill tradition, which includes Tennessee Williams, Sam Shepard, Lillian Hellman, Lanford Wilson, Beth Henley, and numerous others. Among these are the disruption of the surface of family life by repressed or buried secrets, the blurring of the line separating "psychological" and "physical" realities, and the transformation of everyday diction and syntax into a heightened vernacular poetry. Wilson's approach recalls Ellison's comparison of T. S. Eliot and Louis Armstrong. Emphasizing Eliot and Armstrong's parallel interest in "the artful juxtapositioning of earlier styles," Ellison observes that the jazz tradition makes no distinction between the sources of those styles. Both Eliot's juxtaposition of ragtime and Shakespeare in *The Waste Land* and Coltrane's modal revoicing of "Chim Chim Cheree" anticipate Wilson's combination of Robert Johnson and O'Neill, who himself drew on African-American traditions. Perhaps the most important reason that Wilson has attracted relatively little of the harsh criticism directed against Marsalis is that he clearly understands the principle behind Ellison's caution that the Eliot-Armstrong analogy "is not a matter of giving the music fine airs—it doesn't need them—but of saying that whatever touches our highly conscious creators of culture" will be treated with equal seriousness in their work (*Shadow* 221). Combining a firm belief in the transcendent virtue of art with his awareness of the presence of these virtues in African-American vernacular traditions, Wilson's description of the carvings on the piano in *The Piano Lesson* sums up his neoclassical perspective: "The carvings are rendered with a grace and power of invention that lifts them out of the realm of craftsmanship and into the realm of art" (xvii).

Wilson as Jazz Visionary: Five Improvisations

In *The Repeating Island*, Antonio Benitez-Rojo explores the "chaotic"—in the scientific sense of a complex system in which recurring patterns cycle through multiple states of potential equilibrium—interaction of European binary systems with Native American, Asian, and African traditions. Rather than subordinating one sensibility to the other (illegitimate universalism) or creating a synthesis that reduces the tensions created by the juxtaposition (a *mulatto* or *mestizo* aesthetic), Benitez-Rojo recommends a polyrhythmic literature that can be read "as a stream of texts in flight, in intense differentiation among themselves and within whose complex coexistence there are vague regularities, usually paradoxical" (27). In addition to "ironizing a set of values taken as universal," polyrhythmic texts "communicate their own turbulence, their own clash, and their own void, the swirling black hole of social violence produced by the *encomienda* and the plantation, that is, their otherness, their peripheral asymmetry with regard to the West" (26). Derived in large part from the African traditions that generated gospel, blues, and jazz, Benitez-Rojo's polyrhythmic culture, which receives stunning literary voice in Eduardo Galeano's *Memory of Fire* trilogy, provides a useful point of reference for discussion of Wilson's jazz neoclassicism.

Because the concept of the organizing thesis derives primarily from European analytical traditions, criticism organized around a central proposition risks repressing the chaotic potential, and thereby subverting potential uses, of polyrhythmic texts, such as Wilson's plays. To this point, this chapter's examination of jazz neoclassicism and the fragmentation of contemporary African-American cultural discourse has been structured to accord with Eurocentric academic conventions. As Benitez-Rojo observes, the point of polyrhythmic discourse is not to destroy or replace binary discourses, but to understand them as part of a larger chaotic context in which other voices sound freely. This formulation suggests the appropriateness of an additional, not alternative, critical methodology based on the polyrhythmic formal structures of the oral tradition. The remainder of this essay represents my polyrhythmic response to a sequence of interrelated calls I hear in Wilson's major plays. Rather than attempting to demonstrate thematic consistency or support a thesis, I will present a series of "improvisational" responses to Wilson's visions of the universal themes—life and death, men and women, success and failure—in black America—the specific source and focus of his jazz-inflected voice.

Responding to Harrison's description of Wilson's plays, my improvisations follow a "modal structure" founded on the "distribution of related and nonrelated ideas." From *Ma Rainey's Black Bottom* through *Two Trains Running,* many of Wilson's most interesting and powerful passages juxtapose ideas to clarify the function of black music (understood as both cultural resource and economic commodity) in response to the chaotic fragmentation of African-American communities, reflected most clearly in class and gender tensions. Resonating with the "intense differentiation" of African-American experience, between people and across time, Wilson's jazz call envisions the transformation of "vague" and "paradoxical" regularities into the foundation for a healthy and healing community.

Ma Rainey and the Devil

The black metafiction that provides the title for August Wilson's first major play, "Ma Rainey's Black Bottom" realizes the process it describes, calling on later black artists to maintain blues realism in a system designed to steal their voices: "I done showed you all my black bottom / You ought to learn that dance" (*Ma Rainey* in *Three Plays* 70). There's no self-delusion in Ma's assessment of the white folks' "love" for her: "They don't care nothing about me. All they want is my voice. Well, I done learned that, and they gonna treat me like I want to be treated no matter how much it hurt them" (64). And there's no self-delusion in Wilson's response. Knowing full well that the devil is a "White fellow . . . got on good clothes and everything. Standing there with a clipboard in his hand" (*Fences* in *Three Plays* 117), Wilson knows that plenty of black folks, especially the men hell-hounded out of the church by their own demons, their ambitions, share Levee's response: "the only thing I ask about the devil . . . to see him coming so I can sell him this one [soul] I got" (*Ma Rainey* 34).

The market's still active.

So it comes down to a battle over which of the "two versions" of "Ma Rainey's Black Bottom" we're going to hear. But before we can get to that, we need to know what "we" means, who we are. Grounded in the deep blues, Cutler tells Levee not to confuse the white man's version with reality: "it ain't what you say, or what Mr. Irvin say . . . it's what Ma say that counts" (28). Slow Drag, the bass player in charge of the black bottom of the sound, gives his amen: "Ma say what happens with her" (28). Toledo, the only literate member of the band, provides an Afrocentric critique of Levee's willingness to sell his soul, to play the songs he thinks the white man wants to hear: "as long as he looks to white folks for approval . . . then he ain't never gonna find out who he is and what he's about. He's just gonna be about what white folks want him to be about" (29). It's not even a matter of being what the white folks want him to be; the devil's satisfied to control the question, set the terms of the contract.

And make no mistake. The devil sets the terms for anyone who wants, who needs, the money or the fame, or the good reviews. The devil lies to Levee and Levee kills Toledo for telling him the truth: "We done sold Africa for the price of tomatoes. We done sold ourselves to the white man in order to be like him. Look at the way you dressed. . . . That ain't African. That's the white man" (78). But Ma tells a deeper truth, a black variation of a neoclassical riff on the transcendent value of art: "White folks don't understand about the blues. They hear it come out, but they don't know how it got there.

They don't understand that's life's way of talking. You don't sing to feel better. You sing cause that's a way of understanding life" (67).

For Ma's people—and, make no mistake, "the colored folks made Ma a star" (78)—understanding develops through call and response. As Sterling Brown sang in "Ma Rainey," the people respond to Ma's response to the call of their own burdens, their lived blues. The process requires individuals not to seek a synthesis, to deny the extreme aspects of their own experience, but to assert their subjectivity in response to other, equally personal and equally extreme, assertions of experience. Call and response is African-American analysis: a process that, by admitting diverse voices and diverse experiences, approximates "universality" more clearly than any individual analysis. The communal critique of Levee takes its force from the convergence of Cutler's voice with Slow Drag's and Toledo's. Toledo's blood is Wilson's amen.

Gabriel's Trumpet and the Black Women's Blues

When Ma Rainey talks about the blues, they're the black folks' blues. When, three decades later, the characters in *Fences* live the blues, they live black *men's* blues and black *women's* blues. Wilson's most classically tragic play, *Fences* explores what that means in a world where jazz—the source of new visions—has fallen into desperate hustles and calls without response.

Troy and Bono, the black men who carry the South in their blood and on their backs, have heard the walking blues in their fathers' lives. Bono's father was "just moving on through. Searching out the New Land" (*Fences* 146); Troy's father "felt a responsibility toward us. . . . Without that responsibility he could have walked off and left us . . . made his own way" (147). Like the tormented figures in D. H. Lawrence's *Studies in Classic American Literature* in flight from oppression and women and civilization and sometimes just responsibility and always from their selves, black men with the walking blues reach out for freedom or nature or truth or money or a visionary gospel city in the North, a "different idea of myself" (163) or even just "second base" (164). Betraying his father and his son and most basically Rose, Troy voices his betrayal as a profoundly American black man's blues: "Rose, you're not listening to me. I'm trying the best I can to explain it to you. It's not easy for me to admit that I been standing in the same place for eighteen years" (164–65).

Rose: standing beside him through every one of those years, every one of those days. Calling out in a world where men still leave—male rappers have only recently begun to acknowledge the idea of sexual responsibility—where black women's blues echo without response, Rose's monologue responds to the calls of Toni Morrison and Alice Walker and Gloria Naylor and the real black women in the lives of real black men:

> I been standing with you! I been right here with you, Troy. I got a life too. I gave eighteen years of my life to stand in the same spot with you. Don't you think I ever wanted other things? . . . You not the only one who's got wants and needs. But I held on to you, Troy. I took all my feelings, my wants and needs, my dreams . . . and I buried them inside you. I planted a seed and watched it and prayed over it. I planted myself inside you and waited to bloom. And it didn't take me no eighteen years to find out the soil was hard and rocky and it wasn't never gonna bloom. But I held on to you, Troy. I held you tighter. (165)

So Troy forgets the source, loses what he loves. Rose. Corey, whose own blues propel him to the military. The shadow of Vietnam hangs heavy over the play.

What can the jazz-man say? For Lyons, jazz starts out as an "idea of being" rather than "the actual practice of the music" (115). Only after he gives up on the quick hit, the devil's bargain, does Lyons begin to understand the blues that may make jazz possible: "I'm still playing. It still helps me to get out of bed in the morning. As long as it do that I'm gonna be right there playing and trying to make some sense out of it" (187).

And finally, Gabriel, name echoing with the myth of Louis Armstrong. Pursued by hellhounds, a victim of the last war, determined to tell St. Peter when it's time to open the gate, Gabriel combines the blues and gospel dimensions of the jazz impulse. He knows "the devil's strong" (144); he knows Lyons is living in the white man's "jungle" (145); he loves and honors Rose. Risking the madness that Dostoyevski and Ellison and Melville and Morrison encounter in the universal and absolutely specific depths of human experience, Gabriel transforms his burden, the burden of his family and his community, into visionary jazz: "There is a weight of impossible description that falls away and leaves him bare and exposed to a frightful realization. It is a trauma that a sane and normal mind would be unable to withstand" (192). Rather than surrendering to madness or walking away, Gabriel points back to Africa with a "slow, strange dance, eerie and life-giving. A dance of atavistic signature and ritual." When Lyons attempts to embrace him, Gabriel howls—"an attempt at song, or perhaps a song turning back into itself in an attempt at speech"— which opens the "gates of heaven" (192). Wilson bears witness to Gabriel's jazz vision, his burden and his call. In neoclassical jazz, tragedy is a fragmented world where no one responds.

And remember the cost of accepting, however brilliantly, the fragmentation: Charlie Parker. Jimi Hendrix. Donny Hathaway. Remember that the black women never accepted it, even as they felt it most deeply. Gospel jazz-women, sources: Aretha, Nina Simone, Rose. Remember the sources, remember that the world wasn't always the way it is.

Africa and the Memory of the Wind

Remember the source of division. When the world split. In two. When Joe Turner, "brother of the governor of the great sovereign state of Tennessee, swooped down on us and grabbed everybody there" (*Joe Turner* in *Fences* 269). Bynum knows that devil: "What he wanted was your song. He wanted to have that song to be his" (270). That's how the blues, the men's blues and the women's blues, were born: "Joe Turner split us up. Joe Turner turned the world upside-down" (273).

Joe Turner's Come and Gone reaches farther back than *Fences,* or even *Ma Rainey's Black Bottom.* Back to a world where Jeremy considers withdrawing from the devil's game: "I don't play no contest, Mr. Bynum. Had one of them white fellows cure me of that" (219). Faced with the "realities" of the labor market where he has to pay the devil to keep his job, Jeremy walks on, bluesman in a world where the responses, of communities and individuals, haven't yet been fixed. This is the core of jazz neoclassicism. Not to turn to the past for answers. But to seek the moments when the answers hadn't been provided, when the calls and responses were still open.

Joe Turner's Come and Gone resonates with Loomis's vision of the ancestors, the bones walking across the water, turning into the black people walking out their blues. Seeking reunion with Martha Pentecost, black woman and gospel spirit, Loomis lives the forces creating jazz: "A man driven not by the hellhounds that seemingly bay at his heels, but by his search for a world that speaks to something about himself. He is unable to harmonize the forces that swirl around him, and seeks to recreate the world into one that contains his image" (216). Or, as Bynum phrases it, "Now, I can look at you, Mr. Loomis, and see you a man who done forgot his song. Forgot how to sing it" (267). The birth of tragedy—Ma Rainey's and Nietzsche's and Robert Johnson's—the loss of a world where "All you got to do is sing it. Then you be free" (287).

The song is on the wind. Where the children, Reuben and Zonia, setting out to sing their own versions of the (not yet) male/female blues, can still hear the call and response between Bynum and the ancestors: "First he say something . . . and the wind it say back to him" (275). With his deep memories of Africa, his communion with the ancestors, his memories of his father's "Healing Song," Bynum understands the burden of the individual, the jazz artist, who passes the tradition on to the community in a chaotically changing world: "That song was hard to carry. I fought against it. Didn't want to accept that song. I tried to find my daddy to give him back the song. But I found out it wasn't his song. It was my song. It had come from way deep inside me. I looked long back in memory and gathered up pieces and snatches of things to make that song. I was making it up out of myself." And, like all African art, the song *worked:* "And that song helped me on the road" (268). The song of the wind, materializing into Miss Mabel, who helps Reuben: "She says, 'Didn't you promise Eugene something?' Then she hit me with her cane. She say, 'Let them pigeons go.' Then she hit me again" (276). The ancestor—conceived as spirit or memory or magic or even neurons firing, an echo in mind—commands respect for the ancestors; responsibility to the community; reverence before the symbols of the spirit. Demands that we live up to our promises. Commands freedom. The ancestors as source of moral direction. The grandmother as manifestation of the moral energy in the universe, the one who knows that there are times when you just plain *do right* or you ain't a man, much less a human being (and the voices of the orisha, the ancestors, the elders resound with a blues humor filled with all *kinds* of double meanings, in theory and practice).

And think what difference it would have made had white folks, white men, ever dealt with the simple question: "Didn't you promise something?"

Bynum knows that, in the world, as it is, he can no longer hope for a response to his father's "Healing Song." So he sings a "Binding Song" for the black men and black women falling away from the gospel vision, from Bertha, who holds the community together as it forgets what Bynum knows, grows deaf to the voices on the wind: "Bertha moves about the kitchen as though blessing it and chasing away the huge sadness that seems to envelop it. It is a dance and demonstration of her own magic, her own remedy that is centuries old and to which she is connected by the muscles of her heart and the blood's memory" (283).

Playing the Changes

As always, there's a white man "going around to all the colored people's houses looking to buy up musical instruments. He'd buy anything. Drums. Guitars. Harmonicas. Pianos" (*Piano* 11). As always, there's the piano, the one Berniece and Boy Willie's father died for, "the story of our whole family" (45): white folks and money and the threat of black blood. A house full of ghosts, a family full of ghosts. An American obsession: Hawthorne and Henry James, Poe and Charles Chesnutt, Faulkner and David Bradley, Charlotte Perkins Gilman and Eugene O'Neill. Toni Morrison's Beloved. Ancestors. The past burdens the present.

While the present closes paths, circumscribes responses. Yet and still, Wining Boy "give that piano up. That was the best thing that ever happened to me, getting rid of that piano. That piano got so big and I'm carrying it around on my back. I don't wish that on nobody. See, you think it's all fun being a recording star. Got to carrying that piano around and man did I get slow" (41). Playing for money, the devil's game, forecloses possibilities, fixes your options: "I'm walking around with that piano. Alright. Now, there ain't but so many places you can go. Only so many road wide enough for you and that piano" (41). Haunted, Berniece seconds the emotion: "When my mama died I shut the top on that piano and I ain't never opened it since. I was only playing it for her. . . . Say when I played it she could hear my daddy talking to her. I used to think them pictures came alive and walked through the house. Sometime late at night I could hear my mama talking to them. I said that wasn't gonna happen to me. I don't play that piano cause I don't want to wake them spirits. They never be walking around in this house" (70). Above all, Berniece hopes to shield Maretha: "She got a chance I didn't have. I ain't gonna burden her with that piano" (70).

As if it were possible. Because, like it or not, the spirits are in the house, the voices on the wind. The only question is on what terms. As always, the devil, Sutter's ghost, defines what it means to be a man. Boy Willie learns the lesson well: "They mistreat me I mistreat them right back. Ain't no difference in me and the white man" (38). A different phrasing: they're both willing to kill to own, to control. The ghosts of the yellow dog: Morrison's Seven Days. From the crossroads where the southern cross the dog. Yellow, the minstrel shade: white turning black, and black turning white. Boy Willie's "Bible say an eye for an eye, a tooth for a tooth, and a life for a life" (89). Like Morrison's Pilate, Maretha, already living the black women's blues, sees that ghost: Boy Willie threatening Wining Boy, his doubled self, locked together with Sutter's ghost in "a life-and-death struggle fraught with perils and faultless terror" (106). Berniece has seen it before, suffered it, borne the burden like Margaret Walker's Vyry, Morrison's Dorcas, Naylor's Lorraine: "you're all alike. All this thieving and killing and thieving and killing. And what it ever lead to? More killing and more thieving. I ain't never seen it come to nothing. People getting burned up. People getting shot. People falling down their wells. It don't never stop" (52).

But the cycle of violence is, *can be,* broken. Berniece, growing into herself as ancestor, returns, remembers, sings: "It is an old urge to song that is both a commandment and a plea. With each repetition it gains in strength. It is intended as an exorcism and a dressing for battle. A rustle of wind blowing across two continents" (106). The wind crying out for the ancestors and the self: "I want you to help me . . . Mama Berniece . . . Mama Esther . . . Papa Boy Charles . . . Mama Ola" (107). Men and women. The song come down from Mama Ola who "polished this piano with her tears for seventeen years. For seventeen years she rubbed on it till her hands bled. Then she rubbed the blood in . . . mixed it up with the rest of the blood on it" (107).

Down at the crossroads, the place where we "cultivate the art of recognizing significant communications, knowing what is truth and what is falsehood, or else the lessons of the crossroads—the point where doors open or close, where persons have to make decisions that may forever after affect their lives—will be lost" (Thompson 19). Home of Eshu, the interpreter, of Legba, home of the devil. The phrasing makes all the difference. And the universal lesson to be learned from the piano is that the past, the African past, the slave past, the free past, never dies. We can lock the energies up, carve them into wood and try to forget, contain, repress them. We can let them kill us. Or we can go down to the crossroads for the power to exorcise the devil, casting out "the spirit of one James Sutter" (*Piano* 104) in the name of the ancestors as well as the holy spirit. Go down to the crossroads where, as Wining Boy knows, the ancestors sing: "I done been to where the Southern cross the Yellow Dog and called out their names. They talk back to you, too" (34). The crossroads where the ancestors, like the piano, *function,* give themselves to the present as sources of power: "I can't say how they talked to nobody else. But to me it just filled me up in a strange sort of way to be standing there on that spot. I didn't want to leave. It felt like the longer I stood there the bigger I got" (35). Boy Willie believes, responds: "They like the wind you can't see them. But sometimes you be in trouble they might be around to help you" (86). The song on the wind, the song Berniece sings, binds, creates the possibility of healing; Sutter's ghost exorcised, Maretha and Boy Willie hug, the black man and black woman reconcile, respond.

The Piano Lesson teaches us that art—even or especially the neoclassical art of an economically successful playwright who looks at the community he grew up in, the community he writes about, and knows "most of it is no longer there" (Moyers 171)—must be *functional.* Wilson sketches a process, responds to the call of a desperately fragmented world. What we make of it is, the ancestors willing, up to us.

Jazz Coda

Structured like a jam session—the voices entering, echoing, calling, responding, never quite resolving, improvising on the changing times—*Two Trains Running* revoices Wilson's concerns in response to the world of Malcolm X and Martin Luther King, a world where "they killed the dreamer" (52), a world where the music is locked up in a broken jukebox that "ain't gonna do nothing but break again if they do fix it" (56). A world where the spirit's in danger of being subdivided, part for the dead Prophet in a coffin full of hundred dollar bills, part for ancient Aunt Ester, who asks only that you throw your money in the river, *if* you want to get right with yourself, if you really want to heal.

A world where Sterling, twenty years before N.W.A., celebrates the gangsta vision: "That's all a man need is a pocketful of money, a cadillac and a good woman" (67). Where Risa, daughter of Gloria Naylor and Toni Morrison, of Leon Forrest and Gayl Jones, takes a razor blade to her own legs, her own soul, to survive in a world that has no earthly idea of her name.

Sterling sets out to kill the devil: the Alberts who, yet and still and always, steal his money and his dreams. But he never makes it to the devil's door. Instead, he turns to Aunt Ester, daughter of the orisha, sister of Morrison's Pilate and Bambara's Minnie Ransom who asks simply: "Are you sure, sweetheart, that you want to be well?" What turns Sterling's steps toward the healer, what empowers him to break the cycle of violence, to turn away from the devil's game, is Risa's voice: "I didn't know it mattered to nobody. I heard you calling me" (68). For Sterling and Risa, the future seems possible.

Reconciling but not resolving, Wilson offers us his vision: a binding song for desperate times.

Epilogue:
Improvisations toward a New Phrasing: West Afrocentrism, Meta-Funk, and the Interiors of *Jazz*

▲ ▲ ▲ ▲

"Deep water ain't drowning," wrote James Baldwin, but there are times when it is. As we near the end of the twentieth century, calls sound, responses echo; the elders—Baldwin, Audre Lorde, Miles Davis—become ancestors, the changing same changes: gospel to house, the blues to rap, jazz to funk. Versions, inevitably partial. So the questions, now, for me, are, as simply as I can phrase them: "what versions can we imagine? which ones do we explore? what actions do they call for? where do we take it from here?"

The ecologist Gregory Bateson observes that most complex phenomena alternate between opening the system to new energies and measuring how those energies change the system's equilibrium. Seen in these terms *Playing the Changes* examines how a given form of expression, a constructed tradition, responds to new voices, whether expressed in primary texts or in new critical phrasings. In response to Bateson, this epilogue advances two new (tentative) phrasings—centered on the concepts of West Afrocentrism (or "Recuperation") and the "Funk Principle" (or an aesthetic of sampling)—and focuses attention on Toni Morrison's *Jazz*, which, as Morrison's novels often do, provides a clear measure of where we—and I use the term in Baldwin's expansive sense—stand today. As Morrison calls out at the end of *Jazz*, which responds to calls emanating from the Harlem Renaissance, European-American modernism, and a deep history in which Africa was just beginning to experience its difference from what was not yet Europe: "If I were able I'd say it. Say make me, remake me. You are free to do it and I am free to let you because look, look. Look where your hands are. Now" (229).

▲ ▲ ▲ ▲

From the beginning, *Jazz* affirms and extends the calls of Morrison's ancestors. The world of the novel is permeated by double consciousness: daylight razors "the buildings in half" (7); Viole(n)t wonders "who on earth that other Violet was that walked about the City in her skin; peeped out through her eyes and saw other things" (89). Recognizing the broad ramifications of Du Bois's formulation (as have numerous feminist critics including Elaine Showalter), Morrison insists that the experience of division must be understood not only in relation to race and gender but also to the split between village and city. Reworking ideas from her essay "City Limits, Village Values: Concepts of the Neighborhood in Black Fiction," Morrison describes the "wave of black people running from want and violence" (33), country people who, when "they fall in love with a city, it is forever. . . . As though there never was a time when they didn't love it." In love with the city, the Harlem Renaissance cradle of jazz, many "forget what loving other people was like" (33).

As the people change, their love changes, the music changes. The blues, linking the brutal experiences of the South and the North, continue to teach them that "laughter is serious. More complicated, more serious than tears" (113); the new music sounds an urban blues of "clarinets and lovemaking, fists and the voices of sorrowful women" (7). Simultaneously, discontinuously, the new music holds out promises unthinkable in the South: "You would have thought everything had been forgiven the way they played" (196). Morrison portrays a modernist Harlem Renaissance dreaming responses to Ezra Pound's modernist clarion to "make it new": "At last, at last, everything's ahead. The smart ones say so and people listening to them and reading what they write down agree: Here comes the new." (7) Liberating and dangerous, Nietzschean, the new music "made you do unwise disorderly things. Just hearing it was like violating the law" (58).

However contagious the energy, however dizzying the journey to the promised freedom of the North, however seductive the thought of transgression, of breaking the tables of the (white man's) law, however dizzying the journey to what Robert Hayden called the "mythic North . . . [the] star-shaped yonder Bible city," Morrison refuses to disremember the price of the ticket: the loss of the past, the village self, the gospel church which Violet leaves in the first paragraph, never to return: "There goes the sad stuff. The bad stuff. The things-nobody-could-help stuff. The way everybody was then and there. Forget that. History is over, you all, and everything's ahead at last" (7).

Everything. Murder. The loss of memory. A (post)modern city-scape recalling both Bigger Thomas's Chicago and what Showalter calls the "wild zone" of women's double consciousness (spatial, experiential, metaphysical) where calls die unanswered, where deep water washes jazz visions away in silence, where Morrison's characters, destroyed like Charlie Parker, Billie Holiday, Sly Stone, sink into "indecent speechless lurking insanity" (179).

▲ ▲ ▲ ▲

The most influential engagement with the problem of double consciousness during the Harlem Renaissance, Countee Cullen's "Heritage" questions, with an obsessiveness at once individual and communal, "What is Africa to me?" An ironically tinged touchstone for celebrations of Africa during the Black Arts Movement, Cullen's phrase elicits the persona's feeling of alienation from the "Quaint, outlandish heathen gods / Black men fashion out of rods." Playing a "double part," he stops his thumbs against his ears to drown out the sound of "Great drums throbbing through the air" even as he responds, internally, to the Garvey movement's call for a militant black Jesus with "dark rebellious hair" whose "Patience wavers just so much as / Mortal grief compels." In the final lines, however, Cullen's despair—articulated perfectly in his choice of "overly controlled" iambic tetrameter couplets—leads him to repress his ancestry, to

> Quench my pride and cool my blood,
> Lest I perish in the flood.
> Lest a hidden ember set
> Timber that I thought was wet
> Burning like the merest wax,
> Lest the grave restore its dead.
> Not yet has my heart or head
> In the least way realized
> They and I are civilized.
>
> (107–8)

Listening to the drumbeats of a Fifth Avenue protest march sounding the black community's "complicated anger" (59) over the riots in which her parents, and so many others, met their fiery deaths, Dorcas hears the drums as "only the first part, the first word, of a command" (60). Suggesting, but not realizing, a vision of community, for Dorcas, "the drums were not an all-embracing rope of fellowship, discipline, and transcendence. She remembered them as a beginning, a start of something she looked to complete" (60).

Protecting her memory of her parents' death—the wood chip that "entered her stretched dumb mouth and traveled down her throat because it smoked and glowed there still" (60–61)—the drums call Dorcas into the city where she will meet her death, the blues city that sends "secret messages disguised as public signs" (64).

▲ ▲ ▲ ▲

In a provocative dissertation titled after black South African pianist Abdullah Ibrahim's lyrical meditation on African American roots, Judylyn Ryan's "Water from an Ancient Well: The Recuperation of Double-Consciousness in African-American Narrative" meditates on the meaning of the drum for African American women. Using the poem "When and If the Drum Is a Woman" as a touchstone for her constructive critique of Stepto's paradigms of ascent and immersion, Ryan distinguishes a "wholesome" diasporic (African American) consciousness from Dorcas and Cullens's experience of a hyphenated (African-American) consciousness that circumscribes, frames, and attempts to contain energies, communities, and movements. As Ryan notes, Stepto establishes a symbolic geography of Afro-American experiences organized around a North-South polarity. This formulation implies both that black experience originates in slavery and that highly literate black intellectuals have no options other than isolation in the white world or a return to an enslaved community with few options save to repeat the cycle of ascent and immersion. Acknowledging the descriptive accuracy of Stepto's formulation for many people and texts, Ryan revises his symbolic geography to provide a broader, more useful, Afrocentric frame of understanding that avoids the limitations of Molefi Kete Asante's Nile Valley Afrocentrism (which among other things propagates uncritical patriarchal attitudes). The core of Ryan's project lies in its reframing of ascent and immersion in relation to two new narrative structures: a "narrative of dispersion" and a "narrative of recuperation." Responding to the "voice of exile" Du Bois heard in the depths of the "sorrow songs," Ryan's "narrative of dispersion" focuses on the exile of Africans from the "symbolic east" of their tribal homelands to a "symbolic west" characterized by the experience of double consciousness. One of the most destructive effects of double consciousness, enforced by physical violence and the racist Africanist discourse that erases African history (Miller), is that it transforms the "symbolic west" into the symbolic south. Reflecting both on consciously Pan-Africanist texts and on the implicit African elements in diverse forms of African American expression ("folk" or "high," "literary" or "musical," to employ terms that must be radically redefined in response to Ryan's call), Ryan suggests that post-immersion narratives frequently manifest a desire for recuperation, for a return (physical or spiritual) to the wholesome consciousness of the "symbolic east."

Ryan's formulation draws attention to an important, and often overlooked, mode of African American literature, that created by writers born in Africa or the Caribbean who received their "higher" education or live in the symbolic west, usually in Great Britain or the United States. Calling for a radically increased awareness of what Robert Farris Thompson calls the "Black Atlantic" tradition (which I would rephrase as "West Afrocentric," in part to emphasize the importance of African American communities geographically closer to the Asian Pacific sphere), Ayi Kwei Armah's *Two Thousand Seasons* and Maryse Conde's *I, Tituba, Black Witch of Salem* redefine our understanding of the African American tradition as profoundly as did *Native Son, Their Eyes Were Watching God, Invisible Man,* or *Song of Solomon.*

The prologue to Armah's *Two Thousand Seasons* provides an exceptionally moving outline of dispersion and recuperation. Armah calls on the "hearers, seers, imaginers, thinkers, rememberers" to "communicate truths of the living way to a people fascinated unto death"; "to link memory with forelistening, to join the uncountable seasons of our flowing to unknown tomorrows even more numerous"; and "to pass on truths of our origins to a people rushing deathward, grown contemptuous in our ignorance of our source, prejudiced against our own survival" (xi). Even as he nears despair over the dispersed Africans who have surrendered to the values of their places of exile, those whose "bodies are mere corpses, awaiting final burial" (xiv), Armah calls for a faith in the future, for a sense of the living self as ancestor: "Remember this: against all that destruction some yet remained among us unforgetful of origins, dreaming secret dreams, seeing secret visions, hearing secret voices of our purpose. Further: those yet to appear, to see, hear, to utter and to make—little do we know what changes they will come among. Idle then for us to presume despair on their behalf; foolish when we have no knowledge how much closer to the way their birth will come, how much closer than our closest hopes" (xv).

Following his epic re-membering of the arrival and seeming triumph of Africa's masters (both Christian and, Ali Mazrui's "triple heritage" notwithstanding, Islamic), Armah (a Ghanaian who has studied and taught in the United States) turns his attention to recuperation. The chapter of *Two Thousand Seasons* titled "The Return" makes it clear that recuperation does not mean a simple return to a remembered homeland or a decision to remain in a "separatist" community, however necessary such a community may have been at certain stages of the process. Writing in a collective voice out of the oral traditions that encode community memory, Armah considers the options open to those who have managed to escape from the physical control of their oppressors. A third of the escapees, "unwilling to risk a return to the dangers of known pasts, afraid to follow any future vision" (148), choose to withdraw from the struggle, thereby leaving themselves vulnerable to unresisting recapture. An even larger group responds to the "call of return," attempting to go back to the homeland from which they were originally dispersed: "To the listening ears of these nostalgic souls it did not matter, could not matter that it was at home they had first been betrayed into destruction's whiteness. Perhaps it was also their hope that their specific betrayals, their single sales were mere unhappy accidents. . . . Ah, blind illusion of nostalgic spirits. Ah, self-murdering deafness of ears forever cut off from the quiet, reasonable call of our way" (149).

Concerned primarily with envisioning the terms on which recuperation can be realized, which necessarily entails reengagement with the destructive forces, Armah calls on the dispersed community, Africans and African Americans throughout the diaspora, to "seek the necessary beginning to destruction's destruction" (151). Acknowledging risk, he knows this struggle involves "real dangers, but nothing beside the present danger of despair in the face of the illusion, massive, stone-like, of the permanence of this white destruction" (205). Armah concludes by reiterating a West Afrocentric "vision of creation, yet unknown" (206):

> There is no beauty but in relationships. Nothing cut off by itself is beautiful. Never can things in destructive relationships be beautiful. All beauty is in the creative purpose of our relationships. . . . The mind that knows this, the destroyer's traps will never hold that mind. The group that knows this and works knowing this, that group itself is a work of beauty, creation's work. Against such a group the destroyers will set traps for the body, traps for the heart, traps to destroy the mind. Such a group none of the destroyers' traps can hold. (206)

Responding to the West Afrocentric call in more concrete terms, Conde (born in Guadaloupe and currently teaching at the University of California–Berkeley) establishes the dispersion pattern in the first paragraph of *I, Tituba*, which describes the rape of an African American woman aboard the slave ship "Christ the King," an "act of aggression . . . of hatred and contempt" (3). Immediately thereafter, she establishes the fundamental values of recuperation through West African ancestor Mama Yaya's teaching that "everything lives, has a soul, and breathes. That everything must be respected. That man is not the master" (9). Still, Conde makes it clear that double consciousness cannot, simply, be erased. When Tituba tells Mama Yaya—whose presence is as real as those of any of the "material" European-Americans—that "I don't want to return to the white man's world," Mama Yaya replies simply: "There's no way of escaping it" (19).

Which does not mean there's no way of reframing it, of envisioning new possibilities within it. Developing her skills as a healer, Tituba finds herself limited by the natural environment around Boston, which lacks "certain items required for practicing my art: the trees in which the invisible spirits repose, the condiments for their favorite dishes, and the plants and roots for healing" (45). Moving toward the multicultural forms exploited by jazz artists, Tituba takes the first step toward recuperation, saying, "I decided to make substitutions" (45). After establishing her ability to survive—"Mama Yaya had said it over and over again: 'What matters is to survive!'" (136)—Tituba imagines a renewed connection between individual courage and communal resistance: "I began to imagine another course for life, another meaning, another motive. The fire engulfs the top of the tree. The Rebel has disappeared in a cloud of smoke. He has triumphed over death and his spirit remains. The frightened circle of slaves regains its courage. The spirit remains. Yes, another motive for life" (136). When she returns to Barbados, a physical journey that marks the first major stage of what is most profoundly a spiritual process, Tituba reestablishes contact with "the invisible trio" that will accompany her *through* (and, reflecting the West African apprehension of death as a crossroads between material and spiritual worlds, not just *to*) her (potentially inspirational) "death" on the gallows: Mama Yaya, her mother, Abena ("the Ashanti princess"), and Yao, the silk-cotton tree that roots her struggle in a West African sense of interrelationship.

A final note on recuperation: heard from my location within the European-American institutional world, Conde's call is both powerful and troubling. Although I honor the ancestors—Mama Yaya, Toni Cade Bambara's Minnie Ransom, the "Thought-Woman" T'Seh in Leslie Silko's *Ceremony*—I apprehend them most clearly as voices in my psyche, variously conscious internalizations of what I have learned from real people, energies accessible to us when we relax the barriers our constructions of reality impose. While this construction has proved useful as a way of initiating dialogues within my intellectual communities, it bears a discomfiting similarity to the traditions of ethnographic translation, described most incisively in Marianna Torgovnick's *Gone Primitive,* which inevitably distort, repress—make comfortable—the untranslatable specifics of "other" texts or traditions, usually as part of an unowned but undeniable imperialist agenda. Yet and still, that's how phrasings change, how we decide on which of the countless questions to pursue. The ancestors aren't, never were, perfect. For the future generations, our mistakes are as significant as our successes. Anyway, I've known for a long time that I had a role in the minstrel show.

▲ ▲ ▲ ▲

Even as it gazes out toward the cultural frames of double consciousness, *Jazz* continues Morrison's theoretically resonant exploration of the psyche, the human interior. The problem of interiority takes on special intensity in relation to black people exiled to an increasingly urban world predicated on unfamiliar notions of "individual consciousness." (This should not be taken to suggest a lack of individual awareness in premodern communities, which usually understand the individual as part of the community that gives his/her experience meaning.) Reflecting her long-standing interest in (though not acceptance of) modernist phrasings, Morrison wrote her M.A. thesis on the theme of alienation in the fiction of Virginia Woolf and William Faulkner. Contrasting Faulkner's repudiation of characters who choose alienation, which he views as a moral flaw, with Woolf's endorsement of "the objectivity of detachment" ("Woolf" 2), Morrison describes Woolf's belief that "to live in the privacy of self, remain apart from others and share nothing is her conception of an essential independence without which life is meaningless" (7).

Although Woolf is today well established as a central figure in a tradition of women's modernism, Morrison's thesis (not surprisingly, given the strong pressures against emphasizing issues of race or gender in an era dominated by formalist New Critical methodologies) emphasizes more general modernist concerns, many of which recur in *Jazz*. Both thesis and novel reject Woolf's "objectivity" as a self-protective delusion; the narrator of *Jazz* admits to being "confused in my solitude into arrogance, thinking my space, my view was the only one that was or that mattered" (220). Nonetheless, *Jazz* shares many of Woolf's concerns, including those reflected in the passages from Woolf's diaries that frame the younger Morrison's academic inquiry. Her chapter on Woolf opens with a diary passage describing life as "tragic . . . a little strip of pavement over an abyss," followed immediately by an excerpt prefiguring the dilemma of the migrants in *Jazz*. Woolf observes: "as the current answers don't do, one has to grope for a new one and the process of discarding the old when one is by no means certain what to put in their place, is a sad one" ("Woolf" 5). Later, Morrison quotes a passage from *Mrs. Dalloway* that parallels Morrison's descriptions of Joe and Violet in *Jazz:* "there is a dignity in people, a solitude; even between husband and wife a gulf; and that one must respect" (8). Observing that Woolf finds alienation a source of "insight into death as well as life" (18), Morrison concludes her chapter with a statement that resonates against Felice's claim that Dorcas chose her own death: "In death only the alienated find freedom and refuge from time" (23).

There is no reason, of course, to believe that Morrison the mature jazz artist would share her younger self's responses to Woolf. Still, the diary passages Morrison quotes suggest that she shares Woolf's belief that recreating the self requires a deep awareness of interior processes. Morrison's apprehension of these processes combines elements of Woolf's stream of consciousness lyricism with elements of Du Bois's and Cullen's equally self-aware encounters with specifically African-American experiences of consciousness.

Although it shifts shapes almost continually, as I will discuss in the final section of this epilogue, the elusive narrative voice of *Jazz* echoes several of Woolf's premises at the outset of the novel. Contemplating the pressure of the city, the narrator recommends self-control as defense against attacks from the outside: "If you don't know how, you can end up out of control or controlled by some outside thing" (9). Aware that many people, uprooted from their villages, flee first to the city and then to themselves, the narrator describes Dorcas's as "an inward face—whatever it sees is its own self" (12). And although "they wouldn't like it" because it would force them to confront the "seep of rage" (16) that Cullen identified as fundamental to the Harlem Renaissance, Violet's customers seek "the space that need not be filled with anything other than the drift of their own thoughts" (16). Intimating the risk that accompanies any real confrontation with experience, with self *or* other, Morrison's narrator revoices a recurring (post)modernist theme when she describes the "private cracks" (22) in the foundation of Violet's interior world. Echoing Woolf and other psychological modernists such as Hemingway, Willa Cather, and Henry James, Morrison describes Violet as she

> wakes up in the morning and sees with perfect clarity a string of small, well-lit scenes. In each one something specific is being done: food things, work things; customers and acquaintances are encountered, places entered. But she does not see herself doing these things. She sees them being done. The globe light holds and bathes each scene, and it can be assumed that at the curve where the light stops is a solid foundation. In truth, there is no foundation at all, but alleyways, crevices one steps across

all the time. But the globe light is imperfect too. Closely examined it shows seams, ill-glued cracks and weak places beyond which is anything. Anything at all. (23)

This vision of a world without certainty can be understood either (in high modernist terms) as a source of alienation requiring a Woolfean withdrawal to the interior or (in jazz terms) as a call to dive into the deep water. Even as she creates a vision that, like the explicit statements of her thesis, implicitly repudiates Woolf's choice, Morrison maintains her awareness that a highly developed sense of interior process is necessary to the call-and-response dynamic, to jazz, in an urban world where so many individuals, like Violet, respond to their brutal experience by "drowning in it, deep-dreaming" (108).

▲ ▲ ▲ ▲

Beneath it all, the music, the changing same. King Sunny Ade's "Ase," the power that animates the world; Bob Marley's "Exodus," the awareness of dispersion, the call for renewal; Aretha Franklin's "Spirit in the Dark," the gospel base; Max Roach's "All Africa," in which Roach sounds his drums alongside those of Nigerian percussionist Olatunji and Afro-Cuban rhythmic genius Machito, while Abbey Lincoln calls out tribal names and Olatunji responds with Yoruba proverbs on the themes of freedom, liberation, recuperation; Sly and the (interracial, male and female) Family Stone's "Thank You (Falettinme Be Mice Elf Again)" metamorphosing into "Thank You for Talkin' to Me Africa"; George Clinton's funk fables; Public Enemy's "Fear of a Black Planet"; Queen Latifah's "Mama Gave Birth to the Soul Children"; Adeva's house revoicing of "Respect"; Sweet Honey in the Rock, calling us to hear the ancestors' words in the voice of the fire. All calling for new phrasings, all echoing the ones that came before. As James Brown shouts, "There It Is."

Underneath the blues, gospel, and jazz impulses: what I've played around with calling the "funk principle." As almost every African-American musician points out, it really doesn't matter whether you call it jazz or blues (Louis Armstrong and Earl Hines's "West End Blues"; Billie Holiday's "God Bless the Child"; Muhal Richard Abrams's "Blu Blu Blu"); gospel or soul (Sam Cooke's "A Change Is Gonna Come," Aretha's "Border Song [Holy Moses])"; funk or jazz (Miles Davis's "Jack Johnson," Parliament's "Motor Booty Affair"). As long as the bass holds the groove (present or implied), maintains a heartbeat grounding individual processes in the community and keeping the spirits on the dance floor moving, you can layer *anything* on top of it, exploring the outer limits of the mind, meditating on the soul of theory and the theory of soul, inviting the more contemplative orisha to do *their* thing. The bass is history, the gospel/blues realities; on the higher frequencies, funk speaks in all possible tongues, explores as many histories and structures, releases as many repressed Barthean myths, as the Funkateers can imagine. Funkentelechy, the Mothership Connection, Electric Pygmies, and Atomic Dogs. Playing all sorts of games with funk theorist Greg Tate's four p's of (post)modernism: pluralism, parody, politics, and pop culture. As Tate reminds us: "As George Clinton learned, you got to free Negroes' asses if you want their minds to bug" (126). Though it ain't quite as easy to escape the Placebo Syndrome and make it real, same goes for white folk.

Bringing it back home to the words on the page, Darius James's hilarious *Negrophobia,* younger cousin of Ishmael Reed's *Mumbo Jumbo* and grandson of Zora Neale Hurston's *Mules and Men,* exemplifies the potential of funk literature. Funking around with his own genealogy, James's character "Talking Dreads" (whose name reminds us that head Talking Head David Byrne collaborated with Brian Eno— who'll be back in just a minute—on an adaptation of Amos Tutuola's surrealist recuperation *My Life in the Bush of Ghosts*) associates *Negrophobia* with the music of Sun Ra, Fanon's *Black Skin, White Masks,* and Ralph Bakshi's film *Streetfight,* a remake of Disney's remake of Joel Chandler Harris's remake of the tar baby story. Identifying himself with Scatman Carrothers's subversive minstrel introduction, "Talking Dreads" says: "Once, I tap-danced in the dreams of a filmmaker known for animating urban animal fables of a pornographic nature. I sang to him in a whisper, *'I'm a nigger man. Watch me dance'*" (131). Reframing Harris's Uncle Remus as Remus/Harris reframed Brer Rabbit, James presents a hitherto unpublished fragment from *The Untold Tales of Uncle Remus* in which Uncle Remus "shuffled his withered organ between the cheeks of the child's smooth white bottom," shouting, *"Slap it an' slick it!* Now ROLL DAT BONE!" before, under some compulsion, hobbling off "in the direction of the North Star" (72) and into the "Church of Uncle H. Rap Remus" where the "throngs of Rastafarians clothed in black leopard-head-hooded animal-hair hides" might well recuperate Ellison's trickster credo "change the joke and slip the yoke" into something like "change the frame and ice the game," if only they weren't quite so stoned (72).

Identifying "the fusion funkbomb Einstein Clinton's theorems made possible" (156) as the spirit informing both the hip-hop aesthetic of sampling and black poststructuralist literary theory, Tate celebrates George Clinton as "a cat who could tune in on everybody else's signals and fit 'em in on his wavelength band" (43). Yeah,

well . . . sadly enough, Tate is also right on target when he observes
"that since I heard a snotty white DJ say he stopped thinking
Parliament/Funkadelic was stupid disco when Brian Eno cited them
as an influence, I've known George Clinton was right when he said
that as soon as white folks figured out funk was intellectually acceptable they'd try to hop on board the Mothership" (201). Which ain't
really the point.

▲ ▲ ▲ ▲

The point is in the new voices calling and responding to the ancestors, to each other, to their changingly constructed worlds. Many of
the most compelling younger writers carry on the musical mainstream of African-American literature, charting the currents that
flow from gospel to motown and house, from blues to rap and reg-
gae, from jazz to funk and hiphop. Ricardo Cortez Cruz's *Straight
outta Compton,* taking its name from N.W.A.'s controversial rap al-
bum, for example, remolds the jazz tradition in a way analogous to
what Tate describes as the "fundamental hiphop" technique of "making old records talk via scratching or sampling" (124). Invoking Billie
Holiday and Public Enemy, Farley Jackmaster Funk and Clint East-
wood, Gil Scott-Heron and Madonna, M. C. Lyte and Branford Marsalis, Cruz joins Darius James and Xam Cartier (*Muse-Echo Blues*) in
moving the jazz impulse from a modernist to a (post)modernist
frame (reflecting not an argument with African-American ancestors,
but a changing assessment of the dominant conceptions of literacy
in the European-American institutional world).

So all respect to the new voices that have joined the chorus since
the late seventies, and apologies to those unnamed (Yusef Komunya-
kaa, Baron James Ashanti, Ai, Carolyn Beard-Whitlow, Thylia Moss,
Michael Warr):

Colleen McElroy, whose West Afrocentric masterpiece "The Griots
Who Know Brer Fox" (1979) honors the blues elders, "old drunks
lost among the tenements" who can:

> . . . spin a new Brer Rabbit story for a nickel;
> tell you how he slipped past the whistle-slick fox
> to become
> > the Abomey king. . . .
> > The face is anonymous,
> > > you can find it anywhere
> but the words are as prized
> as the curved tusks of the bull elephant.

(29)

Paul Beatty, hiphop poet-performer, who sings a hard-edged blues for streets riddled by AIDS, rape, crack, and still finds the strength to envision a recuperative reunion of Clinton's Mothership and Marcus Garvey's Black Star Line:

> then my prison issue wishes dove deep
> much deeper than any ocean
> much deeper than any stellar medium
> thinkin from my heart about planet Africa
> where is our liner now
>> our flagship
>> our spaceship.

(60–61)

Patricia Smith, whose "Life according to Motown" enters the tradition of great poems on black women singers: Sterling Brown's "Ma Rainey"; Sherley Anne Williams's sequence on Bessie Smith, "Regular Reefer"; and the two great Billie Holiday tributes: Rita Dove's "Canary": "Fact is, the invention of women under siege / has been to sharpen love in the service of myth. / If you can't be free, be a mystery" (64); and Langston Hughes's "Song for Billie Holiday," which in the space of nine lines using just eleven different words, charts the interior process necessary to the power of call and response. Hughes's persona first attempts to get rid of the blues: "What can purge my heart / Of the song / And the sadness?" Almost imperceptibly, he/she begins to respond to Holiday's call: "What can purge my heart / But the song / Of the sadness?" (*Selected Poems* 102). The culmination of Hughes's blues minimalism, the perfect response to Holiday's delicate devastating voice, comes when the persona feels the song entering and emanating from his/her own enriched and aching interior: "What can purge my heart / Of the sadness / Of the song?" (102).

Christopher Gilbert, whose "Listening to Monk's 'Mysterioso' I Remember Braiding My Sisters' Hair" responds with honesty and grace to the inclusive call of the sisters, whose experience, at the start of the poem remains "just beyond a man's grasp." Contemplating the way his sisters "take turns braiding each others' hair" into "a flow that hurt and grace could mean," Gilbert struggles to articulate what the patterns mean to him, can mean to us (31). Like Monk's music, at its best composed as much of silence as of sound, promising a process taking us beyond the limits we think are ours:

> this coming into newness, this dis-continuous mind in you looking up, finding
> an otherness which trusts what you'll become—

for me, my sisters once offering,
"You want to learn to braid my hair."

(32)

Metaphysical funk.

▲ ▲ ▲ ▲

As Monk knew, as Morrison knows, life is grounded in mystery, African before European, the mystery of our sources: the wild woman who gives birth to Joe before vanishing into the forest, leaving her son to call out to the white oak tree (recall Conde's Yao) whose response he cannot understand: "'Give me a sign, then. You don't have to say nothing. Let me see your hand. Just stick it out someplace and I'll go; I promise. A sign. . . . You my mother?' Yes. No. Both. Either. But not this nothing" (178).

Against the nothing, in *Jazz* as in *Beloved*—which closes with the caution "This is not a story to pass on" (275) even as it passes it on— Morrison constructs jazz possibilities out of the (post)modernist, dispersed chaos (which, as the scientists suggest, signifies a more complex, relational, masked sense of order): "Now I have to think this through, carefully, even though I may be doomed to another misunderstanding. I have to do it and not break down. Not hating him is not enough; liking, loving him is not useful. I have to alter things" (161). Morrison's narrator assumes visionary tones: "I want to be the language that wishes him well, speaks his name, wakes him when his eyes need to be opened" (161).

Nearing the mysterious source of calls and responses, this voice recalls the epigraph that "precedes" *Jazz,* a quotation from *The Nag Hammadi,* a collection of Coptic texts recovered in Egypt in 1945. Morrison quotes from the section titled "The Thunder: Perfect Mind," a relatively brief section narrated by a female figure who speaks in a variety of voices, all of which resound with her immense generative power:

> I am the name of the sound
> and the sound of the name.
> I am the sign of the letter
> and the designation of the division.

These apparently contradictory qualities recur in the narrative voice in *Jazz,* which resists classification as omniscient (as it seems when recounting the Faulknerian fable of Golden Gray) or limited (when engaging in village gossip or reflecting on its own inability to envision Joe and Violet's reconciliation). Like Morrison's, the voice of "The

Thunder: Perfect Mind" insists on the ongoing dialogue between interior and exterior, a dialogue that creates, enforces, and, potentially, subverts the terms of the divisions that define human discourse, whatever their manifestation in a specific time or place:

> For what is inside of you is what is outside of you,
> and the one who fashions you on the outside
>   is the one who shaped the inside of you.
> And what you see outside of you,
>   you see inside of you;
>   it is visible and it is your garment.
>
> (*Nag Hammadi* 302)

In the specific urban context that divides selves and communities in *Jazz*, this *African* voice provides renewed access to the gospel foundation, the vision of community and possible salvation, lost as the village became city. Morrison's choice of a narrative voice echoing that of a visionary African woman seems particularly significant in light of the *Nag Hammadi*'s editors attempts to minimize the African elements of the collection, which they describe as "originally a Greek literary productivity" (13), and to dismiss the "antithetical, paradoxical" voice of "The Thunder: Perfect Mind" as "difficult to classify" (296). Asserting what can now be understood as a recuperated consciousness, the text anticipates just such a response:

> Why then have you hated me, you Greeks?
> Because I am a barbarian among [the] barbarians?
> For I am the wisdom [of the] Greeks
>   and the knowledge of [the] barbarians.
> I am the judgment of [the] Greeks and of the barbarians.
> [I] am the one whose image is great in Egypt
>   and the one who has no image among the barbarians.
>
> (299)

Framing her excavation of the multilayered African American past with this invocation of the feminine, African energy that centers, creates, decenters, recreates the *process* that shapes meaning, Morrison grounds her jazz vision in the gospel impulse. Acknowledging her own limitations, the narrative voice—at this point, the voice of Morrison's lost villages—echoes the gospel image of the "home in that rock," responding to the wild woman not as destructive nightmare, but as "a playful woman who lived in a rock" (221). As she prepares to sound her final call—"Look where your hands are. Now" (229)—the narrative voice provides one of the most affirmative images in Morrison's fiction, of Joe and Violet at rest: "the mattress, curved like a preacher's palm asking for witnesses in His name's sake, enclosed them each and every night and muffled their whispering, old-time love" (228). A gospel response: to blues lives down home and up north; to jazz calls that drive folks crazy even as they make them possible; to "the voices of women in houses nearby singing 'Go down, go down, way down in Egypt land. . . .' Answering each other from yard to yard with a verse or its variation" (226). Peace.

Works Cited

▲ ▲ ▲ ▲

Adams, Henry. *The Education of Henry Adams*. 1909. New York: Library of America, 1983.

Adell, Sandra. *Double-Consciousness/Double Bind: Theoretical Issues in Twentieth-Century Black Literature*. Urbana: University of Illinois Press, 1994.

Andrews, William. *The Literary Career of Charles W. Chesnutt*. Baton Rouge: Louisiana State University Press, 1980.

————. *To Tell a Free Story: The First Century of Afro-American Autobiography, 1760–1865*. Urbana: University of Illinois Press, 1986.

Anozie, Sunday. *Structural Models and African Poetics*. London: Routledge and Kegan Paul, 1981.

Armah, Ayi Kwei. *Two Thousand Seasons*. London: Heinemann, 1973.

Asante, Molefi Kete. *Kemet, Afrocentricity, and Knowledge*. Trenton, N.J.: Africa World Press, 1990.

Baker, Houston. *Blues, Ideology, and Afro-American Literature: A Vernacular Theory*. University of Chicago Press, 1984.

————. "Generational Shifts and the Recent Criticism of Afro-American Literature." *Black American Literature Forum* (Winter 1981): 3–21.

Baldwin, James. *Another Country*. New York: Dial Press, 1962.

————. *Going to Meet the Man*. New York: Dial Press, 1965.

————. *Go Tell It on the Mountain*. 1953. New York: Dial Press, 1963.

————. *Just above My Head*. New York: Dial Press, 1979.

————. *Notes of a Native Son*. New York: Bantam Books, 1964.

————. *The Price of the Ticket*. New York: St. Martins/Marek, 1985.

————. "Sonny's Blues." In *Going to Meet the Man*. New York: Dial Press, 1965.

Bambara, Toni Cade. *The Salt Eaters*. New York: Random House, 1980.

Baraka, Amiri. *The Autobiography of LeRoi Jones/Amiri Baraka*. New York: Freundlich, 1984.

———— [LeRoi Jones]. *Blues People: Negro Music in White America*. New York: Morrow, 1963.

―――. "The Changing Same (R&B and New Black Music)." In *The Black Aesthetic*. Ed. Addison Gayle, Jr. Garden City, N.Y.: Doubleday, 1971.

―――. *Raise Race Rays Raze*. New York: Vintage, 1972.

Barthes, Roland. "Myth Today." 1956. In *Mythologies*. Trans. Annette Lavers. New York: Hill and Wang, 1984.

Bateson, Gregory. *Mind and Nature*. New York: Dutton, 1979.

Baxter, Charles. "Assaulting the Audience in Modernism." In *Modernism: Challenges and Perspectives*. Ed. Monique Chefdor, Richardo Quinones, and Albert Wachtel. Urbana: University of Illinois Press, 1986.

Beatty, Paul. *Big Bank Take Little Bank*. New York: Nuyorican Poets Cafe, 1991.

Benitez-Rojo, Antonio. *The Repeating Island: The Caribbean and the Postmodern Perspective*. Trans. James E. Maraniss. Durham, N.C.: Duke University Press, 1992.

Benston, Kimberly W. "*Cities in Bezique*: Adrienne Kennedy's Expressionist Vision." *CLA Journal* 20 (1976): 235–44.

Blake, Susan. "Folklore and Community in *Song of Solomon*." *MELUS* 7, no. 3 (1980): 77–82.

Bloom, Harold. *The Anxiety of Influence*. New York: Oxford University Press, 1973.

Bone, Robert. "Richard Wright and the Chicago Renaissance." *Callaloo* no. 28 (Summer 1986): 446–68.

Bradbury, Malcolm, and James McFarlane. "The Name and Nature of Modernism." In *Modernism*. Ed. Malcolm Bradbury and James McFarlane. New York: Penguin Books, 1976.

Bradley, David. *The Chaneysville Incident*. New York: Harper and Row, 1981.

Brady, James. "In Step with Wynton Marsalis." *Parade Magazine*, 16 Aug. 1992, 18.

Brecht, Bertolt. "Against Georg Lukacs." In *Aesthetics and Politics*. London: Verso, 1980.

Bree, Germaine. "Michel Leiris: Mazemaker." In *Autobiography: Essays Theoretical and Critical*. Ed. James Olney. Princeton, N.J.: Princeton University Press, 1980.

Brooks, Gwendolyn. *Beckonings*. Detroit: Broadside, 1975.

―――. *Blacks*. Chicago: Third World Press, 1987.

―――. *Report from Part One*. Detroit: Broadside Press, 1972.

Brown, Lorraine A. "'For the Characters Are Myself': Adrienne Kennedy's *Funnyhouse of a Negro*." *Negro American Literature Forum* 9 (1975): 86–88.

Brown, Sterling. *The Negro in American Fiction*. 1937. New York: Atheneum, 1969.

Bullins, Ed. Introduction to *The New Lafayette Theatre Presents*. Ed. Ed Bullins. Garden City, N.Y.: Anchor Press/Doubleday, 1974.

―――. *New Plays from the Black Theatre*. New York: Bantam, 1969.

―――. "A Short Statement on Street Theatre." *Drama Review* 12 (1968): 11–12.

―――. *The Taking of Miss Janie*. In *Black Thunder: An Anthology of Contemporary African-American Drama*. Ed. William B. Branch. New York: Mentor, 1992.

―――. *The Theme Is Blackness*. New York: Morrow, 1973.

Cash, W. J. 1941. *The Mind of the South*. New York: Knopf, 1973.

Chefdor, Monique. "Modernism: Babel Revisited?" In *Modernism: Challenges and Perspectives*. Ed. Monique Chefdor, Richardo Quinones, and Albert Wachtel. Urbana: University of Illinois Press, 1986.

Chesnutt, Charles W. "Baxter's *Procrustes*." In *The Short Fiction of Charles W. Chesnutt*. Ed. Sylvia Lyons Render. Washington, D.C.: Howard University Press, 1974.

——. *The Conjure Woman*. 1899. Ann Arbor: University of Michigan Press, 1969.

Christian, Barbara. "The Race for Theory." *Cultural Critique* 6 (Spring 1987): 51–64.

Cleaver, Eldridge. *Soul on Ice*. New York: Dell, 1964.

Coleman, Wanda. "On Theloniousism." *Caliban* 4 (1988): 67–79.

Collins, Patricia Hill. *Black Feminist Thought*. Boston: Unwin Hyman, 1990.

Conde, Maryse. *I, Tituba, Black Witch of Salem*. Trans. Richard Philcox. Charlottesville: University Press of Virginia, 1992. Original French edition, 1986.

Cone, James. *Malcolm, Martin, and America*. Maryknoll, N.Y.: Orbis, 1991.

——. *The Spirituals and the Blues*. 1968. Maryknoll, N.Y.: Orbis, 1991.

Crouch, Stanley. Liner notes to Wynton Marsalis, *Black Codes From the Underground*. Columbia CK 43651 (1985).

——. Liner notes to Wynton Marsalis, *Blue Interlude*. Columbia CK 48729 (1992).

——. Liner notes to Wynton Marsalis, *Levee Low Moan*. Columbia CK 47975 (1991).

——. Liner notes to Wynton Marsalis, *The Majesty of the Blues*. Columbia CK 45091 (1989).

——. Liner notes to Wynton Marsalis, *Thick in the South*. Columbia CK 47977 (1991).

——. Liner notes to Wynton Marsalis, *Uptown Ruler*. Columbia CK 47976 (1991).

Cruz, Ricardo Cortez. *Straight outta Compton*. Normal, Ill.: Fiction Collective, 1992.

Cullen, Countee. "Heritage." In *My Soul's High Song: The Collected Writings of Countee Cullen*. Ed. Gerald Early. New York: Doubleday, 1991.

Culler, Jonathan. *On Deconstruction: Theory and Criticism after Structuralism*. Ithaca, N.Y.: Cornell University Press, 1982.

Curb, Rosemary. "Fragmented Selves in Adrienne Kennedy's *Funnyhouse of a Negro* and *The Owl Answers*." *Theatre Journal* 32 (1980): 180–95.

Davis, Francis. *In the Moment: Jazz in the 1980s*. New York: Oxford University Press, 1986.

Davis, Thadious. *Faulkner's "Negro": Art and the Southern Context*. Baton Rouge: Louisiana State University Press, 1983.

DeArman, Charles. "Milkman as the Archetypal Hero: 'Thursday's Child Has Far to Go.'" *Obsidian* 6, no. 3 (1980): 56–59.

Delany, Samuel R. *The Motion of Light in Water: Sex and Science Fiction Writing in the East Village, 1957–1965*. New York: Arbor House, 1988.

Dixon, Melvin. "The Teller as Folk Trickster in Chesnutt's *The Conjure Woman.*" *CLA Journal* 18 (1974): 186–97.

Dove, Rita. *Grace Notes*. New York: W. W. Norton, 1989.

Du Bois, W. E. B. *The Souls of Black Folk*. 1903. New York: Library of America, 1986.

———. *Writings*. New York: Library of America, 1986.

Dumas, Henry. *Ark of Bones and Other Stories*. Ed. Eugene B. Redmond. New York: Random, 1974.

———. *Play Ebony, Play Ivory*. Ed. Eugene B. Redmond. New York: Random, 1974.

Eagleton, Terry. *Literary Theory: An Introduction*. Minneapolis: University of Minnesota Press, 1983.

Early, Gerald, ed. *Lure and Loathing: Essays on Race, Identity, and the Ambivalence of Assimilation*. New York: Allen Lane, 1993.

Eliot, T. S. *Selected Prose of T. S. Eliot*. New York: Harcourt Brace Jovanovich, 1975.

———. "Ulysses, Myth, and Order." In *Selected Essays of T. S. Eliot*. New York: Harcourt Brace Jovanovich, 1975.

———. *The Waste Land*. New York: Boni and Liveright, 1922.

Ellison, Ralph. *Going to the Territory*. New York: Random House, 1986.

———. *Invisible Man*. 1952. New York: Vintage, 1989.

———. *Shadow and Act*. 1964. New York: Vintage, 1972.

Fabre, Genevieve. *Drumbeats, Masks, and Metaphor*. Cambridge, Mass.: Harvard University Press, 1983.

Fabre, Michel. "Bayonne or the Yoknapatawpha of Ernest Gaines." *Callaloo* 1 (1978): 110–24.

———. *The Unfinished Quest of Richard Wright*. New York: William Morrow, 1973.

Fanon, Frantz. *Black Skin, White Masks*. New York: Grove, 1968.

Faulkner, William. *Absalom, Absalom!* 1936. In *Novels 1936–1940*. New York: Library of America, 1990.

———. *Go Down, Moses*. 1942. New York: Vintage, 1973.

———. *Intruder in the Dust*. New York: Random House, 1948.

———. *Light in August*. 1932. New York: Vintage, 1972.

———. *The Sound and the Fury*. 1929. New York: Vintage, 1954.

Ferguson, SallyAnn. "Chesnutt's 'The Conjurer's Revenge': The Economics of Direct Confrontation." *Obsidian* 7, nos. 2–3 (1981): 37–42.

Fiedler, Leslie. *The Inadvertent Epic: From "Uncle Tom's Cabin" to "Roots."* New York: Simon and Schuster, 1979.

Figueroa, Carlos. Liner notes to David Murray, *Ming's Samba*. Columbia CK 45834 (1989).

Fisher, Dexter, and Robert Stepto, eds. *Afro-American Literature: The Reconstruction of Instruction*. New York: Modern Language Association, 1979.

Forrest, Leon. *The Bloodworth Orphans*. 1977. Chicago: Another Chicago Press, 1987.

———. "In the Light of the Likeness—Transformed." In *Contemporary Authors Autobiography Series*, vol. 7. Detroit: Gale Research, 1988.

———. "Souls in Motion." *Chicago,* July 1985.

———. *There Is a Tree More Ancient than Eden.* 1973. Chicago: Another Chicago Press, 1988.

———. *Two Wings to Veil My Face.* 1983. Chicago: Another Chicago Press, 1988.

Foucault, Michel. *Madness and Civilization.* 1961. New York: Vintage, 1973.

———. *Power/Knowledge: Selected Interviews and Other Writings.* New York: Pantheon, 1980.

Frank, Joseph. "Spatial Form in Modern Literature." In *The Widening Gyre.* Bloomington: Indiana University Press, 1968.

Franklin, John Hope. Foreword to *Chant of Saints: A Gathering of Afro-American Literature, Art, and Scholarship.* Ed. Michael S. Harper and Robert B. Stepto. Urbana: University of Illinois Press, 1979.

Frye, Northrop. *The Anatomy of Criticism.* Princeton, N.J.: Princeton University Press, 1957.

Gaines, Ernest. *The Autobiography of Miss Jane Pittman.* New York: Bantam, 1971.

Gates, Henry Louis. "'The Blackness of Blackness': A Critique of the Sign and the Signifying Monkey." *Studies in Black American Literature* 1 (1984): 129–82.

———. "Introduction: The Language of Slavery." In *The Slave's Narrative.* Ed. Charles T. Davis and Henry Louis Gates. New York: Oxford University Press, 1985.

———, ed. *Black Literature and Literary Theory.* New York: Routledge, 1990.

Gayle, Addison, Jr. *The Way of the New World.* Garden City, N.Y.: Doubleday, 1976.

Gennart, John. "Jazz Criticism: Its Development and Ideologies." *Black American Literature Forum* 25 (Fall 1991): 449–523.

Gibson, Donald. *The Politics of Black Writers.* Westport, Conn.: Greenwood Press, 1981.

Giddins, Gary. *Rhythm-a-ning: Jazz Tradition and Innovation in the 80's.* New York: Oxford University Press, 1985.

———. *Riding on a Blue Note: Jazz and American Pop.* New York: Oxford University Press, 1981.

Gilbert, Christopher. *Across the Mutual Landscape.* Port Townsend, Wash.: Graywolf Press, 1984.

Gioia, Ted. *The Imperfect Art: Reflections on Jazz and Modern Culture.* New York: Oxford University Press, 1988.

Grimes, Johanna L. "Leon Forrest." In *Afro-American Fiction Writers after 1955: Dictionary of Literary Biography,* vol. 33. Ed. Thadious M. Davis and Trudier Harris. Detroit: Bruccoli Clark, 1984.

Gross, Harvey. *Sound and Form in Modern Poetry.* Ann Arbor: University of Michigan Press, 1968.

Harris, A. Leslie. "Myth as Structure in Toni Morrison's *Song of Solomon.*" *MELUS* 7, no. 3 (1980): 69–76.

Harris, Joel Chandler. *Uncle Remus: His Songs and Sayings.* 1880. New York: Penguin Books, 1982.

Harris, Norman. "'Who's Zoomin' Who': The New Black Formalism." *Journal of the Midwest Modern Language Association* 20 (1987): 37–45.

Harris, Trudier. *Black Women in the Fiction of James Baldwin*. Knoxville: University of Tennessee Press, 1985.

Harris, William J. *The Poetry and Poetics of Amiri Baraka: The Jazz Aesthetic*. Columbia: University of Missouri Press, 1985.

Harrison, Paul Carter. "August Wilson's Blues Poetics." In *Three Plays* by August Wilson. Pittsburgh: University of Pittsburgh Press, 1991.

———. *The Drama of Nommo*. New York: Grove Press, 1972.

Hatch, James. "Speak to Me in Those Old Words, You Know, Those La-La Words, Those Tung-Tung Sounds." *Yale/Theatre* 8 (Fall 1976): 25–34.

Henderson, Stephen. *Understanding the New Black Poetry: Black Speech and Black Music as Poetic References*. New York: William Morrow, 1973.

Hill, Herbert, ed. *Anger and Beyond*. New York: Harper, 1966.

hooks, bell. *Yearning: Race, Gender, and Cultural Politics*. Boston: South End Press, 1990.

Hughes, Langston. *The Langston Hughes Reader*. New York: Braziller, 1958.

———. *Selected Poems*. New York: Vintage, 1974.

Hurston, Zora Neale. *Moses, Man of the Mountain*. 1939. Urbana: University of Illinois Press, 1984.

———. *Mules and Men*. 1935. Bloomington: Indiana University Press, 1978.

Irwin, John T. *Doubling and Incest/Repetition and Revenge: A Speculative Reading of Faulkner*. Baltimore: Johns Hopkins University Press, 1975.

Jaffe, Dan. "Gwendolyn Brooks: An Appreciation from the White Suburbs." In *The Black American Writer: Volume II*. Ed. C. W. E. Bigsby. Deland, Fla.: Everett/Edwards, 1969.

James, Darius. *Negrophobia*. New York: Citadel, 1992.

Jones, Gayl. *Corregidora*. 1975. Boston: Beacon Press, 1986.

———. *Liberating Voices: Oral Tradition in African-American Literature*. Cambridge, Mass.: Harvard University Press, 1991.

Jordan, June. "Notes toward a Black Balancing of Love and Hatred." In *Civil Wars*. Boston: Beacon Press, 1981.

Jost, Ekkehard. *Free Jazz*. Vienna: Universal Edition, 1974.

Joyce, Joyce A. "The Black Canon: Reconstructing Black American Literary Criticism." *New Literary History* 27 (Winter 1987): 335–44.

Karenga, Ron. "Black Cultural Nationalism." In *The Black Aesthetic*. Ed. Addison Gayle, Jr. Garden City, N.Y.: Anchor, 1972.

Karl, Frederick R. *Modern and Modernism: The Sovereignty of the Artist, 1885–1925*. New York: Atheneum, 1985.

Kelley, William Melvin. *A Different Drummer*. Garden City, N.Y.: Anchor, 1969.

Kennedy, Adrienne. "Cities in Bezique: The Owl Answers, A Beast Story." In *Kuntu Drama*. Ed. Paul Carter Harrison. New York: Grove Press, 1974.

———. *Funnyhouse of a Negro*. In *Black Drama*. Ed. William Brasmer and Dominick Consolo. Columbus, Ohio: Charles E. Merrill, 1970.

———. "A Growth of Images." *Drama Review* 21 (1977): 41–48.

———. *A Movie Star Has to Star in Black and White*. In *Word Plays 3*. New York: Performing Arts Journal Publications, 1984.

Kenner, Hugh. *The Pound Era.* Berkeley: University of California Press, 1971.

Kenney, William Howland. *Chicago Jazz: A Cultural History, 1904–1930.* New York: Oxford University Press, 1993.

Kent, George. *Blackness and the Adventure of Western Culture.* Chicago: Third World Press, 1972.

King, Richard. *A Southern Renaissance: The Cultural Awakening of the American South, 1930–1955.* New York: Oxford University Press, 1980.

Knight, Etheridge. "Answers to Questions Asked after a Reading." In *The New Naked Poetry.* Ed. Stephen Berg and Robert Mezey. Indianapolis: Bobbs-Merrill, 1976.

————. *Born of a Woman: New and Selected Poems.* Boston: Houghton Mifflin, 1980.

————. *Poems from Prison.* Detroit: Broadside Press, 1968.

Kozol, Jonathan. *Savage Inequalities.* New York: Crown, 1991.

Kubitschek, Missy Dehn. *Claiming the Heritage: African-American Women Novelists and History.* Jackson: University Press of Mississippi, 1991.

Lee, Dorothy H. "*Song of Solomon:* To Ride the Air." *Black American Literature Forum* 16 (1982): 64–70.

————. "The Quest for Self: Triumph and Failure in the Works of Toni Morrison." In *Black Women Writers, 1950–1980.* Ed. Mari Evans. Garden City, N.Y.: Anchor Books, 1984.

Lincoln, C. Eric. *The Black Muslims in America.* Boston: Beacon, 1973.

Litweiler, John. *The Freedom Principle: Jazz after 1958.* New York: Quill, 1984.

Locke, Alain. "The New Negro." In *The New Negro.* Ed. Alain Locke. 1925. New York: Atheneum, 1968.

Lorde, Audre. *Chosen Poems, Old and New.* New York: Norton, 1983.

McElroy, Colleen. *Winters without Snow.* Berkeley: I. Reed Books, 1979.

Madhubuti, Haki [Don Lee]. "The Achievement of Gwendolyn Brooks." *Black Scholar* (Summer 1972): 32–41.

————. *Dynamite Voices.* Detroit: Broadside Press, 1971.

Malcolm X, with Alex Haley. *The Autobiography of Malcolm X.* New York: Grove, 1965.

Marable, Manning. *The Crisis of Color and Democracy: Essays on Race, Class, and Power.* Monroe, Maine: Common Courage Press, 1992.

————. *Race, Reform, and Rebellion.* 2d ed. Jackson: University Press of Mississippi, 1991.

Marcus, Greil. *Mystery Train: Images of America in Rock 'n' Roll Music.* New York: E. P. Dutton, 1982.

Martin, Jay. "Joel Chandler Harris and the Cornfield Journalist." In *Critical Essays on Joel Chandler Harris.* Ed. R. Bruce Bickley, Jr. Boston: G. K. Hall, 1981.

Matthews, Fred. *Quest for an American Sociology: Robert Park and the Chicago School.* Montreal: McGill-Queen's University Press, 1977.

Miller, Christopher L. *Blank Darkness: Africanist Discourse in French.* Chicago: University of Chicago Press, 1985.

Miner, Madonne M. "Lady No Longer Sings the Blues: Rape, Madness, and

Silence in *The Bluest Eye.*" In *Conjuring.* Ed. Marjorie Pryse and Hortense Spillers. Bloomington: Indiana University Press, 1985.

Moore, MacDonald Smith. *Yankee Blues: Musical Culture and American Identity.* Bloomington: Indiana University Press, 1985.

Morrison, Toni. *Beloved.* New York: Knopf, 1987.

———. "City Limits, Village Values: Concepts of the Neighborhood in Black Fiction." In *Literature and the Urban Experience: Essays on the City and Literature.* Ed. Michael C. Jaye and Ann Chalmers Watts. New Brunswick, N.J.: Rutgers University Press, 1981.

———. *Jazz.* New York: Knopf, 1992.

———. *Song of Solomon.* New York: Alfred A. Knopf, 1977.

———. *Tar Baby.* New York: Alfred A. Knopf, 1981.

———. "Virginia Woolf's and William Faulkner's Treatment of the Alienated." Master's thesis, Cornell University, 1955.

Moyers, Bill. *A World of Ideas.* New York: Doubleday, 1989.

Mudimbe, V. Y. *The Invention of Africa: Gnosis, Philosophy, and the Order of Knowledge.* Bloomington: Indiana University Press, 1988.

Murray, Albert. *The Hero and the Blues.* Columbia: University of Missouri Press, 1973.

———. *Stomping the Blues.* New York: Vintage, 1976.

The Nag Hammadi Library. Ed. James M. Robinson. San Francisco: Harper, 1990.

Naylor, Gloria. *Linden Hills.* New York: Ticknor and Fields, 1985.

Olney, James. "Autobiography and the Cultural Moment: A Thematic, Historical, and Bibliographical Introduction." In *Autobiography: Essays Theoretical and Critical.* Ed. James Olney. Princeton, N.J.: Princeton University Press, 1980.

Olsen, Tillie. *Silences.* New York: Delta/Seymour Lawrence, 1978.

Ostendorf, Berndt. *Black Literature in White America.* Totowa, N.J.: Barnes and Noble, 1982.

Painter, Nell Irvin. *Standing at Armageddon: The United States 1877–1919.* New York: Norton, 1987.

Perkins, David. *A History of Modern Poetry.* Cambridge, Mass.: Harvard University Press, 1976.

Phillips, Kevin. *The Politics of Rich and Poor: Wealth and the American Electorate in the Reagan Aftermath.* New York: Random House, 1990.

Poirier, Richard. *The Performing Self.* New York: Oxford University Press, 1971.

Poland, Albert, and Bruce Mailman. *The Off-Off Broadway Book.* Indianapolis: Bobbs-Merrill, 1972.

Pound, Ezra. *Essays.* Norfolk, Conn.: New Directions, 1954.

Pynchon, Thomas. *Gravity's Rainbow.* New York: Viking, 1973.

Quinones, Richardo. "From Resistance to Reassessment." In *Modernism: Challenges and Perspectives.* Ed. Monique Chefdor, Richardo Quinones, and Albert Wachtel. Urbana: University of Illinois Press, 1986.

Radano, Ronald. "Jazzin' the Classics: The AACM's Challenge to Mainstream Aesthetics." *Black Music Research Journal* (Spring 1992): 79–95.

———. *Jazz Recast: Anthony Braxton's Cultural Critique.* Chicago: University of Chicago Press, 1993.

Rampersad, Arnold. *The Art and Imagination of W. E. B. Du Bois.* Cambridge, Mass.: Harvard University Press, 1976.

Redmond, Eugene. *Drumvoices.* Garden City, N.Y.: Anchor, 1976.

Reed, Ishmael. *Flight to Canada.* New York: Random House, 1976.

———. *Mumbo Jumbo.* New York: Doubleday, 1972.

———. *Shrovetide in Old New Orleans.* Garden City, N.Y.: Doubleday, 1978.

Reiss, Timothy. *The Discourse of Modernism.* Ithaca, N.Y.: Cornell University Press, 1982.

Rich, Adrienne. "Disloyal to Civilization: Feminism, Racism, Gynephobia." In *On Lies, Secrets, and Silence.* New York: Norton, 1979.

Robinson, Lillian S., and Lise Vogel. *Sex, Class, and Culture.* New York: Methuen, 1978.

Rosenberg, Ruth. "And the Childern May Know Their Names: Toni Morrison's *Song of Solomon.*" *Literary Onomastics Studies* 8 (1981): 195–219.

Ross, Dorothy. *The Origins of American Social Science.* New York: Cambridge University Press, 1991.

Ryan, Judylyn. "Water from an Ancient Well: The Recuperation of Double-Consciousness in African-American Narrative." Ph.D. diss., University of Wisconsin, 1990.

Sanders, Charles. "'The Waste Land': The Last Minstrel Show?" *Journal of Modern Literature* 8 (1980): 23–38.

Scheub, Harold. "Oral Narrative Process and the Use of Models." In *Varia Folklorica.* Ed. Alan Dundes. Paris: Mouton, 1978.

———. *The Xhosa Ntsomi.* Oxford: Clarendon Press, 1975.

Schuller, Gunther. "Third Stream." In *The New Grove Dictionary of Jazz,* vol. 2. Ed. Barry Kernfeld. New York: MacMillan, 1988.

Showalter, Elaine. "Feminist Criticism in the Wilderness." In *Writing and Sexual Difference.* Ed. Elizabeth Abel. Chicago: University of Chicago Press, 1982.

Sidran, Ben. *Black Talk.* 1971. New York: Da Capo, 1981.

Smith, Barbara. *Toward a Black Feminist Criticism.* Brooklyn: Out and Out Books, 1980.

Smith, David Lionel. "The Black Arts Movement and Its Critics." *American Literary History* 3 (Spring 1981): 93–110.

Smith, Patricia. *Life according to Motown.* Chicago: Tia Chucha Press, 1991.

Snead, James. *Figures of Division: William Faulkner's Major Novels.* New York: Methuen, 1986.

Soyinka, Wole. "The Critic and Society: Barthes, Leftocracy, and Other Mythologies." In *Black Literature and Literary Theory.* Ed. Henry Louis Gates. New York: Methuen, 1984.

Spencer, Jon Michael. *Blues and Evil.* Knoxville: University of Tennessee Press, 1993.

———. *Protest and Praise: Sacred Music of Black Religion.* Minneapolis: Fortress Press, 1990.

Spiller, Robert, et al., eds. *The Literary History of the United States.* 4th ed. 1974.

Sprinker, Michael. "Fictions of the Self: The End of Autobiography." In *Autobiography: Essays Theoretical and Critical.* Ed. James Olney. Princeton, N.J.: Princeton University Press, 1980.

Stepto, Robert. *From behind the Veil: A Study of Afro-American Narrative.* Urbana: University of Illinois Press, 1979.

——. "I Thought I Knew These People: Richard Wright and the Afro-American Literary Tradition." In *Chant of Saints: A Gathering of Afro-American Literature, Art, and Scholarship.* Ed. Michael S. Harper and Robert B. Stepto. Urbana: University of Illinois Press, 1979.

Styron, William. *The Confessions of Nat Turner.* New York: Random House, 1967.

——. *Lie Down in Darkness.* Indianapolis: Bobbs-Merrill, 1951.

Sundquist, Eric J. *Faulkner: The House Divided.* Baltimore: Johns Hopkins University Press, 1983.

Tate, Greg. *Flyboy in the Buttermilk: Essays on Contemporary America.* New York: Simon and Schuster, 1992.

Taylor, Walter. *Faulkner's Search for a South.* Urbana: University of Illinois Press, 1983.

Tener, Robert L. "Theatre of Identity: Adrienne Kennedy's Portrait of the Black Woman." *Studies in Black Literature* 6 (1975): 1–5.

Thompson, Robert Farris. *Flash of the Spirit: African and Afro-American Art and Philosophy.* New York: Random House, 1983.

Toll, Robert. *Blacking Up.* New York: Oxford University Press, 1974.

Tolson, Melvin. *Harlem Gallery.* New York: Twayne, 1965.

Toomer, Jean. *Cane.* New York: Liveright, 1975.

Torgovnick, Marianna. *Gone Primitive: Savage Intellects, Modern Lives.* Chicago: University of Chicago Press, 1990.

Van Deburg, William. *New Day in Babylon: The Black Power Movement in American Culture.* Chicago: University of Chicago Press, 1992.

Van Doren, Carl, William Peterfield Trent, John Erskine, and Stuart Sherman, eds. *The Cambridge History of American Literature.* 1917.

Walker, Alice. *In Search of Our Mothers' Gardens.* New York: Harcourt Brace Jovanovich, 1983.

Watt, Ian. *The Rise of the Novel: Studies in Defoe, Richardson, and Fielding.* Berkeley: University of California Press, 1964.

Werner, Craig Hansen. *Paradoxical Resolutions: American Fiction since James Joyce.* Urbana: University of Illinois Press, 1982.

West, Cornel. *The American Evasion of Philosophy: A Genealogy of Pragmatism.* Madison: University of Wisconsin Press, 1989.

——. *Prophetic Fragments.* Trenton, N.J.: Africa World Press; Grand Rapids, Mich.: William B. Eerdmans, 1988.

Wideman, John E. "Surfiction." *Southern Review* 21 (1985): 633–40.

Wilkerson, Margaret B. "Adrienne Kennedy." In *Dictionary of Literary Biography: Afro-American Writers after 1955: Dramatists and Prose Writers.* Ed. Thadious M. Davis and Trudier Harris. Detroit: Gale Research, 1983.

Williams, Martin. *Jazz in Its Time.* New York: Oxford University Press, 1989.

Williams, Sherley Anne. "The Blues Roots of Contemporary Afro-American

Poetry." In *Chant of Saints: A Gathering of Afro-American Literature, Art, and Scholarship*. Ed. Michael S. Harper and Robert B. Stepto. Urbana: University of Illinois Press, 1979.

————. *Dessa Rose*. New York: William Morrow, 1986.

Willis, Susan. "Eruptions of Funk: Historicizing Toni Morrison." *Black American Literature Forum* 16 (1982): 34–42.

Wilson, William Julius. *The Truly Disadvantaged*. Chicago: University of Chicago Press, 1987.

Wilson, August. Foreword to *Romare Bearden: His Life and Art* by Myron Schwartzman. New York: Abrams, 1990.

————. *The Piano Lesson*. New York: Plume, 1990.

————. *Three Plays*. Pittsburgh: University of Pittsburgh Press, 1991.

————. *Two Trains Running*. *Theater* 22.1 (Winter 1990–91): 41–72.

Wolfe, Bernard. "Uncle Remus and the Malevolent Rabbit: 'Takes a Limber-Toe Gemmun fer ter Jump Jim Crow.'" In *Critical Essays on Joel Chandler Harris*. Ed. R. Bruce Bickley, Jr. Boston: G. K. Hall, 1981.

Woodward, C. Vann. *The Burden of Southern History*. Rev. ed. Baton Rouge: Louisiana State University Press, 1968.

Wright, Richard. *American Hunger*. New York: Harper and Row, 1977.

————. *Black Boy*. New York: Harper, 1945.

————. "Blueprint for Negro Writing." In *Richard Wright Reader*. Ed. Ellen Wright and Michel Fabre. New York: Harper and Row, 1978.

————. Foreword to *Blues Fell This Morning* by Paul Oliver. London: Horizon Press, 1960.

————. *How "Bigger" Was Born*. New York: Harper, 1940.

————. Introduction to *Black Metropolis* by St. Clair Drake and Horace R. Cayton. New York: Harcourt Brace, 1945.

————. *Native Son*. New York: Harper, 1940.

————. "Portrait of Harlem." In *New York Panorama*. New York: Random House, 1938.

————. *Twelve Million Black Voices*. New York: Viking, 1941.

Yellin, Jean Fagan. *The Intricate Knot: Black Figures in American Literature, 1776–1863*. New York: New York University Press, 1972.

Index

▲ ▲ ▲ ▲

"Love Note II: Flags," 146
"Lovers of the Poor," 158
"Love Song of J. Alfred Prufrock, The,"
183, 194–95
"Love Supreme, A," 250
Lukács, Georg, 204, 215
Lumumba, Patrice, 114, 116
Lyric mode, 175–76

McElroy, Colleen, 299
McFarlane, James, 66, 183
McKay, Claude, 142, 174
McMillan, Terry, 265
McPherson, James Alan, 34
Ma Rainey, 280–81
"Ma Rainey" (poem), 281, 300
Ma Rainey's Black Bottom (play), 277, 279–81, 283
"Ma Rainey's Black Bottom" (song), 280
Machito, 297
Madheart, 111
Madhubuti, Haki (Don L. Lee), 93, 124, 142, 158
Madonna, 299
Magical realism, 255
Mailer, Norman, 32
Majesty of the Blues, The, 270–71
Major, Clarence, 241
Malcolm X: jail as ritual ground for, 31, 40; Knight's eulogy for, 125–26; Lorde on, 136; Brooks and, 158; Baldwin and, 227, 231; compared to King, 247–48; on Fard, 260; Wilson and, 287; mentioned, 123
Malone trilogy, 84
"Mama Gave Birth to the Soul Children," 297
Mammy, 40, 68
"Man Who Lived Underground, The," 208
Mao Zedong, 123
Marable, Manning, 106, 107, 108, 236
Marchand, Roland, 188
Marcus, Greil, 206, 253
Marley, Bob, 242, 297
Marquez, Gabriel Garcia, 255
Marrow of Tradition, The, 5
Marsalis, Branford, 274, 299
Marsalis, Wynton: and jazz audience, 175; on black codes, 270; and classical music, 270; Crouch on, 270–72; neoclassicism

and, 270–75; and Monk, 271; and Ellington, 271–72; critical response to, 272; neoconservatism and, 272–74; media image of, 274; compared to Wilson, 275–76, 278
Marshall, Paule, 26, 135–36
"Mars Jeems's Nightmare," 19, 21, 23
"Martha," 138
Martin, Roberta, 244
Marvin X, 108, 119
Marx, Karl, 189
Marxism: Baraka and, 97, 99–100; Wright and, 188, 201; view of aesthetics, politics, 214
Mascon, 70, 71, 72
Masking: Hurston on, 3; and double consciousness, 9; Brer Rabbit and, 15; Chesnutt and, 16–23; Gaines and, 35, 39–41; Morrison and, 63, 73–74, 77, 78, 81; and myth, 67–69; in tar baby story, 71; as trap, 73; in autobiography, 86–87; nationalist rejection of, 91; political implications of, 106; Kennedy and, 114, 116; Baldwin and, 238. *See also* Signifying
Masters, Edgar Lee, 119, 177
Matriarchy, 137
Maud Martha, 93
"Maxie Allen," 147
Mazrui, Ali, 292
MC Lyte, 299
"Me and the Devil Blues," 206, 253
Melville, Herman, 24, 87, 183, 222, 282
Memory of Fire, 279
"Men of Careful Turns," 158
"Mentor," 138
Meridian, 135
Mestizo aesthetic, 278
Metafiction, 4
Metamorphoses, 23
Metaphysical funk, 301
Metaphysical picaresque, 192, 194–96, 200
"Midnight Blues," 150
Miller, Christopher, 85
Miller, James, 135
"Mill Hand's Lunch Bucket," 276
Minimalism, 300
Minstrelsy: Ostendorf's definition, 10–11, 16; and plantation tradition 10–16, 25; stereotypes, 12; subversion of hierar-

149–54, 163, 165–66, 172, 174, 177–78, 180; and Afro-Modernism, 162–63, 167–71, 179–80; modernism and, 164; Tolson and, 165–66, 172, 174, 177–78, 180; and lyric mode, 175; Wright and, 206; as community expression, 213; and black literature, 218; Baldwin and, 227, 239; in Chicago Renaissance, 241–44, 246, 249–52; and European avant-garde, 248; Leon Forrest and, 255; and black language, 266; Wilson and, 277; economics of, 279; and functionality, 279; developing tradition, 297–98. *See also* Blues; Gospel music; Jazz
Mussolini, Benito, 214–15
"My Dreams, My Works, Must Wait till after Hell," 145–46, 158
Myers, Amina Claudine, 222, 241, 243, 249, 252
My Life in the Bush of Ghosts, 298
Mystery Train, 206
Myth: of American history, 32; regional, 33; Faulkner and, 35; of Flying African, 39, 72; Kelley's use of, 39; Jones's use of, 43; of tar baby, 63, 70–71; Barthes on, 63–67; and history, 63–65, 69, 71–72, 75; political implications of, 64; racial, 64, 67–68, 73, 75, 76, 78, 81, 115; modernist conceptions of, 64–67, 131–33; Eliot on, 65–66, 72, 132–33, 259; postmodern approach to, 66–67; Afro-American approaches to, 67–69; Morrison and, 67–68, 72–83; plantation tradition and, 68, 75, 76; Christian, 72, 261; Gullah, 72; of Icarus, 72; of Philomela/Persephone, 72; of scapegoat, 72; of safety, 73, 75, 76, 81–83; double consciousness and, 82; Greek, 131; Dumas and, 131–35; of Afro-American past, 133; Lorde and, 133, 137, 139; African, 133–35, 137, 261; ascent, immersion as, 134; matriarchal, 137; black women and, 139; Tolson and, 164; Wright and, 190; Forrest and, 257, 259; Hurston and, 259–60; of city, 289. *See also* Countermyth; Monomyth
Mythologies, 198
"Myth Today," 63–65

Nag Hammadi, The, 301–2
Narrative of ascent. *See* Ascent, narrative of

Narrative of descent. *See* Descent, narrative of
Narrative of dispersion. *See* Dispersion, narrative of
Narrative of endurance. *See* Endurance, narrative of
Narrative of hibernation. *See* Hibernation, narrative of
Narrative of immersion. *See* Immersion, narrative of
Narrative of recuperation. *See* Recuperation, narrative of
Narrative of repudiation. *See* Repudiation, narrative of
Nationalism. *See* Black nationalism
"Nationalism Vs PimpArt," 109
Nation of Islam, 122, 222, 230, 236–37, 242, 247, 254, 260–61
Native Americans. *See* American Indians
Native Son: on liberalism, 34; compared to Brooks, 142; as modernist text, 183, 185–86, 201–5; criticisms of Bigger Thomas, 185, 197; relation to blues, 186, 202–11; advertising in, 187–89; film in, 187–88; journalism in, 187–88; Boris Max in, 189–90, 210–11; image of city in, 191–93, 290; murders of Mary, Bessie, 192, 199; as metaphysical picaresque, 192–97; Bigger's consciousness, 193–97; form of, 197–203; sense-making in, 197–202; treatment of articulation, 197–99; Bigger as modernist artist, 199–202; black women in, 209–10; response of left to, 216; and *Go Tell It on the Mountain,* 217; sociological approach to, 246
Naturalism, 190–91, 243
Naughty by Nature, 266
Naylor, Gloria: response to Faulkner, 35, 52, 56, 58, 60; and minstrelsy, 62; use of myth, 67; and black women's writing, 265; images of black women, 285; mentioned, 278, 287
Neal, Larry, 92, 104, 106
"Need: A Choral of Black Women's Voices," 140
"Negro and Language, The," 164
"Negro Hero," 147, 158
Negro in American Fiction, The, 28
Negrophobia, 4, 34, 299
Neo-abolitionists. *See* Abolitionists

CRAIG HANSEN WERNER is a professor of Afro-American studies at the University of Wisconsin–Madison. He has previously published *Adrienne Rich: The Poet and Her Critics*, *Dubliners: A Pluralistic World*, and *Paradoxical Resolutions: American Fiction since James Joyce*. A member of the multicultural performance group Abreaction, he has collaborated with composer Geoff King on *Game Theory* and *The Virus*.